The
|D|I|Y|
ENCYCLOPEDIA

The
|D|I|Y|
ENCYCLOPEDIA

BLACK CAT

Acknowledgements

Photographers:
Jon Bouchier, R W Burns, Simon Butcher, Paul Forrester,
Jem Grischotti, Oliver Hatch, Ian McKinnell, Keith
Morris, Ian O'Leary, Polycell, Roger Tuff.

Artists:
Drury Lane Studios, Bernard Fallon, Nick Farmer, Tony
Hannaford, Val Hill, Trevor Lawrence, Linden Artists,
David Pope, Peter Robinson, Roger Courthold Associates,
Mike Saunders, Ian Stephen, Will Stephen, Universal
Advertising, Craig Warwick, Brian Watson, Gary Watson,
David Weeks.

Cover tiling picture:
Bathroom sanitary ware and fittings, C P Hart; Cristal
tiles, H & R Johnson Tiles Ltd; blind, Luxaflex; set design,
Lizi Freeman; photography, Rupert Watts.

First published 1987 exclusively for W H Smith and Son Limited
by Macdonald and Co (Publishers) Ltd
This edition published 1993 by Little, Brown under the Black Cat imprint
© Macdonald and Co (Publishers) Ltd 1987

Little, Brown and Company (UK) Ltd
165 Great Dover Street
London SE1 4YA

ISBN 0 316 90718 9

Material in this book has previously appeared in Jobmate (Whinfrey
Strachan Ltd) and Know How (Orbis Publishing Ltd).

Typeset by Peter MacDonald, Twickenham

Printed in Portugal by Resopal

CONTENTS

Chapter 1
PAINTING &
DECORATING

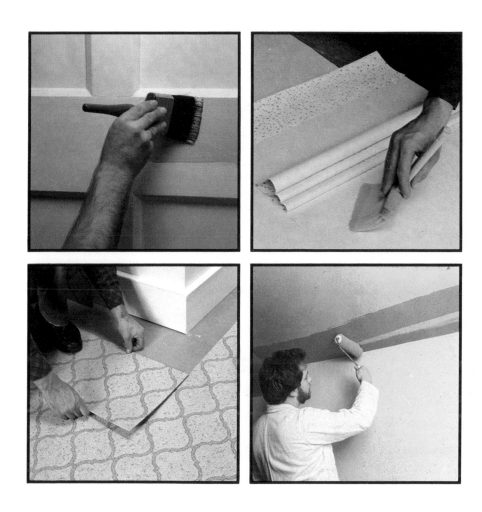

PAINTING PREPARATION

No matter what sort of decorating you intend to do, the surface you are covering must be sound. If you paint, paper or tile over cracks or loose plaster you're wasting your time and money.

CRACKS

There are two types of cracks – a structural one will be large, deep, and often wider at one end than the other; this has been caused by subsidence and you should seek the advice of a professional before any attempt is made to repair it. The second type is usually just a crack in the plaster layer.

For such superficial cracks, first detach all loose material and brush out thoroughly. Dampen the crack with water then fill it with cellulose filler. Smooth this on with a filling knife. Sand down when dry.

WEAK PLASTER

Old plaster may be loose against its backing, and if this is the case in any more than small areas, complete replacement may be necessary. Weak plaster sounds hollow when tapped gently.

Use a club hammer and a bolster chisel to chip out the weak area, working from the outside edges of the patch. With the patch removed you fill in as for holes.

Very large holes in a lath and plaster wall need to be replastered. You start with an undercoat plaster to fill to about 6mm (¼in) from the surface. This provides a key for two coats of finishing plaster applied with a float. Between coats, scratch lines through the surface to form a key for the following coat. As the final coat dries, 'polish' it quickly by applying water and smoothing with the float. This is a difficult skill to master.

First, though, you have to expose the laths, removing all loose plaster to make sure that the filling goes between the slats. If the slats are damaged then treat as plasterboard (see page 9); otherwise, build up the filler in layers.

FILLING A DEEP CAVITY

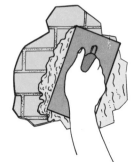

1. To fill a deep cavity, first apply undercoat plaster to the hole.

2. Apply a first coat of finishing plaster, smoothing upwards, then from side to side.

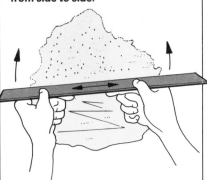

3. To level, use a batten with a side-to-side sawing action.

4. As the plaster hardens, cut it back with a trowel.

FILLING SURFACE CRACKS

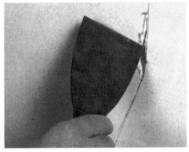

1. Remove loose material from cracks with a stripping knife.

2. Brush out the crack thoroughly so there's no dust left.

3. Press the filler to the wall surface, leaving it slightly proud.

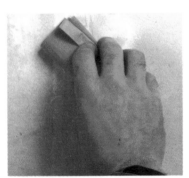

4. When the filler is dry use glass-paper to make the surface flush.

REPAIRING HOLES IN THE CEILING

1. To repair a hole in the ceiling, start by pulling out broken laths.

2. Moisten paper and scrape back a 50mm (2in) margin around the hole.

3. Nail the plasterboard panel to the joists, grey side down.

4. Spread two coats of finishing plaster on the patch. Polish when it starts to set.

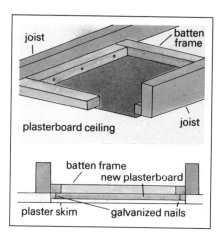

To repair a damaged external corner, nail a batten vertically along the edge of one wall and fill the hole on the other as described on page 8. When this patch is dry remove the batten and repeat on the other wall. If the damage to an exposed corner is extensive, cut back the plaster beyond the damage and square off to neaten edges. Then fix an expanded metal corner-piece to the underlying wall with dabs of plaster, and plaster over it using the batten technique.

Internal corners are a bit trickier. There are two methods. Either fill one side, smooth with batten, then leave to dry before doing the other; or fill both, and when semi-dry, smooth dry with an angle trowel.

GAPS

Where gaps occur between woodwork and walls (eg, near windows, architraves and skirting boards), a flexible sealant will fill them. This is bought in cartridges with a nozzle which can be directed straight into the gap. Alternatively, partly fill the gap with strips

Always overfill a large hole, and to get it flush use a batten (long enough to bridge it) in a sawing action to reduce excess or redistribute it till the required level is reached. Finally smooth with a filling knife and sand when dry.

If holes aren't too large but are deep, press in balls of wet newspaper, then skim a layer of plaster or cellulose filler over the top. If you can get above a hole in the ceiling then expanded metal can be used as a support for the filler.

Large holes in plasterboard must be patched with plasterboard offcuts. Cut a hole big enough to expose the nearest wooden supports. On a ceiling, if you can get at it from above, the hole can be cut square and battened along each side, the battens being nailed to the joists. Use 30-40mm (1¼-1½in) galvanized nails to fix the plasterboard in place. When secure, plaster over using a creamy mixture of finishing plaster and allow to dry; apply two coats.

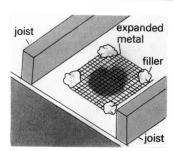

1. Support holes with expanded metal if you can get above them.

REPAIRING LARGE HOLES

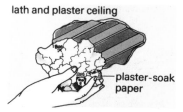

2. For backing support, line holes in lath and plaster ceilings with wedges of plaster-soaked paper.

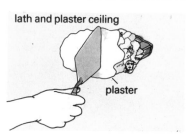

3. Build up the repair with layers of plaster. When set, dampen edges and apply last coat of filler.

of folded newspaper and apply cellulose filler over the top. If they're wide, use thin wood to fill and filler to finish, then sand down when dry.

MOULD

Mould appears as grey, green or black patches, and first should be treated with a fungicidal solution or alternatively with a solution of three parts water to one part household bleach. If the problem persists, you'll have to tackle the underlying cause – this may be damp or condensation.

STRIPPING WOOD

Stripping wood of old paint or varnish is done because you're after a natural finish or because the painted surface has degenerated to such an extent that further coats of paint simply can't produce a smooth finish. Both varnishes and paints act as sealants, giving a durable finish. But which one you choose might depend on the wood itself – and you won't know what that's like until you've stripped it. If you're unsure of its quality, it's advisable to strip a test area first.

Sanding by hand using glass-paper wrapped around a wood or cork block is hard work and only advisable where small areas of flaking paint are involved. Always sand backwards and forwards *with the grain of the wood*, not across it. Scratches across the grain will always be highlighted by a clear finish.

HEAT STRIPPING

Heat stripping removes paint or varnish quickly. Blowtorches with gas canister attachments are light to use and a flame spreader nozzle makes the job easier (it can be bought separately). Light the blow-torch and hold it a little way from the surface. Move it back and forth until the paint starts to wrinkle and blister, then scrape it off. Wear gloves to save your hands from being burnt by the falling paint, and cover areas below where you are working with a sheet of non-flammable material to catch the scrapings. In awkward areas, especially overhead, you should wear protective goggles for safety's sake.

Blowtorches have largely been superseded by the hot air electric stripper. Resembling a hand-held hair dryer, it is used in much the same way as a blowtorch – being played over the paint until it is melted by the blast of hot air. Hot air strippers have become popular because they don't cause the paint to ignite and are unlikely to scorch the wood.

CHEMICAL STRIPPING

Chemical strippers are available in liquid, gel and paste forms. Their methods of application and re-

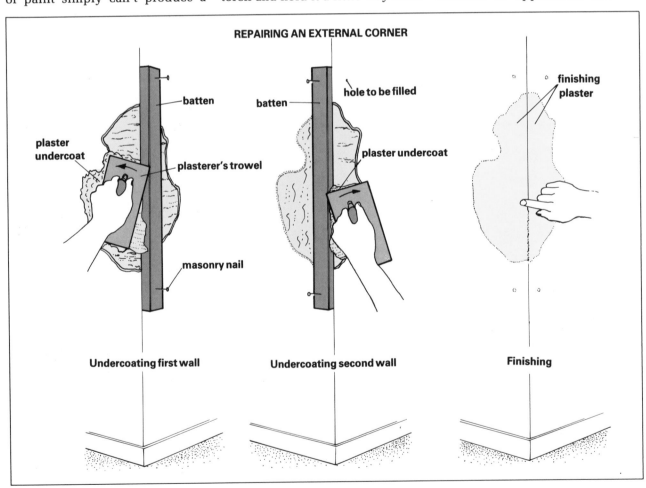

REPAIRING AN EXTERNAL CORNER

batten

plaster undercoat

plasterer's trowel

masonry nail

Undercoating first wall

batten

hole to be filled

plaster undercoat

Undercoating second wall

finishing plaster

Finishing

USING SCRAPERS

A triangular shavehook needs two hands when paint is thick. Angle the blade so as not to gouge the wood.

A combination shavehook has round, straight and pointed edges; it is useful for stripping mouldings.

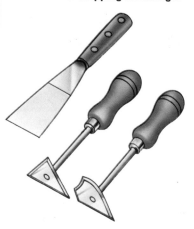

Shavehooks and a scraper are essential tools for paint stripping.

SEALING GAPS

Gaps between woodwork and walls can be filled with a flexible sealer.

moval vary, so always remember to read the manufacturer's instructions before you begin. If you are dealing with a large area of wood they can work out to be very expensive – they're also very messy.

Liquid and gel strippers are stippled on to the surface with a brush and left till the paint bubbles before scraping. Several applications can be necessary. Artists' brushes rather than paint brushes are useful when applying these strippers to mouldings or beading in windows and No 2 steel wool is useful for removing it.

After liquids or gels have been used, the surface must be cleaned down with white spirit or water (it depends on the stripper used) to remove any trace of chemical, and must be left till completely dry before any stain or seal is applied.

Pastes are mostly water soluble and are supplied in tubs ready-mixed or in powder form to be made up. They are spread in thick 6mm (¼in) layers over the wood which must then be covered with strips of polythene which adheres – when you press it – to the paste. They have to be left for between 2 and 8 hours, after which the paste can be removed, simply by lifting it, together with the paint, from the wood.

PAINTING WINDOWS AND DOORS

A good paint system comprises primer, undercoat and top coat of gloss. The primer stops the paint soaking into porous areas and provides a good key between the bare wood and the paint film. The undercoat helps build up the paint film and at the same time obliterates the colour of the primer, so that the top coat is perfectly smooth and uniform in colour.

If bare wood has knots in it you should brush a special sealer called knotting over them to stop the resin oozing up through the paint film and spoiling its looks. If the knots are 'live' – exuding sticky yellowish resin – use a blowtorch

or hot air stripper to draw out the resin and scrape it off before applying knotting.

PAINT ON PAINT

If existing paintwork is flaking off and is in generally poor condition, you will have to remove the entire paint system (see page 10). You then treat the stripped wood as described above.

Where the paintwork is in good condition, clean it and sand it down lightly to provide a key for a fresh undercoat and top coat.

If the paintwork is basically sound but needs localized attention, you can scrape or sand dam-

CHEMICAL STRIPPERS

1. Liquid strippers are stippled on to wood with a brush.

2. Leave until paint is bubbling, then use a scraper to remove it.

HEAT STRIPPING

Play the flame on to the paint and scrape off when it begins to bubble.

aged areas back to bare wood and 'spot-treat' with primer. Then apply a fine surface filler to bring the patch level with the surrounding area. Apply undercoat and top coat over the entire surface.

FINAL PREPARATION

Before painting doors and windows remove all the 'furniture' – handles, fingerplates, keyholes, hooks etc. – so you can move the brush freely without interruption.

All your brushes should be dry – this is something to remember if you are painting over several days and have put them to soak overnight in white spirit or a proprietary brush cleaner. They should be rinsed, then brushed on newspaper till the strokes leave no sign.

The same principle applies to wood as it does to any other large surface area – ie, you divide it into manageable sections and complete one before moving on to another – but if you're using an oil-based gloss paint don't let the completed area dry to such an extent that you cannot blend in the new.

For small areas, special shaped or narrow brushes are available and can make painting easier.

Tie a length of string across the paint kettle to wipe off excess paint.

HOW MUCH PAINT?

In all cases coverage per litre depends on the wood's porosity and the painter's technique.
Wood primer: 9-15 sq metres (95-160 sq ft)
Aluminium primer: 16 sq metres (170 sq ft)
Primer/undercoat: 11 sq metres (120 sq ft)
Undercoat: 11 sq metres (120 sq ft)
Runny gloss or satin: 17 sq metres (180 sq ft)
Non-drip gloss or satin: 13 sq metres (140 sq ft)
Runny emulsions: 15 sq metres (160 sq ft)
Non-drip emulsions: 12 sq metres (130 sq ft)

CLEANING BRUSHES

To ensure the long life of brushes: remove excess paint from the bristles with the back of a knife; wash out solvent-based paint in white spirit followed by soapy, then clean water – the soap restores flexibility and softens the brush. Wash out non-drip paint in a hot water/washing-up liquid solution then rinse in clean cold water. Hang up brushes, bristles down, to dry (drill a hole near the ferrule to take a nail).
At the end of a job a build-up of paint can be difficult to remove – soak the brush in a proprietary brush cleaner.
If leaving brushes overnight before continuing a paint job, suspend them in a jam-jar containing white spirit (using the drilled hole as shown).

STORING BRUSHES

Store dry brushes wrapped in aluminium foil held in place with elastic bands. Don't distort the bristles.

HOW TO APPLY PAINT

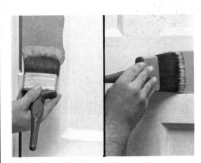

1. Apply paint along the grain.

2. Blend a second strip into the first.

3. Reload and brush across the grain.

4. 'Lay off' the paint with very light brush strokes along the grain.

5. Paint an adjoining area and blend into the first by about 50mm (2in).

6. Brush *towards* edges or paint will be scraped off and form a ridge.

WHAT CAN GO WRONG WITH PAINT

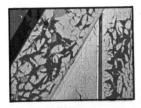

Lifting and flaking may occur if the surface is damp or powdery.

Blistering occurs if damp or resin is trapped beneath the paint film.

If paint is applied too thickly it can run, sag or 'curtain'.

Crazing is caused if a previous coat of paint was not completely dry.

Rain or condensation droplets on wet paint result in cratering.

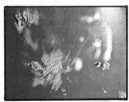

Wrinkling or shrivelling may occur if paint is applied too thickly.

STAINS AND VARNISHES

When it comes to giving wood a clear finish, you can choose from a variety of traditional or modern materials, including oils, wax, French polish and different types of varnish. Some are suitable for exterior use, others for interior use only.

TYPES OF VARNISH AND STAINS

The easiest clear varnishes to obtain, and most widely used, are those containing polyurethane resin. Polyurethane varnish is available in gloss, satin or matt finishes.

Some polyurethane varnishes have added pigments and are known as coloured sealers. It's quicker to use one of these rather than a wood stain followed by a clear finish, but you won't get the same depth of colour, and if the varnish chips, timber of a different colour will show through.

Wood stains are colouring pigments suspended in water, oil or spirits. Water-based stains penetrate the wood more deeply than other types and are therefore suitable for use on wood which will be subject to hard wear. Oil stains are easier to apply without blotching than water-based ones and, since they dry quite slowly, any overlaps are less likely to show.

Spirit stains are available in a wide range of colours. They dry quickly so you have to work at speed; but this also means you can apply the varnish sooner.

Don't use a polyurethane varnish over oil stains or a chemical reaction will spoil the finish.

PREPARING THE SURFACE

Ensure that the surface is clean, dry, smooth and free from any old paint or varnish. Large cracks and dents can be filled with a matching wax crayon or with a proprietary wood filler. If you do decide to use a filler, don't try to smooth it flat as you apply it with the knife or you'll risk spreading it round – it tends to show up in the nearby grain if it is rubbed in when wet.

Finally, you should make sure

PAINTING WINDOWS

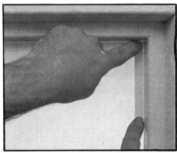

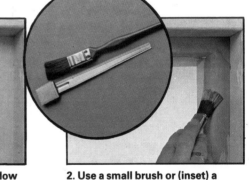

1. Stick masking tape to a window pane to keep paint off the glass.

2. Use a small brush or (inset) a cutting-in brush or sash paint pad.

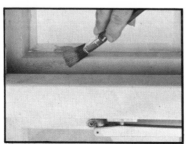

3. Paint along the grain, and remove tape before the paint is fully dry.

4. An alternative to masking tape is a paint shield or plywood offcut.

the surface is dust-free by wiping it with a clean, dry cloth or a fine brush. It's a good idea, too, to wipe it with a cloth soaked in turpentine to remove any greasy fingermarks that may be left on the surface.

STAINING WOOD

You can apply the stain with a brush or a folded lint-free rag. Aim to get the colour you want in one coat; a second coat can be applied if needed to get a darker finish.

VARNISHING WOOD

For a good finish on open-grained hardwoods like oak, mahogany and walnut you will have to apply a grain-filler to the wood surface before using varnish.

Polyurethane varnish is brushed on, working with the grain of the wood. You should sand down the surface lightly with flour-grade glasspaper between coats, and wipe with a damp cloth.

WALLS AND CEILINGS

Most walls and ceilings are plastered and this, when in sound condition, is ideal as a base for emulsion and other paints. But it is not the only surface finish you are likely to come across.

The walls may well be covered with a decorative paper and even painted on top of that. At the very worst there may be several layers of paper and paint, making it very difficult to achieve a good finish. Here it is better to strip the surface and to start again from scratch.

Plain white relief wallcoverings and woodchips are intended to be painted, and actually look 'softer' after one or two redecorations.

CHOOSING PAINTS

Vinyl emulsion is the most commonly used type of paint for walls

VARNISHING WOOD

1. Apply varnish in a generous coat, working with the grain of the wood.

2. Allow to dry, then rub down with fine glasspaper between coats.

BLEACHING WOOD

1. In a two-stage process, apply the first solution and leave it to work.

2. Brush on the second solution and leave; remove any crust that forms.

3. Neutralize the bleach with a solution of white vinegar and water.

STAINING WOOD

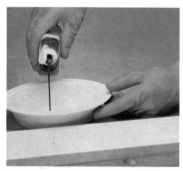

1. Shake the can well and pour the stain into a wide dish.

2. Use a cloth pad, and apply the stain liberally for even coverage.

3. For greater grain contrast, wipe each strip with a rag after allowing a minute or so for penetration. Leave to dry for 24 hours, then varnish.

and ceilings. It is easy to apply and comes in a wide range of colours. You will have a choice of two finishes: matt or silk.

A matt finish is preferable on a surface which has defects since a shiny paint tends to highlight faults.

Emulsion comes in three forms – traditional liquid, non-drip jelly and, the most modern, solid. This is supplied in a tray and liquefies as it is applied with brush or roller.

TOOLS AND EQUIPMENT

Few specialized tools are needed for wall and ceiling paintwork. If you are content to work with only a brush you will require two sizes: one 100-125mm (4-5in) size for the bulk of the work, and a smaller 25mm (1in) brush for working into corners.

Rollers or large paint pads make the job of painting large areas of wall or ceiling much quicker and will also help to achieve a better finish. But you will still need a small brush for working into corners and for dealing with coving, cornices, etc.

A good quality lamb's-wool roller gives a better finish and tends to hold paint better than a cheap foam roller.

PREPARING THE SURFACE

Walls which have been stripped will need a thorough washing to remove all traces of old paste. Emulsion-painted walls also need washing to remove surface dirt. In both cases, use warm water with a little household detergent added. Then rinse with clean water.

If you decide to leave the wall-paper on the walls, wash it down before you paint. Avoid overwetting the paper, particularly at joins. When the surface is dry, check the seams; if any have lifted, stick them down with paste.

Ceilings should be washed in small areas at a time and rinsed thoroughly before you move on to another section.

If the plaster is sound but covered in superficial cracks you should consider covering it completely with lining paper, wood-chip or other relief wallcovering before painting it. If it is coming away in chunks or sounds hollow behind the cracks, then the wall should be replastered.

PAINTING SEQUENCES

If possible paint in daylight. Painting is always done from the high-

PAINTING DOORS AND SASH WINDOWS

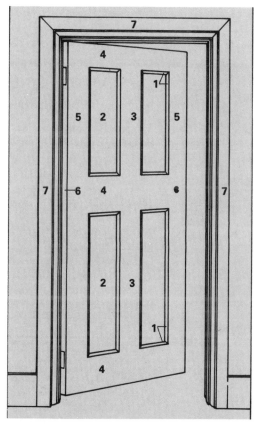

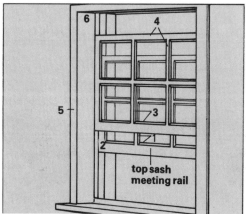

If you have to shut the door or window after painting, work first on the surfaces that come into contact when closed, to give them time to dry thoroughly. *Left*: Always start with the panel or bead inside edge sections on a panelled door (1). *Above right*: For a casement window, follow the same pattern as for a door. *Lower right*: Paint a sash window in the same way, but first pull down the top sash and lift the bottom one to get at the top sash meeting rail. You need only paint those sections of the runners (5) that show when the window is open. Don't get paint on the cords as it will weaken them.

PAINTING PROCEDURE

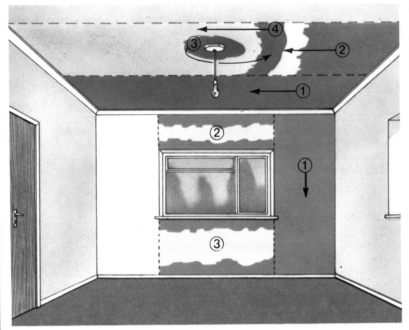

Paint the ceiling in bands (1,2); go round a ceiling rose (3) then finish the band (4). On walls work downwards (1), painting above a window (2) then below (3).

PAINTING WITH A ROLLER

1. Before using a roller, paint round the outside edge with a brush.

2. Push roller back and forth in the paint at the shallow end of the tray.

3. Run the roller parallel to the strip of paint you have brushed on.

4. Reverse the direction of the roller to join the two strips into one band.

est point downwards, so ceilings are tackled first. Paint the whole ceiling in 1-2m wide bands across the room.

Always paint working away from the window so you can see which areas have been painted. Work quickly so that painted areas are joined up before edges dry, or a 'seam' line will be evident later.

Walls are treated similarly, starting at the top and working downwards in sections about 1m wide, cutting in at the ceiling and at return walls.

PAINTING TIPS

The number of coats required will depend on the previous colour and condition of the surface and the type of paint. If another coat has to be applied, be sure that the previous one is fully dry first. Modern vinyl emulsion paint may cause the paper underneath to swell and bubble; however, as the water in the paint dries out, the paper and paste behind the paint surface will begin to flatten again.

TEXTURED FINISHES

Textured finishes can provide a relatively quick form of decoration and are ideal for improving the appearance of old, though structurally sound, ceilings. Since the material is flexible it will cover hairline cracks and will keep them filled despite any normal future ceiling movement.

There are two types of textured compound – powder form for mixing with water and ready mixed.

TOOLS AND EQUIPMENT

You will need a brush or roller to apply the finish. The most suitable type of brush is a 100 or 125mm (4 or 5in) distemper brush. The type of roller used will affect the pattern created. A foam roller is normally recommended to apply self-texturing compounds.

You may also require equipment for filling cracks or joints, such as a caulking tool, jointing tape knife, filling knife, filler and so on.

Where you intend to texture the surface after painting on the finish you will also need a patterning tool. Proprietary tools available include combs, stipple brushes and pads and special 'swirl' brushes.

PREPARING THE SURFACE

Textured finishes can be applied to bare or painted surfaces but the surface must be sound.

All porous surfaces should first be treated with a stabilizing primer recommended by the manufacturer of the finish so that the setting of the texture material is not spoilt by suction. Surfaces requiring such treatment include brick, render, concrete, plaster and wallboards.

Cracks or joints any more than 1.5mm (1/16in) wide should first be filled (see pages 8-9).

Painted surfaces should be clean, sound and sanded lightly to provide a key for the finish. Distemper and low-quality emulsion paint may not hold the texture; test by pressing adhesive tape on a small area first and remove any painted surface that has a tendency to come away when the tape is peeled off. If the surface has been painted in a dark colour it's best to paint over it with a light colour emulsion before you apply the texture.

Use masking tape to protect window frames and also window reveals, light fittings, ventilator grilles and so on. If the finish does get on any of the areas, wipe it off with a damp rag immediately.

APPLYING TEXTURED FINISHES

If you intend using a patterning tool, working on a deep, even coat of texture will give the best results. Apply the finish in bands across the room until the entire wall or ceiling is covered.

The drying time for textured finishes depends on atmospheric conditions. You will normally have at least 4 hours to complete your patterning, but complete one wall or ceiling at a time as far as possible.

A random pattern will usually be quicker to achieve than a regular one where you will have to take care in matching up the pattern. In the latter case, it may be better to

---

PAINTING LARGE AREAS

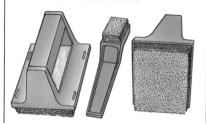

1. For painting ceilings, use a pad of about 190×100mm (7½×4in) for the main area, and a smaller pad or a brush for touching-in work.

2. Use scaffold boards and step-ladders so that you don't have to keep moving ladders. You can hire scaffold boards or mobile platforms.

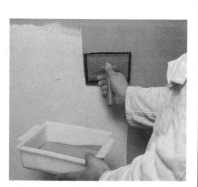

3. Thin the paint a little when using a pad, and paint in bands.

PAINTING THE WALL WITH A BRUSH

1. Use a small brush to cut in at angles before tackling larger areas.

2. Working downwards, cover the first band with crossways strokes.

3. At top of wall, finish each band by covering with downward strokes.

4. At the bottom two-thirds of the wall finish off by brushing upwards.

MAKE YOUR OWN COMB

You can make a comb with a wooden handle and a rigid plastic blade (cut, for example, from an old ice cream carton). Use a sharp knife to cut your own designs out of the plastic – they need not be regular.

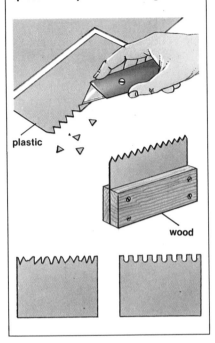

plastic

wood

PROPRIETARY TOOLS

You can buy various tools for patterning textured finishes. They include combs, patterned rollers, various types of brushes and a 'lacing' tool for smoothing high points, which may otherwise break off or cut people.

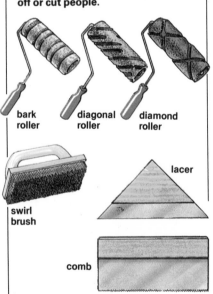

bark roller

diagonal roller

diamond roller

lacer

swirl brush

comb

spread the texture on in strips and pattern each strip as you go rather than covering the whole wall or ceiling and then patterning it.

FINISHING OFF

After patterning, it is normal to 'lace' the pattern (to dull any sharp ridges) just as the material begins to dry. Even after it has dried you may still need to remove sharp points which may cut people; use the blade of a filling knife to knock them back, or wrap fine glasspaper round a sanding block and sand them down.

Textured finishes can usually be covered with either an emulsion or oil-based paint, but check the manufacturer's recommendations.

TEXTURED FINISHES

1. A plain but striking effect is produced by a diagonal roller.

2. A swirled effect can be created by using a coarse nylon mitt.

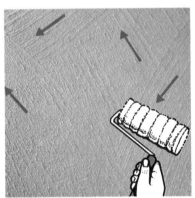

3. Here a 'bark' effect roller has been used in a random sweeping motion.

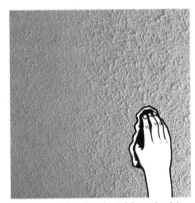

4. Coarse stippling is achieved with a sponge wrapped in plastic.

5. Use a sponge to make circles against a 'bark' effect background.

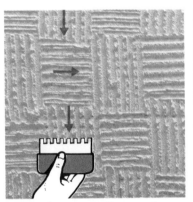

6. This criss-cross pattern can be made with a serrated scraper.

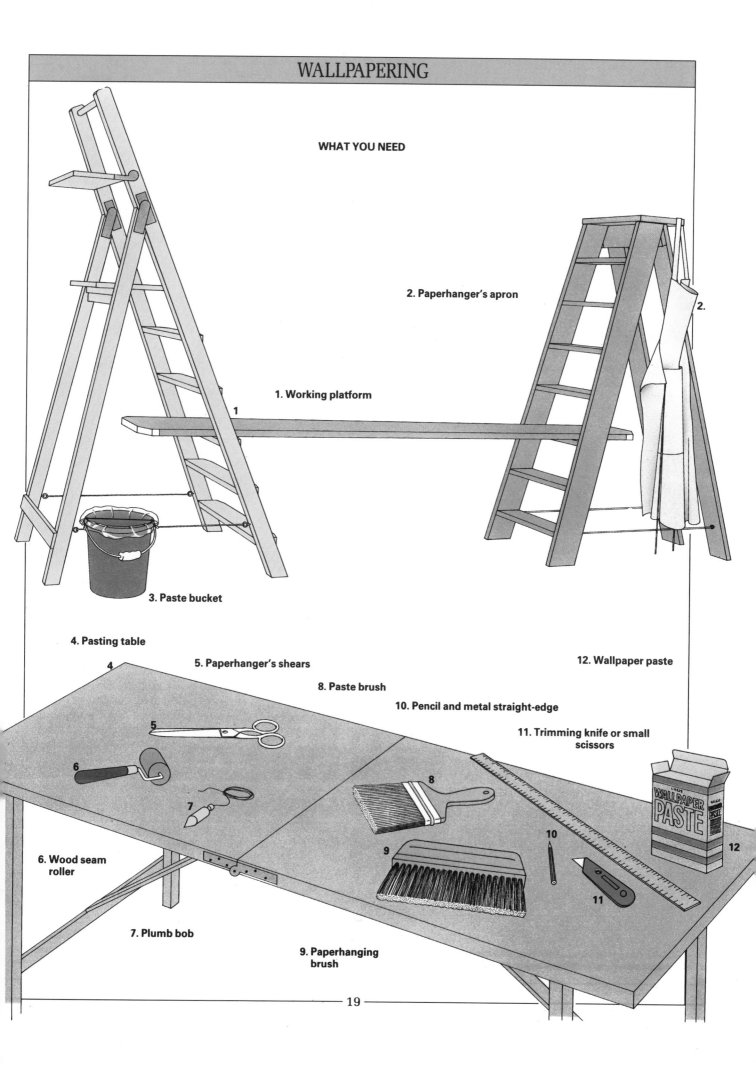

WHAT YOU NEED

2. Paperhanger's apron

1. Working platform

3. Paste bucket

4. Pasting table

5. Paperhanger's shears

8. Paste brush

10. Pencil and metal straight-edge

11. Trimming knife or small scissors

12. Wallpaper paste

6. Wood seam roller

7. Plumb bob

9. Paperhanging brush

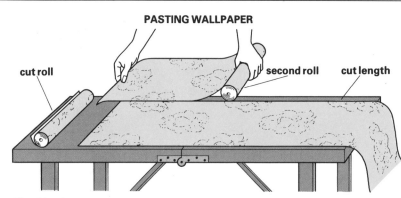

order of hanging

window area

projection

Start papering either at a window wall or in the centre of a chimney breast.

PAPERING WALLS

In rooms full of awkward corners and recesses, pick a paper with a random, busy design which the eye doesn't try to follow.

The most difficult patterns to hang are those with a regular small and simple repeat motif. The loss of pattern continuity will be easy to spot if even slight errors are made. The same is often true of large repeat designs.

The easiest papers for the beginner to handle are medium weights and vinyls.

STRIPPING OLD WALLPAPER

Never hang new coverings over existing wallpaper – the old may lift and bring the new with it.

To remove ordinary wallpaper use hot water with washing-up liquid or proprietary wallpaper stripper to soak the surface. Scrape off old paper in strips with a broad-bladed scraper; wash down again to remove stubborn bits.

Washable or painted wallpaper is more difficult. Always score the surface coating with a serrated scraper before soaking and scraping. For large areas a steam stripper (available from hire shops) is a real time-saver.

ADHESIVES

A cellulose-based adhesive is used for all standard wallcoverings. There are two types, ordinary and heavy-duty, which relate to the weight of the paper being hung. Certain brands of paste are suitable for all types of wallcoverings – less water being used for mixing when hanging heavy papers.

Since vinyls and washable wallcoverings are impervious, mould could attack the paste unless it contains a fungicide. Fungicidal paste is also needed if the wall has previously been treated against mould or if there is any sign of damp.

Some wallcoverings (like polyethylene foam, some hessians and foils) require a specially thick adhesive which is pasted on to the

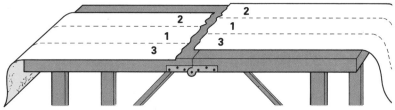

PASTING WALLPAPER

cut roll   second roll   cut length

1. Matching lengths: with patterned papers, cut the second and all subsequent lengths before pasting the previous one.

2. Paste the paper in strips, starting with the centre and brushing out to the edges in a herringbone pattern; make sure you cover thoroughly.

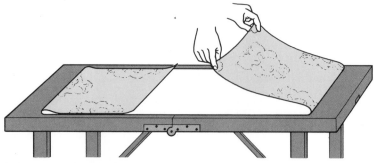

3. Fold a pasted length of paper, paste to paste, and leave for the recommended soaking time before hanging.

HANGING WALLPAPER

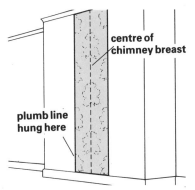

plumb line hung here

1. The first length of paper to be hung turns on to a window wall.

centre of chimney breast

plumb line hung here

2. If there is a chimney breast, start by centring the pattern on this.

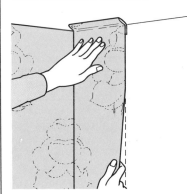

4. Mark the paper at top and bottom with creases, and then trim.

6. Mark a new vertical on the return wall and hang the offcut to this.

wall. Follow manufacturers' instructions.

Glue *size* (a watered down adhesive) is brushed over the walls before papering to seal them and prevent the paste from soaking into the wall. It also ensures all-over adhesion and makes sliding the paper into place easier. You can make size from most adhesives, or buy it separately.

Sizing can be done several days or an hour before papering.

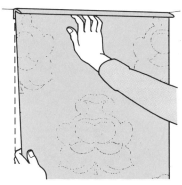

3. Hang the first length against a vertical guideline.

5. At an internal corner, turn a strip of paper on to the return wall.

7. Take no more than 25mm (1in) around an external corner.

Measure the height of the wall you want to paper using a steel tape measure and cut a piece of paper from the roll to this length, allowing an extra 50mm (2in) top and bottom for trimming.

Lay the first length of paper pattern side up on the table and unroll the paper from which the second length is to be cut next to it. Move this along until the patterns match, then cut the second length using the other end of the first as a guide. Subsequent lengths of paper are cut in exactly the same way, with each matching the length that preceded it.

PASTING AND SOAKING

Paste the paper carefully to ensure that all parts, the edges especially, are well covered. Work from the centre outwards in herring-bone style. Cover two-thirds of the length, then fold the top edge in so paste is to paste. Move the length along the table and paste the remainder, folding the bottom edge in, paste to paste.

Soak medium weight papers for 3-4 minutes, heavyweights for about ten. Lightweight papers and vinyls can be hung immediately.

Wallcoverings must be hung absolutely vertical. Mark a vertical on the first wall 25mm (1in) less than a roll's width from the corner, using a plumb bob and line.

Open out the paper and offer the top edge up, placing the pattern as you want it at the ceiling with waste above. Smooth the paper on to the wall with the paperhanging brush, using the bristle ends to form a crease between wall and ceiling, and at corners.

As soon as the paper is holding in place, work down the wall, brushing the rest of the length in position, opening out the bottom fold when you reach it. Again use the bristle ends to form a good crease where paper meets the skirting board.

The next step is to trim off the waste paper at the top and bottom. Run the back of the scissors along the crease between the ceiling or skirting and the wall. Gently peel paper away from the wall and cut carefully along the crease line. Finally brush the paper back in place.

READY-PASTED WALLPAPERS

With these you won't need pasting table, bucket and pasting brush but you will need a special light plastic trough made for the purpose. Put it below where the first length is to be hung and fill with water – covering the floor with layers of newspaper to soak up accidental spillages. Don't try to lift the trough; slide it along the floor as the work progresses.

Cut each length so patterns are matching, then roll the first one loosely from the bottom up with the pattern inside. Place it in the trough and press it down so water can reach all the parts covered with paste. Leave for the required soaking time, then pick the length up by the two top corners and take it to the ceiling line. Press on to the wall, using a sponge to mop up and push out air bubbles. Press firmly on the edges with the sponge or a seam roller, then trim waste.

LINING WALLS

It's advisable to line walls and ceilings with lining paper before you hang a relief wallcovering. Lining paper is also useful for creating a smooth surface on walls which are to be painted. It can be hung either vertically or horizontally. If vertically, ensure that the joins will not coincide with the joins in any wallcovering to be hung over it.

Never overlap the edges of the lining paper; they should be butt joined.

DEALING WITH CORNERS

Hang the last full length before the corner. Measure from the last length to the corner at the top, middle and bottom of the gap.

Take the largest measurement; for an internal corner add 12mm (½in) and for an external corner 25mm (1in) to give you the width to cut from the next length. The offcut left is used on the 'new' wall and overlaps the 12mm (½in) or

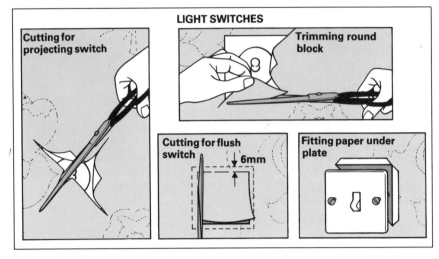

LIGHT SWITCHES
Cutting for projecting switch
Trimming round block
Cutting for flush switch ↓6mm
Fitting paper under plate

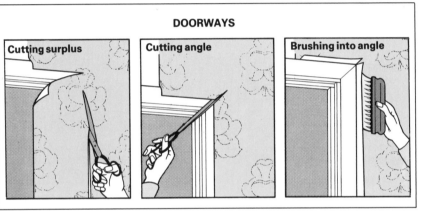

DOORWAYS
Cutting surplus
Cutting angle
Brushing into angle

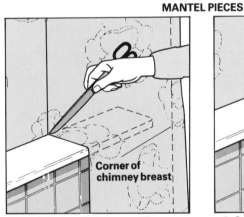

MANTEL PIECES
Corner of chimney breast

1. Mark the mantel piece outline on the paper.

2. Cut off the surplus paper, leaving 25-50mm (1-2in) for fine trimming.

25mm (1in) strip turned round the corner. You won't be able to match the pattern perfectly but this will not be noticed. Never try to take a lot of paper round a corner.

On an external corner the overlap of the edges of the two strips of paper which cover the corner should be positioned where they will be least obvious (eg. on a chimney breast it is better to make the overlap on the side wall rather than have it on the wall facing into the room). To stick down overlapping edges of vinyl, a latex adhesive is needed.

HANGING A FRIEZE

1. To fix a pasted frieze, pin a batten to the wall and check that it is level.

2. Hold the pasted frieze up to the wall, then smooth it into place.

3. Where you need to join lengths of frieze, carefully butt the cut ends.

WINDOW REVEALS

Pattern matching is the problem here. Before you begin work on the window wall, take a roll of wallcovering and estimate how many widths will fit between the window and the nearest corner. If it looks as though you will be left with a join within about 25mm (1in) of the window opening you should alter your starting point slightly so that, when you come to the window, the seam will have moved from the edge of the reveal.

Place a length of paper against the recess and mark the right-angle, adding 12mm (½in) where the top and side of the recess fall. Cut the length to shape. Measure inside the top and side of the recess, deduct 6mm (¼in) from the depth of each and cut pieces of paper to size, matching the pattern as near as possible. Paste and hang these offcuts, butting them up to the back of the recess. Paste and hang the prepared length for the front wall, turning the extra 12mm (½in) into the recess so it overlaps the pieces already hung.

CHIMNEY BREASTS

Special rules apply to chimney breasts. For a start, since they are a focal point in the room, any pattern must be centralized. The design of the paper will affect where you begin to hang the wallpaper. Where one length of paper contains a complete motif, you can simply measure and mark off the

central point of the chimney breast and use a plumbline to help you draw a vertical line down the centre. You can then begin hanging the wallpaper by aligning the first length with this line.

On the other hand, if it is the type of paper where two lengths, when aligned, form a motif, you will first have to estimate the number of widths which will fit across the chimney breast and then draw

a line as a guide for hanging the first length of paper so the combined motif will be centred.

Your order of work should be from the centre outwards; you will have to turn the paper round the corners at the sides so you form an overlap join with the paper to be applied to the sides of the chimney breast. Follow the techniques described earlier for measuring and papering round external corners.

PAPERING AROUND A WINDOW

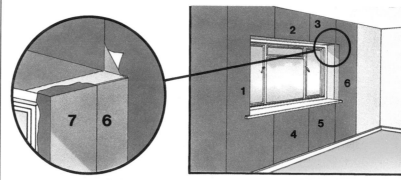

1. The papering sequence: piece 7 fills the gap left on the reveal by piece 6.

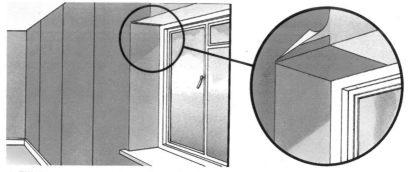

2. Fill the narrow gap left on the underside of the reveal with a small offcut.

FIREPLACE SURROUNDS

Brush the paper down on to the top part of the wall and then cut it to fit along the back edge of the mantelshelf. You can then cut the lower half to fit the contours of the surround. Gradually work downwards, pressing the paper into each shape, withdrawing it to snip along the crease line, then brushing it back into place.

If there is only a small distance between the edge of the mantelshelf and the corner, it's a lot easier if you hang the paper down to the shelf and then make a neat horizontal cut line in the paper. You can then hang the lower half separately and join the two halves to disguise the cut line.

FRIEZES AND BORDERS

A border can be used to bridge the gap between ceiling and wall or to hide any unevenness.

Borders need to be applied to a smooth, clean, dry wall area and if

1. Fold long lengths of paper into concertinas for ease of carrying.

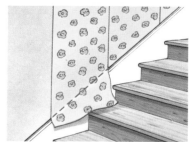

2. Where the skirting is angled take care to measure the *longer* side.

the walls are covered with heavily embossed paper which has been painted over, a border may not adhere securely to the surface.

It's well worth doing a trial run on a small area of wall first, to make sure it will stick, rather than risking wasting time and money on doing the whole room.

For paper friezes, use ordinary wallpaper adhesive. If the frieze is vinyl or you are sticking it to a vinyl surface, use a heavy-duty or ready-mix tub paste.

PAPERING STAIRWELLS

Because the lengths of paper for the wall at the sides of the stairs will all be of a different size it is better to cut and paste one length at a time. First hang the longest one, then work round the stairwell from this length.

A problem unique to stairwells is the length of paper you are handling. Fold the pasted paper in concertinas and then gather up the folds and drape the folded-up length over your arm to carry it.

Because the weight of the paper may cause it to stretch or tear as you are hanging it, try to get someone to help you take the weight rather than just leave it loose.

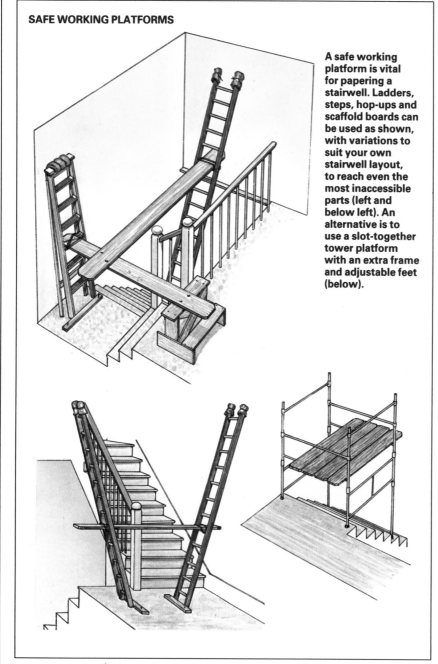

SAFE WORKING PLATFORMS

A safe working platform is vital for papering a stairwell. Ladders, steps, hop-ups and scaffold boards can be used as shown, with variations to suit your own stairwell layout, to reach even the most inaccessible parts (left and below left). An alternative is to use a slot-together tower platform with an extra frame and adjustable feet (below).

PAPERING CEILINGS

All ceiling papering starts from a line which is strung or marked across the ceiling 10mm (⅜in) less than the width of the paper away from the wall. The 10mm (⅜in) on the length of paper which runs next to the wall allows for the walls being out of square and its overlap is trimmed off at the wall and ceiling junction. You can chalk a line and snap it against the ceiling between two tacks to make a mark, or just pin it temporarily in place and butt the first strip of paper against it.

It makes sense to get all the lengths measured and cut out in advance. Cut all the strips, including those which will be trimmed for chimney breasts, to full room dimensions plus 100mm (4in) excess for trimming.

The surface to which you fix the paper must be clean and sound. New plasterboard, often used in modern construction, needs painting with a primer/sealer before decoration.

THE EQUIPMENT YOU NEED

You will need the same equipment as for papering walls, with the addition of a safe working platform that spans the width of the room. You should check with your

PAPERING CEILINGS

Top left: Order of hanging, working away from the window. Top right: Marking the ceiling with a chalked string line. Above: Fold the paper into concertina folds as you paste. Right: Support the folded paper with a spare roll while brushing out with the other hand.

supplier that the paper of your choice is suitable for ceilings – some heavier types may not be – and ask him to provide a suitable adhesive.

HANGING THE PAPER

The secret of successful ceiling papering is to use the correct folding technique as you paste, so that the paper can be transferred to and laid out against the ceiling surface in a smooth manner. Each fold of the concertina should be around 300mm (1ft) wide, apart from the first, which can be shorter.

Assemble the working platform securely at the correct height across the whole length of the room, beneath the area where the first strip is to be pasted.

The last-to-be-pasted section of each length is first to go on the ceiling; tease off this first section and brush it into place. Continue to unfold the concertina in sec-tions, brushing it down as you go and checking it is straight against the guideline.

When you trim, make sure the paper butts exactly up to covings, but allow a 5-10mm (¼-⅜in) over-lap down the surface of the walls you intend to paper later. Except with embossed papers, you should roll the butt joints between strips with a seam roller.

If a chimney breast falls parallel to the run of the paper, mark a rough line on the paper at the ap-proximate position of the chimney breast. Cut out the marked piece, leaving an excess of about 15mm (⅝in) for fine trimming when the whole strip is in place.

If the strip ends at a chimney breast there are fewer problems. External corners are dealt with by making a V-cut so that one flap of the paper can be folded down the inside alcove edge of the chimney breast.

CEILING COVING

Covings are of various materials. Fibrous plaster covings are avail-able in different styles, mostly tra-ditional. Plasterboard or gypsum covings are elegant and simple to install. Of the various plastic types there are covings and ceiling cen-tres made from glass fibre and from cellular plastics such as polyure-thane and expanded polystyrene: these are light and easy to handle. There are also covings made from a plastic resin product that looks like genuine plasterwork and can be sawn, drilled and sanded like wood; and, unlike the other plas-tics, it is fire-resistant.

TYPES OF ADHESIVES

Manufacturers usually recom-mend a suitable adhesive. They come ready-mixed or, for fixing

PAPERING ROUND OBSTACLES

1. Make a small slit where the edge of the paper meets a ceiling rose.

2. Hang the next length so it butts up against the previous one.

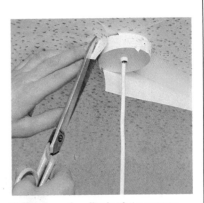

3. Again make slits in the paper to fit it round the rose.

4. Turn off the power, remove rose cover and press overlap into place.

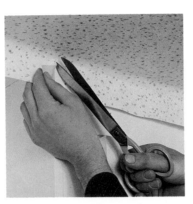

5. Where paper meets an alcove make slits in line with the corners.

6. Brush the paper into place, then trim the overlap along the wall.

plasterboard or gypsum coving, in powder form – you mix the adhesive with water.

Polystyrene should be stuck with a special expanded polystyrene adhesive. However, if the ceiling is uneven, you will get better results with a ceramic wall tile adhesive; this also can be used to fill any gaps between the coving and ceiling or wall.

CUTTING COVING

Corners will have to be mitred, and there is a different technique for internal and external angles. Some preformed coving comes with a template to make cutting easier; if not, you will need to use a mitre box. For cutting you will need a fine-toothed saw. Polystyrene coving comes with special pre-formed corners.

FIXING COVING

Slightly roughen the surface of the wall and ceiling where the coving will be fixed. If it is very porous seal it with a coat of diluted emulsion or PVA adhesive.

Spread the adhesive on to the back edges of the coving. Push each length firmly into position and hold it in place until it sticks.

If plaster coving does not hold in place after a few seconds then support it with nails until the adhesive sets. Drive masonry nails into the wall immediately above and below the edges of the cove (not through it) at about 300mm (1ft) centres. Remove the nails later.

Scrape off surplus adhesive which squeezes out from under the coving. Butt up successive lengths of cove and use excess adhesive to fill the joints.

FIXING CEILING CENTRES

A ceiling centre is a focal point, and it is essential to choose the right size for the room. They range from 150mm (6in) to 685mm (2ft 3in) in diameter. To help you decide on the size, make a paper template to gain an impression of the finished effect.

Ceiling centres are fixed in the same way as coving. Use a cardboard template round which to draw a guide line before preparing the surface in the same way as for fixing coving. Make the template about 6mm (¼in) smaller than the actual ceiling centre so that areas where paper or paint have been removed will be covered.

Heavier types may need extra support from nails or screws: make sure the heads are countersunk or punched home and fill the gaps with adhesive or other filler.

Where the ceiling centre has a hollow in the middle, it may be

FIXING COVING

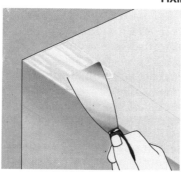

1. Use a piece of coving as a ruler to draw guide lines on the wall and ceiling, then prepare the surface by removing all old wallpaper, flaking paint or distemper from between the guidelines. Fill any cracks and leave the filler to harden.

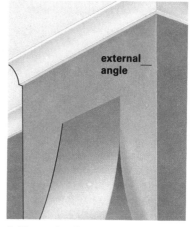

2. Use a mitre box or paper template to cut mitres for angles.

3. Place ceiling edge of the coving in the bottom of the mitre box.

4. If a paper template is provided, mark a line and saw along it.

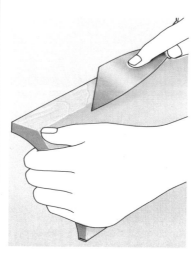

5. Spread a thick layer of adhesive on to the back of the cove.

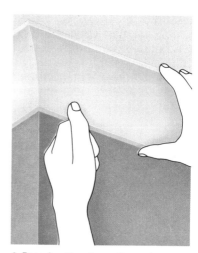

6. Pressing the piece of cove into position will ensure a firm grip.

FIXING A CEILING CENTRE

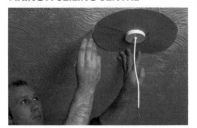

1. Mark the area with a paper template.

2. Apply adhesive and fix in position.

possible to leave the existing ceiling rose in place and fit the new ceiling centre over it. With other types you may have to remove the existing rose and replace it with a terminal connector strip which will fit in the space available before fixing the ornament. Alternatively, you can rewire the light so access can be gained from above.

SUSPENDED CEILINGS

A suspended ceiling can be both decorative and practical. You can install one simply to conceal an ugly (though sound) existing ceiling, or to create a concealed lighting scheme by combining translucent panels with fluorescent lights mounted on the original ceiling. A suspended ceiling also improves the acoustics of a room.

The panels are supported on a metal grid of main tees (which span the shorter dimension of the room) and cross tees (which span the main tees). The whole assembly is then supported on edge trims fixed to the walls; the tees are actually held in place by their own weight. Joins are usually needed in the edge trim and main tees to achieve the required length. The ends simply butt together and in

the case of the main tees are usually secured with a clip.

You may need some form of intermediate support linking the suspended and the original ceiling in order to stop sagging. These supports are certainly necessary at joins in main tees and may be needed elsewhere along the main tees. At joints, special brackets may be used to clip the joints together and provide support. Over the rest of the ceiling, it is more usual to use a length of galvanized wire twisted through a hole in the tee and attached to a screw eye driven into the ceiling.

FITTING THE EDGE TRIM

The first stage is to mark the position of the edge trim on the walls, bearing in mind that, where you are using fluorescent lights above the ceiling, a gap of at least 100mm (4in) will be needed between the

original ceiling and the translucent panels. If you are installing opaque mineral fibre panels a gap of 50-75mm (2-3in) is enough.

Make a mark with a pencil at the appropriate level – the minimum ceiling height is 2.3m (7ft 6in) – and continue the line right round the room, using a spirit level and a long, straight timber batten as a guide. Fix the edge trim in place using masonry nails or screws and wall plugs.

Any cutting to length can be done with a hacksaw; clean up the cut ends with a file. Butt joins are adequate for joining straight lengths of trim, but at corners it is usual to use a mitre or overlap join.

Because the main and cross tees are not fixed to the edge trim, you can always make slight adjustments to their positions as you put up the ceiling in order to equalize the sizes of the border panels.

SUSPENDED CEILING COMPONENTS

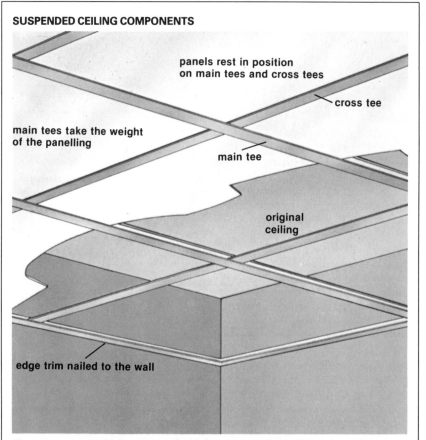

panels rest in position
on main tees and cross tees

cross tee

main tees take the weight
of the panelling

main tee

original
ceiling

edge trim nailed to the wall

The components which make up the kit for a suspended ceiling as supplied by the manufacturer. Main tees are supported on the edge trim fixed at the sides of the room and in turn support the cross tees and panels which are held in place by their own weight and do not require extra fixing.

JOINING EDGE TRIM NEATLY

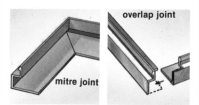

overlap joint

mitre joint

To mark off an overlap join neatly, use one piece of trim as a rule to draw the cutting line on the other. Either cut mitres or remove part of each piece as shown.

ADDING EXTRA SUPPORT

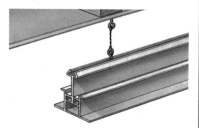

Loop wire through a hole drilled in the tee or joint clip. Hook it over screw eyes fixed to the joists.

FITTING CROSS TEES AND PANELS

Once all the main tees are in position the bulk of the work is over. All you need do now is add the cross tees and slot in the panels.

Cut the border panels to size with scissors or a fine-toothed saw.

FLUORESCENT FITTINGS

If you have an existing pendant fitting, undo the rose cover. An old-fashioned two-terminal rose should be replaced with a four-terminal junction box connected to the existing mains cable. A three-terminal loop-in rose can be retained; disconnect the flex and connect a length of new cable to line the flex terminals of the rose to a new three-terminal junction box nearby. The new cable is connected to this.

Cables are connected to this junction box and run from there to the individual fluorescent fittings or starter-and-ballast units. Fly leads connect the units with the individual tubes. The existing switch arrangement will then control all the fittings as one.

A final point to remember: if the existing light fitting is not earthed, you should run a single earth core from the junction box back to the earthing point on your main fuse box or consumer unit.

FITTING MINERAL FIBRE TILES

There are several ways of fixing mineral fibre tiles. They can be stuck to the ceiling with a fireproof adhesive recommended by the manufacturer, used in conjunction with metal grids or other components to form suspended ceilings, or bevelled tongued-and-grooved tiles can be secret-nailed though the tongue to battens fixed to the joists.

ASSEMBLING A SUSPENDED CEILING

1. Mark a true horizontal line all round the room for the edge trim.

2. Carefully drive in a masonry nail at one end of the first trim.

3. Lay the main tees in position on the edge trim. On long spans and at joins in the tee, add intermediate supports to prevent sagging.

4. Add cross tees and drop the first whole panels into place.

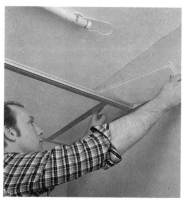

5. Cut border pieces to the width you need with scissors or a fine-toothed saw; slip them into place.

6. Offer up each panel in turn, then slide the next cross tee into place.

TACKLING TILING PROBLEMS
Plan for symmetry *round* the features that are the focal points of a wall. Here are some guidelines:

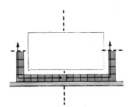

Wall with one window; plan the tiling from a centre-line drawn vertically through the window.

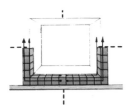

Recessed windows; again work from a line drawn vertically through the window, but make sure that whole tiles are placed at the front of the sill and sides of the reveals.

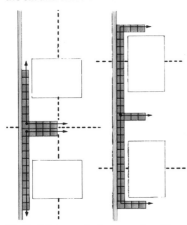

Wall with two windows; unless the space between the windows is exactly equal to a number of whole tiles, start your tiling from a centre line drawn between the two.

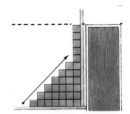

Wall with door placed close to a side wall; plan the tiling to start one tile's width from the frame; if the frame is not exactly vertical, you can cut tiles to fit the remaining space.

TILES AND TILING

Within each range of tiles there are usually three types. *Spacer* tiles have small projections on each edge called lugs which butt up to the neighbouring tile. *Border* tiles are squared off on all sides but are glazed on two adjacent edges – these give a neat finish to outer corners and top or side edges. *Universal* or *continental* tiles have no lugs and are square on all edges. If tiles do not have lugs you have to include grouting space in your calculations – this can be created using pieces of cardboard or cross-shaped plastic spacers sold in packets.

Tiles are sold by the sq metre, sq yard, boxed in 25s or 50s, or can be bought individually.

ADHESIVES AND GROUTING

The choice of both of these depends on where the tiles are to be fixed. In a watery situation (eg, a shower cubicle or a steamy kitchen) it is important to use a waterproof variety of both, even though you might have to wait 4-5 days before exposing the tile surface to use. It is not worthwhile buying

TILING AROUND A PIPE
Cut a tile into two along a line corresponding with the centre point of the pipe. Mark semi-circles on the tile, score, and nibble away waste with pincers or a file saw.

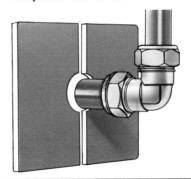

ordinary and waterproof adhesive for a job – you might as well use all waterproof.

All ceramic tile adhesives are like thin putty and can be bought ready mixed in tubs or in powder form to be made up with water. They are what is known as thin-bed adhesives in that they are designed to be applied in a thin layer on a flat even surface. The spread is controlled by a notched comb (usually provided by the manufacturer but cheap to buy where you bought the tiles) to make furrows of a specified depth. When the

TILING PREPARATION

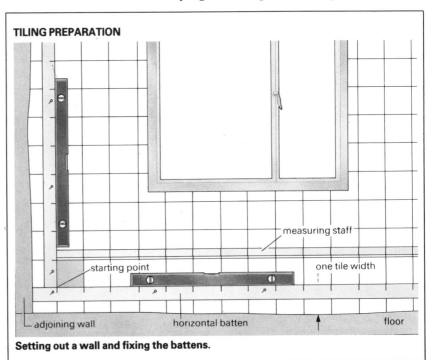

measuring staff

starting point

one tile width

adjoining wall   horizontal batten   floor

Setting out a wall and fixing the battens.

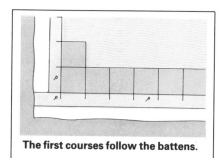

The first courses follow the battens.

HOW TO CUT A TILE

1. To cut a tile, score with a cutter.

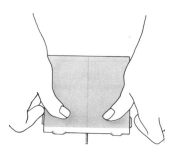

2. Then break it over a matchstick.

3. Cutting with pincers.

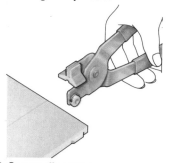

4. Oporto tile cutter.

tiles are pressed on with a slight twist, the adhesive evenly grips the tile.

Grout gives the final finish to the tiled area, filling the spaces between the tiles and preventing moisture getting behind them and affecting the adhesive. Grouting can be done 12-24 hours after the last tile has been pressed into place. Grout can be standard or waterproof (with added acrylic), and both are like a cellulose filler when made up.

If you only make up one lot of grouting, you can colour it with special grouting tints – but remember that it's hard to make other batches match the colour. Waterproof grouting cannot always take these tints.

Press grout between the tiles with a sponge or squeegee and wipe off any excess with a damp sponge. Even up the grouting by drawing a pencil-like piece of wood (eg, dowelling) along each row first vertically, then horizontally. Do this within 10 minutes of grouting so it is not completely dry.

Leave the tiles for 24 hours before polishing with a clean dry cloth. Wash clean only if a slight bloom remains.

Tiles should never be fixed with tight joins for any movement of the wall or fittings will cause the tiles to crack. Similarly where tiles meet baths, basins, sinks or other fittings, flexibility is needed, and grout that dries rigid cannot provide it. These gaps must be filled with a silicone rubber sealant.

TOOLS FOR TILING

A *tile cutter* is essential for scoring the glaze of tiles before breaking them. There are many proprietary types available. *Pincers* are used for nibbling away small portions of tile after you have scored a line with the cutter. Ordinary pincers are perfectly adequate for most jobs, but special tile nibblers are available. An alternative for cutting shaped tiles accurately is a small hacksaw-type saw. *Additional tools* are hammer, spirit level, rule, pencil and a sponge.

GROUTING

1. When grouting a large expanse, a rubber float is less tiring to use; work upwards, then across.

2. On smaller areas, use a sponge or squeegee to press grout in.

HOW TO HANG TILES

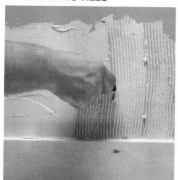

1. Spread tile adhesive, then 'comb' with a notched spreader.

2. When positioning tiles, twist them slightly but don't slide them.

SUITABLE SURFACES

The ideal surface for tiling is one that's perfectly flat, dry and firm. Small irregularities will be covered up, but major hollows, bumps or flaking need to be made good.

Plastered walls and asbestos cement sheets are perfect for tiling

TILING CORNERS

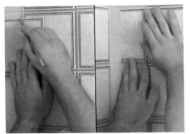

1. At internal corners, mark the tile, then break it and fit in position.

2. File the remaining part until it fits the adjacent area.

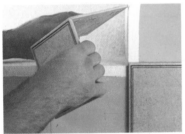

3. On a window sill, use a whole tile at the front; overlap the tile below.

4. Glazed edges of universal tiles finish external corners.

but wait a month after any new plastering to allow the wall to dry out completely. Unless the surface has been previously painted, apply a coat of plaster primer.

Plasterboard is also ideal for tiling as long as it's firmly fixed. Prepare by dusting and wiping down with white spirit, then treat with primer.

Old emulsion paint should be cleaned thoroughly with sugar soap or detergent to remove all traces of dust and grease. Gloss paint needs to be cleaned thoroughly; remove any flaking paint, then roughen up the whole surface with a coarse abrasive.

Do not tile directly on to wallpaper, as this can come away with the adhesive. Strip it completely.

Wood and chipboard are both perfect as long as they are flat and adjacent boards cannot shift. Treat with an ordinary wood primer.

Laminates are suitable provided entire sheets are soundly fixed and absolutely flat. Joins and minor blemishes can be covered up, and the smooth surface must be roughened with a coarse abrasive.

Old ceramic tiles are an ideal surface if flat and sound. Loose tiles will have to be refixed. Small sections or mis-shapen pieces can be built up level with neighbouring tiles – use cellulose filler.

PLANNING ON THE WALL

Plan to give a tiled wall a balanced appearance – with equal sized part tiles in the corners and no narrow slivers around windows, doors etc. To do this, all you need is a tiling gauge which you can make. A tiling gauge is like a long ruler, except that it's marked off in tile widths, including the grout joins. Use a long straight piece of timber about 25mm (1in) square.

Holding the gauge against the walls, first vertically, then horizontally, tells you instantly where whole tiles will fit in and where cut tiles will be needed.

First you must find the centre of each wall. Measure the width – doing this at three places will also tell you if the corners are vertical (hang a plumb line or use a spirit

TILING AROUND FIXTURES

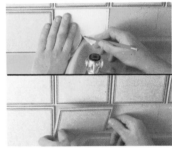

1. At awkward corners use card to make a tile-sized template.

2. Where tiles meet fixtures, seal the joins with silicone caulking.

level to make absolutely sure) – and halve it to find the centre. Use the tiling gauge to mark this vertical centre line with a pencil, then hold the gauge against it. Move it up or down until you have at least a whole tile's width above the floor or skirting board – this can be adjusted slightly if you would otherwise be left with a thin piece of tile at ceiling height – then mark off the tile widths on the vertical line.

Now hold the tiling gauge horizontally, and move it to right or left of the vertical line if thin pieces of tile would have to be cut near windows or fittings, or to make cut tiles at both ends of the wall equal. Following this adjustment, mark the wall and draw in a new vertical line if necessary. The wall can now be marked horizontally with tile widths. Keeping to the same horizontal, mark up adjacent walls in the same way.

Never assume that corners, door frames etc. are vertical, or that the floor, skirting or work surface is horizontal. Fix vertical and horizontal battens to the wall to serve as a guide to fixing the tiles.

FIXING THE BATTENS

First fix a length of straight 50× 25mm (2×1in) battening across the full width of the wall – use a spirit level to ensure that the batten is horizontal. Use masonry nails to fix it in place, but don't drive them fully home as they will have to be removed later. The batten provides the base for your tiling and it's important that its position is correct.

If more than one wall is being tiled, fix battens around the room at the same height, using the spirit level to check the horizontal. The last one you fix should tie up perfectly with the first. If there are gaps, at the door for example, check that the level either side is the same, using a straightedge and spirit level to bridge the gap. Once the horizontal battens are fixed, fix a vertical batten to give yourself the starting point for the first tile. Use a spirit level or plumb line to check that it is truly vertical.

FIXING TILES

Begin tiling from the horizontal base upwards, checking as you work that the tiles are going up accurately both vertically and horizontally. Work on an area of approximately 1 sq metre (1 sq yd) at a time, spreading the adhesive and fixing all the whole tiles using spacers as necessary. Wipe away excess adhesive on the surface of the tiles before it dries.

Next, deal with any tiles that need to be cut. You may find that the gap into which they fit is too narrow to operate the adhesive spreader properly. In this case spread the adhesive on to the back of the tiles.

When all the tiling above the base batten has been completed wait for 24 hours, then remove the battens and complete the tiling.

TECHNIQUES WITH TILES

To cut tiles, lightly score the glaze with a tile cutter to break the surface. Place the tile glazed side up with the scored line over matchsticks and firmly but gently press the tile down on each side. Smooth the cut edge with a file.

To remove a narrow strip of tile, score the line heavily by drawing the tile cutter across the tile more firmly several times in the same place. Then use pincers to 'nibble' the waste away in small pieces and smooth the edge.

Use a cardboard template for awkwardly shaped tiles. Place the template on a tile and score a line with the tile cutter. Any straight score marks can be deepened – use a straight edge for support. Then carefully nibble away the waste with pincers. If there's a large amount to be cut away, score the waste part to divide it into sections, then nibble away. Alternatively, use a tile saw to make the cut; first secure the tile in a vice.

TILING AROUND FITTINGS

When tiling around electrical fittings disconnect the electricity

---

TILE SHAPES
Most mosaics are square or rectangular, but other shapes are also available – round, hexagonal and Provençale are the commonest.

Ceramic tiles for walls are usually square or oblong in shape. The commonest sizes are shown below.

▼200×200mm   6×6in▼

100×100mm▲
▲4¼×4¼in   50×50mm ▲

FIXING SHEET TILES

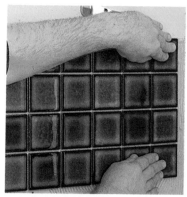

1. Press the first sheet into place, carefully checking its position.

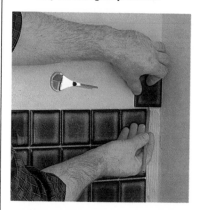

2. Mark off tiles which need cutting to fill gaps at the end of the wall.

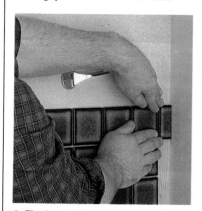

3. Fix the cut tiles in place, leaving a grouting gap.

and remove the wall plate completely so that you can tile right up to the edge of the wall box. This is much neater and easier than trying to cut tiles to fit around the perimeter of the plate. This same principle applies to anything easily removable. The fewer objects you have to tile around the better.

Fittings such as towel rails and soap dishes, shelves and the like have a ceramic base equal to one or two tiles. Leave a gap in the tiling where you want a fitting to be positioned. When the tiles have been in place for 24 hours and the adhesive has fully set, position the fitting (having spread adhesive on the back) and secure it in position with adhesive tape. Allow 24 hours before removing the tape.

TACKLING TILING PROBLEMS

Whenever a fitting, a door or a window interrupts the clean run of a wall, it becomes the focal point of

the wall. So you have to plan for symmetry round the features.

On a wall with one window, plan the tiling from a centre-line drawn vertically through the window.

In the case of a recessed window, again work from a centre-line drawn vertically through it. But make sure that whole tiles are placed at the front of the sill and

the sides of the reveals; place cut tiles closest to the window frame.

On a wall that has two windows, unless the space between the two windows is equal to a number of whole tiles, start from a centre-line drawn between the two.

If there is a door in the wall, and it is placed fairly centrally, plan your tiling from a centre-line

FIXING THE BATTENS

1. Fix battens in place so they are equally spaced at intervals.

2. Insert packing pieces to ensure the battens are perfectly flat.

ATTACHING WALLBOARDS

1. Place a board so that its edge comes to the middle of a batten.

2. Drive in the pins 150mm (6in) apart at alternate angles.

3. With the board secured to the uprights, you can pin it to the cross battens. Stretch a piece of string across the board so that all the pins will be in line.

4. Butt-join the boards, placing the second tightly against the first.

5. Punch nail heads down, then cover the nail heads with stopping.

6. Fix the skirting board: you may need to pack out the wall behind.

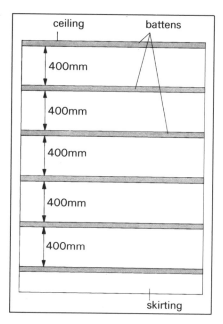

drawn vertically through the door. If, however, the door is very close to a side wall, plan the tiling to start one tile's width from the frame. If the frame is not exactly vertical, cut tiles to fit the space.

TYPES OF MOSAICS

Most mosaic tiles are supplied on backing sheets. This means that the sheet itself can be cut to fit the tiles round doors, windows, light switches and fittings. In effect, it keeps the cutting of tiles themselves to a minimum.

The tiles are available glazed or unglazed, and in various shapes. The number on a sheet varies from 12 to about 80, depending on the size and shape of each tile. Some sheets come with a paper facing over the front of the tiles, and this has to be removed after the adhesive has set so that the grouting can be completed. The disadvantage in using such sheets is that you cannot see the overall effect of the tiles right away. To overcome this problem, most mosaic tiles are now produced with either a nylon or perforated paper backing. The added advantage with this type is that you can, if you wish, make minor adjustments to the placing of each tile during laying, by cutting through the backing mesh with a sharp knife and sliding the tile to its ideal position.

WALL BOARDS

There are two basic types of board: those made from plywood, usually finished on one side with a decorative hardwood veneer, and those made from hardboard. There is nothing to stop you using plywood as wallboards, but if you do, make sure that the surface veneer is free from unmatched joins, patches, knots or other defects so that it looks reasonably attractive.

Hardboard versions come in a greater variety, largely because hardboard, being fibrous, can be moulded and coloured to resemble a great many other materials. You can get hardboard wallboards that look like tongued-and-grooved boards, tiles, Tudor or Jacobean-style panelling, some that look like plaster or stone, and so on. The size of the sheets is invariably 2440×1220mm (8×4ft).

When choosing wallboards it pays to shop around. You'll find that there are many variations not only in price and style but also in quality.

Find the centre of the wall and from this work out how many whole board widths are needed to cover the length of the wall, and how many cut boards you will need to complete the job. If the cut boards will be too narrow, move the starting point along by half the width of a board and try again. Next, work out the positions of the horizontal joins. You may decide to go for a random arrangement so the joins will appear less obvious. Alternatively, you can arrange the horizontal joins systematically to form a regular pattern.

FIXING BATTENS

If you are going to fix the boards to battens, lengths of 50×25mm (2× 1in) sawn timber will be suitable. These should be treated with preservative before fixing. Fix them to the walls with screws and wallplugs or masonry nails.

It's up to you whether you run the battens vertically or horizontally, or both. Whichever way you

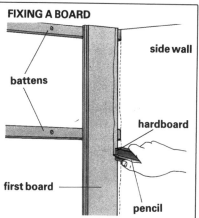

1. Scribing the first board to wall.

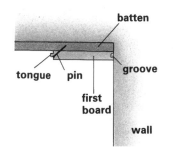

2. The groove fits into the corner.

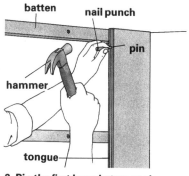

3. Pin the first board at an angle through the tongue.

choose they should be equally spaced and close enough together to stop the boards buckling; this spacing depends on the thickness of the boards and their strength so it's worth asking your supplier for advice.

FIXING THE WALLBOARDS

You can use nails or screws to fix the boards to the battens. If you decide to make a decorative feature of the screws they should be evenly spaced. You can also glue the panels to the battens using

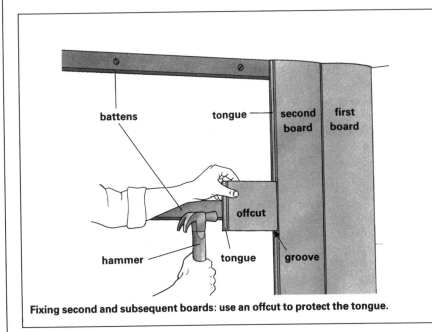

Fixing second and subsequent boards: use an offcut to protect the tongue.

Labels: battens, tongue, second board, first board, offcut, hammer, tongue, groove

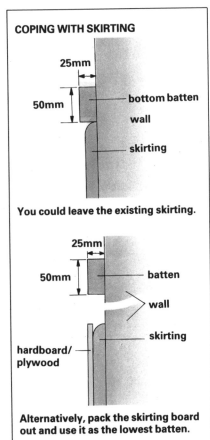

COPING WITH SKIRTING

25mm, 50mm, bottom batten, wall, skirting

You could leave the existing skirting.

25mm, 50mm, batten, wall, skirting, hardboard/plywood

Alternatively, pack the skirting board out and use it as the lowest batten.

special panel adhesive applied to the battens. If the adhesive doesn't hold the panels immediately, fix them temporarily with nails, driving these only partly home so they can be easily removed later.

The logical extension to glueing the boards to battens is to glue them directly to the wall, again using special adhesive. The wall needs to be pretty flat for this method to work. Also, it must be clean, dry and sound.

If you are using a handsaw to cut the boards, work with the decorative face uppermost to reduce the chances of damaging it. If you are using a power jig saw, work with the decorative face downwards. Always score the cutting line first before sawing to reduce the risk of tearing or fraying the cut edges.

COPING WITH OBSTACLES

For light switches, power sockets and so on you should follow the same procedure as if you were cladding the wall with tongued-and-grooved boards (see below) unless you have opted to glue the boards directly to the wall. In this case you can simply remove the faceplate while the board is fixed in position and then replace it.

You will have to cut the necessary hole in the board using a jig saw or pad saw so that it measures about 3mm (⅛in) less all round than the faceplate. This allows the faceplate to conceal any roughly cut edges.

To cope with an internal corner, cover one wall as completely as possible without scribing to fit (unless the join is very irregular). Then cover the adjacent wall, butting the edge of the covering tight against that on the first wall. You could conceal the angle further with scotia moulding or quadrant beading, glued in place with PVA woodworking adhesive. At an external corner, try to butt-join the boards as best you can so the overlap conceals the cut edge which is most clearly visible. From some viewpoints the cut edge will still be visible, so if you are using a wooden or wood-effect board, fit a covering moulding (birdsmouth or angle moulding) stained to match the main board surface.

FINISHING

Many boards, particularly those made from pressed hardboard, are pre-finished and don't need any additional treatment. Those made from veneered plywood or some other 'natural' timber finish need only be varnished, preferably using a polyurethane varnish.

WALLBOARDS AND INSULATION

You can place insulation behind the wallboards – provided, of course, they are supported on battens. Simply fit the insulation, either glass fibre blanket or slabs of polystyrene foam, in between the battens and cover it with polythene sheeting, stapled in place, to act as a vapour barrier and prevent condensation problems.

TONGUED AND GROOVED BOARDS

Tongued and grooved boarding comes in widths of 100mm and 150mm (4 and 6in) and is cut to the length required. The surface may be untreated or prefinished. An untreated surface may come sanded ready for finishing; if not, sand it before you fix it in place on the wall so it will be ready to receive the finish you choose.

USING BATTENS

The most common method of fixing is to fit timber battens to the walls, then fix the wall covering to the battens. The boards can be fixed vertically or horizontally.

TACKLING INTERNAL AND EXTERNAL CORNERS

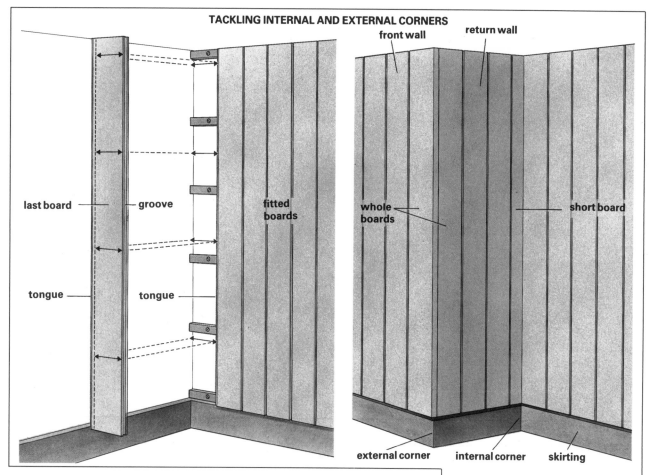

last board — groove — fitted boards — front wall — return wall — whole boards — short board

tongue — tongue — external corner — internal corner — skirting

Use 50×25mm (2×1in) softwood, treated with wood preservative, for the battens. Cut them to the required length and fix them to the wall 400-450mm (16-18in) apart at right-angles to the way in which the boarding is to run. For vertical boarding, fix the top batten at ceiling level and the bottom one at top of skirting level. Where necessary use hardboard packing pieces to ensure the battens are level.

Prise off all architraves around windows and doors and replace them with battens. Skirtings are usually best left in place to form a recessed plinth with the bottom batten fixed directly on top of it. However, if the cladding is to go all the way to the floor, the skirting can be used as the bottom fixing as long as it is the same thickness as the battens, that is 25mm (1in). If it is thicker than this, it should be replaced with battens; if thinner, it can be made up to the batten thick-

ness using hardboard or plywood of the appropriate thickness.

Fix battens around plug sockets and check that any new cable runs are safely tucked behind conduit channels; cut the battens to accommodate any new runs. Then you can bring the socket outlet through to the level of the new surface.

FIXING THE BOARDS

Start fixing the boarding in a corner and make sure the first length is truly vertical or horizontal by checking with a plumb line or spirit level. It may be necessary to trim the grooved edge of the first length to follow the line of the side wall or ceiling. To do this, scribe a line along the edge of the board by running a pencil flat against the adjacent surface. Trim back to the scribed line with a flat plane.

To fix the first length in position without any nails or pins showing, use a small amount of contact adhesive. Drive the panel pins ob-

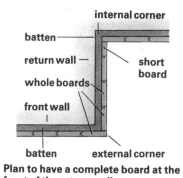

internal corner — batten — return wall — short board — whole boards — front wall — batten — external corner

Plan to have a complete board at the front of the return wall.

liquely through the tongue into the battens behind, then use a nail punch to sink the heads of the pins slightly below the surface of the tongue.

The second length of boarding must be closed tightly on to the first. Slide the grooved edge over the tongue of the first length and, using an offcut of the tongued and grooved boarding, slip the groove of the offcut on to the tongue of the second length. Tap the tongue side

FIXING CORK TILES

1. Spread adhesive for the first tile.

2. Press the tile firmly into place.

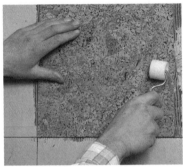

3. Roll the tile with a wallpaper seam roller to get a better bond, particularly at the edges.

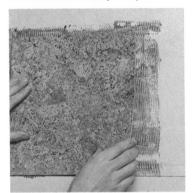

4. Position a tile to be cut over the last whole tile in the row.

5. Marking up the tile to be cut.

6. Cut the tile with a sharp knife.

7. Fix the cut tile to the wall.

8. Tiling the side of a chimney breast.

of the offcut gently so that the joint between the first and second lengths closes up; do this before pinning along the entire length of the board. Put up all subsequent lengths in the same way.

When you come to the end of the run you may need to trim away part of the last length to fit the remaining space. Measure the space carefully and transfer the measurements to the piece of boarding. Take measurements at a number of places in case the adjacent surface is badly out of true. Trim the boarding, cutting off the tongue side. Fix the board using contact adhesive.

At external corners where the boards are laid vertically, trim off the tongue of the last length of board on the return wall and form a square edge so it lies flush with the front face of the battens on the front wall. Plan the boarding so you have a complete board at the end of the return wall – it may mean you have to fit a narrower board in the internal corner.

Drive pins through the square edge into the battens in the same way as you drive them through the tongues. Trim the grooved edge of the first board on the front wall so it will lie flush with the face of the board on the return wall. Glue it in place and pin it through the tongue.

CORK TILES AND SHEET

Cork tiles, panels and sheet come in various sizes. Most are pre-sealed, either waxed or treated with a sealant, which makes them washable and suitable for the steamy atmosphere of a kitchen or bathroom. Some come unsealed, including some of the heavily textured types and the very open granular tiles.

TOOLS AND EQUIPMENT

You will need a sharp knife to trim the cork, a straightedge, a notched adhesive spreader (sometimes supplied with the adhesive) or a pasting brush, a plumbline and chalk or pencil, a T-square or set square, a wallpaper seam roller and (for sheet cork) a wallpaper hanger's roller (which is wider than a seam roller). You will also require a tape measure and, to cut bark-type cork, a fine-toothed tenon saw.

PREPARING THE SURFACE

If you are going to cover with cork a wall which has already been decorated you should strip off old wallpaper, scrape off any flaking paint and fill any deep holes; cut and replaster any crumbling 'live' areas. If the plaster is porous, prime with a solution of one part PVA primer to five parts water.

Gloss or emulsion painted walls can be keyed by rubbing over with glasspaper to roughen the surface, but as the paint can sometimes cause the adhesive to break down, most cork suppliers recommend lining a painted wall with heavy lining paper before fixing the cork in position. Follow the instructions supplied with the particular product you intend using. If you are going to use lining paper, remember to cross-line the walls, that is, hang the paper horizontally just as you would before hanging a good quality wallpaper or fabric wallcovering.

If you are hanging a sheet cork wallcovering and using a heavy-duty wallpaper paste to fix it, it may be necessary to prime the wall surface first with a coat of size or diluted wallpaper paste.

FIXING THE CORK

The tiles should always be centred on a focal point or wall, so you end up with cut tiles or panels of equal width in the corners or at the edge of a chimney breast. Once you have established your central point and squared up the wall for the first line of tiles, tiling should be quite straightforward; the tiles are fixed with contact adhesive applied to the back of the tile and the wall or with an adhesive which is applied to the wall only.

Sheet cork is hung in different ways. The crucial thing here is to hang the lengths of cork to a true

vertical and to plan the layout so cork which has to be cut to fit in width will come at the corners where any unevenness (due to the walls being out of square) will be least likely to be noticed.

With some types of cork sheet you use a special cork adhesive, applied to the wall. With others you apply a heavy-duty wallpaper adhesive to the back of the cork or to the wall – check with the manufacturer's instructions.

Unlike wallpaper, which you trim after fixing, each length of cork should be cut exactly to fit before you hang it. The joins between the lengths of cork shouldn't be rolled with a seam roller, as this will simply make the joins more obvious and spoil the overall look.

If you inadvertently get adhesive on the front of the cork you may be able to remove it by rubbing with your finger when the adhesive is partly set. If it dries before you notice it, rub it gently with a cloth moistened with white spirit (turps). You may then need to re-seal or retouch the surface with wax polish when the cork is dry in order to hide the marks.

If you put up cork tiles, panels or sheet cork which are not sealed you can seal them with a transparent polyurethane varnish (a matt finish looks best). Dust the surface thoroughly and apply two or three coats of varnish.

DECORATIVE MOULDINGS

Mouldings, beadings and decorative trims can be used in a wide variety of ways for decorative effect. For example, they can add character and style to an ordinary chest of drawers, a plain built-in wardrobe with flush doors, or a solid but dull door; they can be used to transform completely a plain box-like room, to make a long wall seem shorter or a tall one less high.

If you have a large room with bare-looking walls, try dividing up the longer walls with 'frames' made of moulding; the areas inside

the frames can then be decorated to contrast with the rest of the wall area. In a traditional setting you could have paper, flock, fabric or other wallcovering, with the outside decorated in a contrasting or co-ordinating colour and the beading treated so that it stands out. This may make it possible for you to choose a luxury wallcovering

FIXING CORK SHEETS

1. Apply adhesive within lines marked on the wall.

2. Trim the first length, then fix in place and smooth with a wide roller.

3. Fix the next length by butting the cork up against the first length.

which would work out prohibitively expensive if applied to the whole wall.

TYPES OF MOULDINGS

There are several types of decorative mouldings available now: the fibrous plaster and rigid polyurethane ones come in narrow widths as mouldings, and also as plaques. These can be used to decorate walls and there are various widths, lengths and designs available.

Wooden mouldings also come in different sizes, shapes, widths and lengths, and include copies of period mouldings. They are usually supplied ready for sanding and finishing in random lengths. It's also possible to have special ones made to order, to make good a gap where the original is missing, or to match other mouldings in the room or on furniture. Mouldings can be bought from specialist suppliers, from wood yards and builders' merchants and, in some cases, direct from the supplier.

At the planning stage you need to check that the mouldings you intend to buy are suitable for the use you have in mind. Remember that wood, plaster and rigid polyurethane mouldings can all be used on plaster, but it is better to use wood on wood. Fibrous plaster can chip if knocked really hard, so it's not practical for use on doors or furniture. Heavy or very definite forward-projecting moulding collects the dust and can be easily knocked.

ESTIMATING PANEL SIZES

Where you are making panels on a wall with mouldings you should aim to have them of a size where they're most effective. Therefore you should make a template from paper (preferably brown) and fix it to the walls with sticky tape; adjust until you get the size right. Make sure the depth of the beading relates to the size of the panel; if it's too thick it will look too heavy and if too thin it will seem flimsy.

'PANELLING' A DOOR

To panel a simple flush door, use narrow moulding, pinning it in

PANELLING A DOOR

1. To panel a door, before you attempt to fix the beading use paper templates to work out how many panels you want and their sizes.

2. Mark off the positions of the beading on the door.

3. Measure the exact dimensions of the panels and mark up the beading.

4. Complete the first panel, then fix the others in the same way.

rectangular shapes, or a combination of rectangles and squares if the door is large enough to take it. You may decide instead simply to create a 'frame' within a door, as on a wall; there's no necessity to form definite panels. The moulding can become part of the decorative treatment or can be different, so it stands out in relief.

To ensure a visually successful result when you panel a door with mouldings there are several steps you can take.

Measure the door and decide whether you want four or six rectangular panels, or possibly four rectangular and two square ones (this treatment will make the door look shorter).

Work out accurately where each piece of beading is to come and draw out the shape on the door as a guide line (use the same technique for applying mouldings to wardrobe doors or built-in cupboard doors).

PROPER PREPARATION

There is no point in trying to fix mouldings or beadings to a rough, untreated surface. Do any cleaning, smoothing, sanding, and fill any holes first.

Prepare the mouldings as necessary. In some cases, as with fibrous plaster, rigid polyurethane and similar products, no preparation is necessary, although the back which is to be fixed to the wall may need sanding smooth.

FIXING THE MOULDINGS

Mark the correct positions for the mouldings using a spirit level, straightedge and try-square to make sure you get the levels right and form true right-angles.

It's usual to stick the fibrous plaster, polyurethane and resin compound type in position, using the manufacturer's recommended adhesive. With a very long length it may be necessary to pin it in position temporarily, using very fine panel pins which can be removed when the adhesive is dry (you can in fact put the pins under the moulding just to hold it in place, and this won't damage the beading and leave unsightly holes which need filling).

With wooden mouldings, the panel pin method, without sticking, is sometimes more practical,

PANELLING A WALL

1. To panel a wall, mark true vertical guidelines using a spirit level.

2. Fix moulding with adhesive, temporarily pinning it if necessary.

3. With the verticals and horizontals in place, fill in with the corner piece.

particularly if you are likely to want to remove them at a later stage. With heavier mouldings it is usually recommended that they be stuck and a few panel pins also be used as a form of insurance. Hide the pins by using a nail punch to tap the head below the surface. Fill the holes to conceal the head.

COPING WITH CORNERS

To mitre the corners when you are fixing panels, squares or rectangles you will need a mitre box to get a true right angle at the corners. Carpenters' mitre boxes are usually a little too clumsy for delicate beadings and a picture framer's mitre box is better. If you don't want to buy one (and they are quite expensive) you can hire one, or alternatively perhaps borrow one. It is also possible to buy moulding ready cut to size and angled; however, you will have to make absolutely sure that your measurements are totally accurate when ordering.

With some ranges of moulding and beading (including the DIY pre-packaged type) you can buy special corner pieces, some of which are curved, which make mitring unnecessary.

DRY LINING WITH PLASTERBOARD

Traditionally the walls of your house were coated with plaster to give a smooth, flat and hard surface which could be decorated with paint or wallcoverings. But plastering – apart from being time-consuming – demands a degree of skill with specialist tools to get a faultless finish. The alternative is to clad the bare brick or block walls with sheets of plasterboard, fixed to a timber framework or stuck directly to the masonry. You can also clad existing plastered walls where the old plaster is uneven, cracked or damaged.

BENEFITS OF DRY LINING

This technique of cladding walls, known as 'dry lining', will give a surface every bit as good as a traditionally plastered wall – albeit

slightly more flimsy – and can be decorated in exactly the same way. Dry lining has a number of advantages over plastering. Large areas, for instance, can be covered quickly with plasterboard, and as there's no drying out time, you can decorate the wall immediately. It's easy, also, to insulate outside walls at the same time as dry lining them, and afterwards you'll have a wall

FIXING A DADO

1. Fixing a dado: work out the height at which to position the rail.

2. Mark off the position of the rail, then pin it in place.

3. At a corner you will have to cut the rail so it forms a mitre join.

that's resistant to cracking, especially that which is due to traffic vibration.

There are basically two ways of fixing dry linings to a wall. The standard method is to nail the sheets of plasterboard to a framework of timber battens fixed to the wall surface. A second technique, suitable where the existing wall surface is sound and the plaster smooth, is to bond special thermal plasterboard direct to the wall surface using adhesive. This is an ideal way to improve standards of wall insulation, particularly in older houses with solid walls that can't have cavity wall insulation installed.

TYPES OF PLASTERBOARD

There are several types of plasterboard available, but it's usual to use a general purpose gypsum plasterboard such as Gyproc Wallboard for dry lining. This has one grey side for plastering and one ivory-coloured side for direct decorating.

Tapered-edge wallboards are needed for dry lining, and in this case the ivory-coloured surface of the boards should be tapered down the two long edges so that after the edges have been concealed with special filler and tape and the surface sealed, the wall will be ready for decorating.

For external walls you should choose 'vapour check' plasterboard, which has a water-vapour resistant blue-tinted polythene film bonded to the grey side, while the ivory side is left exposed for decoration. Again, choose the tapered-edge boards so the joints can be fitted neatly.

Dry lining provides an excellent opportunity to improve thermal insulation of external walls. One way to do this is to fix insulating glass fibre quilt or mineral wool blanket between the battens to which the plasterboard is fixed, but a more effective and convenient method is to line and insulate the wall in one operation, using a special 'thermal board', which consists of standard gypsum plasterboard bonded to a backing of expanded polystyrene. Like ordinary plasterboard, thermal board is available with tapered edges for flush jointing and an ivory surface for direct decoration.

'Vapour check thermal board', the best type to use on external walls, also has a vapour barrier between the wallboard and the expanded polystyrene, in the form of a polythene membrane.

WALLBOARD SIZES

Plasterboard can be purchased in various thicknesses and sizes. Those commonly used are 9.5mm (⅜in) and 12.7mm (½in) thick.

Thermal board is composed of

FITTING THE WALLBOARDS

1. Thermal wallboard is best cut with a saw.

2. For a flush window, cut the board to fit exactly; the edge can be finished with a timber surround.

3. Use a footlifter to lift the board into place, then nail it to the battens.

4. On long walls, butt the tapered edges of the boards tightly together.

5. At external corners, cut away the backing by the thickness of a board.

6. At a corner, have a paper-covered edge overlapping a cut edge.

9.5mm or 12.7mm plasterboard bonded to 12.7,19,27,37 or 52mm (½, ¾, 1, 1⅜ or 2in) thick polystyrene, giving boards ranging from 22 to 65mm thick. The most widely used thicknesses are 25, 32 and 40mm (1, 1¼ and 1½in), consisting of of 12.7mm plasterboard bonded to 12.7, 19 and 27mm (½, ¾ and 1in) thick polystyrene respectively.

The standard width of all boards is 1200mm (4ft) and the normal length is 2400mm (8ft), although 1800 and 2700mm (6 and 9ft) long boards can also be obtained. Bearing the floor-to-ceiling height of the room in mind, try to choose a size that requires the minimum of jointing. In some cases it may be better to fit the boards horizontally.

DAMP AND CONDENSATION

Dry lining isn't a means of curing a damp wall. Although you'll prevent the dampness from showing through on your new wall surface, you'll only be concealing the defects. In cases of rising or penetrating damp therefore, you must cure the problem and allow the walls to

CLADDING REVEALS

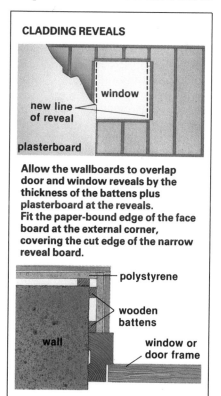

Allow the wallboards to overlap door and window reveals by the thickness of the battens plus plasterboard at the reveals.
Fit the paper-bound edge of the face board at the external corner, covering the cut edge of the narrow reveal board.

USING A FOOTLIFTER
The plasterboard sheets must be fitted tightly into the ceiling angle while you nail them to the battens. To do this, make a 'footlifter' from 225×100×50mm (7×4×2in) timber.

dry out thoroughly before dry lining them.

Condensation, however, can be reduced by using special vapour check plasterboard. Ordinary plasterboard with a minimum of 250 gauge polythene sheeting stapled to the wall battens immediately behind the plasterboard will also do the job; any joins in the polythene should be overlapped by at least 25mm (1in) to make sure of a good seal.

PREPARING THE WALLS

Before starting the job, make sure that the room is properly prepared. When carrying out any replumbing or rewiring work, bear in mind the thickness of the plasterboard or thermal board plus battens.

After the electricity supply has been switched off any socket outlets and light switches should be removed and a check made that there's sufficient cable to allow them to be reset on the new wall surface. If necessary you may have to modify the cables to suit the new surface.

Dry lining provides a good opportunity to conceal water pipes beneath the plasterboard in the cavities formed by the timber battens or in grooves formed by channelling out of polystyrene if you're using thermal board fixed directly to the wall. Ordinary 15mm copper pipe is easy to conceal, but with thicker 22mm copper or plastic pipes it may be necessary to chase grooves in the wall surface in order to cover the pipework.

If heavy fittings, such as kitchen

wall units, are eventually to be fixed to the wall, work out their positions in advance. You can then allow for extra battens to be fixed to the wall surface, in addition to the battens supporting the boards; this will enable the heavy fittings to be fixed securely.

Where you're fixing the dry lining over an existing plastered wall, surface fixtures such as skirting boards and door and window architraves should be carefully removed for re-use. Tap the original plaster surface all over to ascertain that it is sound. If it sounds hollow, this means that it's loose and may weaken the adhesion of the wallboards. The best precaution for such 'blown' areas is to hack off the loose plaster to reveal the masonry.

New deeper window sills will be required. If these are wood, either you can fit new ones, or plane the front edge of the existing ones square, allowing an extension piece to be glued and screwed to the sill once the thermal board has been fitted.

If you're also going to re-line a ceiling with plasterboard, fix the

SEALING JOINTS
Use special corner tape for external angles. The board surface is then sealed and painted or wallpapered.

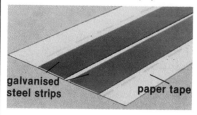

Three tools you need for jointing are: (A) a 100mm (4in) taping knife; (B) a 200mm (8in) applicator for filler and finish, and (C) a jointing sponge for feathering edges and final finish.

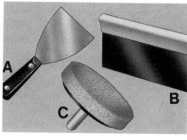

FIXING BOARDS USING ADHESIVE

Spread on the adhesive in bands as shown, with the outer bands approximately 50mm (2in) inside the guidelines. Then immediately fix the thermal wallboard with wallplugs and screws.

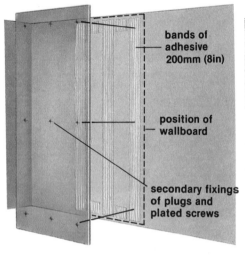

bands of adhesive 200mm (8in)

position of wallboard

secondary fixings of plugs and plated screws

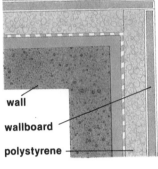

wall

wallboard

polystyrene

For neat external corners, cut away the polystyrene backing to take the full thickness of a board with its backing.

sheets before starting on the wall lining.

SETTING OUT THE BATTENS

The majority of walls – especially brick and block walls prior to plastering – are usually uneven, and to achieve a straight and flat finish this must be corrected by fixing a framework of battens to fix the plasterboard on to.

Begin by marking the wall vertically in board widths, then mark the intermediate batten positions, according to the thickness of the board you're using. These should be 400mm (16in) for 22 and 28mm (⅞ and 1in) boards, and 600mm (2ft) for 25, 32, 40, 50 and 65mm (1,1¼, 1½, 2 and 2½in) boards.

Where there are door and window openings, work from these, allowing the thickness of the board and batten combined to determine the new line of the door or window reveal.

Fix a horizontal batten along the wall about 25mm (1in) above the floor. Fix another horizontal batten at the top of the wall, then check with the straightedge that the face of the battens are plumb.

Screw vertical battens to the wall at each side of the room, and at the previously marked centres, so that when the boards are fixed

all the edges will be supported. The boards are usually fixed in single sheets between floor and ceiling, but where it's easier to fix them horizontally then you'll need extra horizontal battens to ensure that all edges are supported. Fix the battens using wallplugs and zinc-plated screws at 600mm (2ft) centres.

Cut the boards about 25mm (1in) shorter than the floor-to-ceiling height and fix them ivory face outwards (if you just intend to decorate the finished surface) starting at one side of the room. Use a home-made 'footlifter' (as illustrated on page 43) under the lower edge of the board, to lift the plasterboard and press it up tightly against the ceiling.

Secure the board in place by driving galvanized plasterboard nails at 150mm (6in) centres into each batten. Use 30mm (1¼in) long nails for 9.5mm thick board and 40mm (1½in) long nails for 12.7mm thick board. The nails at each side of the board should be no closer than 13mm (½in) from the edge.

Drive in the nails so they just dimple the surface of the board, but don't break the paper covering. Work across the wall, butt-joining adjacent boards.

CUTTING THERMAL BOARD

Cut holes for switch and socket boxes as necessary using a pad saw or keyhole saw. Drill a small hole in the corner where each cut out is required so that the saw can be started. Where boards have to be cut in L-shapes – around window reveals, for example – then it's probably best to cut the plasterboard with a fine-tooth tenon saw.

Try to arrange the work so that a bound edge will coincide with external corners, such as around window reveals. The bound edge of the face board should cover the cut edge of the reveal board. Wherever possible, cut edges should be fitted into internal corners. Where cut edges are unavoidable at joins, leave a gap of 3mm (⅛in) between the boards so that the joint can be filled neatly.

Once the wall is fully boarded you can fill the joints. There are two methods: one uses jointing tape, joint filler and joint finish; the other uses jointing tape plus just one compound called Jointex. The technique is shown in the photo sequence opposite.

When the joint treatment has dried, the boards should be sealed prior to painting or wallpapering. In the latter case, the sealer makes subsequent removal of the wallpaper possible. One coat of wallboard primer can be applied, or one coat of Drywall Top Coat.

DRY LINING WITH ADHESIVE

Thermal board can be fixed as described by nailing the boards to battens. However, the expense of battens and the time spent fixing them can be saved by fixing thermal board direct to dry, sound, flat-faced walls using panel adhesive.

Prepare the wall by removing any wallpaper and water-soluble and flaking paint, to leave a clean, dry surface. To improve adhesion, painted walls should be rubbed down with coarse abrasive paper to give a good key for the adhesion. Remove skirtings and architraves, and carry out any rewiring or replumbing as necessary.

Sufficient adhesive should be

spread on about 6mm (¼in) thick, then combed out with a notched spreader – the type commonly used for tiling walls is ideal; or you could cut 13mm (½in) wide by 10mm (⅜in) deep notches in the joint filler applicator.

Hold the board in position with the wallboard surface outermost, then press it back firmly against the wall, applying even pressure with a heavy straightedge. Check that the edge and face of the board is vertical. The board is then immediately given a secondary fixing of wallplugs and screws, using nine fixings in three rows of three; one row 50mm (2in) in from the top and bottom edges and the third row across the centre. The screws, which should be long enough to sink about 35mm (1½in) into the wall, should be inserted so that the heads dimple the paper surface without tearing it. The plugs you use should incorporate a slim

sleeve thinner than the screw head diameter.

After all the boards have been fixed, fill the joints, angles and screw heads as for conventional plasterboard. The surface of the wall should also be sealed in the same way ready for decoration.

SKIRTINGS AND ARCHITRAVES

If damage or rot demands the removal of a skirting, a bolster chisel makes a useful lever for prising boards off. Start at an external corner; otherwise take the overlapping board at an internal corner, or start at the point where the skirting meets the doorway.

Usually skirting boards are fixed in place with nails, but you must be alert for screws (their heads may be covered with filler or even

wooden plugs). Unscrew them first if this is possible, otherwise cut away a little plaster above the skirting board, then slip a cold chisel behind the skirting to chop through them before you finish prising the board off.

In certain places – for example, the backs of alcoves – the skirting board is held in position by the two pieces at right-angles to it. So, unless you remove at least one of those first, cutting the board out is your only option. Drill a series of holes in line down the face of the skirting, and use a chisel to chop out the waste between the holes so you can prise out the two ends of the board.

External corners are invariably mitred. Use a deep mitre block or box or a circular saw set to a 45° bevel and drive light nails through the completed joint. Where walls meet at odd angles, for example round bay windows, you'll have to

FINISHING THE JOINTS

1. Finish wallboard joints with joint filler and jointing tape.

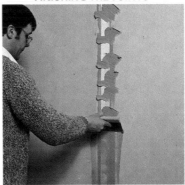

2. Apply a new layer of filler over the tape using the special applicator.

3. Moisten the jointing sponge and feather the edges – that is, wipe off surplus filler from the joint edges. Take care not to disturb the filler in the main joint.

4. At external corners bed in corner tape in the same way.

5. Once the filler has set apply a thin layer of joint finish.

6. When the first coat has dried apply a second coat of finish.

SCRIBING AND FIXING SKIRTING
Use an offcut of skirting to scribe the profile on the back of the board: the end will then fit neatly.

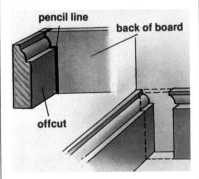

Fix skirtings in the order shown below to ensure that any slight gaps in scribed joints aren't immediately obvious when seen from the centre of the room.

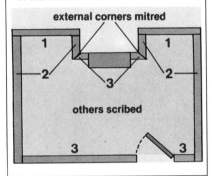

FIXING MOULDINGS

To replace old skirting nail packing pieces to the wall to bring the new skirting out to the level of the old plaster.

To replace modern skirting just nail through the plaster (which probably extends to the floor) into the wall behind.

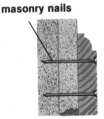

Replacing architraves: these are inset slightly from the edge of the door (or window) frame or lining; conceal the join with the plaster.

gauge each angle with a sliding bevel, and measure it with a protractor. Then reset the bevel to half the angle, and mark the pieces accordingly.

On internal corners, however, a mitre will tend to separate and show a gap, because when you fix the second board against the wall, it will tend to move away slightly from the first board. The answer is to scribe the profile of the moulding on to the second board. Cut it out so that its end fits snugly into position over the first board, then cut it to length at the other end. (Plain boards, of course, can just be butt-jointed.)

The fixing itself depends largely on what's behind the old skirting. If it's fairly recent, the plaster will probably run right down to the floor, the skirting being simply nailed on top of it. Nail the new piece on in the same way, using masonry nails long enough to pass through both layers of plaster and into the brickwork behind – say 63mm (2½in).

For a hollow timber-framed stud partition use ordinary oval or lost-head nails, making sure they pass through the cladding and into the timber sole plate (into the studs, too, in the case of wide skirtings). Ordinary nails will also do for solid walls of soft blocks, and for medium-hard blocks you can use cut nails. If for any reason nails don't hold, use screws and wall-plugs.

Older skirtings can present more problems because the plaster usually doesn't go right to the floor. In fact, it sometimes overlaps the top of the skirting, which means you need to take special care during removal so as not to dislodge too much of it.

Obsolete types of skirting are often very wide, and sometimes even made in two sections across the width. If, as is almost certain, you're replacing them with something narrower, you'll have to be prepared to extend the plaster downwards accordingly.

The skirting will probably have been nailed, either into timber plugs wedged into the joints in the

mortar, or to short vertical battens ('grounds') on the face of the brickwork. There may also be a continuous batten along its upper edge. Your best plan is to make use of these existing plugs or battens. However, you may well have to add packing pieces of your own to bring the skirting forward, the aim being to get its back as nearly as possible flush with the face of the plaster. You may have to replace

FIXING SKIRTING BOARDS

1. To fit skirting boards, use a sliding bevel to gauge the angle at which to cut the end meeting the door.

2. If necessary insert packing pieces to bring the board to the right level.

3. Mark on the board face where the packing pieces are, and nail it on.

plugs or battens that have split or been riddled by woodworm.

Here again, nailing right through is the quickest method. But you may find you can only get a secure fixing and the right alignment by screwing or nailing the packing on first, then nailing or even screwing the skirting to that.

A very uneven floor may mean you have to scribe the lower edge of the board to fit, but such gaps are usually noticeable only when very thin sheet floorcoverings are laid; carpets will usually hide them.

ARCHITRAVES

The idea of an architrave is to hide the join between a door or window frame or lining and the surrounding plaster.

A loose architrave can be nailed back in place to the door frame, or even screwed to the surrounding masonry if you drill right through it with a masonry bit and insert wallplugs to take the screws. But removal and fixing are both easier than for skirting, so replacement is usually the best option. You just lever the existing architrave off and nail the new one on.

On a brick or block wall, you usually nail through the moulding's inner edge and into the door-frame, lining or 'wrought grounds'

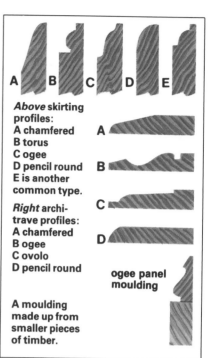

Above skirting profiles:
A chamfered
B torus
C ogee
D pencil round
E is another common type.

Right architrave profiles:
A chamfered
B ogee
C ovolo
D pencil round

ogee panel moulding

A moulding made up from smaller pieces of timber.

with 25mm (1in) oval nails, lost-head nails or panel pins. But if necessary you can nail through the middle of the moulding and into the wall itself, using cut nails for medium-hard blocks if you like, and masonry nails for bricks and hard blocks. If there are rough (concealed) grounds between the plaster and the frame or lining, nail into those. On a stud wall, nail into the studs.

At the bottom the upright pieces butt against the floor and the ends of the skirting. At the top the corners are mitred. A good idea is to start by cutting off three pieces of moulding which are manageable but still slightly too long. Then you can mark off the heights of the two upright ones (which may of course differ a bit, depending on whether the floor is flat or level), mitre their top ends and fix them loosely to the wall.

This makes it easy to mark off the exact length of the top piece. Mitre its ends, position it, and make any adjustments – by moving the uprights slightly, and even shaving the mitred ends with a sharp chisel or block plane if necessary. Then nail all three pieces finally in place, and pin the mitres from the top as for skirting boards.

REPLACING AN ARCHITRAVE

1. Cut the moulding into three over-long pieces; and mark the height.

2. If possible, use a mitre box to cut the upper end of each upright.

3. Nail each of the uprights lightly in position parallel to the frame.

4. Place the top piece upside-down on the uprights and mark it off.

5. Make any necessary adjustments, then nail all three pieces firmly.

RESTORING DAMAGED DECORATIONS

In even the most well-regulated households the decorations may become damaged: paint gets chipped, paper begins to peel or gets marked and stained, vinyl can become scuffed, and wallcoverings may tear or blister. It is, however,

TORN WALLPAPER

1. To repair torn wallpaper, place a matching piece over the damage.

2. Tear round the edges of the patch, tearing away from the front so that the backing will not show.

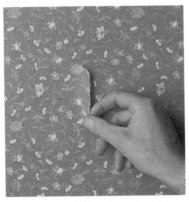

3. Paste the patch, then press it into place: match the pattern exactly.

often possible to mend the damage without having to redecorate.

TORN WALLCOVERINGS

Torn wallpaper can usually be patched fairly simply. Cut a piece slightly larger than the damaged area, then place it over the hole, making quite sure that the pattern matches. Cut through both layers with a sharp knife to a square or oblong shape (unless there is a definite motif in the pattern, in which case you should follow the shape of this). Peel away the old wallcovering and, using a suitable adhesive, stick the new piece in place. Roll the patch lightly with a seam roller and leave it to dry.

Many vinyl wallcoverings have a paper backing. Don't leave the backing of the old wallcovering in place; cut right through it and strip it back to the wall surface before fixing the new piece.

PEELING OR BLISTERED PAPER

If wallpaper is coming apart at the seams you can easily stick it back down again. Where overlapping vinyl edges are loose, use a latex adhesive to secure them.

One method of dealing with blisters is to half-fill a syringe with a suitable paste and inject this into the centre of the blister. Allow the paste to penetrate the back of the paper (it should take about five minutes), then flatten the blister firmly with your fingers. Wipe off any surplus paste and then go over the area lightly with a roller until the paper lies completely flat. If you cannot get hold of a syringe, make a cross-shaped cut and peel back the tongues before pasting them and pressing them back into place.

DAMAGED FLOORING MATERIALS

All types of floor tiles can get damaged and will therefore need to be replaced. You can remove individual ceramic or quarry tiles using a hammer and chisel, but you must wear goggles or safety glasses. Break up the damaged tile using a cold chisel and, working from the centre towards the edges, chip out the fragments and smooth the sur-

face underneath. A bolster chisel is useful for removing old adhesive. Put the new tile in place and check not only that it fits, but also that it sits level with the rest of the tiles. Remove the tile, spread a layer of ceramic floor tiling adhesive on the tile and press it into position. Scrape off any surplus adhesive with the trowel and leave this area of the floor unwalked on for at least 24 hours. You can then

BLISTERED PAPER

1. Make a cross-shaped cut in the blister with a sharp knife.

2. Pull back the edges carefully and apply paste to the back of the paper (or the wall) with a small brush.

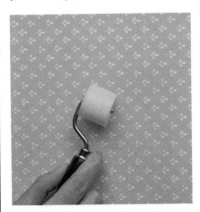

3. Push the flaps back firmly, then roll with a seam roller to flatten.

grout the tile edges. Wipe away the surplus with a clean sponge while it's still wet.

Remove a damaged cork tile by cutting along the edges with a sharp knife and straightedge. Prise the tile from the floor using an old chisel (bevelled side down) and a mallet. Do take care when doing this as cork can easily crumble, and surrounding tiles might get damaged. Once the tile has been removed, clean away the old adhesive from the floor. If removing the tile from a wooden floor, then you'll have to lift the paper felt and remove the panel pins. Brush out any debris left in the space, make sure that your replacement tile has straight edges and cut it to fit. If necessary, press a new piece of felt paper in position and trim the edges neatly. Apply a recommended adhesive directly to the floor and fit the tile. If the floor is wood, hammer a pin into each corner. Remove surplus adhesive from the tile, leave to dry and then reseal.

Thermoplastic and vinyl tiles can also be replaced in much the

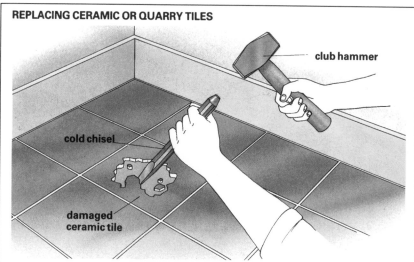

REPLACING CERAMIC OR QUARRY TILES

club hammer

cold chisel

damaged ceramic tile

Remove a damaged tile by chipping it away from the centre outwards.

same way. It's important to remove old adhesive on the floor, either by using a hammer and chisel or a hot air stripper and scraper.

PATCHING SHEET VINYL

Cushioned and printed vinyl can be repaired fairly easily with a patch, so it's wise always to save offcuts at the time of installation. Lay the new section over the damaged area, matching the pattern. Cut through both layers with a sharp knife, using a straightedge and allowing a margin round the damaged area. If your vinyl has a 'tile' pattern it's a good idea to cut through the imitation grout line.

PATCHING VINYL

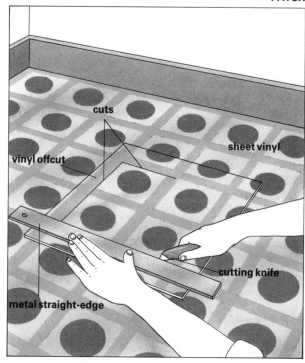

cuts

sheet vinyl

vinyl offcut

cutting knife

metal straight-edge

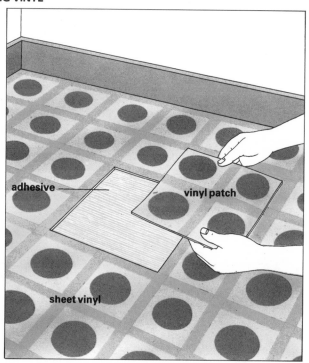

adhesive

vinyl patch

sheet vinyl

Place a spare piece of vinyl over the damaged area with the pattern matching, and (left) cut through both layers of material. Spread adhesive on the floor and (right) place the patch in position.

REPAIRING A DAMAGED WOOD FLOOR

mallet

damaged
parquet blocks

chisel

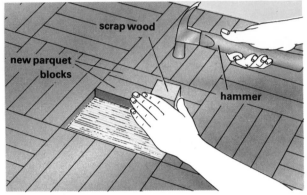

scrap wood

new parquet
blocks

hammer

Remove the damaged wood – either individual 'fingers' or a complete tile – using first a chisel , then a crowbar if necessary. Spread adhesive on the floor, fit the new wood and tap it into place.

Otherwise try to follow other lines in the design. Remove the damaged piece and the old adhesive and make sure the sub-floor is clean and smooth. Spread the recommended flooring adhesive on the back of the patch and on the floor; press the patch into position, remove any surplus adhesive and allow the adhesive to dry.

HARDWOOD FLOORING STRIPS

Replacement areas of hardwood strip flooring are easy to obtain, but do remember to get the correct pattern. Remove the damaged strip or section using a mallet and chisel and make sure you work from the centre towards the edges to avoid damaging the surrounding cover-ing. Clean the floor thoroughly and then apply a thin layer of adhesive. Paper-backed strips should be laid with the paper uppermost, but those with felt backing should have the felt side laid downwards. Individual strips can be carefully planed to make them fit. Replacements should be gently rubbed down with glasspaper and sealed.

DAMAGED CORK

1. Rub an individual tile with glasspaper to remove stains.

2. Brush away the dust and reseal.

REPLACING A DAMAGED WOOD STRIP

1. Remove the damaged strip.

2. Scrape away the old adhesive.

3. Apply a thin layer of adhesive.

4. Press in the new strip and reseal.

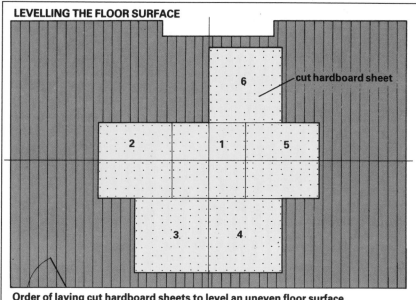

LEVELLING THE FLOOR SURFACE

cut hardboard sheet

6

2   1   5

3   4

Order of laying cut hardboard sheets to level an uneven floor surface.

LAYING A NEW FLOOR

The floor surface on which you intend to lay the new floorcovering should be free of dust and dirt, so go over it first of all with a vacuum cleaner. Then check that the subfloor is in sound condition.

If it is a timber floor, repair any damaged boards, and if the floor has been treated with stains and polishes these will prevent the new floor adhesive from adhering properly, and will have to be removed with a proprietary floor cleaner. Where floorboards are uneven or there are gaps between, the best plan is to cover them up with flooring-grade chipboard, plywood or flooring quality hardboard, either nailed or screwed down securely. Remember to stagger the sheets of material to avoid continuous joins. Then, if there is any floor movement it will not disturb the tiles fixed on top and cause them to lift or be moved out of alignment. Use 12mm thick, water resistant, resin-bonded plywood over floorboards when laying ceramic or quarry tiles.

Punch home protruding nails and countersink any screws. If a board squeaks because it is loose, fix it with screws rather than nails.

Hardboard sheets 1220mm (4ft) square will be a manageable size. To condition them, brush water at the rate of ½ litre (⅔ pint) per 1220mm (4ft) square sheet on to the reverse side of the sheets. Then leave them for 48 hours stacked

flat back to back in the room where they are to be laid, so that they will become accustomed to its conditions.

When fixed they will dry out further and tighten up to present a perfectly flat subfloor.

You can begin fixing the hardboard in one corner of the room. It's not necessary to scribe it to fit irregularities at the walls; small gaps here and there at the edges of the boards will not affect the final look of the floor.

To fix the hardboard sheets in place use hardboard pins. Drive these in at 150mm (6in) intervals round the edges and 225mm (9in) apart across the middle of the sheets. Begin nailing in the centre of a convenient edge, and work sideways and forwards so that the sheet is smoothed down in place. On a floor where there are water pipes or electric cables below, use pins of a length which will not come out on the underside of the floorboards.

The sheets should normally be fixed with their smooth side down

LAYING HARDBOARD SHEETS

1. Nail sheets of hardboard, rough side up, to the old floor surface.

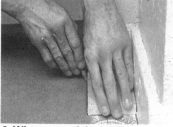

2. Where part of the wall protrudes, use a scribing block to provide a guide when marking off the contour of the wall on the hardboard.

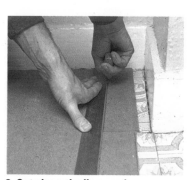

3. Cut along the line you have marked on the hardboard.

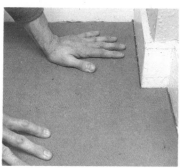

4. Butt the hardboard up against the bottom edge of the skirting.

REPAIRING A CRACK

1. Widen the crack with a club hammer and cold chisel.

2. Dust out, apply PVA adhesive, then fill the crack with mortar.

so that the floorcovering adhesive will grip more securely. Also, the pin heads will be concealed in the mesh.

Nail down the first sheet and work along the wall. When you come to the end of a row of sheets, you will have to cut a sheet to fit. Don't throw the waste away; use it to start the next row so the joins between sheets will not coincide.

When you come to the far side of the room you will have to cut the sheets to width. As before, you need not worry about scribing them to fit the exact contours of the wall.

On a solid floor, check to see if there are any holes or cracks and to find out whether it is truly level and smooth. Fill in all holes and small cracks with a sand/cement mortar. Large cracks could indicate a structural fault and, if in doubt, you should call in an expert. To level an uneven floor, use a self-levelling compound, applying it according to the manufacturer's instructions.

LEVELLING COMPOUNDS

There are two main types of levelling compounds: they are either water-based or latex-based. Both types come as a powder which is then mixed to a slurry and spread over the floor in a very thin layer – no more than 4mm (³⁄₁₆in) thick. They must be trowelled out to an even thickness but there is no need to finish off the surface as they are self-smoothing and any trowel marks will disappear.

The water-based compound is the more common and the more easily obtainable. It is also the easier type to use. It is most suitable for levelling concrete floors and Terrazzo or quarry tiles.

The latex-based compounds are harder-wearing and slightly flexible. Some types can be used to smooth joints and nail holes in a timber floor whereas the water-

based compound would crack and break up as the timber flexed. It is also best to use a latex compound on an impervious surface such as vinyl tiles, as it bonds to them more successfully. Even harder-wearing acrylic-based compounds are also available.

CERAMIC AND QUARRY TILES

Floor tiles are usually thicker than ceramic wall tiles – generally at least 9mm (³⁄₈in) thick – very strong and have a tough hardwearing surface to withstand knocks as well as wear and tear from the passage of feet.

TYPES OF TILES

Square tiles are commonest, in sizes from 150×150mm (6×6in) to 250×250mm (10×10in). Besides square tiles you can choose oblong ones in several sizes, hexagons or other interlocking shapes. Surfaces are usually glazed but are seldom as shiny as those of wall tiles, or scratch marks would inevitably become apparent as grit was trampled in. Most floor tiles are semi-glazed; others have a matt, or unglazed finish.

PLANNING

The first whole tile you lay will determine where all the other tiles are laid, so it is important to get this positioning correct. Choose the corner in which you wish to

1. To use a levelling compound, pour out about half a bucketful at a time.

LEVELLING CONCRETE FLOORS

2. Working outwards from a corner, spread the compound over the floor.

3. Minor trowel marks disappear, but try to leave surface level.

CUTTING FLOOR TILES

Because of the high-baked clay back, floor tiles can be hard to snap by hand. Save time and breakages by buying a tile cutter with angled jaws, or hire a special floor tile cutter from a tool hire shop.

start tiling and, laying your tile gauge (a long batten marked off in tile increments) parallel to one of the walls, measure how many whole tiles will fit along that side of the room. There will almost certainly be a gap left over. Measure this gap, and divide the answer by two to find the width of the cut tiles that will fill the gap at each end of the row. (These should be of equal size.)

If these cut tiles turn out to be less than a quarter of a tile-width across (and therefore tricky to cut), reduce the number of whole tiles in the row by one. The effect of this is to increase the width of each cut tile by half a tile – much easier to cut.

Return to the corner and with your tile gauge parallel to the wall along which you have been measuring, move it so the end of the gauge is the width of one cut tile away from the adjacent wall. Mark this position off on the floor – it

indicates where one edge of the first whole tile in that row will fall.

Repeat this same measuring process along the adjacent wall to establish the positioning of the row at right-angles to the one you've just set out; you will then be able to mark off where the other edge of this same first tile will fall, and so fix its position precisely. Once that is done, every other tile's position is fixed right across the floor.

You can then place this first tile in position. Mark off and cut the boundary tiles between it and the corner. Remember to allow for the width of the grouting gap when measuring each cut tile.

Each cut tile should be measured individually because the wall may not be perfectly straight. You may then go ahead with laying whole tiles, starting from your original corner.

The first thing you have to do is establish a right-angled starting point for the first whole tile. Temporarily nail timber battens in place to indicate the starting point and to serve as a guide for the rest of the tiling. Where you are laying the tiles on mortar and the mortar is simply used as an adhesive, the thickness of the battens should equal twice the thickness of the tiles. Where the mortar is to double as a screed their thickness should equal the thickness of the screed – usually 50mm (2in) – plus the thickness of a tile.

Then, if you are tiling on mortar, use the gauge rod to work out the position of another batten four

DON'T FORGET DOORS

Tiling will raise the floor level. Remove inward-opening doors before starting to tile or they will not open when the tiles are laid.

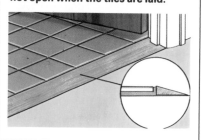

tiles in from one of the battens already in place, and temporarily nail this batten in position. You now have a 'bay' formed by the three battens and it is within such bays that you work across the floor, spreading the mortar and bedding the tiles area by area.

LAYING TILES

In the corner area spread floor tile adhesive evenly on the floor over an area of about 1 sq m (11 sq ft) – it is important to work on only a small area at a time, otherwise the adhesive may have begun to dry out by the time you reach it. With a gentle, twisting motion, place the first tile in the corner, and use light hand pressure to bed it firmly in the adhesive. Place the second tile alongside the first, using the same gentle pressure as before, and placing spacers between the tiles if they don't have spacer lugs. Continue laying tiles, building up a rectangular area, until you reach

LAYING GRANITE TILES

1. First spread an even layer of mortar between battens.

2. Smooth the mortar with a notched dragging board.

3. Bed the tiles by hand, using a tiling gauge as a guide.

the edge of the adhesive bed. As you lay the tiles, it is worth checking every now and again that adequate contact with the adhesive is being made and that there are no voids beneath the tiles – any gaps or hollows under the tiles will become weak points later on.

Use a spirit level to check that the tiles are level; if any are too low, lever them off the bed as quickly as possible with a wide-bladed trowel, add adhesive and reset them, pressing them down gently.

With the first square metre of tiles laid, you can spread another layer of adhesive over a further area, and lay the next area of tiles.

You can proceed with the tiling in 1 sq m sections until all the tiles are in place, then leave them for at least 48 hours before walking on them, otherwise there is the risk that they will be knocked out of place or bedded too deeply. When 48 hours (or longer – check the manufacturer's instructions) are up, you can remove the spacers. Check with the adhesive manufacturer's instructions to see whether you need to allow extra time after this before you begin grouting.

CUTTING TILES

You will have to cut each tile individually since you will almost certainly find variations around the room. Place the tile which is going to be cut against the wall and on top of the adjacent whole tile. Mark it off for cutting.

Using a straightedge as a guide, score the tile surface and edges with a scribing tool. You *can* use a hand tile cutter to cut and break the tile along the scoreline, but it's probably worthwhile hiring a special floor tile cutter to make the job easier.

To cut a tile to give an L-shape, you will need to use tile nips to nibble away at the waste area. Use a tile file, carborundum stone or coarse glasspaper to smooth off the rough edge. For curved shapes (to fit round a WC pedestal, for example) you will need to make a template and again use tile nips to nibble away at the tile.

GROUTING THE TILES

Mix the grout according to the manufacturer's instructions; make up only a small amount at a time and, as with adhesive, work in areas of 1 sq metre (11 sq ft). Apply it with the straight edge of a rubber float, or a sponge or squeegee, making sure the joints are properly filled. Pack the grout firmly into the joints and smooth off using a small rounded stick (not a finger, as grout may irritate the skin).

Remove excess grout (and adhesive) as soon as possible. If it sets it will be difficult to remove.

CORK AND VINYL TILES

Vinyl tiles are ideal for use on kitchen and bathroom floors because they are waterproof and resistant to oil, grease and most domestic chemicals.

The tiles come in a wide variety of patterns and colours, with a smooth gloss finish or a range of sculptured and embossed designs. They can be bought with or without a cushioned backing. Cushioned tiles are softer and warmer underfoot, but more expensive than uncushioned tiles. However, even among tiles without a cushioned backing there is a wide vari-

LAYING CERAMIC TILES

1. First establish a starting point.

2. Pin two guide battens to the floor.

3. Spread adhesive in the corner.

4. Lay the first tile in position.

5. Continue laying tiles along the first row, butting them against the batten to keep the edge straight. Use a spacer to create even gaps.

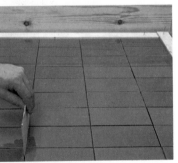

6. Lay tiles area by area.

LAYING WHOLE TILES

1. Start by applying adhesive to a quarter of the floor.

2. Place the first whole tile in the centre right angle.

3. Lay a row of tiles following the guidelines, treading each tile down gently but firmly.

4. Work across the floor, taking each quarter in turn.

ation in price. The cost of a tile is usually a fair indication of its quality.

You can use cork floor tiles in bathrooms, dining rooms and in children's rooms; anywere, in fact, where any other resilient floor-covering could be used. They are warmer and quieter than most other floorcoverings. Where spills and accidents are inevitable, such as in kitchens, bathrooms and children's rooms, it is wiser to use pre-sealed types of tiles. Cheaper seal-it-yourself types are, however, perfectly adequate for living rooms, bedsitting rooms and halls.

LAYING CORK AND VINYL TILES

You should start laying cork or vinyl tiles from the middle of the floor.

Very narrow cut strips at the edges will tend to give an unbalanced look, especially if you are laying the tiles in a dual colour or chequerboard pattern. So set out the tiles dry (in other words, not stuck down) to find out which position for the first tile gives you borders with the largest cut tiles. In a regularly-shaped room this will be quite straightforward; two or three dry runs should make things clear. But in an awkwardly shaped room, especially if it has a lot of alcoves or projections, you will have to make several of these practice runs. When you finally decide on your final starting position, draw round the outline of the first tile to be placed.

If you are laying tiles which require adhesive, you should apply this to as large an area as you can cope with in one go: possibly a square metre (1 sq yd). Butt all the tiles accurately up against each other, and check that they are precisely aligned. Then apply firm hand (or foot) pressure to bed them firmly in place.

Normal practice is to stick down all the full tiles, leaving a border of cut tiles to be fitted round the edges afterwards.

If you are laying self-adhesive tiles, you simply peel off the backing paper and press each tile into place. Where you have to cut tiles,

CUTTING BORDER TILES

1. To cut a border tile, place it on the last whole tile in a particular row.

2. Scribe a line on the tile, using another tile as a guide.

3. Remove the tile to be cut and make a deeper mark; the tile should then break through cleanly.

4. Place the cut border tile in place against the skirting.

don't peel off the backing until the cutting-to-size is completed. Should a tile be misplaced, lift it quickly and re-lay it correctly; the adhesive 'grabs' quickly and later attempts to lift the tile will probably tear it.

CUTTING TILES

Vinyl tiles can be quite easily cut using a sharp knife and a straightedge. For an intricate shape make a template first.

Border tiles can be marked up for cutting in the usual way; that is, you take the tile to be cut, place it on the last complete tile in the row, place another tile to rest on top of these tiles but jammed hard against the wall and use this tile as a guide for marking off the cutting line on the first tile (see page 55). A problem with this method is that it may leave a narrow border in which it is difficult to apply adhesive, with the consequent risk that the border tiles will not adhere properly.

Another method, which avoids this problem, is to lay the field except for the last full tile in each row. Then take a tile and place it against the last full tile in the field. Place another tile on top of the first one and jammed against the wall. Use this second tile as a guide to cut through the first (and it will itself become the last full tile fixed in the relevant row).

The two tiles can temporarily be placed on top of the field, adjacent to the position they will occupy, while you cut the rest of the border. When you come to stick the border tiles down you will have plenty of room in which to wield your adhesive spreader and ensure adequate coverage.

SHAPED TILES

Use either a strong, sharp pair of scissors or a stiff, sharp knife held against a metal straightedge to ensure clean cuts.

Cut shaped tiles by making a card template of the shape you require and tracing it on to the tile to be cut. Alternatively, lay a new tile on top of the last whole tile in the row nearest the corner and another

TILING AN L-SHAPE

1. Positioning the tile to be cut.

2. Use another tile as a guide.

3. Measuring the second cut.

4. Testing if the cut tile fits exactly.

whole tile over that with its far edge flush with the skirting board. Use the near edge of the top tile as a guide to draw a line across the tile to be cut. Slide this on top of the last whole tile in the row around the corner, but don't twist it – the line on it must remain parallel with the first skirting marked out. Place the guide tile over the tile to be cut once more, with its far edge pressed up against the skirting board, and draw another line using its near edge as a guide. Finally cut out the L-shaped part.

To fit a tile around a pipe, make a card template of the required shape and trace the shape on to the tile. Cut a slit directly from the hole made for the pipe to the skirting board.

For other awkward shapes, tiles can be cut using a card template or a special tool called a shape-tracer or contour gauge. This comprises a series of tightly packed wires which, when pressed against a shaped object, forms its outline. The outline can then be transferred to the tile to be cut.

TILING ROUND AN ARCHITRAVE

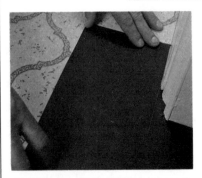
1. Make a template of the area round the architrave.

2. When the template fits, use it to mark the required shape on the tile.

TOOLS, EQUIPMENT AND FITTINGS

For cutting and laying foam-backed carpet you will need: a handyman's knife plus spare blades; an old broad-bladed knife or scissors; a staple gun (useful for fixing lining to floorboards); a steel tape measure.

To anchor the perimeter of foam-backed carpet in place, use either double-sided carpet tape or carpet tacks (best on long-pile carpets that conceal the tack heads). Use only rustproof tacks or rust marks could form around the fixing points if the tacks ever got wet. Space the tacks at 150mm (6in) intervals around the room; closer spacing will be needed at corners and other awkward areas. You will need two lengths of tacks: to fix the carpet around the edges use 19mm (¾in) tacks – these will go through a double thickness of carpet and into the floor; in corners, where three thicknesses of carpet result from folding under the edges, use 25mm (1in) tacks.

At door thresholds, use proprietary edging strips to finish off the carpeted area. Different types are available for linking two carpets (A) or one carpet and one smooth floorcovering (B).

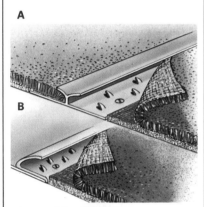

ORDER OF WORKING

First unroll the carpet in the room where it will be laid, and position it roughly, with an even overlap at the skirting boards all round. Check that the excess will fit into alcoves beside chimney breasts, and other recesses such as bay windows and door openings.

Make the first trim along the longest uninterrupted wall (1), then follow the sequence illustrated.

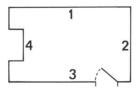

CUTTING IN AT DOORWAYS

At doorways carpet should extend to a point under the centre of the door. To get an accurate fit round architraves and door stops, start making release cuts in the overlap at one side of the opening, until the tongue falls neatly into the door opening. Trim to fit neatly under the threshold strip.

COPING WITH BAY WINDOWS

It's easier to cope with odd-shaped bay windows by trimming the two flanking walls first. Then pull the carpet down the room until its edge is across the 'mouth' of the bay. Measure the depth of the bay, and cut a strip of wood to match this measurement. Use it to trace off the profile on the carpet, marking the line with chalk. Trim along the marked line and slide the carpet back into place against the wall with the bay.

FITTING ROUND PIPEWORK

Where pipes to radiators come up through the floor, you will have to cut the carpet to fit neatly round them. To do this, make an incision in the edge of the carpet, parallel with one edge of the pipe. Measure the distance between wall and pipe, and cut out a small circle in the carpet at this distance from the edge, then fit the carpet round the pipe.

STAIR CARPETS

Before you lay a carpet runner which does not completely cover the width of the treads, mark out the positions of the carpet edges to help you get the borders equal.

FIXING METHODS

There are three ways of fixing stair carpet. They are:

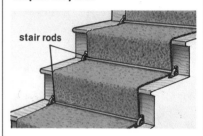

stair rods

● using stair rods which are anchored with side clips; this is the simplest method and the rods form part of the stair decoration

tacks

● tacking the carpet down with special carpet tacks

● using tackless gripper strips or right-angled metal stair grippers (A) – a pinless type is available for foam-backed carpets (B)

CHECK PILE DIRECTION

Always make sure the pile of the carpet is facing *down* the stairs to prevent uneven shading and to ensure longer wear. If you move a carpet runner, never be tempted to reverse the pile direction.

TRIMMING AROUND A CHIMNEY BREAST

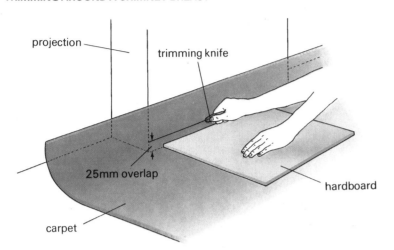

projection

trimming knife

25mm overlap

hardboard

carpet

1. Trim along the front edge of the chimney breast, leaving a 25mm (1in) overlap.

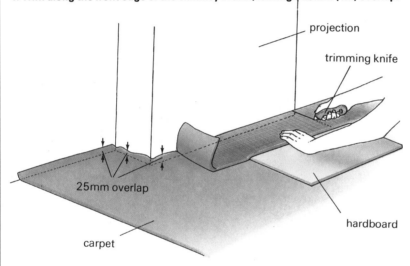

projection

trimming knife

25mm overlap

carpet

hardboard

2. Cut to fit from the corners of the chimney breast back to the wall, leaving a 25mm (1in) overlap.

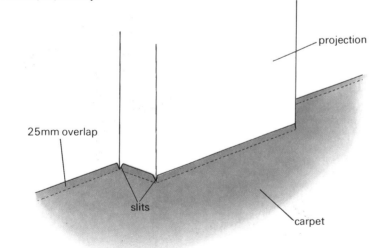

projection

25mm overlap

slits

carpet

3. Cut slits at internal and external corners to allow the carpet to lay properly.

USING CARPET TAPE

1. Using carpet tape: stick double sided self-adhesive tape down all round the edge of the room. Do not remove the release paper yet.

2. Press carpet into the base of the skirting board with the back of an old knife or a pair of scissors; press hard enough to leave a score mark.

3. Turn back the carpet and cut off the excess with a sharp knife, using the score mark made by the back of the old knife or scissors as a guide.

4. Peel off the release paper from the border tape and press the carpet firmly into place, working round the room wall by wall.

STRIPPING AND SEALING FLOORBOARDS

Old floorboards may not look much when you first expose them, but if you sand them smooth to take off all the uneven top layers which are engrained with dirt you'll be surprised how beautiful they can become, especially after they've been stained and coated with varnish to make the grain pattern clear.

First fill any gaps and make sure there are no protruding nails or screws. These should be driven well below the surface.

The first sander you use looks a bit like a lawn mower, but is in fact a giant belt sander. It has a revolving rubber-covered drum set on a wheeled frame which can be tilted backwards to lift the drum from the floor. You wrap a sheet of abrasive round the drum to provide the sanding surface. This type of sander can be hired. The second sander is a sort of heavy-duty orbital sander, and it is used to tackle the parts the main sander cannot reach.

After machine sanding there will be small unsanded patches left, usually at the edges of the floor, and these will have to be sanded by hand or scraped with a shave hook or some other form of scraper.

SANDING PROCEDURE

To prevent dust from permeating other areas of the house, keep the doors closed. Close the windows too, to allow the dust to settle so it can be vacuumed up.

Sanding is extremely dusty and very noisy work, so you should wear the appropriate equipment to protect yourself. A mask, to prevent you from breathing in dust, is a must; you should also consider ear muffs to protect your ears from the din, and goggles so that dust and flying bits of grit don't get into your eyes.

For a truly smooth finish you should first sand with a coarse paper to remove the roughest bits,

SANDING FLOORBOARDS

1. Go over the entire floor, punching all nail heads well below the surface and countersinking any screws.

2. Cut thin fillets of wood to fill gaps between boards. Hammer them in, protecting the edges with an offcut.

3. Plane the fillets flush with the surrounding surface, taking off a little at a time.

4. Start sanding the floor, running the sander diagonally across the boards to remove the rough surface.

5. Sand a strip down the length of the room, working in the same direction as the boards.

6. Sand this strip again, dragging the sander backwards. Repeat for the rest of the floor.

7. Use a small sander to sand round the perimeter, using progressively finer grades of paper.

8. To finish, apply at least two, preferably three, coats of polyurethane varnish.

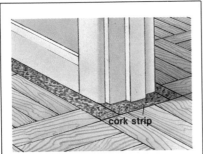

Leave a gap round the perimeter of the room. This allows for expansion, and also means that you can fill in with cork strips instead of cutting flooring pieces to intricate shapes.

then use a medium paper and finish off with a fine grade paper.

Use the large sander in a diagonal direction across the boards in order to flatten them out and to remove thoroughly the top dirt-engrained layer. Then work in strips this time along the boards. Work down a strip then, with the machine on, move back along the strip. Switch off when you reach your starting point.

When the floor has been sanded in strips using first coarse, then medium and fine abrasives, you can use the small sander on the perimeter of the floor.

BLEACHING AND STAINING

If you feel that the boards are too dark to leave as they are after sanding you can apply bleach to lighten them. You may want to change the colour of the boards: you could use coloured polyurethane varnish, but it's better to use wood stains which colour the timber itself and then seal with clear polyurethane varnish. Polyurethane varnish is by far the best choice for sealing the floor, simply because it is so hard-wearing and easy to look after. You'll need to give the floor two or three coats. You can choose a high gloss, satin or matt finish.

LAYING HARDWOOD PANELS

A hardwood floor can add real elegance to a room. In addition to its decorative qualities the flooring

LAYING HARDWOOD PANELS

1. Prepare to lay panels by snapping a chalked line along a straight wall.

2. Using the chalked line as a guide, spread on the adhesive.

3. Lay the first row of panels along the wall, 12mm (½in) away from it.

4. Lay all the whole panels before cutting and laying border panels.

5. Use a spare panel as a guide to mark a panel to be cut to size.

6. Use a tenon saw to cut panels; work with the panel face side up.

will be hard-wearing, durable and easy to clean and maintain.

An attractive hardwood floor can cost less than the price of a good quality carpet with underlay. And the timber will stand up better to spills and dirt.

CHOOSING THE FLOORING

The type of hardwood flooring which is most widely available is mosaic flooring, which comes in panel form. Normally, mosaics are

the most flexible of the various types of flooring and therefore the easiest to lay.

PREPARATION

The floor must be in sound condition and level. The more level it is the less sanding you will have to do when finishing.

You should also condition the flooring. Buy it at least a week before you intend laying it, then unpack it and leave it in the room where it will be laid so it can adjust to the atmosphere; stack it so the air can circulate freely around it.

SETTING OUT

Start laying mosaic panels, strips and wood blocks alongside the longest uninterrupted wall in a room. You should check first that the position in which you intend to lay your first row won't mean you have to cut very narrow pieces to fit on the other side of the room. Dry-lay a row of panels across the room, and, if necessary, adjust your starting point, then snap a chalked line down the room to serve as a guide when you are fixing the first row. A tip: if you want, instead of snapping a chalked line you can make a mark at each end of the room in the relevant position, drive in a nail at each mark and then tie a length of string so it's tightly stretched between them.

LAYING AND CUTTING FLOORING

If you are using a bitumen-based adhesive, spread it on the floor so it covers an area only slightly larger than the piece of flooring you are laying, then very carefully place the flooring in position. This type of adhesive is very messy.

The normal procedure is to lay all the whole pieces of flooring first and then to fill in with the cut pieces at the borders. Cutting should be done with a fine-toothed saw; check that it's sharp before you start cutting. Intricate shapes are best cut with a power jigsaw. If you first make a cardboard template of the shape, the job will be much easier.

If you are using cork strips, to fill in the gaps you should leave for expansion at the perimeter of the room, you may find that some of the intricate cutting which would otherwise be required will not be needed. Round a fluted architrave in a doorway, for example, you can simply cut the flooring as if it were a square corner and then fill in with the flexible cork strip.

FINISHING THE FLOOR

If you have laid flooring which is not pre-finished, you will have to

LAYING PANELS IN AN ALCOVE

1. Place the panel to be cut over the last whole panel at the corner.

2. Repeat the marking procedure at the end of the other row.

3. Cut the panel to an L-shape, spread on adhesive and lay it in position.

4. Finish by fitting the cut border panels at the back of the alcove. Mark them up in the usual manner.

SEALING THE FLOOR

1. Sand the floor to provide a clean, even surface, removing any high spots between the panels.

2. Remove dust arising from the sanding, then brush on a thin coat of special wood flooring sealer over the panels.

3. For a good finish, buff the dry sealer gently with fine sandpaper to provide a key for the second coat.

4. You can use moulding rather than cork to cover the expansion gap round the perimeter of the room.

give it a sanding first to smooth it over. In fact, one of the advantages of using an unfinished type of flooring is that sanding may in any event be necessary to remove the odd high spot here and there.

You can tackle the floor in a small room by hand or with a portable powered orbital sander, but on larger rooms you will need a heavy-duty floor sander and an edging sander for the borders.

Finally, you'll have to seal the floor. Floor sealers come in matt and gloss versions and you will need two or three coats, according to how fine a finish you want. For a good-looking result, it's worth sanding each coat (except the final one, of course) lightly with very fine glasspaper to provide a key for the following coat. If you do this, wipe the floor surface between coats, using a cloth moistened with white spirit, to pick up any dust. If you wish, you can apply a little polish to the flooring once the sealer is properly dry.

LAYING SHEET VINYL

Before laying vinyl, slacken the roll and leave it in a warm room overnight so it will soften, relax any strain in the sheet and be easy to work.

FITTING A SINGLE SHEET

Since walls are rarely straight, you must cut the vinyl to fit the contour of the walls. If you are working in a small room which can be covered with a single width and the vinyl is very flexible, you can lay it out so it overlaps all round and cut it into the edges of the wall with a trimming knife.

Use a metal straightedge to push the vinyl into the angle between the floor and the wall. If the vinyl is not flexible enough, or if you feel more confident having a cutting guide, then make a template.

MAKING A TEMPLATE

Lay a sheet of felt paper – or any stiff card – on the floor to be covered. Rough-trim the paper to fit

FIXING WOOD STRIP FLOORING

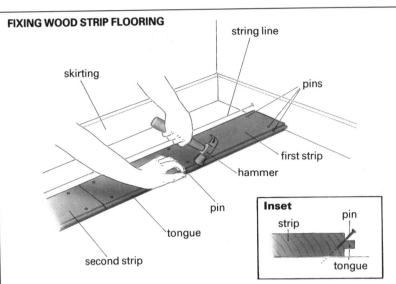

1. Tongued and grooved strip flooring is fixed by pinning through the tongues into the boards below. Hammer in the pins at an angle as shown.

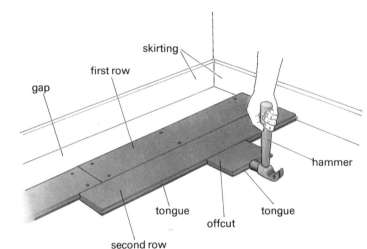

2. When you tap the next board into place the pins in the first board will be hidden. Use an offcut to protect the tongue of the board being tapped.

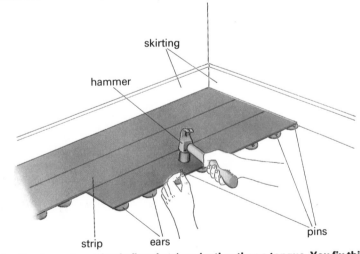

3. Another type of wood strip floor has 'ears' rather than a tongue. You fix this type of board by pinning through the ears.

the required area, leaving a gap of about 16mm (⅝in) around the wall and the fittings. When fitting the template – and later the vinyl – on the floor, you will have to make a single cut from the back of the fitting cut-out to the nearest edge: as long as you follow lines on the pattern, this will not show once the vinyl is laid.

If you have to use more than one sheet, overlap the sheets and draw two check marks across the overlap to ensure the sheets can be repositioned accurately later. Once the paper is lying flat and has been roughly fitted, secure it with either drawing pins or heavy weights to prevent any movement.

Use a pair of compasses with a locking device set at about a 25mm (1in) radius, and with the pointer vertical against the wall or fitting, trace the outline of each in turn on to the template with a felt tip pen. Pipes and supports which are true circles can be squared off using a straightedge on three or four sides.

To transfer the outline to the vinyl, lay out the vinyl face up and position the template accurately on top of it, using pins or heavy weights to prevent any movement.

Check that the compasses are still at the same radius and, keeping the point always on and at right-angles to the marked outline, follow the outline so the felt tip

pen marks the vinyl. Any squared-off pipes can now be traced back using a straightedge, and an accurate circle (the diameter of the pipe) drawn on the vinyl.

FITTING LENGTHS

If the room is too large to be covered by a single sheet, you will have to use a different procedure. Measure the width of the room and cut a length of vinyl from the roll, allowing an extra 75mm (3in). Tackle the area by the door first: this is going to have the most wear and you should always allow a full width of vinyl around it. Lay the vinyl square to the door opening.

Using a square-cut wood block

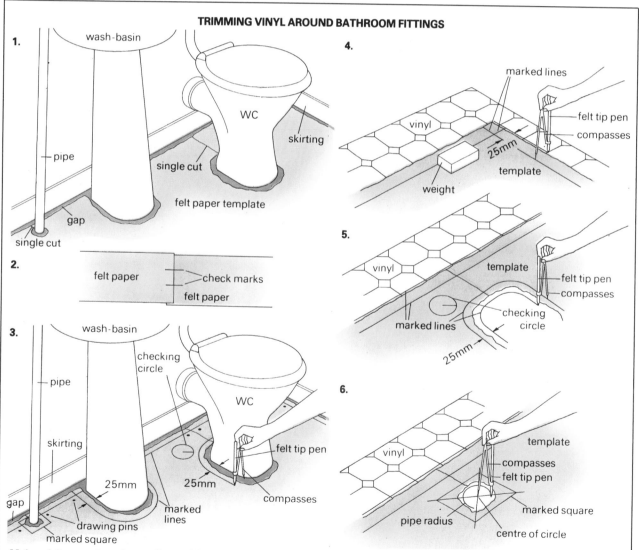

TRIMMING VINYL AROUND BATHROOM FITTINGS

Make a felt paper template to fit roughly round awkward fittings. Secure the template to the floor, trace the outline of fittings on to it, then transfer these marks to the vinyl. For pipes, make a square mark then draw a circle within the square.

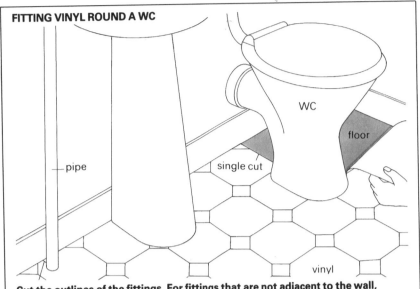

FITTING VINYL ROUND A WC

WC

floor

pipe

single cut

vinyl

Cut the outlines of the fittings. For fittings that are not adjacent to the wall, make a single cut from the cut-out to the nearest edge, following the pattern.

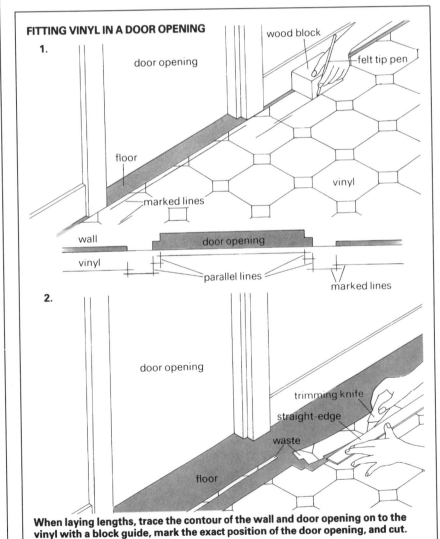

FITTING VINYL IN A DOOR OPENING

1.

wood block

door opening

felt tip pen

floor

vinyl

marked lines

wall

vinyl

door opening

parallel lines

marked lines

2.

door opening

trimming knife

straight-edge

waste

floor

When laying lengths, trace the contour of the wall and door opening on to the vinyl with a block guide, mark the exact position of the door opening, and cut.

125×75×25mm (5×3×1in), with a felt tip pen on the side furthest from the wall, follow the contour of the wall on either side of the door and across the door opening to mark the outline on the vinyl. Mark on lines parallel to the door opening from the edge of the wall outlines already marked to ensure the vinyl fits snugly in the door opening and the edge is not visible when the door is closed. A shape-tracer is ideal for marking out the outline of an architrave to achieve a really neat finish. You can now cut along the marked lines on each side of the door. Place a straight-edge on the vinyl and cut along the outline with a trimming knife.

Reposition the first length of vinyl against the wall with the door, then mark a guideline on the floor along the opposite edge. Place the wood block centrally on this edge and mark lines at either end of the block on both the vinyl and the floor.

Slide the vinyl the length of the block along the edge guideline so that the marks transferred from either end of the block coincide. With the block positioned length-ways against the wall, mark a line on the vinyl as you move the block along the wall. Trim off the surplus with a straightedge on the marked line. Reposition the vinyl along the guideline once more and check for fit.

Repeat for the opposite wall, sliding the vinyl the length of the block in the opposite direction.

To lay the second length, overlap the trimming edges on both lengths and check that the pattern aligns and matches exactly. Measure the size of one pattern repeat; the repeat dimension is marked from the wall to the edge of the vinyl to be cut, following the contour of the wall along the width of the vinyl. The surplus, which is never more than the measured dimension of the repeat, can then be trimmed off in the usual way.

Before cutting along the over-lapping lengths, spread a 50mm (2in) strip of vinyl adhesive at the ends of the vinyl sheets, stopping within 150mm (6in) of the join, to prevent the lengths of vinyl slipping out of position. Place an offcut of vinyl under the overlapping lengths to protect the blade of the knife as it cuts. Make a vertical cut along the overlap as near to the centre as possible – along the border if you have a tile pattern – through both sheets of vinyl. Remove the surplus vinyl and the

lengths will lie neatly together. When laying the final length of vinyl, position it against the wall opposite the door and then draw it away until the pattern matches the previous length on the overlap. Measure the width of one pattern repeat and mark a line the same measurement as the pattern width on to the edge of the vinyl, follow-

ing the contours of the wall; trim off the excess as before. Slide the last length against the wall and trim the overlap.

Vinyl can be loose laid when just one sheet is used to cover a small area, although you should still stick down the area around a door. When laying more than one length you should always stick

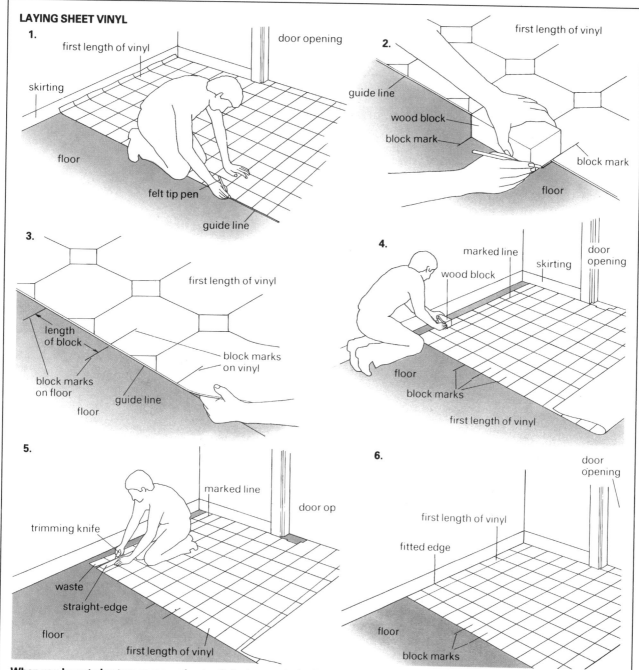

LAYING SHEET VINYL

When you have to lay two or more sheets of vinyl to cover the floor, fit the first to the wall and mark the other edge on the floor. Mark each end of a block on both vinyl and floor, pull vinyl the length of the block away from the wall and trace the contour of the wall on the end of the vinyl. Cut the vinyl then push it back to the wall: the block marks will align.

MATCHING VINYL LENGTHS

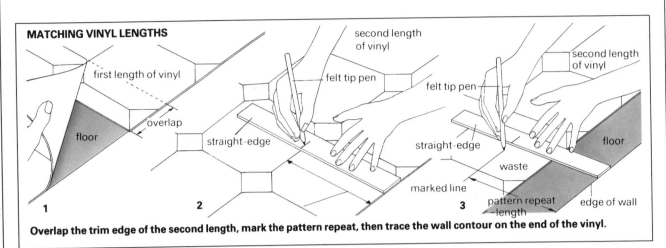

Overlap the trim edge of the second length, mark the pattern repeat, then trace the wall contour on the end of the vinyl.

USING ADHESIVES TO SECURE VINYL FLOORS

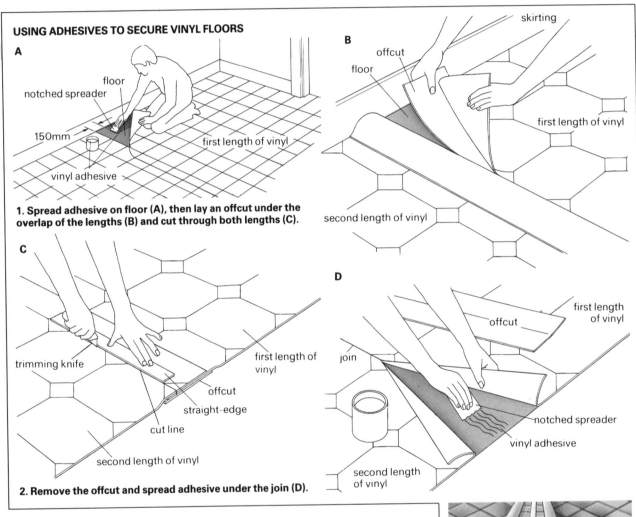

1. Spread adhesive on floor (A), then lay an offcut under the overlap of the lengths (B) and cut through both lengths (C).

2. Remove the offcut and spread adhesive under the join (D).

down the vinyl at the ends and along each seam with adhesive or double-sided adhesive tape, as recommended by the manufacturer. Some recommend sticking down the whole floor covering – and certainly the centre sheet if more than two are to be laid – especially when laying cushioned vinyl. Any shrinkage will be in the length of the vinyl. If you make sure you stick down the sheets at each end, you will overcome this problem and each length will be secure.

Always wipe off excess adhesive at once with a clean cloth.

You can secure the seams of 'lay-flat' vinyls with double-sided tape.

Chapter 2
HOME
PLUMBING

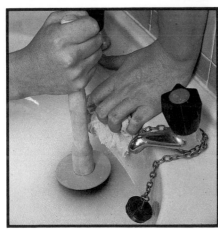

THE HOUSE WATER SYSTEM

The water supply for your house comes via a communication pipe from a sub-main under the road and ends at the water authority's stop valve. This is usually situated under the pavement about 300mm (1ft) outside the boundary of your property. It lies about 1 metre (39in) deep under a hinged metal cover. It should only be operated by the water authority, and requires a special key to turn it. In an emergency you may be able to turn it yourself, and in some old houses it may be the only way of turning off the water supply.

After this stop valve the water enters the service pipe and from this point all the pipes become your responsibility. The service pipe comes underground into the house and when it rises above the ground it is called the rising main.

Your main stop valve is usually to be found on the rising main just above floor level, often close to the kitchen sink. It's where you turn off the water if there is a burst pipe, and this valve should always be turned off if you leave the house empty for any length of time.

In an old house the stop valve may be in the cellar, under the stairs, under the floor near the front door, or even under a cover in the front path; failing these, the authority's stop valve can be used.

DRINKING WATER

At least one branch will leave the rising main – this is the supply pipe to the kitchen sink tap and it provides all drinking and cooking water direct from the mains supply. Other branches may feed an outside tap or indoor appliances.

The rising main terminates at the cold water storage cistern, but the pipework in between depends on whether the cold water supply system is 'direct' or 'indirect'.

DIRECT SYSTEM

In this type of system all the cold water supplies are taken direct

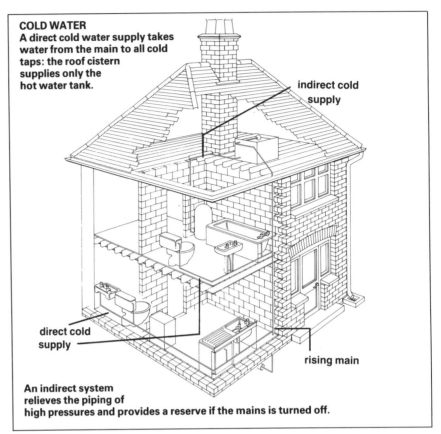

COLD WATER
A direct cold water supply takes water from the main to all cold taps: the roof cistern supplies only the hot water tank.

indirect cold supply

direct cold supply

rising main

An indirect system relieves the piping of high pressures and provides a reserve if the mains is turned off.

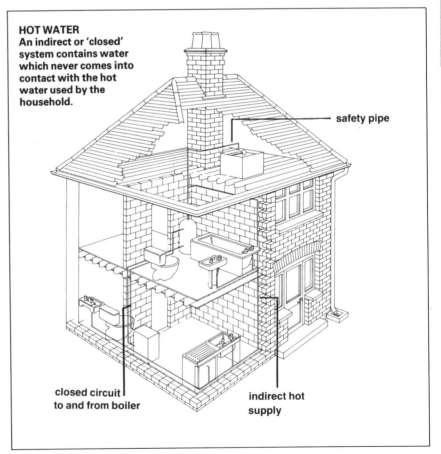

HOT WATER
An indirect or 'closed' system contains water which never comes into contact with the hot water used by the household.

safety pipe

closed circuit to and from boiler

indirect hot supply

THE HOUSE WATER SYSTEM

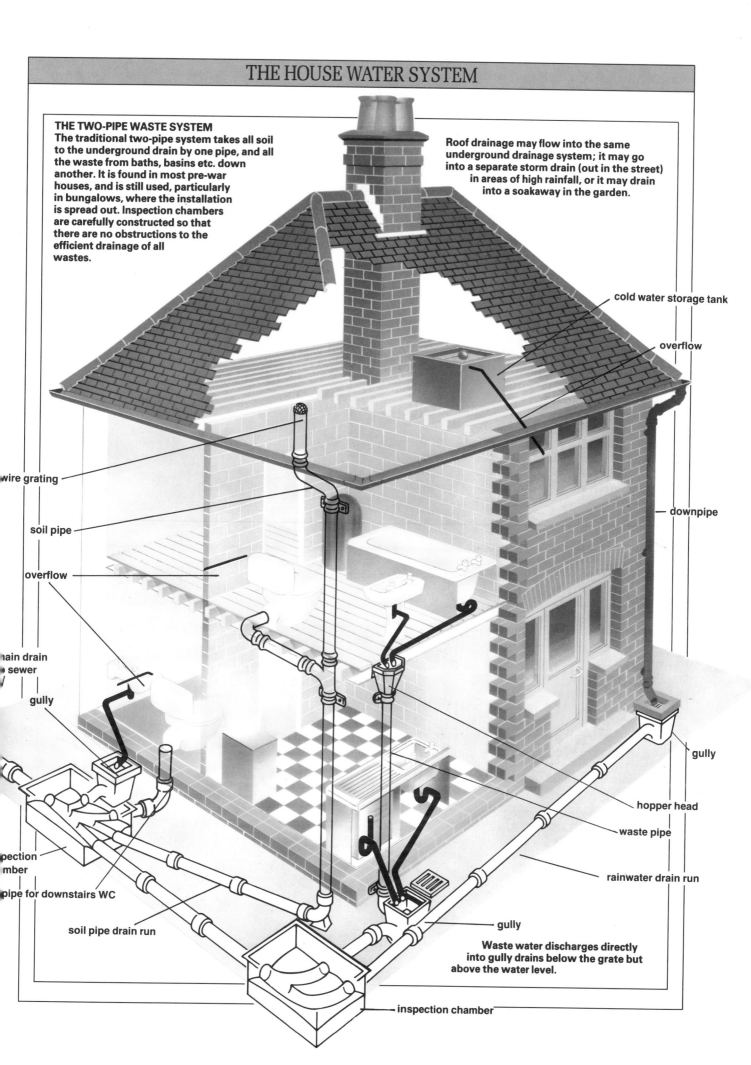

THE TWO-PIPE WASTE SYSTEM
The traditional two-pipe system takes all soil to the underground drain by one pipe, and all the waste from baths, basins etc. down another. It is found in most pre-war houses, and is still used, particularly in bungalows, where the installation is spread out. Inspection chambers are carefully constructed so that there are no obstructions to the efficient drainage of all wastes.

Roof drainage may flow into the same underground drainage system; it may go into a separate storm drain (out in the street) in areas of high rainfall, or it may drain into a soakaway in the garden.

cold water storage tank

overflow

downpipe

wire grating

soil pipe

overflow

main drain sewer

gully

gully

hopper head

waste pipe

inspection chamber

pipe for downstairs WC

soil pipe drain run

rainwater drain run

gully

Waste water discharges directly into gully drains below the grate but above the water level.

inspection chamber

from the rising main and the cold water storage cistern is used only to supply the hot water tank. Although common in some areas, this system is generally not favoured by water authorities.

INDIRECT SYSTEM

With the exception of a direct supply at the kitchen sink for drinking purposes, all cold water supplies are taken from the cistern. This is the system favoured by most water authorities and is the system usually installed in new houses.

CISTERNS

The 'tank' in your loft or attic is in fact a 'cistern'. A cistern is not sealed, but it should have a loose cover to prevent contamination of the water by dust and other debris. The top and sides should be insulated, but not the underside (to allow rising warm air from rooms below to prevent the water in the cistern from freezing). In a direct cold water system there is only one distribution pipe from close to the bottom of the storage cistern and this connects to the hot water tank or cylinder. In an indirect cold water system there will be a similar direct connection to the hot water tank or cylinder, and in addition one or more distribution pipes to other appliances – basins, baths and WC cisterns.

HOT WATER SYSTEMS

Cold water which is supplied to the hot water tank or cylinder is heated in two different ways – indirect (closed) and direct (open) systems.

In indirect hot systems the cold water supplied to the hot water cylinder never actually goes to the boiler. Instead it is heated in the cylinder by a coiled pipe or jacket containing a small quantity of hot water which continuously circulates through the boiler.

In the case of direct hot water systems, cold water is circulated via the hot water tank or cylinder to the boiler, where it is heated, and returned to the hot water tank or cylinder. There is no separate feed and expansion cistern.

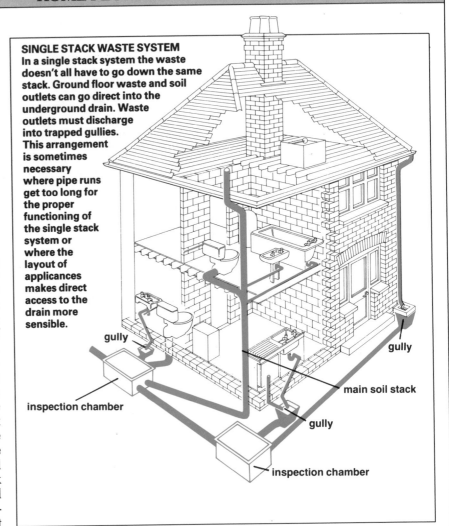

SINGLE STACK WASTE SYSTEM
In a single stack system the waste doesn't all have to go down the same stack. Ground floor waste and soil outlets can go direct into the underground drain. Waste outlets must discharge into trapped gullies. This arrangement is sometimes necessary where pipe runs get too long for the proper functioning of the single stack system or where the layout of appliances makes direct access to the drain more sensible.

gully

gully

main soil stack

inspection chamber

gully

inspection chamber

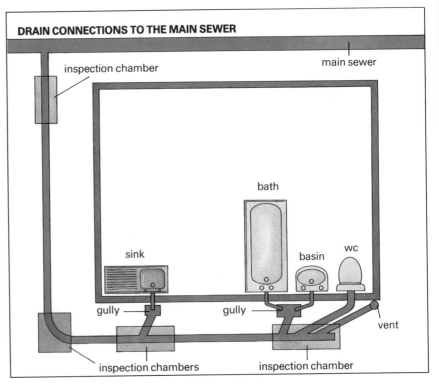

DRAIN CONNECTIONS TO THE MAIN SEWER

inspection chamber

main sewer

bath

sink

basin

wc

gully

gully

vent

inspection chambers

inspection chamber

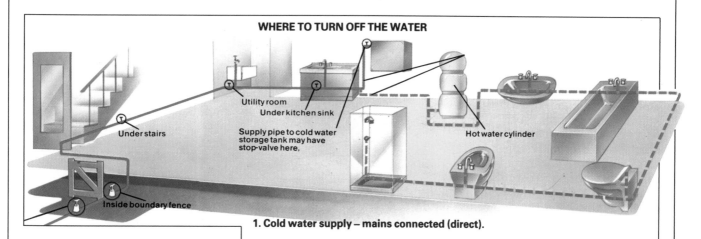

WHERE TO TURN OFF THE WATER

Under stairs

Utility room

Under kitchen sink

Supply pipe to cold water storage tank may have stop-valve here.

Hot water cylinder

Inside boundary fence

1. Cold water supply – mains connected (direct).

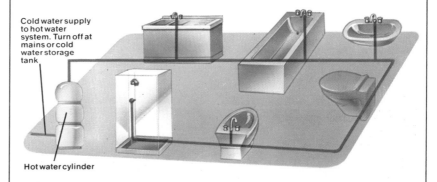

Stop-valve usually located by side of cold water storage tank supplying bathroom and other cold water outlets.

Ball-valve

Stop-valve isolating hot water system

Hot water cylinder

2. Cold water supply – cistern supply (indirect).

Cold water supply to hot water system. Turn off at mains or cold water storage tank

Hot water cylinder

3. Hot water supply.

DRAINAGE SYSTEMS

There are basically two distinct drainage systems: two-pipe drainage systems which are found in older houses and the newer single-stack or one-pipe systems.

With two-pipe systems there are two main vertical drainage stacks on the outside wall of the house – one taking waste water from basins and sinks, and the other taking soil water from WCs.

Single-stack systems are now more common than two-pipe systems. In this case all discharges flow into a single stack which has an open-ended outlet for ventilation just above roof level.

With both systems waste water goes through a trap which fills with water each time the waste pipe empties.

PLUMBING EMERGENCIES

Plumbing emergencies have the habit of occurring at the worst possible times, so you need to be prepared by knowing where to turn off the water supply.

TOOLS AND EQUIPMENT

An emergency plumbing tool kit should comprise the following: two fairly large adjustable spanners; stop-valve 'key'; penetrating oil; pipe repair tape, epoxy resin plastic putty, or a pipe repair clamp; electric hot air paint stripper or hair dryer; flexible sink-waste clearing auger; length of thin wire; sink waste rubber plunger; and drain-clearing chemical.

WATER LEAKS

With any leak, the first step is to stop the flow of water. Where you turn off the water depends on the type of supply.

In the case of cold water supply pipes connected directly to the mains, there may, in fact, be two stop valves (see page 68). If there is an indoor stop valve the only possible complication is if it hasn't been touched for years and is stuck fast. Applying a little penetrating oil and then tapping the handle with a hammer or working it with a spanner will usually loosen it. You should then drain the system: just above the rising main stop valve there should be a drain cock. With the stop valve turned off the drain cock can be used to drain this part of the cold water system.

Where the cold water supply

pipes come from a storage tank they will usually supply the bathroom cold taps, the WC cistern and the hot water cylinder. To close off the water supply in these pipes there's often a stop valve immediately alongside the cold water tank where the pipe exits. Turn this off first and then open all cold water taps. They'll quickly run dry. If there isn't a stop valve, you have to drain the whole tank, so first you stop water entering the tank by either turning off the mains or by tying up the ball-valve in the tank so that it remains closed. Then you open all the taps in the house.

Hot water pipes are all supplied from a hot water cylinder, which in turn gets its cold water either from the cold tank or from the mains. Since hot water leaves the hot water storage cylinder from the top, it's only the pressure of water going in at the bottom of the cylinder that forces the water out. Turn off the supply of cold water and you stop the flow.

EMERGENCY PIPE REPAIRS

Leaks from compression joints are best cured by remaking the joints using two spanners. In an emer-

CLEARING BLOCKAGES
Lead traps are very soft and may bend or split if you use force to open the rodding eye, so insert a piece of scrap wood into the U-bend. Follow the diagrammatic sequence shown on the right.

1.

gency all pipes can be temporarily repaired with a repair kit, of which there are several types. One type is based on a two-part epoxy resin plastic putty: two strips of differently coloured putty are kneaded together and packed firmly round the dried and cleaned pipe, where it will harden to form a seal.

A valuable aid is a multi-size reusable pipe repair clamp. It consists of a rubber pad which fits over the hole (it's not necessary to turn off the water) and a metal clamp. Position the pad and one side of the clamp over the hole, and link the two parts of the clamp

2.
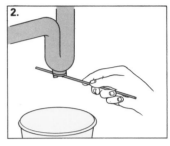

3.
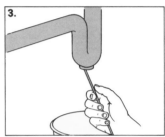

4.
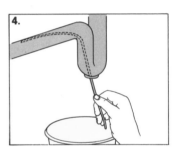

5.
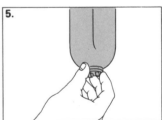

BOTTLE TRAP
1.

2.
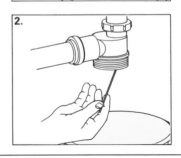

EMERGENCY PIPE REPAIRS
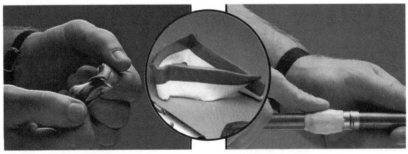
1. You can make a quick repair using a proprietary plastic putty.
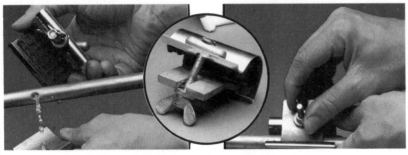
2. There's no need to turn off the water when using a pipe clamp.

CLEARING BLOCKAGES

1. Fish out hair with a wire hook.

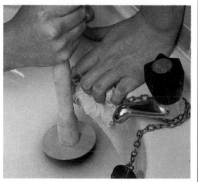

2. Using a force cup.

TYPES OF TRAP
On old systems you may find lead traps; modern ones are of plastic.

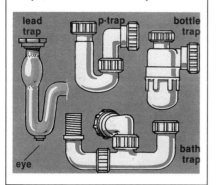

TURNING OFF MAINS WATER
If a stop valve is in the front garden near the path, about a metre (39in) down, you may have to use a home-made wooden key to reach the tap.

together, making sure that the pad is still in place. Tighten the wing nut fully. This method of repair cannot be used to mend leaks occurring at fittings.

Another proprietary product uses a two-part sticky tape system to build up waterproof layers over the leak. The area round the leak should be dried and cleaned and then three layers of tape are wound round the pipe.

Don't re-open the stop valve fully when turning on the supply until a permanent repair is made.

FROZEN PIPES

These must be thawed as soon as possible to prevent ice building up and bursting the pipe or pushing a joint apart. If damage to the pipe has occurred, turn off the supply to the pipe before thawing it.

An electric hot air stripper is ideal for thawing pipes. A hair dryer is also suitable, but slower. Don't use a gas blowtorch because of the risk of starting a fire.

Thaw out first those parts of a pipe most likely to have frozen – unlagged areas, pipes close to the eaves, and at bends.

BLOCKED WASTE OUTLETS

The outlet of a sink, usually the trap immediately beneath the sink itself, is the commonest site of waste-pipe blockage. Usually the obstruction can be cleared quickly with a sink-waste plunger.

First press a damp cloth firmly into the overflow outlet, holding it securely with one hand. Lower the plunger into the flooded sink so that the cup is positioned over the waste outlet, and plunge it up and down sharply several times.

If plunging proves unsuccessful you'll have to gain access to the trap. Brass and lead U-shaped traps have a screwed-in plug at the base. With plastic U-shaped and bottle traps the lower part can be unscrewed and removed. Before attempting this, put the plug in the sink and place a bucket under the trap. Then probe into the trap and into the waste pipe itself. You can buy purpose-made flexible sink waste augers for this purpose, but

you'll find that a piece of expanding curtain wire with a hook on the end can be equally effective.

Partial blockage of a wash basin waste-pipe is caused by hair suspended from the grid of the outlet. You may not see this from above, but probing with a piece of wire will often produce festoons.

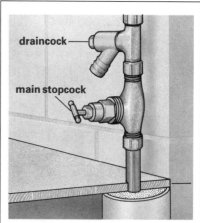

A draincock and stopcock together.

MAKESHIFT PIPE REPAIRS
If you don't have the right materials to hand, bandage insulating tape round the pipe and hole, cover with a piece of garden hosepipe bound on with wires, then wrap more tape over this.

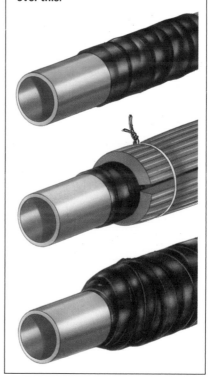

TAP REPAIR AND REPLACEMENT

Basically a tap can leak at the spout, in which case the washer and perhaps the seating will need attention, and at the spindle when the tap is turned on, which means either the packing in the gland or the 'O' ring has failed.

REPLACING WASHERS

With conventional pillar taps, first turn off the water supply. Turn on the tap fully so it drains before you start work. The spindle of a pillar

EQUIPMENT
You will need a pipe wrench and adjustable spanner to remove headgear; a cranked basin spanner to remove and replace taps; and also, penknife, penetrating oil, wool vaseline, PTFE plastic thread sealing tape, jumper, washer and seating parts. A thin screwdriver and cross-headed screwdriver may also come in useful.

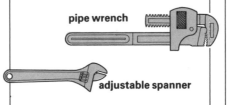

pipe wrench

adjustable spanner

REPLACING A WASHER

1. Hold spout to remove headgear.

2. Remove and replace the washer.

REPLACING WASHERS

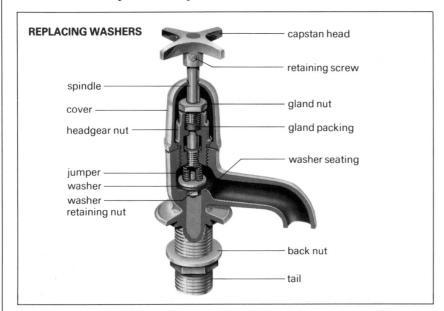

- capstan head
- retaining screw
- spindle
- cover
- headgear nut
- gland nut
- gland packing
- washer seating
- jumper
- washer
- washer retaining nut
- back nut
- tail

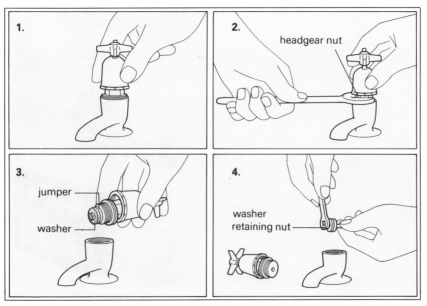

1.

2. headgear nut

3. jumper / washer

4. washer retaining nut

tap usually rises out of a dome-like easy-clean cover, which should be unscrewed. You can then raise the cover sufficiently to slip the jaws of a wrench under it to grip the 'flats' of the headgear – the main body of the tap which has a nut-shaped section to it. If you can't do this you'll need to take off the tap handle and cover: first remove the tiny grub-screw in the side of the handle, which can then be pulled off. While doing this, hold the tap steady: if the entire tap turns you may damage the sink.

You should now see the jumper, with washer attached, resting on the valve seating within the body of the tap (sometimes it gets stuck and lifts out with the headgear). Often the washer is held in position on the jumper by a tiny nut: this has to be undone with pliers before the washer can be replaced. This may be difficult, so it's probably better to fit a new washer and jumper complete.

A tap with a shrouded head is treated in the same way once the head itself has been removed. The commonest method of attaching the head is by a screw beneath the plastic 'hot' or 'cold' indicator: use a small screwdriver to prise this off, then unscrew the headgear to reach the interior of the tap.

REPAIRING A POOR SEATING

If a tap continues to drip although you've changed the washer, this is usually because the valve seating has become scored. You can cure this with a reseating tool, which you can buy or perhaps hire. Turn off the water, insert the tool into the body of the tap and turn it to cut a new seating.

An alternative method is to use a nylon 'washer and seating set'. With the water supply turned off, the headgear and the washer and jumper are removed from the tap end and the nylon liner is placed in position over the seating. The jumper and washer are inserted into the headgear, which is then screwed back on to the tap. The action of turning the tap to the off position will force the liner into and over the old seating to give a watertight joint.

Yet another method is to use a domed washer: this increases the surface area in contact with the waterway and so effectively cuts off the flow when the tap is turned off even though the top of the valve seating may not be smooth.

REPACKING A GLAND

This is necessary if water flows up the spindle towards the handle when the tap is turned on. To make a repair you don't have to cut off the water supply, but you must be able to get at the gland adjusting nut – the first nut through which the spindle passes. Tightening this nut by about half a turn may be enough to stop the leakage, but eventually all the available adjustment will be taken up and you'll then have to repack the gland. Remove the gland adjusting nut, take

REPLACING AN 'O' RING

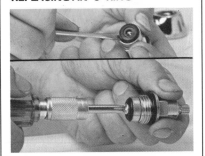

1. Getting access to an 'O' ring seal.

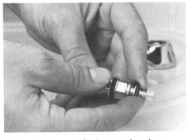

2. Work off worn 'O' rings and replace.

retaining screw
shrouded-head
'O' ring seal
head nut
'O' ring seal
washer stem
washer

Shrouded-head tap with 'O' ring.

tail
back nut

REPAIRING A POOR SEATING

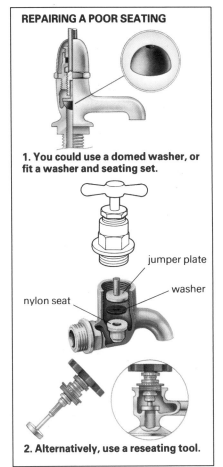

1. You could use a domed washer, or fit a washer and seating set.

jumper plate
washer
nylon seat

2. Alternatively, use a reseating tool.

FITTING PILLAR TAPS

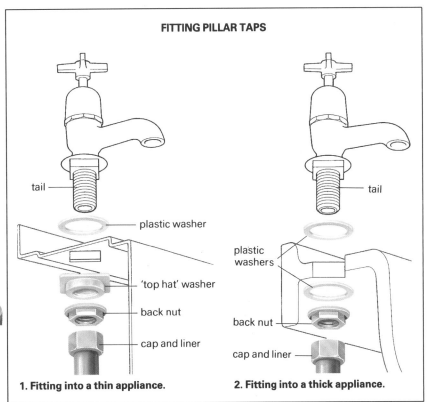

tail
plastic washer
'top hat' washer
back nut
cap and liner

1. Fitting into a thin appliance.

tail
plastic washers
back nut
cap and liner

2. Fitting into a thick appliance.

TYPES OF BASIN

pedestal basin

bracket support basin

inset 'vanity' basin

single rail basin support
either cantilevered or
screwed into the wall

basin support with towel
rail, screwed to the wall

FITTING A VANITY BASIN
A new vanity basin should be
supplied with a template to guide
you in cutting the work surface.

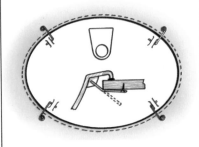

out the old gland packing material
and replace it with knitting wool
saturated with petroleum jelly.
Wind the wool round the spindle
and pack it down tightly before
replacing and tightening the gland
adjusting nut.

REPLACING AN 'O' RING

Many modern taps have an 'O' ring
seal instead of a packed gland or
stuffing box. If an 'O' ring fails,
simply undo the gland adjusting
nut, pick out the old 'O' ring and
replace it with a new one.

REPLACING BASIN TAPS

First cut off the hot and cold water
supplies to the taps. The most difficult part of the job is likely to be
removing the old fittings. If you
look under the basin you will find
that the tails of the taps are connected to the water supply pipes with
small, fairly accessible nuts, and
that a larger – often inaccessible –
back-nut secures the tap to the
basin. The nuts of the swivel tap
connectors joining the pipes to the
taps are usually easy to undo with
a wrench or spanner; the back-nuts
can be extremely difficult.

There are special wrenches and
basin or 'crowsfoot' spanners that
should turn them. In some cases it
may be necessary to disconnect
the swivel tap connectors and to
disconnect the trap from the waste
outlet, then lift the basin off and
place it upside-down on the floor.
Allow some penetrating oil to soak
into the tap tails before tackling
the now accessible nuts with your
wrench or crowsfoot spanner.
Hold the tap while you do this to
stop it swivelling and damaging
the basin.

To fit a new tap, first fit a plastic
washer on to the tap tail. Push the
tail through the hole in the basin.
Slip flat plastic washers over the
tails where they protrude from
beneath the basin, screw on the
back-nuts and tighten them up. To
make tightening easier use top-hat
washers – these are essential if the
taps are fitted to a thin material
like stainless steel.

Finally, wrap the tails of the taps
with 4-5 turns of PTFE tape and

BASIN COMPONENTS

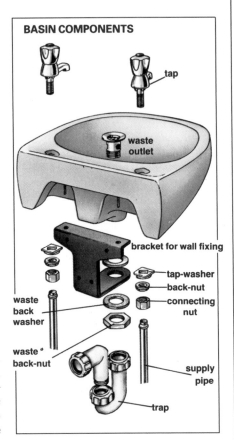

tap

waste
outlet

bracket for wall fixing

tap-washer

back-nut

connecting
nut

waste
back
washer

waste
back-nut

supply
pipe

trap

connect the swivel tap connectors
to the tails. The connectors may
need new fibre washers. The tails
of modern taps are shorter than
those of older ones, and the tap
connectors may not reach. In this
case, bridge the gap by fitting a
special extension adaptor to the
tap tails.

INSTALLING A
WASHBASIN

You will need the following tools:
pipe wrench; adjustable spanner;
basin wrench (crowsfoot); PTFE
tape; plumbers' mastic; and hacksaw or pipe cutter.

A washbasin can be the pedestal
type, wall hung, or the inset type
for fitting into a vanity unit. The
dimension from side to side is
specified as the length and that
from back to front as the width.
Most standard basins are between
550 and 700mm (22-28in) long,
and 450-500mm (18-20in) wide.
It's a good idea to choose the taps

and waste fittings at the same time as the basin. As an alternative to shrouded head or pillar taps you could fit a mixer, provided the holes at the back of the basin are suitably spaced; but remember that because of the design of most basin mixers, you shouldn't use them if the cold supply is directly from the mains.

TRAPS

A 'deep seal' trap with a 75mm (3in) depth of seal should be fitted. The modern bottle trap is one of the most common types used. It's neater looking and takes less space than a U-trap, but it discharges water more slowly. You can buy traps with telescopic inlets that make it easy to provide a push-fit connection to an existing copper or plastic branch waste pipe.

CONNECTING THE WATER SUPPLY

It's unlikely that you'll be able to replace a basin without making some modification to the pipework. If you're installing new supply pipes, how you run them will depend on the type of basin you're putting in. With wall-hung or pedestal types, the hot and cold pipes are usually run neatly together up the back wall and then bent round to the tap tails. But as a vanity unit will conceal the plumbing there's no need to run the pipes together.

To make it easier to bend the required angles you can buy flexible corrugated copper pipes which you can bend by hand. They are available with a swivel tap connector at one end and a plain one at the other, on which you can use capillary or compression fittings.

PREPARING THE BASIN

Before you fix the basin in position you'll need to fit the taps and the waste: it's much easier to do this at this stage than later. To fit the taps all you have to do is remove the back-nuts and slip flat plastic washers over the tails (if they're not there already). The taps can then be positioned in the holes in the basin.

When this has been done more plastic (or top-hat) washers have to be slipped over the tails before the back-nuts are replaced. It's very important not to overtighten these as it's quite easy to damage a ceramic basin.

Because some vanity unit basins are made of a thinner material, you may find that the shanks of the taps fitted into them will protrude below the under-surface of the basin. The result is that when the back-nut is fully tightened, it still isn't tight against the underside of the basin. Fit a top-hat washer over the shank so the back-nut can be screwed up against it.

Mixers usually have one large washer or gasket between the base of the mixer and the top of the basin and you fix them in exactly the same way (see page 79).

When you've fitted the taps you can then fit the waste. With a ceramic basin you'll have to use a slotted waste to enable water from the overflow to escape into the drainage pipe. Getting this in place means first removing the back-nut so you can slip it through the outlet hole in the basin – which itself should be coated with a generous layer of plumbers' mastic. Make sure that the slot in the waste fitting coincides with the outlet of the basin's built-in overflow. You then have to smear jointing compound on the protruding screw thread of the tail, slip on a plastic washer and replace and tighten the back-nut. As you do this the waste flange will probably try to turn on its seating, but you can prevent

FITTING A PEDESTAL BASIN

1. Stand the basin on its pedestal to check the height of the pipes.

2. Fit the taps: do this before fixing the basin to the pedestal.

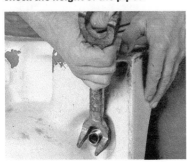

3. Tighten up the back-nut.

4. Remove any surplus mastic.

5. The pedestal conceals the pipes.

6. Connect the waste pipes.

this by holding the grid with pliers as you tighten the back-nut.

Finally, any excess mastic that is squeezed out as the flange is tightened against the basin should be wiped away.

A vanity unit will probably be supplied with a combined waste and overflow unit. This is a flexible hose that has to be fitted (on a ceramic basin, it's an integral part of the appliance). The slotted waste is bedded in in exactly the same way as a waste on a ceramic basin. You then have to fit one end of the overflow to the basin outlet

and slip the 'banjo' outlet on the other end over the tail of the waste to cover the slot. It's held in position by a washer and back-nut.

FITTING THE BASIN

Once the taps and waste have been fixed in position, you are ready to remove the old basin and fit the new one. First cut off the water supply. If the existing basin is a pedestal model you'll have to remove the pedestal, which may be screwed to the floor. Take off the nut that connects the basin trap to the threaded waste outlet and un-

screw the nuts that connect the supply pipes to the tails of the taps. These will either be swivel tap connectors or cap and lining joints. Lift the basin clear and then remove the brackets or hangers on which it was resting.

You'll probably need some help when installing the new basin as it's much easier to mark the fixing holes if someone else is holding the basin against the wall. With a pedestal basin, the pedestal will determine the level of the basin. The same applies with a vanity unit. But if it is set on hangers or

FITTING A VANITY UNIT

1. Cut a hole in the vanity unit with the help of the template provided.

2. Prop the basin up while you install the mixer unit.

3. Fit the water inlet assembly with the basin still propped up.

4. Next insert the waste outlet on its rubber flange.

5. Turn the basin over; secure the outlet and pop-up waste controls.

6. Put a strip of mastic around the hole before positioning the basin.

7. Fix the basin to the underside of the top of the vanity unit.

8. Fit the inlet pipes and screw on the waste trap.

9. Turn the water back on, then replace the doors of the vanity unit.

brackets, you can adjust the height for convenience.

Once the fixing holes have been drilled and plugged, the basin can be screwed into position and you can tackle the plumbing. Before you make the connections to the water supply pipes you may have to cut or lengthen them to meet the tap tails. If you need to lengthen them you'll find it easier to use corrugated copper pipe. The actual connection between pipe and tail is made with a swivel tap connector – a form of compression fitting.

Finally you have to connect the trap. You may be able to re-use the old one, but it's more likely you'll want to fit a new one. And if its position doesn't coincide with the old one, you can use a bottle trap with an adjustable telescopic inlet.

INSTALLING A BATH

As with many other plumbing projects the most difficult part is likely to be the removal of the old fitting rather than the installation of the new one.

TOOLS AND EQUIPMENT

To replace a bath, you're likely to need the following tools: crowsfoot wrench; adjustable spanner; adjustable wrench; hacksaw (possibly); and spirit level.

You'll also need the new bath itself; new overflow connection, waste outlet and PVC trap; taps or mixer and new inlet pipe if you are replacing them; and plumbers' mastic.

Measure up carefully before you buy a new bath to make sure it fits. It should come complete with supports, carcase and side panels, otherwise you'll need to buy these as well.

BATH TYPES

Most baths sold today have outside dimensions of about 1675mm (66in) long, 750mm (30in) wide, and 550mm (21in) high. Shorter baths are available for particularly small bathrooms.

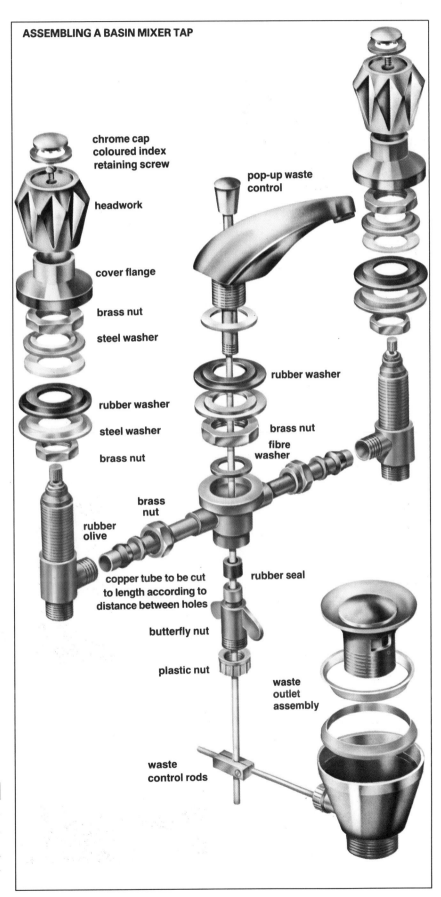

ASSEMBLING A BASIN MIXER TAP

chrome cap
coloured index
retaining screw

headwork

cover flange

brass nut

steel washer

rubber washer

steel washer

brass nut

pop-up waste control

rubber washer

brass nut

fibre washer

brass nut

rubber olive

copper tube to be cut to length according to distance between holes

rubber seal

butterfly nut

plastic nut

waste outlet assembly

waste control rods

KNOW YOUR BATH

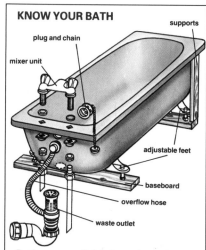

supports
plug and chain
mixer unit
adjustable feet
baseboard
overflow hose
waste outlet

Baths are available in various sizes to suit different bathrooms and they also come with different bottom mouldings to make them safe, and often have handles to help the less active to get in and out.

Plain traditional rectangular

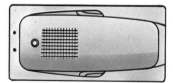

Off-rectangular with handles

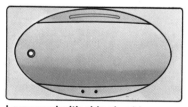

Large oval with side plumbing

Corner bath

It is possible to replace your old cast iron bath with a new one made of the same material, but more modern in styling. However, these baths are expensive and extremely heavy. Carrying one into the bathroom and fitting it requires considerable strength (you'd need at least one strong helper) as well as care. There are other snags with enamelled cast iron baths: they normally have a slippery base that can make them dangerous to use – particularly by the very young and the elderly, although some are available with a non-slip surface. Furthermore, the material of which they are made rapidly conducts heat away from the water, and while this didn't matter too much in the old days, when energy was plentiful and cheap, large amounts of hot water cost rather more today.

One economical alternative is an enamelled pressed steel bath. This is lighter and cheaper than enamelled cast iron, but can be more easily damaged in storage or installation.

For do-it-yourself installation a plastic bath is the obvious choice. They are available in a number of attractive colours and any surface scratches can be easily polished out. They are light in weight and one man can quite easily carry one upstairs for installation. They are both comfortable and economical to use and many of them have a non-slip base to make them safe.

But plastic baths do have their snags. They are easily damaged by extreme heat. You should beware of using a blowtorch in close proximity to one and a lighted cigarette should never be rested, even momentarily, on the rim. A fault of early plastic baths was their tendency to creak and sag when filled with hot water and, sometimes, when you got into them. This has now been overcome by the manufacturers who provide substantial frames or cradles for support; but these frames must be assembled and fixed exactly as recommended. Some come already attached to the bath.

A combined plastic waste and

FITTING A BATH

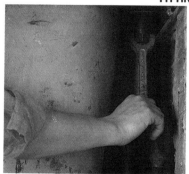

1. First undo the back-nuts.

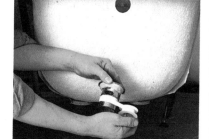

2. Assembling the new plumbing.

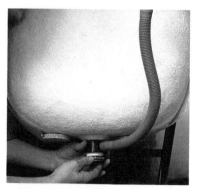

3. Attach the overflow to the outlet.

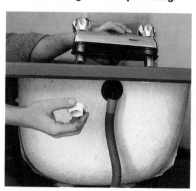

4. Fit the mixer with a rubber gasket.

overflow assembly is likely to be the choice nowadays for any bath, and is obligatory with a plastic bath. If a rigid metal trap is used with a plastic bath, the material of the bath could be damaged as hot water causes unequal expansion.

You obviously won't want to re-use the old bath taps, and you will probably opt for either individual modern pillar taps or a bath mixer. A mixer should be chosen only if the cold water supply is taken from the same cold water storage cistern that supplies the hot water system. It should not be used if the cold water supply to the bathroom comes directly from the mains supply.

FITTING PROCEDURE

To avoid too long a disruption of the domestic hot and cold water supplies you can fit the taps, waste and trap into the new bath before removing the old one. The technique is the same as for fitting a vanity unit – see page 78.

Removing the old bath may well be the most difficult part of the procedure. Turn off the hot and cold water supplies and drain the distribution pipes from the bath taps. If you haven't done so already, remove the bath panel to give access to the plumbing at the foot of the bath. You can try to unscrew the back-nuts holding the taps in position, but it's generally easier to undo the nuts that connect the distribution pipes to the tails of the taps. In order to reach the one nearest the wall you may have to dismantle the overflow, either by unscrewing it or, if it is taken through the wall, by cutting it off flush with the wall. Then undo the waste connection.

The bath is now disconnected from the water supply pipes and from the branch waste pipe and can be pulled away from the wall. Unless you particularly want to save the old bath and have some strong helpers, do not attempt to remove it from the house, or even from the room, in one piece as it will be very heavy. The best course of action is to break it into manageable pieces. Drape an old blanket

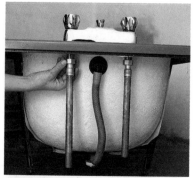
5. Attach inlet spurs to the taps.

6. Fit the waste trap.

7. Position and adjust the feet.

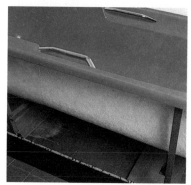
8. Fix the bath panels in position.

over it to prevent flying chips of enamel, and wear goggles to protect the eyes. Then, with a club hammer, break the bath up into pieces that you can easily carry away.

Place the new plastic bath in position and assemble the cradle or other support exactly as recommended by the manufacturer. Ensure that the rim of the bath is level, using a spanner to turn the adjustable feet. It is most unlikely that the tails of the new taps will coincide with the position of the tap connectors of the old distribution pipes. If they don't, the easiest way of making the connections is by means of bendable copper pipe. This is 'corrugated' copper tubing – easily bent by hand. It is obtainable in 15mm and 22mm sizes and either with two plain ends for connection to soldered capillary or compression joints, or with one plain end and a swivel tap connector at the other. For this particular job two lengths of 22mm corrugated copper pipe will be required, each with one end plain

and one end fitted with a swivel tap connector.

Offer the lengths of corrugated pipe up to the tap tails, and cut back the distribution pipes to the length required for connection to the plain ends. Leave these pipes slightly too long rather than too short. The corrugated pipe can be bent to accommodate a little extra length. Now connect the plain ends to the cut distribution pipes using either soldered capillary or compression couplings.

The chances are that the distribution pipes will be ¾in imperial size. If you use compression fittings an adaptor – probably simply a larger olive – will be needed for connection to a 22mm coupling. If you use soldered capillary fittings, special ¾in to 22mm couplings must be used. Remember to keep the blowtorch flame well away from the plastic of the bath.

Connect up the swivel tap connectors of the corrugated pipe and the overflow of the bath. Do this in a logical order: first connect the tap connector to the further tap.

A fibre washer inside the nut of the tap connector will ensure a watertight joint. Then connect up the flexible overflow pipe of the combined waste-and-overflow fitting to the bath's overflow outlet, and, finally, connect the nearer tap to the nearer tap connector.

If you have installed new pipework then you can install the entire trap, waste and water supply pipe spurs before moving the bath into position. Whatever you have decided upon, finish making all the connections, then reinstate the water supply and check for leaks.

Finally, check once more that the rim is level, and fit the side and end panels in position.

CORNER BATHS

Corner baths are available in several slightly different shapes and sizes. It's most important to check the overall dimensions before you order your new bath – they may measure up to 1500mm (about 5ft) along each side, so will only fit in a large bathroom.

A corner bath can be fitted with a pair of pillar taps or a mixer. When choosing taps for your bath, check that the taps you want are compatible with it. In particular, check whether the taps are deep enough to fit through the reinforcing block under the rim of the bath; whether the separation of the tap holes matches the tap dimensions; and whether a remote spout is linked to the mixer with reinforced hose or made-up copper pipework.

FIXING THE FEET

Corner baths are usually secured in place with wall brackets attached to the two straight edges of the bath, and by screwing the adjustable feet to the floor once the bath is in position. Access can be very awkward, however, and a useful alternative method is to position the bath accurately and mark the position for the feet on the floorboards, then remove the bath, take off the feet and screw them to the floor. Finally lift the bath on to the feet and do up the securing nuts.

INSTALLING A CORNER BATH

1. Mark the outline of the bath and waste outlet on the floor.

2. Move the bath away and attach the waste and overflow fittings.

3. Fit the mixer tap body. Secure by fitting the flange from above and tightening the nuts below.

4. Extend the supply and waste pipework, then replace the bath.

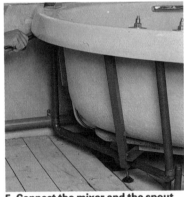

5. Connect the mixer and the spout and the supply and waste pipes.

6. Offer up the bath panel, making sure its top lip engages in the clips.

INSTALLING A SHOWER

Showers have become a part of the modern home, whether fitted over the bath or in a separate cubicle. They save time, space and energy and are quite easy to install once the design is right.

WHY INSTALL A SHOWER?

Showers have many advantages over baths. They are hygienic, as you don't sit in dirty soapy water and you get continuously rinsed. They are pleasant to use; standing under jets of water can be immensely stimulating, especially first thing in the morning. They use a lot less water per wash than a bath, which results in a saving of energy and is also an advantage where water softeners are in use. This economy of hot water usage means that at peak traffic times there is more water to go round. Showers also take less time; they don't have to be 'run' before you can start to wash, and users can't lay back and bask, monopolizing the bathroom. Finally, easy temperature adjustment of a shower affords greater comfort for the user and lessens the risk of catching cold in a cold bathroom.

SHOWER LOCATION

You don't have to install a shower over a bath, or even in a bathroom. A bedroom is one alternative site, but landings and utility rooms are another possibility. Provided a supply of water is available, the pressure head satisfactory and the disposal of waste water possible, a shower can provide a compact and very useful house improvement in many parts of the home.

Where a shower is provided in

SHOWER LOCATION
To install a shower cubicle you need a fairly modest space – one which is not less than 900mm (3ft) square will suffice.

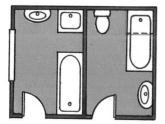

In a bathroom you can install a shower cubicle (left) or a simple shower unit over the bath (right).

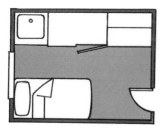

Arrangement for a bedroom shower at the end of built-in wardrobes.

its own cubicle, as distinct from over a bath, it takes up very little extra space. One can be provided in any space which is at least 900mm (36in) square.

In a bathroom a shower will usually go over a bath, which is the easiest and most popular position. In a larger bathroom a cubicle is a good idea.

In a bedroom a shower can be easily fitted at the end of built-in wardrobes.

TYPES OF SHOWER

There are basically two types of shower: those attached to a mixer on a bath, and those independent of the bath, discharging over their own bases, in their own cubicles.

Bath showers may be attached to a mixer head on which you have to adjust both taps, or they may simply fit over the tap outlets. The shower head in either case is detachable and may be mounted at whatever height you require.

Independent showers may be adjustable, or may have fixed position heads; they may have a single control mixer, or a dual control, which means that you can adjust the flow as well as the temperature. Thermostatic mixing valves are also available which can cope with small pressure fluctuations in the hot and cold water supply. These only reduce pressure on one side of the valve if that on the other side falls; they cannot increase the pressure unless they have already decreased it.

If you have a cylinder storage hot water system, which is by far the commonest kind of hot water supply, a conventional shower connected to the household's hot and cold water supplies is likely to be the most satisfactory and the easiest to install.

PRESSURE

The most important requirement for a shower is that the hot and cold water supply pipes must be under equal water pressure. With a cylinder storage hot water system, hot water pressure comes from the main cold water storage cistern supplying the cylinder with water.

The cold supply to the shower must therefore also come from this cistern (or perhaps from a separate cistern at the same level); it must not be taken direct from the cold water main.

The cold water storage cistern must also be high enough above the shower sprinkler to provide a satisfactory operating pressure. Best results will be obtained if the base of the cold water storage cistern is 1.5m (5ft) or more above the sprinkler. However, provided that pipe runs are fairly short and have only slight changes of direction, a reasonable shower can still be obtained when the vertical distance between the base of the cistern and the shower sprinkler is as little as 1m (39in). The level of the hot water storage tank in relation to the shower doesn't matter in the least: it can be above, below or at the same level as the shower. It is the level of the cold water storage cistern that matters.

Yet another design requirement for conventional shower installation sometimes applies: this is that the cold water supply to the shower should be a separate 15mm branch direct from the cold water storage cistern, not as a branch from the main bathroom distribution pipe. This is a safety precaution.

For the same reason it is best for the hot supply to be taken direct from the vent pipe immediately above the hot water storage cylinder – not as a branch from another distribution pipe.

MIXERS

Showers must have some kind of mixing valve to mix the streams of hot and cold water and thus to produce a shower at the required tempereature.

With a bath/shower mixer the tap handles are adjusted until the water flowing through the mixer spout into the bath is at a comfortable temperature. The water is then diverted up to the head by turning a valve.

Then there are manual shower mixers. These are standard equipment in independent shower cu-

CHOOSING THE RIGHT SHOWER TYPE

The type of shower you can install depends on the sort of water supply you have in your home. Various restrictions are in force, largely for safety reasons. For example, you must not supply a conventional shower from a branch off the main bathroom distribution pipe, but from its own branch from the cold water cistern. This is to prevent a person taking a shower from getting a scalding due to sudden drop in pressure when someone turns a cold tap on elsewhere in the house. This chart will help you decide what sort of unit is suitable for your water supply, or help you to solve plumbing problems you may encounter with your preferred choice.

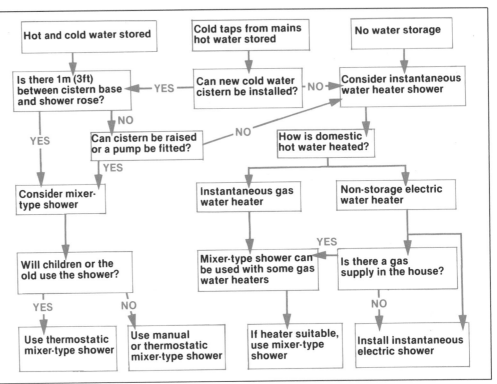

SHOWER TYPES

- bath/shower mixer
- single control mixer
- thermostatic mixer with adjustable head
- dual control mixer with fixed head

bicles and may also be used over a bath. With a manual mixer the hot and cold streams of water are mixed in a single valve. Temperature (and sometimes flow control as well) is regulated by turning large knurled control knobs.

Finally, there are thermostatic shower mixing valves. These may resemble manual mixers in appearance, but they are designed to accommodate small fluctuations of pressure in either the hot or the cold water supplies to the shower. They are thus very useful safety devices. But thermostatic valves cannot, even if it were legal, compensate for the very great pressure difference between mains supply and a supply from a cold water storage cistern. Nor can they add pressure to either the hot or the cold supply. If pressure falls on one side of the valve the thermostatic device will reduce flow on the other side to match it.

Thermostatic valves are more expensive but they eliminate the need to take an independent cold water supply pipe from the storage cistern to the shower and can possibly reduce the overall cost of installation.

SHOWER TRAYS AND WASTE OUTLETS

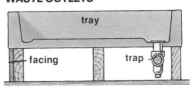

1. You need enough room under the tray for the waste trap and outlet pipe. You can support the tray on timber or bricks.

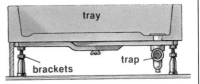

2. You can support it with special supporting brackets. In both the above cases you would face the elevation with panels.

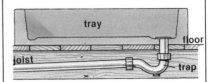

3. Alternatively, you can cut a hole in the floor, if it's made of wood, and run the trap and waste above the ceiling of the room beneath.

Where a shower is provided over an existing bath, steps must be taken to protect the bathroom floor from splashed water. Plastic shower curtains work quite well and provide the cheapest means of doing this; however a folding glass shower screen has a much more attractive appearance and is more effective.

ELECTRIC SHOWERS

You can run your shower independently of the existing domestic hot water system by fitting an instantaneously heated electric one. They need only to be connected to the rising main and to a suitable source of electricity to provide an 'instant shower'.

The shower unit should be connected directly to the cold water mains supply. If this isn't possible, a storage tank may be used to supply the unit; but it must be about 10.75m (35ft) above the shower spray head.

When you are wiring up an instantaneous electric shower, you must ensure that it is permanently connected to its own separate 30A power supply, and is properly earthed; and that it is controlled by a 30A double-pole cord-operated switch mounted on the ceiling.

Never turn on the electricity supply until all the plumbing has been completed, including mounting the handset and hose, and the power supply and earthing connections are made.

USING THE SHOWER

After turning on the unit, you'll have to wait a short while so the water retained in the heater tank and shower fittings from the last shower is drawn off. The water temperature is controlled by the rate of flow through the heater – the slower the flow rate, the higher the temperature, and vice versa. Because the cold water supply is

SHOWER SURROUNDS
Buying a ready-made surround and door in kit form is easy, if expensive. You could use a curtain, which is cheaper but less efficient.

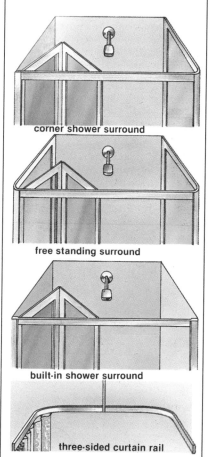

corner shower surround

free standing surround

built-in shower surround

three-sided curtain rail

WATERPROOF SEALS
The surround is no use if it leaks and it is most likely to leak where it meets the tray. Fill this gap with non-setting mastic and then seal with any acrylic or silicone sealant to match the tray colour.

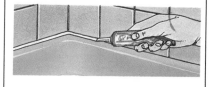

ELECTRIC SHOWERS

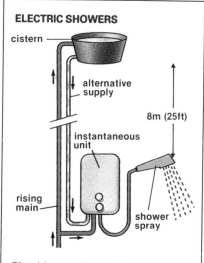

cistern

alternative supply

8m (25ft)

instantaneous unit

rising main

shower spray

Plumbing requirements.

A 30A double-pole cord operated ceiling switch is essential.

FITTING AN ELECTRIC SHOWER

1. Fix the unit on the cubicle wall.

2. Make the connections (see page 82).

3. Turn on water and electricity.

colder in winter than in summer, in winter you may have to put up with a slower flow rate in order to get the water comfortably warm.

To install a shower above a bath, first disconnect the water supply

and drain the cistern. Remove the bath panel – if there is one – and disconnect the tap tails from the supply pipes. Then unscrew and

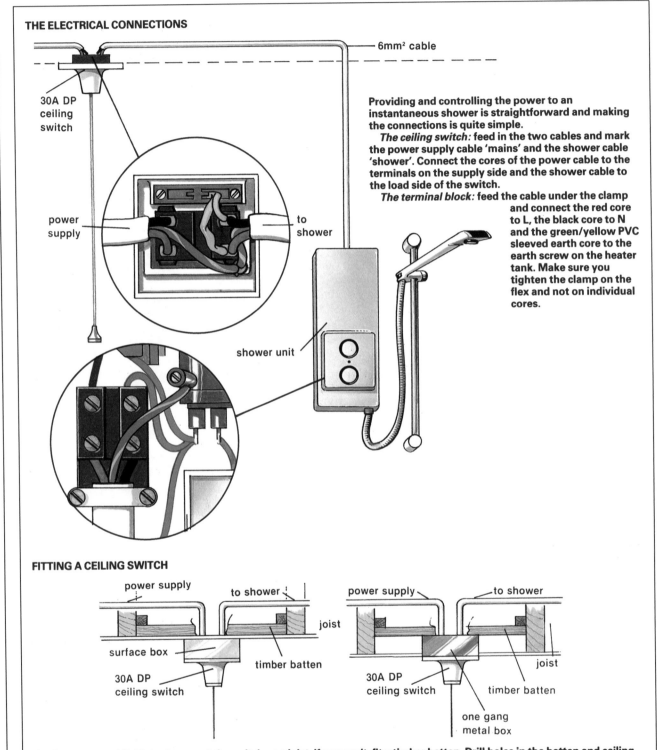

THE ELECTRICAL CONNECTIONS

6mm² cable

30A DP ceiling switch

power supply

to shower

shower unit

Providing and controlling the power to an instantaneous shower is straightforward and making the connections is quite simple.

The ceiling switch: feed in the two cables and mark the power supply cable 'mains' and the shower cable 'shower'. Connect the cores of the power cable to the terminals on the supply side and the shower cable to the load side of the switch.

The terminal block: feed the cable under the clamp and connect the red core to L, the black core to N and the green/yellow PVC sleeved earth core to the earth screw on the heater tank. Make sure you tighten the clamp on the flex and not on individual cores.

FITTING A CEILING SWITCH

power supply | to shower | joist
surface box | timber batten
30A DP ceiling switch

power supply | to shower
joist
30A DP ceiling switch | timber batten
one gang metal box

Surface mounted (left): try to mount the switch on a joist. If you can't, fit a timber batten. Drill holes in the batten and ceiling to admit the cables and remove a knockout from the base of the box. Fix the box to the ceiling and make the connections.
Flush mounted (right): use a pad saw to cut a hole in the ceiling for the mounting box. Fix the box to a batten between the joists and set the batten so the box is flush with the ceiling. Feed the cables through and make the connections.

THE PLUMBING CONNECTIONS – SINK TOP UNIT

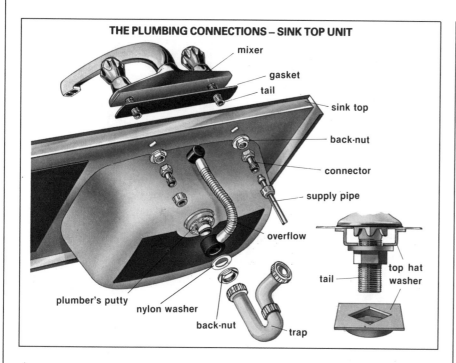

mixer

gasket

tail

sink top

back-nut

connector

supply pipe

overflow

top hat washer

tail

plumber's putty

nylon washer

back-nut

trap

TYPICAL DESIGNS
If you don't have a dishwasher a double bowl is useful – one for washing and one for rinsing.

A double drainer gives you a greater working area at the sink but cuts down on the other work surfaces.

If you're short of space you can dispense with the drainer altogether and use an inset bowl only. There are also units with small subsidiary bowls specially incorporated to house a waste disposal unit. These may also be supplied with trays which fit in or over the bowl, facilitating such tasks as salad preparation.

Disposal sink and trays.

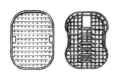

remove the tap back-nuts and take the taps off.

You can now fix the new mixer in place. Finally, decide where you want the shower spray bracket to go, and fix it in place.

INSTALLING A SINK UNIT AND AN INSET SINK

The traditional Belfast sink, made of fireclay and enamelled after baking is occasionally installed, fixed on cantilevered brackets or on leg supports. However, most modern sinks are made of stainless steel or durable plastic material which gives a functional, streamlined finish and is easy to clean.

SINK TOPS

Sink tops fit on top of a sink unit of the same size. While sink units started off as an alternative to the cantilevered support Belfast sink, they are now often inset as part of a work surface. As nearly all sink units are designed on a module basis, the sizes of sink tops correspond to these module sizes.

NEW DEVELOPMENTS

There is no question of being restricted to a single sink with either right or left-hand drainer. Double sinks, one for washing the crockery and cutlery and the other for a hot rinse before air drying, have become more and more popular. The two sinks may be of equal size, around 450mm (18in) in width, or one may be smaller than the other for use in food preparation. A second sink like this might be only 240mm (10in) in width. There are also sinks with double drainers, although these are rather less in demand as they take up a lot of space; they are usually around 2m (6ft 8in) long. Overall sizes of rectangular sinks and drainer units range from about 900mm (3ft) to 1500mm (5ft) in length, and usually measure 500 or 600mm (20 to 24in) deep, to fit metric base units. Some sink tops are still available in the 21in (533mm) size to match old imperial base units. There are also many intermediate sizes, and bowl depths may range between 130 and 180mm (5 and 7in).

Apart from stainless steel, considerable advances have also been made in reinforced plastics, and modern plastic sinks and sink tops seem well able to stand up to anything that is required of them.

Ceramic sinks are also making a comeback, though they are very different from the old Belfast and

INSET SINK ACCESSORIES
A: draining tray
B: chopping board

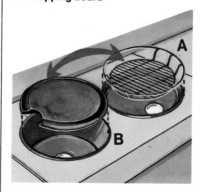

London pattern sinks. Modern ranges include tough inset sinks and tops in an attractive range of colours. There are inset round bowls 450mm (18in) in diameter with an accompanying but separate round drainer 380mm (14in) in diameter. Then there is a conventional rectangular double sink and drainer, all of ceramic ware, at an overall size of 1125×505mm (45×20in). There is also a conventional rectangular single sink and drainer and round double sinks and drainer in one unit. A feature of these new ceramic units is their extreme toughness.

WASTE OUTLETS

In the new ceramic sinks a built-in overflow connects to the slot in a slotted waste outlet that is bedded on mastic in the outlet hole. Stainless steel sinks are provided with a flexible overflow which connects to the slotted 38mm (1½in) waste below the sink but above the trap. Double sinks have only one trap. This is fitted into the outlet of the sink nearest to the drain outlet, the waste from the other sink being connected to it above the level of the single trap.

MIXERS

Individual sink pillar taps are still freely available, but the choice nowadays is more likely to be a sink mixer.

A mixer with a swivel spout is essential where a double sink is installed.

Sink mixers differ from bath and basin mixers in one important respect: they have separate channels for the hot and cold streams of water, which mix in the air as they leave the spout. The reason for this is that it is illegal to mix, in one fitting, water from the main and water from a storage cistern.

There are some exciting new designs of mixers available. With some the mixer unit is fitted into just one of the holes at the back of the sink. The other may be blanked off or used to accommodate a rinsing brush, supplied with hot water by a flexible tube connected to the hot water supply pipe.

INSTALLING A SINK TOP UNIT

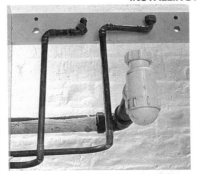
1. Check over the existing plumbing.

2. Press the outlet into position.

3. Run PTFE tape around the thread.

4. Fit the banjo unit.

5. Screw on the back-nut.

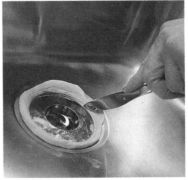
6. Remove excess plumber's mastic.

PUTTING IN A SINK TOP

When you come to install your new sink it's a good idea to make the first job fitting the taps (or the mixer), waste and overflow to it. By doing this you will avoid unnecessary interruption to the rest of the plumbing services. Start by putting in the combined waste and overflow unit, then attach the taps or mixer. If the sink is made of stainless steel the shanks of the taps will protrude through the holes so you won't be able to screw up the back-nuts tight. Use 'top-hat' washers or spacers to accommodate the shanks.

When the sink is in position the tap tails will usually be fairly inaccessible, so it may be a good idea to attach purpose-made extension pieces to bring them to a level below the sink basin where they will be accessible.

When you've got the new sink top ready, you'll have to turn off the main stop valve and drain the hot and cold water pipes which supply the existing sink, which is then removed.

If the supply pipes to the old

taps were chased into the wall, you'll have to excavate the pipes from the wall and pull them forward so that they can be connected to the tails of the new taps.

With the sink unit in position, the next job is to cut the water supply pipes to the correct length to connect to the tails of the taps. Often the sink top simply rests on the sink unit, so the tails of the taps can now be connected to the water supply pipes. Sometimes the top is held to the unit with clips. If the trap of the old sink will connect to the new waste it can be re-used.

INSTALLING AN INSET SINK

Inset sinks can have one, two or two and a half bowls. Some incorporate drainers but, with individual bowls, separate drainers have to be installed alongside.

Many inset sinks are made of

7. Position the mixer unit.

8. Screw on the inlet tail back-nuts.

9. Lift the sink top into position.

10. Screw the old trap to the outlet.

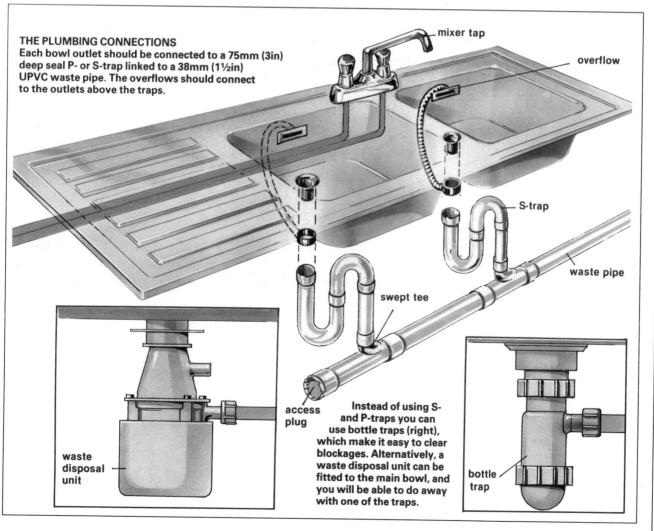

THE PLUMBING CONNECTIONS
Each bowl outlet should be connected to a 75mm (3in) deep seal P- or S-trap linked to a 38mm (1½in) UPVC waste pipe. The overflows should connect to the outlets above the traps.

mixer tap

overflow

S-trap

waste pipe

swept tee

access plug

waste disposal unit

Instead of using S- and P-traps you can use bottle traps (right), which make it easy to clear blockages. Alternatively, a waste disposal unit can be fitted to the main bowl, and you will be able to do away with one of the traps.

bottle trap

stainless steel, but if you choose a plastic or ceramic sink you have the added option of a wide range of colours.

There are various accessories you can fit over the bowl of the sink, such as a draining tray and a chopping board. Ideally, use the chopping board over the sink with a waste disposer so that any vegetable matter can be hygienically flushed away. If you're installing a ceramic sink and you also want a waste disposal unit, make sure the outlet on the sink is compatible with the inlet on the disposer. A ceramic sink can't be cut, so the two must match exactly.

You've got considerable flexibility as to where you position an inset sink – it need not necessarily be directly over a base unit. But wherever you propose to site it make sure there is sufficient depth under the worktop to accommodate the bowls.

Installing an inset sink presents no special difficulties. As with conventional sinks, you may prefer to carry out as much work as possible before putting the worktop in position. But if the worktop is fixed, rather than remove it work *in situ* instead.

First fit the taps, connecting a short run of pipe, or lengths of corrugated flexible pipe, to each of the tap tails at this stage. The waste and overflow unit is usually supplied with the sink, and should be fitted next.

As far as marking out the work surface is concerned, most sink manufacturers supply a template indicating the area of worktop to be removed.

Needless to say the cutting must be done accurately, and for this reason it's best to work on the top surface and not the underside so there's no risk of getting the sink in the wrong place.

Drill a hole through the waste side of the cut-out and then use a jigsaw to cut the hole. You can then fit the retaining brackets or rim round the underside edge. The fixing clips on the sink are secured to these when it's set in its final position.

Usually, inset sinks are provided with a rubber seal or gasket so that when fitted there's a watertight seal between the bowl and drainer and the worktop. If there isn't one, run a continuous bead of non-setting mastic round the perimeter and bed the top firmly on to this.

Once you've lowered the sink into position and clipped it in place, all that then remains is to set the worktop in position on top of the unit and to connect the waste pipe and the hot and cold supply runs.

PLUMBING IN A WASHING MACHINE

A washing machine is normally sited next to an existing sink, so you'll know that the water supply pipes and drainage facilities are close at hand.

Most machines are run off separate 15mm (½in) hot and cold supplies taken from tees inserted in the pipe runs to the sink. You should also insert some form of stop valve into the pipes so that

INSTALLING AN INSET SINK

1. Mark round the template.

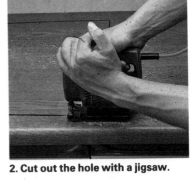
2. Cut out the hole with a jigsaw.

3. Run sealer round the hole.

4. Fasten the inset sink in position.

5. Fit the mixer and waste outlet.

6. Connect wastes to a common run.

the machine can be isolated for repairs.

Use female/male connections to join the copper pipes to the rubber inlet hoses of the machine. These connections are normally an integral part of the stop valves. The discharged water is fed into a rubber drain hose which should be loosely inserted into the top of the stand-pipe. This in turn connects to a 75mm (3in) trap and from here the waste water is taken in 38mm (1½in) pipe to discharge in the gully outside below the grid.

In the case of single-stack drainage, the waste water is conducted to the main drainage stack where

the pipe is connected via a fitting known as a strap boss.

WATER SUPPLY

Cut into the hot and cold supply pipes at a convenient level, after cutting off the water supply and draining the pipes, and insert into them 15mm compression tees. From the outlets of the tees run lengths of 15mm (½in) copper tube to terminate, against the wall, in a position immediately adjacent to the machine. On to the ends of these lengths of pipe fit purpose-made stop-cocks. These are normally provided with back-plates that can be screwed on to the wall

after it has been drilled and plugged. The outlets of the stop-cocks are designed for connection to the machine's inlet hose or hoses.

As an alternative, which is best used where the hot and cold water pipes in the kitchen are in close proximity to the position of the machine, you can use a special patent valve (ie. Kontite Thru-flow valve). This is a 'tee' with a valve outlet designed for direct connection to the washing machine hose. There are compression joints at each end of the tee and the valve is particularly easily fitted because there is no tube-stop in one of these joints. This cuts out the dif-

PLUMBING IN A WASHING MACHINE
Plumbing in a washing machine shouldn't present too many problems. Normally it's sited next to an existing sink, so you'll know that the water supply pipes and drainage facilities are close at hand. Most machines are run off separate 15mm (½in) hot and cold supplies (1 & 2) taken from tees (3) inserted in the pipe runs to the sink. You should also insert some form of stop-valve (4). You'll have to use female/male connections (5) to join the copper pipes to the machine's rubber inlet hoses (6). Used water is fed into a rubber drain hose (7) which should be loosely inserted into the top of the stand-pipe (8). This in turn connects to a 75mm (3in) trap and from here the waste water is taken in 38mm (1½in) pipe (9) to discharge outside in the gully below the grid (10).

Dealing with single-stack drainage: from the trap at the bottom of the stand-pipe (11) the waste water is conducted to the main drainage stack (12) where the pipe is connected via a fitting known as a strap boss (13).

ficult business of 'springing' the cut ends of the pipe into the tee.

Then there are valves which can be connected without cutting a section out of the water supply pipes. With one such valve the

pipe is drained and is then drilled with an 8mm (⁵⁄₁₆in) bit. A back-plate is then fitted to the wall behind it and a front-plate, with a short projecting pipe and a rubber seal that fits into the hole in the

pipe, is clamped to it. The washing machine valve then screws into this front-plate.

Yet another valve is self-tapping and screws its own hole in the water pipe. This, so the makers

KONTITE THRU-FLOW VALVE

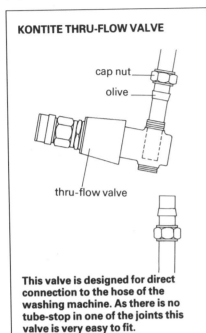

cap nut
olive
thru-flow valve

This valve is designed for direct connection to the hose of the washing machine. As there is no tube-stop in one of the joints this valve is very easy to fit.

OPELLA CONTROL VALVE

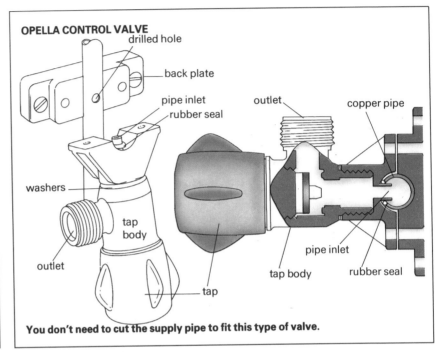

drilled hole
back plate
pipe inlet
rubber seal
washers
tap body
outlet
tap
outlet
copper pipe
pipe inlet
tap body
rubber seal

You don't need to cut the supply pipe to fit this type of valve.

PUTTING IN DRAINAGE

1. Put an inspection elbow in the 38mm (1½in) waste pipe.

2. Terminate the waste pipe below the gully grid.

3. Fix the stand-pipe with the open end 600mm (24in) above the floor.

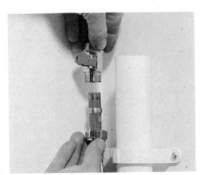

4. Run the water supply and attach a stop-valve at the end.

5. Screw the appliance inlet hose to the threaded part of the stop valve.

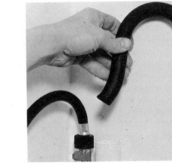

6. Place the outlet hose from the machine in the top of the stand-pipe.

claim, can be done without cutting off the water supply and draining the pipe.

PUTTING IN DRAINAGE

The simplest method is undoubtedly to hook the machine's outlet hose over the rim of the kitchen or utility room sink. However, it is better to provide an open-ended stand-pipe fixed to the wall, into which the outlet hose of the appliance can be permanently hooked. The open end of the stand-pipe should be at least 600mm (24in) above floor level and should have an internal diameter of at least 35mm (1⅜in). A deep seal (75mm or 3in) trap should be provided at its base and a branch waste pipe taken from its outlet to an exterior gully, if on the ground floor, or to the main soil and waste stack of a single stack system if on an upper floor. As with all connections to a single soil and waste stack, this should be done under the supervision of the district or borough council's Building Control Officer. Manufacturers of plastic drainage systems include suitable drainage stand-pipes and accessories in their range of equipment (the trap and pipe being sold as one unit).

It is sometimes possible to deal with drainage by taking the waste pipe to connect directly to the trap of the kitchen sink, and this course of action may be suggested at DIY centres and by the staff of builders' merchants. But it must be stressed that this is not recommended by the manufacturers of the appliances, who believe that it involves a real risk of back-siphonage. This could lead to waste water from the sink siphoning back into the washing machine or dishwasher, which would cause serious problems.

JOINING PIPES

Joining copper pipe is one of the basic plumbing skills. Compression and capillary joints are easy to make and once you've mastered the techniques you'll be prepared for a whole range of useful plumb-

ing projects. If you are making a join into an existing pipe system, remember to turn the supply off.

WHICH TYPE OF FITTING?

A compression joint is made by compressing two brass or copper rings (known as olives or thimbles) round the ends of the pipes to be joined, so forming a watertight seal. There are two main types of compression joint – manipulative and non-manipulative. Manipulative joints are now rarely used in indoor domestic water systems. Because they cannot be pulled apart they are sometimes used for underground pipework, but capillary joints will do equally well in these situations.

Although not the cheapest way to join a pipe, a non-manipulative joint is the easiest to use and requires only the minimum of tools. It comprises a central body made of brass or gunmetal with a cap-nut at each end which, when rotated, squeezes the olive tightly between

WHICH TOOLS?
For cutting pipe you need a wheel tube cutter or hack saw, and a metal file for removing ragged burrs.

For compression joints you need two adjustable spanners or pipe wrenches, and some steel wool to clean the surfaces of the pipes.

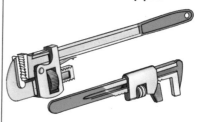

For capillary joints you need a blow torch, steel wool, flux, solder (even if you're using integral ring fittings which already have solder in them), and a glass fibre or asbestos mat to deflect the blowtorch flame from nearby surfaces.

MAKING A COMPRESSION JOINT

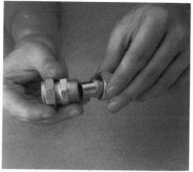

1. In a compression joint, the olive goes on after the cap-nut.

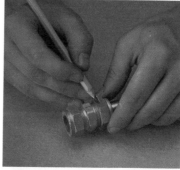

2. Make pencil marks on cap-nut and on the body of the fitting.

3. About 1½ turns is sufficient to give a watertight seal.

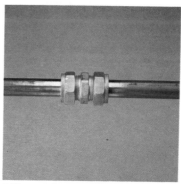

4. Repeat the operation to join the other pipe to the fitting.

the pipe end and the casing. This is the most commonly used type of compression joint and is suitable for most internal domestic plumbing purposes.

A capillary joint is simply a copper sleeve with socket outlets into which the pipe ends are soldered. It is neater and smaller than a compression joint and forms a robust connection which will not readily pull apart. Because it is considerably cheaper than a compression joint it is frequently used when a number of joints have to be made and is also particularly useful in awkward positions where it is impossible to use wrenches.

Some people are put off using capillary fittings because of the need to use a blowtorch. But modern gas-canister torches have put paid to the fears aroused by paraffin lamps and are not dangerous.

Nevertheless there are certain precautions you should always take when using a blowtorch: wear thick heat-resistant gloves; put down a lighted blowtorch on a

MAKING A CAPILLARY JOINT

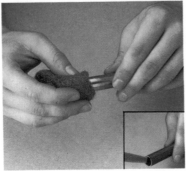

1. For capillary joints, clean the pipe end with steel wool.

2. Use a brush to smear flux over the end of the pipe and in the fitting.

3. Slide the pipe into the fitting and heat the joint with a blow torch.

4. For an end feed fitting, hold the solder to the mouth of the joint.

MATCHING UP PIPEWORK
Matching new pipe to old isn't always as easy as it sounds, because even if your existing pipework is copper it may have been manufactured to imperial sizes – and all new copper pipe comes in metric sizes. Metric/imperial equivalents for the most widely used sizes are given below

Metric (external diameter)	Imperial (internal diameter)
12mm	⅜in
15mm	½in
22mm	¾in
28mm	1in
35mm	1¼in

If you're using integral-ring capillary fittings (where the solder is pre-loaded into the fitting) you'll always need special adaptors to join new copper pipe to old. These adaptors are just ordinary fittings with one end slightly larger than the other.

End-feed capillary fittings can be made to work simply by adding more solder, but it takes more skill.

if you're making compression joints, the 12mm, 15mm and 28mm fittings will work with old ⅜in, ½in and 1in pipe. For other imperial pipe sizes, again you'll need adaptors.

firm flat surface with the flame pointing into space, and clear any flammable material from the area where you are working.

When using a blowtorch, the most convenient place to work is at a bench, but you'll find most jointing work has to be carried out where the pipes are to run. Pipework is usually concealed so this may mean working in an awkward place, such as the roof space, or

stretching under the floorboards. However, always make sure that you are in a comfortable position, and that there's no danger of your dropping a lighted blowtorch.

PREPARING THE PIPES

Before joining pipes, check that the ends are circular and have not been distorted. If they have been dented, cut back to an undamaged section of the pipe using a hack-

PLASTIC PIPES

1. With solvent-weld joints, smear a little adhesive on the pipe ends.

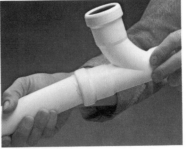

2. A little washing-up liquid helps push-fit pipes to be connected.

saw with a sharp blade or a wheel tube cutter.

The ends should also be square. Use a file to make any correction and to remove any ragged burrs of metal. If you're using a capillary joint it is important to clean up

CISTERN MECHANISMS

There are two sorts of flushing mechanism: the bell type in well-bottom cisterns, and the piston type, which is more popular today.

Well-bottom cistern for replacement of high-level arrangements.

Lever flush cistern for low-level suites.

Slimline flush panel for use where space is restricted.

The mechanism is bagged up inside a new cistern for you to assemble.

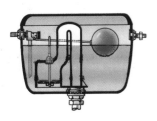

the sides of the pipe with abrasive paper or steel wool.

PLASTIC PIPES

Plastic pipes are widely used for waste water. The pressure of waste water is relatively low and in this case push-fit joints are normally used, although solvent-weld joints may be found.

Plastic pipes may also be used for the hot and cold water supply. Joints may be the push-fit type (Acorn fittings), compression type or solvent-weld type.

REMOVING A WC

1. Remove the old WC: turn off the water and flush and empty the WC.

2. Disconnect or saw off the supply pipe and the overflow.

3. Disconnect the cistern from the pan; a close-coupled one is lifted off.

4. Use a cold chisel to break the joint between pan and outlet.

5. Ease the pan away from the pipe.

6. Stuff the soil pipe with newspaper.

REPLACING A WC

It is quite easy to replace a WC, and not nearly as unpleasant a task as you may think.

HOW TO START

After you have turned off the water supply and flushed the cistern to empty it, the next step is to disconnect the water supply and the overflow and outlet pipes. Begin by unscrewing the cap-nut connecting the water-supply pipe to the cistern's ball-valve inlet. Then undo the back-nut retaining its overflow or warning pipe. Finally undo the large nut which secures the threaded outlet of the cistern to the flush pipe. It should now be possible to lift the old cistern off its supporting bracket or brackets.

If the WC suite is a very old one and screwed to a timber floor, unscrew and remove the pan's fixing screws. Use old rags to mop the water out of the pan. Then, taking the pan in both hands, pull it from side to side and away from the wall. If the connection to the soil pipe is made with a mastic or putty joint, the pan outlet may come easily out of its socket (which will have to be cleaned of all jointing material before the new unit is fitted). If a rigid cement joint has been used then there's no alternative but to use a bit of force. This means deliberately breaking the pan outlet, just behind the trap and above the drain socket, with a club hammer. You can then prise the front part of the pan away from the floor using a cold chisel and hammer. This will separate the pan outlet from the drain. At this point it's a good idea to stuff a bundle of rags or screwed-up newspaper into the drain socket to prevent any debris getting into the soil pipe. Next attack the socket to remove the remains of the pan's outlet. For this, use a small cold chisel and hammer, but do it carefully to avoid damaging the drain socket itself – this will be used again. It's best to keep the point of the chisel pointing towards the centre of the pipe. Try to break it right down to the shoulder of the socket at one point and the rest will then come out fairly easily. Repeat the chipping process to remove all the old jointing material. Remove the rags or newspaper with the fragments of pipe and jointing material. Then with your cold chisel, remove all traces of the cement base that secured the old pan to the floor.

INSTALLING THE NEW PAN

Don't set the pan on a cement base: just use screws and plugs to fix it to the floor. But first, you must get the connection to the drain socket right. Begin by positioning the patent push-fit WC connector in the drain socket. Then offer up the new pan to the patent push-fit socket and move the pan around until it fits snugly. To fix the pan, mark the screw positions on the floor by tapping a nail through the screw-holes, and draw round the base on the floor so that you can replace it in exactly the same position. Drill holes in the floor at the points marked and finally fit the screws.

For fixing the pan, it's advisable to use brass non-corroding screws with a lead washer slipped over each one so that you won't crack the pan as you tighten the screws. Screw the pan down, checking that it is exactly horizontal with the aid of a spirit level laid across the top of the bowl. If it is not dead-level, pack the lower side with thin wood or plastic strips. The latter are more suitable because thin wood rots too easily. Finally check that the outlet of the pan is firmly pushed into the connector and that you have followed any specific fitting instructions from the manufacturer.

FITTING THE CISTERN

Fix the new cistern to the wall at the level above the pan recommended by the manufacturer. In the case of a separate cistern, secure the upper end of the flush pipe to the cistern, usually by means of a large nut, and the lower end to the pan's flushing horn with a rubber cone connector; but with a close-coupled suite, follow the manufacturer's instructions. You will now quite likely have to extend or cut back the water supply pipe to connect it to the new cistern. Complete the job by cutting and fitting a new overflow.

INSTALLING A WC

1. Fit the new pan outlet into the push-fit adaptor. Position the cistern.

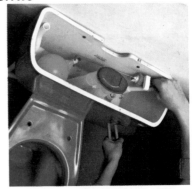

2. Assemble the flushing mechanism before fitting the cistern.

3. Attach the new overflow pipe, finally tightening up the lock-nut.

4. Turn on the water and check that the cistern fills to the correct level.

Chapter 3
CENTRAL
HEATING

CHOOSING A SYSTEM

Choosing a heating system is all about getting comfort with economy, in terms of both installation and running costs. There are three basic rules which influence the planning and operation of any system: (1) have as much warmth as you need but not more; (2) have warmth where you need it, and nowhere else; (3) have warmth when you want it, not any other time.

SCOPE OF THE SYSTEM

First decide on the scope of the system. There are 5 basic choices: full, partial, background, partial background, or selective central heating. The last of these is a happy compromise for most people. No room is denied warmth, but because it is rare to use all the rooms all the time, it is possible to make a 'short list' of those likely to be used simultaneously. Their total heat demand then dictates the size of the heat generator.

WET SYSTEMS

These are the most common type of central heating system. The boiler, which may be gas-fired, oil-fired or for solid-fuel, supplies heat for the room heating circuit and for the provision of domestic hot water. A circulating pump pushes hot water round the heating circuit, but the water rises to the heat exchanger in the hot-water cylinder by normal convection although sometimes even this circuit is pumped. Two cisterns are fitted in the roof space: a cold-water storage cistern, which supplies water to be heated in the hot-water cylinder and also to the cold taps in the house; and a feed-and-expansion cistern for the heating system. The latter keeps the heating circuit topped up and catches any expansion of the heating-circuit water should this occur. Both are fed from the rising main.

PIPEWORK

The simplest form of pipe run is the single-pipe system, where a single loop of pipe has both radiator inlets and outlets connected. Thus, cooled water is returning to the system, gradually reducing the temperature. The two-pipe system prevents this by providing separ-

'WET' SYSTEMS

All wet systems have the following basic features: a heat generator, a self-contained water system with circulating pump, and a number of heat emitters. These allow the production of heat in a central location and its distribution to a number of pre-selected areas.

It is a fallacy that there is such a thing as 'gas central heating' or 'oil central heating'. A wet system is a wet system, whatever form of energy it uses or heat distribution it contains. For that reason, it is possible to examine systems before worrying about the kind of fuel used. Don't concern yourself with outdated concepts of gravity circulation or direct hot water cylinders.

The layout of a typical wet system is shown in this diagram. Hot water from the boiler is pumped round the radiator circuit, while convection carries hot water to the heat exchanger in the hot water cylinder.

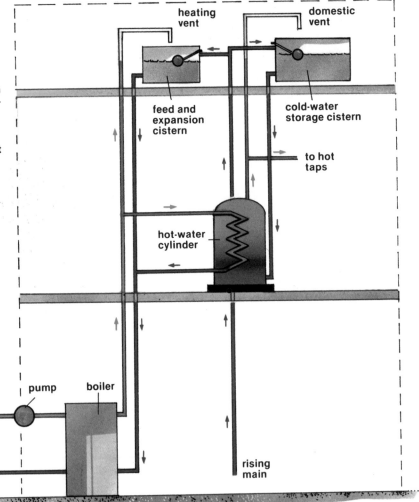

heating vent

domestic vent

feed and expansion cistern

cold-water storage cistern

to hot taps

hot-water cylinder

pump

boiler

flow to radiators

return from radiators

rising main

ate flow and return pipes. The microbore system utilises a 'flow and return' manifold from which individual radiators are serviced by narrow pipes (see illustrations below).

There are three choices of fuel for a wet central heating system: oil, gas or solid fuel. Gas is probably the cleanest and most convenient.

Oil appliances come in pressure jet or vaporizing (mostly wall-flame) varieties. The former are noisier and may need siting in an outbuilding. Solid-fuel heating can have a boiler, a room heater or an open fire with back-boiler as its heat source.

Although boilers are provided with integral controls, there are many others that you can incorporate in your heating system. But don't fall into the trap of believing that controls are certain to bring economies, used incorrectly, they can do just the opposite.

The function of a thermostat is to control the amount of heat the system delivers. The room thermostat is the best known; it is usually fitted in the hall, and is the one instrument which decides when the air temperature requires the switching on or off of the central heating, usually via the pump. It has limitations, and many of these can be overcome by using individual radiator thermostats instead.

A half-way measure is found in zone control, the house being divided into zones (eg, upstairs and downstairs) and the relevant parts of the heating circuit being controlled by special valves.

As well as controlling the quantity of heat your system delivers, you also want to control when it arrives. Time clocks can control individual pieces of apparatus or

SMALL BORE SYSTEMS

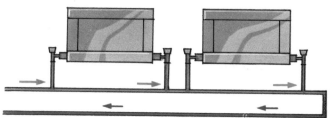

1. Single-pipe system: each radiator in the circuit receives progressively less heat.

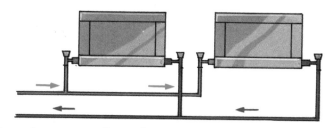

2. Two-pipe system: separate flow and return pipes ensure even heat distribution.

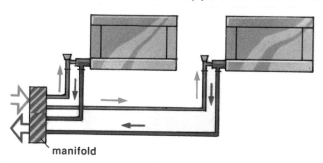

manifold

3. Microbore system: individual radiators are fed from a flow and return manifold.

CHOOSING RADIATORS

Skirting heaters are more efficient but more expensive than panel radiators. The sizes shown are just a few of the wide range available. Heat output figures are for single-panel radiators, with outputs for double-panel radiators shown in brackets.

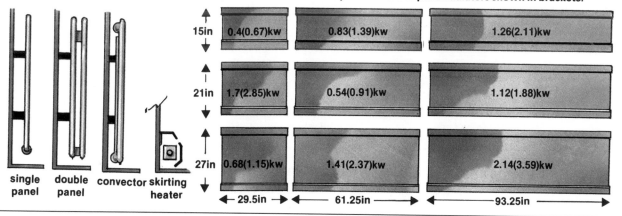

single panel | double panel | convector | skirting heater

15in 0.4(0.67)kw 0.83(1.39)kw 1.26(2.11)kw
21in 1.7(2.85)kw 0.54(0.91)kw 1.12(1.88)kw
27in 0.68(1.15)kw 1.41(2.37)kw 2.14(3.59)kw
29.5in 61.25in 93.25in

INSTALLING THE PUMP

Correct positioning of the pump is essential if it is not to set up a circulation round the boiler's feed and expansion pipes; this could happen if the vent pipe were taken from the heating circuit. When installing the pump, fit isolating valves on either side to allow its easy removal for servicing or repair.

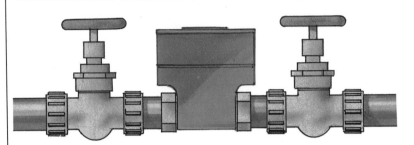

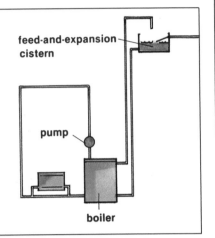

feed-and-expansion cistern

pump

boiler

CALCULATING HEAT LOSSES

A simple plan of each floor in your house – showing the dimensions, desired temperature and number of air changes per hour – will prove useful when calculating heat losses. An example is shown here together with sample calculations for one bedroom, illustrating how the answers are obtained. You can use the data in the plans to practise the calculations.

ground floor

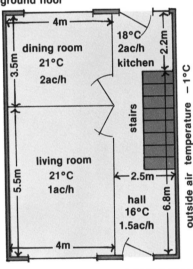

first floor

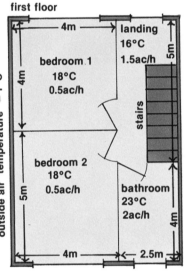

The calculations

	Area m²	U-value W/m²°C	Temp. Diff. °C		Loss W	Gain W
Bedroom 1 (18°C/0.5 air changes per hour)						
Window	2.50 × 5.70 ×		19	=	270.75	
Ext. walls	17.50 × 1.95 ×		19	=	648.38	
Landing wall	10.00 × 2.55 ×		2	=	51.00	
Bed. 2 wall	No heat loss - same temperature					
Floor*	16.00 × 1.43 ×		3	=		68.64
Ceiling	16.00 × 2.00 ×		19	=	608.00	
Air Change	40m³× 0.33 × 19 × 0.5			=	125.40	
					1703.53	
					− 68.64	
		Total loss:			1634.89	

* Heat gain due to higher temperature of room below.

Total heat loss for each room

	Watts
Dining room	2207.20
Living room	2518.04
Kitchen	933.19
Hall	1229.17
Bedroom 1	1634.89
Bedroom 2	1727.95
Landing	1201.37
Bathroom	2092.66
	13544.47

Allowance for domestic hot water	3000.00
Total heat requirement:	16544.47

Building construction   U-value

Roof – tiles over felt, loft, plaster ceiling	2.0
First floor – timber boards on joists, plaster ceiling below	1.43 (down) 1.45 (up)
Ground floor – solid on earth	1.15
External walls – 275mm, ventilated and uninsulated cavity	1.95
Internal walls – 114mm brick, plaster	2.55
Windows – single glazed	5.7
External doors – single glazed	5.7

Note: internal doors have same U-value as a partition wall

Other useful U-values

275mm (11in) cavity wall, insulated cavity	0.6
Ceiling, 140mm (5½in) insulation	0.25
Uninsulated timber ground floor	1.7
Double glazing	2.9

Window/external door areas

Dining room	4.8m²
Living room	3.3m²
Kitchen	1m² (window) 1.8m² (door)
Hall	1.8m² (door)
Bedroom 1	2.5m²
Bedroom 2	2.5m²
Bathroom	1.3m²
Landing	1.3m²

Deduct these figures from the total wall area to get a net figure for walls.

The total heat loss figure for each room gives the size of radiator required for that room. Add up all the heat-loss figures and divide by 1000 for a result in kilowatts. Add a 3kW allowance for domestic hot water and you will get the size of heat generator required for full central heating. For a selective system, take the totals of rooms to be heated simultaneously.

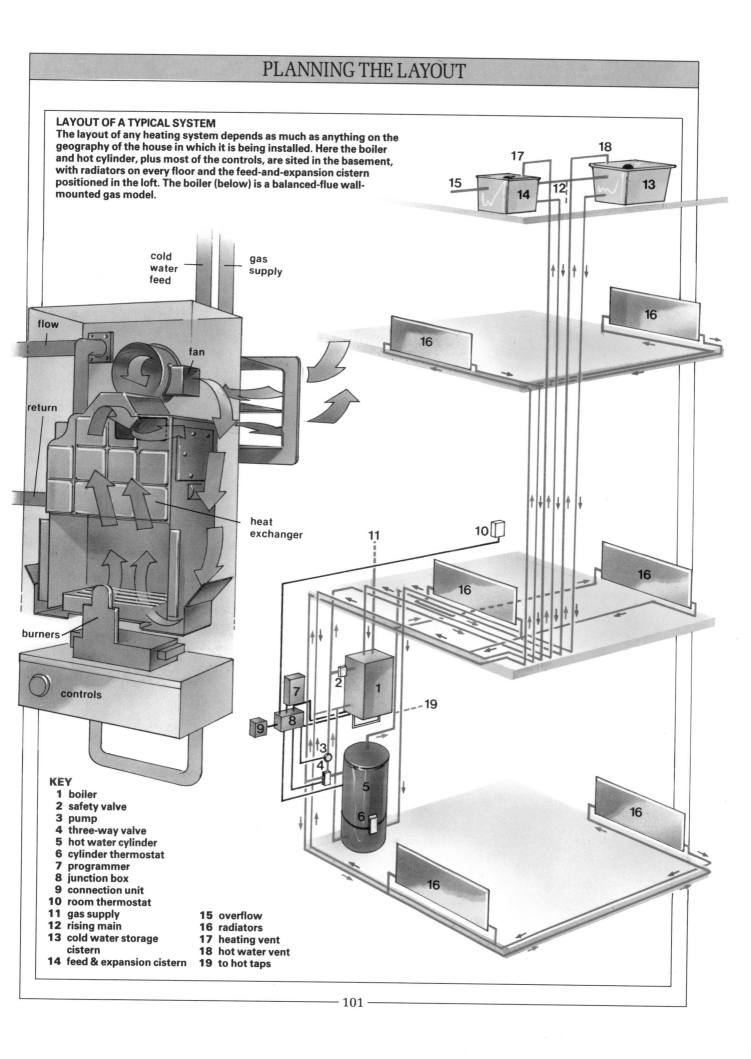

LAYOUT OF A TYPICAL SYSTEM
The layout of any heating system depends as much as anything on the geography of the house in which it is being installed. Here the boiler and hot cylinder, plus most of the controls, are sited in the basement, with radiators on every floor and the feed-and-expansion cistern positioned in the loft. The boiler (below) is a balanced-flue wall-mounted gas model.

cold
water
feed

gas
supply

flow

fan

return

heat
exchanger

burners

controls

KEY
1 boiler
2 safety valve
3 pump
4 three-way valve
5 hot water cylinder
6 cylinder thermostat
7 programmer
8 junction box
9 connection unit
10 room thermostat
11 gas supply
12 rising main
13 cold water storage
cistern
14 feed & expansion cistern

15 overflow
16 radiators
17 heating vent
18 hot water vent
19 to hot taps

whole systems, while elaborate switching mechanisms permit the control of more than one function.

RADIATORS

The rating of radiators is very important when designing a heating system, but it is a highly controversial matter. The only reliable guide is a MARC certificate and, so far, this is only awarded to radiators and convectors of British make.

In houses with single glazing, the old rule about placing radiators under windows still applies. Double glazing should prevent cool downdraughts, and consequently, radiators may be placed where they are most convenient, allowing for short, pipe runs.

PLANNING THE SYSTEM

You would be wise to enlist the aid of a professional to carry out the initial design work, since you are buying an expensive package of parts (even though you may make considerable savings by installing them yourself) and mistakes could cost you dearly. Some companies will undertake the initial calculation and design work, then supply all the necessary components with installation instructions. Others simply plan the installation and

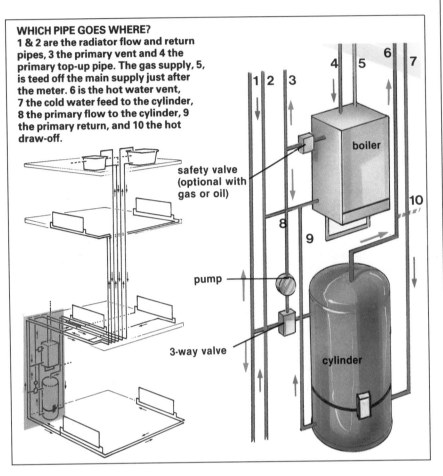

WHICH PIPE GOES WHERE?
1 & 2 are the radiator flow and return pipes, 3 the primary vent and 4 the primary top-up pipe. The gas supply, 5, is teed off the main supply just after the meter. 6 is the hot water vent, 7 the cold water feed to the cylinder, 8 the primary flow to the cylinder, 9 the primary return, and 10 the hot draw-off.

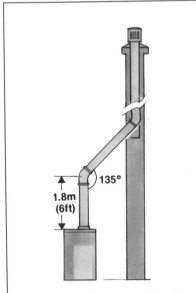

Requirements for a conventional flue: there must be at least a 1.8m (6ft) vertical run from the boiler, and all bends should be 135°, never 90°.

leave you to buy the parts elsewhere. Either way, it will help you appreciate how the decisions are made if you know the basis on which the calculations are made.

In order to determine the total heat output of the system, it is necessary first of all to calculate the heating requirement of each room. Then the output of each emitter (radiator) plus an allowance for providing domestic hot water can be totalled to determine the size of boiler needed.

The room will have an optimum design temperature which can be used for these calculations. For example, the ideal temperature for living rooms is generally considered to be 21°C (70°F). You need to know the difference between this temperature and the 'notional' outside temperature, which for the purpose of calculation is taken to be −1°C (30°F). Thus the difference is 22°C (40°F).

The amount of heat required is that necessary to maintain the

design temperature (here 21°C) by making up for heat lost through the fabric of the building and by air change – warmth escaping through opening doors, etc. Before any calculations are made you measure each room, and its windows and doors, and determine the building materials. The rate of heat transmission is expressed as a 'U' value.

A heat loss sheet is filled in for each room, allowing individual heat-loss calculations to be made for each surface. This is done by multiplying the surface area of each different element by its 'U' value and by the design temperature difference; the resulting figure gives heat loss in watts. By adding together the heat loss figure for each surface, plus an allowance for air change (found by multiplying the volume of the room by the number of changes per hour and by its air change 'U' value of 0.33), you obtain a total heat loss figure for the room.

PREPARING SITE AND BOILER

1. Use a template to mark the wall.

2. Fit the balanced flue ducting.

3. You'll need help to lift the boiler.

4. Fit the combustion chamber cover.

INSTALLING A BOILER

The exact method for installing any boiler varies from one appliance to another, but the following is a guide to a typical installation (in this case a wall-mounted, gas-fired model with a balanced flue).

All boilers come with full installation instructions, which should be followed closely.

POSITIONING THE BOILER

Boilers are heavy, so help will be needed to move them. With wall-mounted units use strong wall fixings such as expanding masonry bolts.

CONNECTING THE HOT WATER CYLINDER

1. Manoeuvre cylinder into position.

2. Complete pipe runs, then solder.

An oil-fired boiler must be sited so that its oil inlet is far enough below the fuel tank outlet to ensure a good gravity feed.

When installing the boiler in a confined space, make sure you allow access for servicing. There should be at least the same amount of room in front of a unit as its depth from front to back. When connecting a conventional gas flue, make sure there is at least a 1.8m (6ft) vertical run from the boiler before any bend. Never put 90° bends in the flue, but rather make them all 135°. Also, never include horizontal runs in the flue.

A conventionally-flued boiler takes its combustion air from the room itself, so an adequate supply is absolutely essential. If the air inlet is at the back of the unit, allow at least a 50mm (2in) gap between one side of the boiler and the nearest cabinet. Don't seal the room completely by draught-proofing.

SORTING OUT THE FLUE

Solid fuel boilers can be connected to existing chimneys, provided the latter are clean, give a good up-draught and are of the correct size. The boiler's stub flue is sealed to the chimney with a closing plate, and you will need to break through the chimney breast to provide access for this work. If the flue is too big, it will have to be fitted with a liner; this is always necessary with oil and gas appliances to prevent the condensation seeping into the brickwork of the chimney. Once the boiler is in place, the liner is fed down the chimney for connection to the stub flue.

CONNECTING TO GAS SUPPLIES

Leave connection to the delivery side of the meter to the gas board, but you can run the supply pipe to that point from the boiler. Take it as close to the meter as possible if it will break into the supply pipe of another appliance.

HOT WATER

If you intend using an immersion heater during the summer, make the secondary connection to the cylinder first. This will allow you to provide hot water to the taps by using the immersion heater until the heating system is ready.

DEALING WITH PIPEWORK

Try to arrange the pipework so that you need the minimum of fittings;

RADIATOR PIPEWORK

With the boiler and cylinder in position, you can fix the radiators (1) and their pipework. The feed-and-expansion cistern (2) is best set in the roof space next to the cold water cistern (3). The expansion pipe (4) from the primary circuit can then be installed so that it discharges over the feed-and-expansion cistern. The expansion pipe from the hot water system (5) should discharge over the main cistern.

The feed-and-expansion cistern should be supplied from a branch of the rising main (6). Fit a high-pressure ball-valve to the supply pipe and install an overflow pipe (7).

The expansion cistern should be used to top up the primary circuit (8); you can introduce a corrosion inhibitor to this circuit when it is first filled. The hot water system (9) is fed by the main cold water storage cistern.

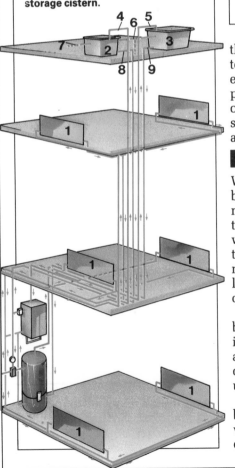

INSTALLING RADIATORS

1. To install the radiators, first screw the brackets into place.

2. Connect the circuit pipework to the radiators.

3. Don't forget to lag all pipes that run under the ground floor.

4. Check that all radiator vent valves open and close easily.

these are places for potential leaks to occur. Compression fittings are easier to use and this will aid the positioning of the boiler, pump, cylinder, etc, but capillary fittings should be used elsewhere as they are neater and cheaper.

POSITIONING RADIATORS

When marking out the wall for the brackets supplied with a radiator, make allowance for the fact that the radiator should be angled up-wards *very slightly* in the direction of the air vent to ensure that no air becomes trapped inside, leading to poor heat emission and corrosion.

Position the radiator so that its bottom edge is just above the skirting board, allowing air to circulate around it and providing sufficient clearance for any pipes to run underneath.

Fit the valves to the radiator before fixing it to the wall, which will be easier, and seal the threads of the couplers with PTFE tape

CISTERN CONNECTIONS

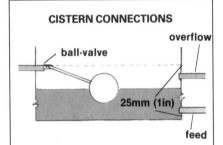

The feed pipe from the feed-and-expansion cistern to the boiler should be fitted 25mm (1in) up from the bottom of the cistern, and the overflow pipe 25mm (1in) below the level of the ball-valve inlet.

Connecting pipework to the cistern.

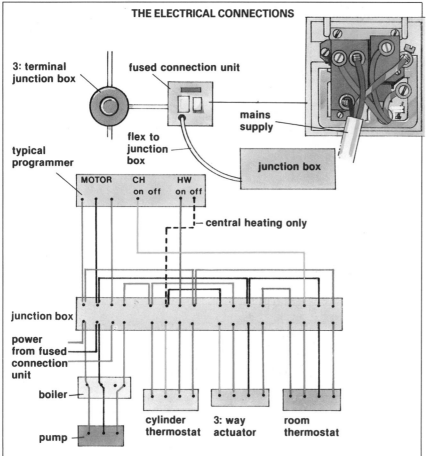

THE ELECTRICAL CONNECTIONS

3: terminal junction box

fused connection unit

typical programmer

flex to junction box

mains supply

junction box

MOTOR | CH on off | HW on off

--- central heating only

junction box

power from fused connection unit

boiler

pump

cylinder thermostat

3: way actuator

room thermostat

Wiring of the controls varies: this is a typical example. A spur from the ring circuit is taken to a multi-terminal junction box via a fused connection unit; the control devices are wired to one side of the junction box, the programmer to the other.

INSTALLING THE CONTROLS

Manufacturers supply installation instructions with their products; follow these to the letter.

A room thermostat needs to be positioned where it will not be subjected to cold draughts or any form of localized heating.

Power for the control system can be taken by means of a spur from a ring circuit; in this case, the cable should terminate at a double-pole fused connection unit fitted with a 3A fuse. Alternatively, a cable could be run direct from a spare fuseway at the consumer unit; fit a 5A fuse or MCB.

MAKING THE CONNECTIONS

Lead a single flex from each control to a centrally-located junction box. In some instances, flexes with more than three cores are needed, and special heat-resistant flex with up to five cores is available specifically for wiring up central heating installations.

Heat-resisting flex must be used anywhere that is subjected to heat, such as inside the boiler casing, at the cylinder thermostat and at the pump; otherwise use ordinary three-core flex.

FILLING THE SYSTEM

Before filling the system, check that all joints are secure, exposing as many as possible. Make up a short length of straight pipe and fit it in place of the pump.

before screwing them into the radiator. Wind this round the thread so that as you tighten the coupler it is forced between the grooves. Similarly, seal any blanking plugs in unused radiator tappings, but don't seal the air vent screw. The control valve is screwed into the

flow tapping and the lockshield valve (which is used to balance the flow of water once the system is operational) into the return tapping, both being at the bottom of the radiator on a pumped system. The air vent should be fitted into one of the top tappings.

INSTALLING THE CONTROLS

1. Install a multi-terminal junction box.

2. Fit the programmer's backplate.

3. Mount the control unit.

4. Run a flex to the site of the room thermostat and connect up.

5. Connect cores to the terminals of the terminal block in the boiler.

6. Fix the motor-driven actuator on backplate of the three-way valve.

7. When the wiring is complete, the pump can be refitted.

Open all the radiator valves and close all the air vents and drain-cocks. Attach a hose to the lowest draincock and lead it outside. Then open the ball-valve at the feed-and-expansion cistern and allow the system to fill.

After curing all leaks (this may mean draining the system), flush out the system by opening the ball-valve and draincock, letting the water flow for about ten minutes. Close the draincock and allow the system to refill. As this happens, bleed the air trapped in each radiator – starting with those at the bottom of the system and working your way upwards – by opening the air vents. Close each vent when water begins to trickle from it. Add a corrosion inhibitor to the water in the cistern as the system fills.

Finally, flush the pump through with tap water, close the valves on either side of the pump position and remove the pipe. Refit the pump, open the valves and bleed any air from the unit by opening its

vent screw. You are now ready to commission the system.

COMMISSIONING THE SYSTEM

The procedure for commissioning a central heating system depends on the type of boiler you have installed. Gas- and oil-fired boilers need specialized equipment, so call in an expert.

SOLID FUEL BOILERS

Prepare the fuel as instructed in the boiler's literature. Push a sheet of newspaper up the flue from inside the boiler, and light it to warm the flue. Light the fire, making sure the hopper lid is shut securely.

Set the damper to the fully open position, or adjust the boiler stat to a high setting, reducing the setting when the fire is established. Make sure the flue is 'pulling' – taking away the flue gases.

THE HEATING CIRCUIT

With a gravity primary circuit to the hot water cylinder, check the progress of the warm water from the boiler by feeling the flow pipe to the cylinder with your hand.

Make sure the pump is adjusted to a low setting and switch it on. With your hand, monitor the progress of the warmth along the heating pipes and into each radiator. When all the radiators are warm, run the pump for a further half hour. Switch it off and bleed each radiator by opening its air vent to expel any air.

BALANCING THE SYSTEM

The design of different parts of the heating system will affect the resistance they offer to the flow of hot water. Areas offering the least resistance will receive most of the circulated water, as this will take the easy route. Therefore, it is necessary to increase the resistance in these sections until all parts of the circuit receive an equal amount of heat. First bleed all the radiators and run the system long enough for it to reach its normal operating temperature. Make sure all the radiator valves are fully open.

Check the temperature of each radiator by hand, and partially close the lockshield valves on the hottest radiators. Allow the system to stabilize for an hour or so and repeat the process. Continue until all radiators feel equally warm.

The next stage requires the use of two clip-on thermometers. Take each radiator in turn; clip one to the flow pipe into the radiator and one to the return. Leave them to stabilize for a few minutes and then check the difference between the readings. Adjust the lockshield valves until the temperature drop across each radiator is the same. With a normal two-pipe circuit, the 'drop' across each radiator should be about 7°C (20°F). It may be difficult to balance the system exactly unless the outside air temperature is −1°C (30°F). If, when all the radiators have been balanced, the temperature drop is more or less than 7°C (20°F) the pump setting should be adjusted.

Chapter 4
HOME
ELECTRICS

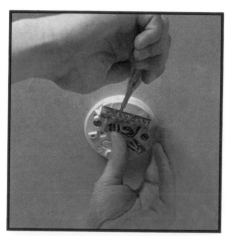
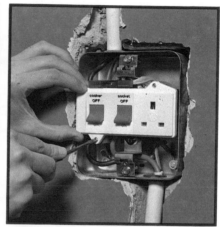
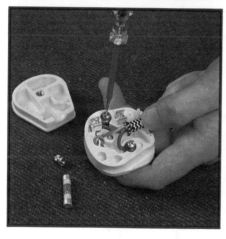

UNDERSTANDING ELECTRICAL SYSTEMS

In order to carry out electrical work it is important to understand how each part of the system functions. If you don't understand electricity then call in a qualified electrician.

LOOK AT YOUR WIRING

In a modern installation – one wired in the last 30 years – there are two wires carrying electric current that lead from the meter to the 'consumer unit'. These wires are called the meter tails – one is termed live, the other neutral.

On the inlet side of the consumer unit there's a switch with which you can turn off the power altogether, but the unit's main job is to direct power throughout the home via a network of cables.

SAFETY WITH ELECTRICITY

● **Never work on a circuit with the current on. Turn off at the mains and isolate the circuit by removing the relevant fuse. Keep this with you until you restore the supply.**

● **Never touch plugs and sockets with wet hands.**

● **Remove the plug from the socket when working on an applicance.**

● **Always use the correct fuse wire when mending a fuse.**

These cables are organized into circuits. There are circuits for lights, power sockets and so on, each with its own fuse in the consumer unit.

In older installations, instead of a consumer unit there may be individual fuse boxes protecting separate circuits. And each of these fuse boxes will have an isolating switch to cut off power to the circuit it controls. Alternatively, the fuse boxes may be supplied from a distribution box which in turn is connected to the meter.

Sometimes, even with a consumer unit you may find separate fuse boxes, probably the result of the system having been extended.

WHAT ARE FUSES?

The main service cable has its fuse; the various circuits have theirs in the consumer unit or fuse box and if you remove the back of a flat-pin plug you'll find a fuse in there.

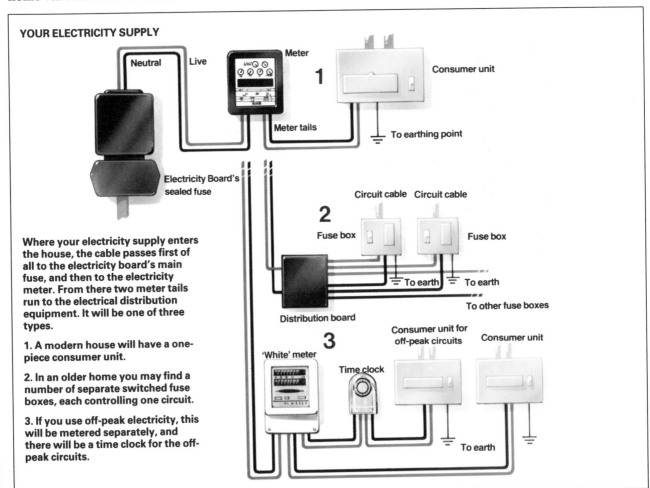

YOUR ELECTRICITY SUPPLY

Where your electricity supply enters the house, the cable passes first of all to the electricity board's main fuse, and then to the electricity meter. From there two meter tails run to the electrical distribution equipment. It will be one of three types.

1. A modern house will have a one-piece consumer unit.

2. In an older home you may find a number of separate switched fuse boxes, each controlling one circuit.

3. If you use off-peak electricity, this will be metered separately, and there will be a time clock for the off-peak circuits.

Fuses are weak links, built in to protect a circuit. Most fuses are just thin pieces of wire. They can be fitted to rewirable fuse carriers, in which case you can replace them, or they may be in ceramic cartridges, in which case you just throw them away and fit another. In any event, the fuse's thickness is described in terms of how much electricity – expressed in amps – is theoretically needed to melt it.

The word 'theoretically' is important because, in fact, fuses are not particularly accurate or reliable. For this reason, a more sensitive device called a miniature circuit breaker (MCB) may be used instead. An MCB is simply a type of switch which turns off automatically when danger threatens. Once the fault responsible for the overload is put right, you switch on again.

EARTHING

The purpose of the earth wire within the cable is to make up the earth continuity conductor (ECC). This is an essential safety feature of any electrical installation. Its role is to act as a 'safety valve' in the event of a fault, causing a fuse to blow or an MCB to trip to isolate a faulty circuit or faulty appliance from the mains supply. In doing so

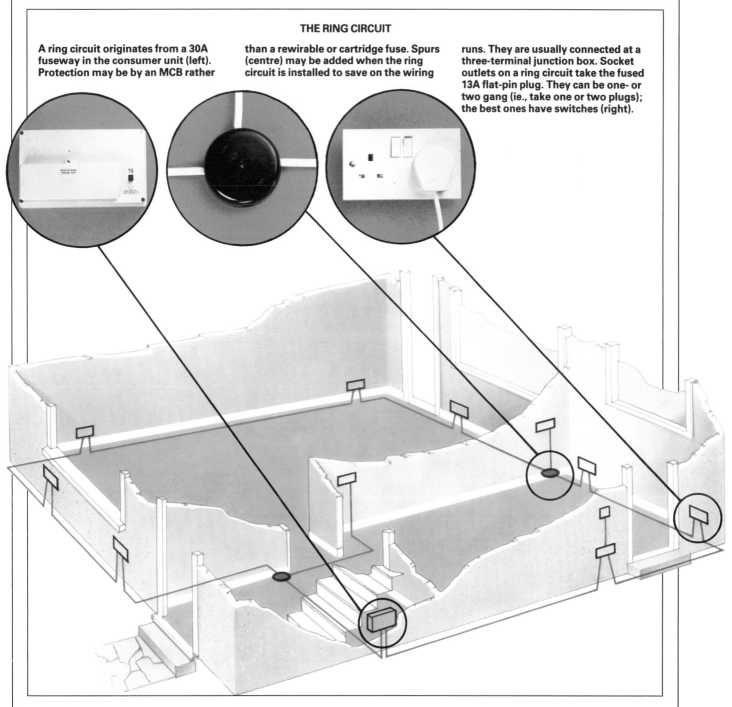

THE RING CIRCUIT

A ring circuit originates from a 30A fuseway in the consumer unit (left). Protection may be by an MCB rather than a rewirable or cartridge fuse. Spurs (centre) may be added when the ring circuit is installed to save on the wiring runs. They are usually connected at a three-terminal junction box. Socket outlets on a ring circuit take the fused 13A flat-pin plug. They can be one- or two gang (ie., take one or two plugs); the best ones have switches (right).

it could prevent the risk of fire or someone being electrocuted.

Earth wires are connected to the metal parts of switches, socket outlets, fittings and appliances (and even plumbing) in a really up-to-date system. Electricity will flow along the line of least resistance, so that if by some mishap any of these parts become live (by coming into contact with a live conductor) the earth wire would offer a line of 'less' resistance. And the extra current passing through one circuit would be sufficient to blow the fuse or activate the MCB.

But, unfortunately, this doesn't always happen, so for added safety a special device called an earth leakage circuit breaker (ELCB) can be fitted to detect the slightest leakage of current to earth. It shuts off the power within milliseconds – quickly enough to save a life – at the first sign of a fault.

TYPES OF CIRCUITS

For getting electricity to the power points, the most common system of wiring is what's called a 'ring' circuit. Wired in 2.5mm^2 two-core and earth cable, most homes have one such circuit for each floor.

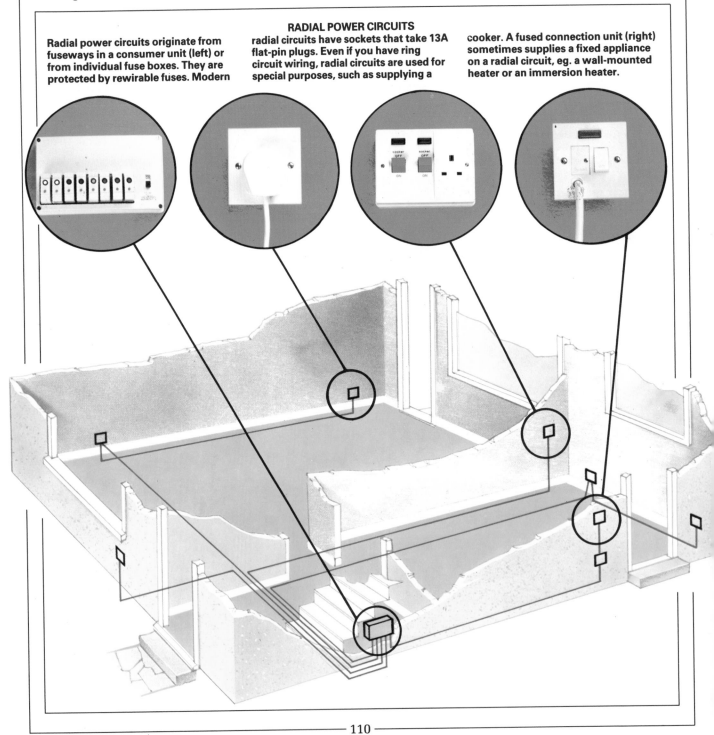

RADIAL POWER CIRCUITS

Radial power circuits originate from fuseways in a consumer unit (left) or from individual fuse boxes. They are protected by rewirable fuses. Modern radial circuits have sockets that take 13A flat-pin plugs. Even if you have ring circuit wiring, radial circuits are used for special purposes, such as supplying a cooker. A fused connection unit (right) sometimes supplies a fixed appliance on a radial circuit, eg. a wall-mounted heater or an immersion heater.

The two cores and the earth wire are connected to their terminals in the consumer unit (or fuse box) and then pass through each power socket in turn before returning to their respective terminals in the consumer unit (fuse box).

Radial circuits consist of a single cable that leaves the fuse box and runs to one or more sockets. In older homes, all power circuits were wired as radials. Any such circuits should be examined by a qualified electrician, and it is best to have them replaced.

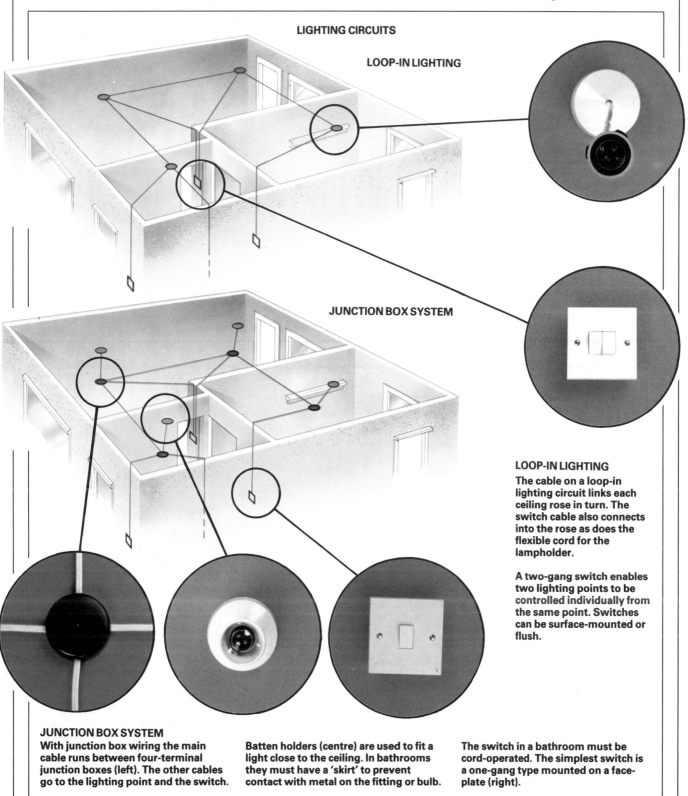

LIGHTING CIRCUITS

LOOP-IN LIGHTING

JUNCTION BOX SYSTEM

LOOP-IN LIGHTING
The cable on a loop-in lighting circuit links each ceiling rose in turn. The switch cable also connects into the rose as does the flexible cord for the lampholder.

A two-gang switch enables two lighting points to be controlled individually from the same point. Switches can be surface-mounted or flush.

JUNCTION BOX SYSTEM
With junction box wiring the main cable runs between four-terminal junction boxes (left). The other cables go to the lighting point and the switch.

Batten holders (centre) are used to fit a light close to the ceiling. In bathrooms they must have a 'skirt' to prevent contact with metal on the fitting or bulb.

The switch in a bathroom must be cord-operated. The simplest switch is a one-gang type mounted on a face-plate (right).

BE PREPARED
Make a list of which circuit does what and keep it by the main fuse box or consumer unit. Keep a fuse wire card containing lengths of each rating, a small screwdriver and a torch near the fuse box or consumer unit. If the consumer unit contains cartridge fuses, keep at least two spare fuses of each rating nearby.

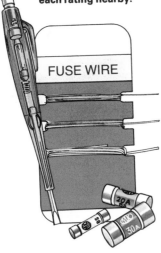

TESTING FUSES
You can test suspect fuses (both circuit and plug types) by holding them across the open end of a switched-on metal-cased torch, with one end on the casing and the other on the battery. A sound fuse will light the torch.

PLUGS AND EARTHING
Most appliances are fitted with three-core flex. When plugged in, the earth wire (green/yellow) is linked to the house earthing and ensures that the appliance is properly earthed. Two-core flex is for double-insulated appliances. The plug shown below is correctly wired.

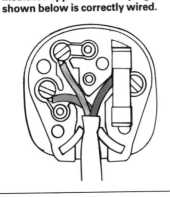

REPLACING CIRCUIT FUSES AT A CONSUMER UNIT

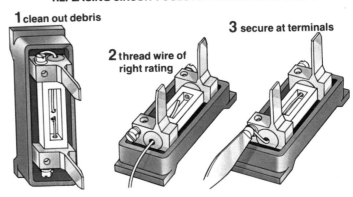

1 clean out debris

2 thread wire of right rating

3 secure at terminals

ELECTRICAL FAULTS

Many electrical breakdowns in the home are caused by only a few common faults. These include:
● overloading of circuits, causing the circuit fuse to blow or the MCB to trip
● short circuits, where the current bypasses its proper route because of failed insulation or contact between cable or flex cores; the resulting high current flow creates heat and blows the plug fuse (if fitted) and circuit fuse
● earthing faults, where insulation breaks down and the metal body of an appliance becomes live, causing a shock to the user if the appliance is not properly earthed and blowing a fuse or causing the ELCB to trip otherwise
● poor connections causing overheating that can lead to fire and to short circuits and earthing faults.

WHEN A PLUG FUSE BLOWS

Standard plug fuses have current ratings of 3A and 13A and are colour-coded red and brown respectively. Fit a 3A fuse for appliances rated at less than 700 watts, a 13A fuse otherwise (and always for colour TV sets).

If an appliance doesn't work, the most likely cause is a blown plug fuse. Replace it with a new one of the correct rating, then put the plug back in the socket and switch on. If nothing happens, check the socket and the circuit fuse.

REPLACING A CARTRIDGE FUSE

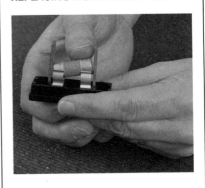

CHECKING A PLUG

Terminal connections must be tight.

Snap in a fuse of the correct rating.

CABLES
(PVC-sheathed and insulated, two core and earth, except E, which is three core and earth)

A 4mm²; *use*: circuits for small cookers, instantaneous water heater (up to 7kW), 30A radial circuit. **B** 6mm²; *use*: circuits to cookers over 12kW (10mm² for large split-level cookers). **C** 2.5mm²; *use*: ring main, power circuit, immersion heater, instantaneous water heater up to 5kW. **D** 1.5mm²; *use*: lighting circuit. **E** 1.0mm²; *use*: two-way switching for lighting circuit.

CABLES AND FLEXES

Two types of wiring are used in the domestic electrical circuits – fixed cables and flexible cords.

Fixed cables are normally concealed and carry electrical current to switches, ceiling lights and socket outlets.

Flexible cords (flexes) connect portable appliances and light fittings to the fixed wiring.

FIXED WIRING

Fixed wiring consists mostly of PVC-sheathed cable containing three copper conductors (cores). The core insulated in red PVC is the 'live' and the one in black the 'neutral', though in lighting circuits in the cable to the switch both the black and red are live. (The black core is required to have a piece of red sleeving on it to indicate this, although this measure is often omitted by incompetent

The earth core is uninsulated when exposed by removal of the sheathing, but it must be sheathed in green/yellow striped PVC sleeving before being connected to the earth terminal.

FLEXES

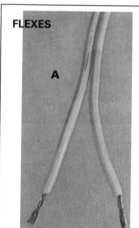 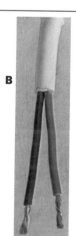 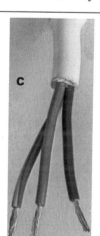 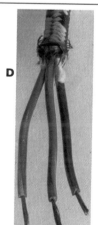 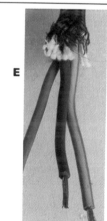 

A Parallel twin unsheathed; *use*: 0.5mm² and 0.75mm² – table lamps and clocks. **B and C** Circular PVC sheathed two-core, and two core and earth; *use*: 0.5mm² and 0.75mm² – plain lighting pendants (two-core); 1.0mm² and 1.5mm² – most appliances (three-core), power tools and most other double-insulated appliances (two-core). **D** Circular braided (rubber insulated); *use*: 1.00mm² and 1.25mm² – heaters and fires. **E** Unkinkable; *use*: 1.25mm² and 1.5mm² electric irons, percolators and kettles. **F** Heat-resisting; *use*: 0.5mm² and 0.75mm² – lighting pendants with 100-200W bulbs; 1.25mm² and 1.5mm² – immersion heater, storage heater.

TOOL KIT

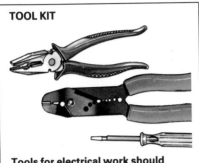

Tools for electrical work should have insulated handles. Top to bottom: electrician's pliers, wire stripper and small screwdriver.

HOW TO STRIP CABLE

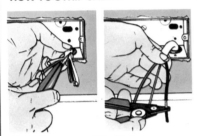

Use a handyman's knife to cut sheathing between the neutral and earth cores, then use wire strippers to remove core insulation.

FLUSH FITTING IN A BRICK WALL

1. Pencil round the mounting box.

2. First drill, then chop out recess.

3. Channel down behind skirting.

4. Thread the cable up from beneath.

electricians.) The third core is the earth and this is uninsulated, but when exposed after the sheathing is removed it must be sleeved in green/yellow striped PVC before connection to the earth terminal. In some circuits, PVC-sheathed cables having one core are used, eg. where a live core is looped out of a switch or a neutral core is looped out of a light, to supply an additional light or lights. Three-core and earth cable is used for two-way switching. The conductors are insulated in red, blue and yellow; the colour coding is for purposes of identification only.

CABLES FOR FIXED WIRING

Most domestic wiring is now supplied in metric sizes which refer to the cross-sectional area of one of the conductors, whether it is composed of one or several strands of wire. The most common sizes of cable are $1.0mm^2$ and $1.5mm^2$, used for lighting, and $2.5mm^2$, used for power circuits.

FLEXIBLE CORDS

Flexible cords are made in various sizes and current ratings and the types you most often come across are: parallel twin unsheathed, circular PVC-sheathed, circular braided, unkinkable, and heat-resisting. Each conductor is made up of a number of strands of copper and it is this which gives the cord its flexibility.

The insulation used round the conductors now conforms to an international colour coding standard – brown denotes the live wire, blue the neutral, and green/yellow the earth, when it is part of the flex.

Transparent or white insulation is used for a flex that carries a low current and where it doesn't make any difference which wires are connected to the live and neutral terminals of an appliance. It is used mainly for table lamps that need no earth.

CONNECTING A NEW SOCKET

1. Strip back the cable sheathing, but avoid damaging the cores.

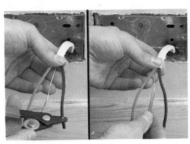

2. Remove insulation from the cores, but sleeve the earth core in PVC.

3. Connect the three cores to the relevant terminals of the socket.

ADDING A POWER POINT

Electrical equipment is now used more and more in the home, so an extra power socket is always useful. Here's how to fit one.

The power supply to the sockets will probably be wired as a ring circuit. You can add a spur to this provided the number of spurs does not exceed the number of sockets on the ring.

The connection could be made at any socket on the ring (unless it already has a spur coming from it), or by using a three-terminal junction box inserted into the cable run. Each spur can have one single or one double socket fitted to it.

TOOLS FOR THE JOB

Electrician's pliers (these have cutting edges on the jaws and insulated handles); wire strippers (can be adjusted to the diameter of the insulation to be stripped); handyman's knife (ideal for cutting back the sheathing of the cable); screwdrivers (a small one for the terminal fixing screws and a medium sized one for the fixing screws on the rose and switch).

CHECKING YOUR CIRCUITS

Although it's very likely that your house has ring circuits for the power supply, it's important to make sure. A ring circuit serves a number of 13A power outlets, and the sockets themselves take the familiar three-pin plugs with flat pins. But having this type of socket doesn't necessarily mean you've

FITTING A JUNCTION BOX

1. Find a nearby socket on the ring.

2. Feed the cable through.

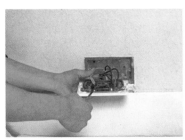

3. Connect the new cable.

4. Installing a junction box.

got a ring circuit – a new radial circuit may have been installed with these fittings, or an old radial circuit simply modernized with new socket outlets.

First you must check whether you've got a modern consumer unit or separate fuse boxes for each of the circuits. Having a consumer unit is a fair indication that you've got ring circuit wiring, and if two cables are connected to each individual 30A fuseway in the unit this will confirm it. Normally each floor of the house will have a separate ring circuit, protected by a 30A fuse or MCB.

If you have separate fuse boxes, look for the ones with 30A fuses. If they have one supply cable going into them and two circuit cables

coming out, this indicates a ring circuit.

It's easy to identify the sockets on any particular circuit simply by plugging in electrical appliances, such as table lamps, turning off the power and then removing a 30A fuse from the fuse box or consumer unit, or switching off a 30A MCB. When you restore the supply, the lamps that remain off will indicate which sockets are on the circuit.

DEALING WITH RADIAL CIRCUITS

Where a house hasn't got ring circuits, then the power sockets will be supplied by some form of radial circuit. In this case you should contact the local electricity authority, or a qualified electrician, before carrying out any work.

FLUSH FITTING IN A PLASTERBOARD WALL

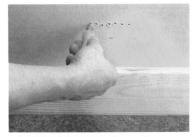

1. Locate the centre of a stud near where you want to install a socket.

2. Use a drill and chisel to remove some wood from the stud so that the box can be fully recessed.

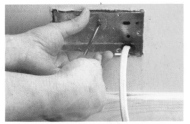

3. Set the box in the recess and fix it in place by screwing to the stud. Connect the cable to the terminals.

HOW TO RECOGNIZE A LOOP-IN CEILING ROSE

You can extend from an existing rose only if it is of the loop-in variety with three banks of terminals: such roses can accommodate up to four cables. If you have older roses, extensions must be made via a junction box.

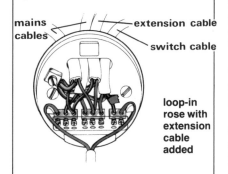

mains cables — extension cable

switch cable

loop-in rose with extension cable added

FLUSH FITTING A SWITCH

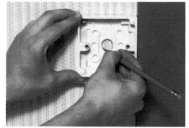

1. Mark the position of the switch box 1.4m above floor level.

2. Channel out a groove to take the switch cable.

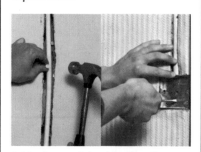

3. Fix the conduit with old nails, then screw the box into place.

ADDING A SPUR TO A RING

Once you've established you're dealing with a ring circuit and what sockets are on it, you'll need to find out whether any spurs have already been added – you can't have more spurs than there are socket outlets on the ring itself. But unless the circuit has been heavily modified, it's unlikely that this situation will arise.

You'll also need to know exactly where any spurs are located. You don't want to overload an existing branch by mistake.

You can distinguish the sockets on the ring from those on a spur by a combination of inspecting the back of the sockets and tracing some cable runs.

FIRST TURN OFF THE POWER SUPPLY. Then undo a socket near where you want to install the new socket.

At a single socket

One cable entering: socket is on the end of a spur. You cannot add another socket to this spur, but you can change the single socket for a double.

Two cables entering: socket may be on the ring, or it could be the intermediate socket on a spur. You'll need to trace the cable runs. If the cable is the only one going to another single socket, then the socket is on a spur. If the cable makes up one of two cables in another socket then it's on the ring.

Three cables entering: socket is on the ring with a spur leading from it. You cannot add another spur from this point.

At a double socket:

One cable entering: socket is on a spur. You cannot connect a new socket from this.

Two cables entering: socket is on the ring. You can connect a spur into this.

Three cables entering: socket is on the ring with a spur leading from it. Checking to see which cable is which is the same as for a single socket with three cables. You can't connect a spur from this socket.

FIXING THE SWITCH

1. Strip back 100mm (4in) of sheathing.

2. The black wire at a switch is live, not neutral: mark it with red PVC tape.

INSTALLING THE SOCKET

It's best to install the socket and lay in the cable before making the final join into the ring, since by doing this you reduce the amount of time that the power to the circuit is off.

You can either set the socket flush with the wall or mount it on the surface. The latter is the easier and less messy method, but the fitting stands proud of the wall and so is more conspicuous. Flush-fixing a socket on a plasterboard wall is a little more involved.

If you choose to surface-mount the socket, all you have to do is to fix a PVC or metal box directly to the wall after you've removed the knockout (if metal, use a grommet) where you want the cable to enter. The socket can then be screwed directly to this.

LAYING IN THE CABLE

New spurs should be in 2.5mm² cable. Because cable is expensive, it's best to plan the spur so that it uses as little as possible. When you channel cable into a wall you'll need to chase out a shallow run, fix the cable in position with clips, then plaster over it. But the best method of all is to run the cable in oval PVC conduiting. It won't give any more protection against an electric drill, but it'll prevent any possible reaction between the plaster making good and the cable sheathing. Always channel horizontally or vertically, and never diagonally, so it's easier to trace the wiring run when you've completed decorating. You can then avoid the cable when fixing something to the wall.

In fact, surface mounting is the easiest method of running cable. All you do is fix special plastic conduit to the wall and lay the cable inside before clipping on the lid. But many people regard this as an ugly solution.

When you're laying cable under ground floor floorboards it's best to clip it to the sides of the joists about 50mm (2in) below the surface so that it doesn't droop on the ground. Cable in the ceiling void can rest on the surface.

When you have to cross joists, you'll need to drill 16mm (⅝in) holes about 50mm (2in) below the level of the floorboards. The cable is threaded through them and so will be well clear of any floorboard fixing nails.

CONNECTING INTO THE CIRCUIT

If you use a junction box, you'll need one with three terminals inside. Connect the live conductors (those with red insulation) of the circuit cable and spur to one terminal, the neutral conductors (black insulation) to another, and the earth wires to the third. Sleeve the earth wires in green/yellow PVC first.

You might decide that it's easier to connect into the back of an existing socket than to use a junction box, although this will probably mean some extra channelling on the wall. Space is limited at the back of a socket so it may be difficult to fit the conductors to the relevant terminals. However, this method is ideal if the new socket that you're fitting on one wall is back-to-back with an existing fitting. By carefully drilling through the wall a length of cable can be linked from the old socket into the new.

ALTERATIONS TO LIGHTING SYSTEMS

Fitting a dimmer switch, putting in a new pendant ceiling light and switch, or changing the position of an existing one, usually presents few problems – even if you have little or no experience of electrical work.

DIMMER SWITCHES

A dimmer switch is particularly easy to install and gives a lot of flexibility in controlling artificial light – it can instantly transform the mood of a room.

Installation is simply a matter of unscrewing the existing switch from its mounting box (don't forget to turn off the power first) and disconnecting the cable. The two conductor wires and the earth are then fixed into the same terminals in the dimmer which is then screwed back to the same mounting box.

CEILING LIGHTS

Installing a new ceiling light requires making a simple connection into a nearby lighting circuit either by inserting a junction box or at an existing loop-in rose and then running a cable to a switch. In order to connect into the circuit you'll first need to know how the lights in your house are wired and which lights belong to which circuit. Then you'll be able to work out whether you can actually add another light to the circuit that is nearest to the new light's position.

FITTING A ROSE AND LAMPHOLDER

1. Fix new rose to the ceiling, then carefully prepare the conductors.

2. Loop-in wiring: wrap red PVC tape round the black wire (inset).

3. Junction box wiring: the red conductor goes to the SW terminal.

4. Connect the conductors to the two terminals of the lampholder.

5. Screw on the lampholder cap and prepare the free end of the flex.

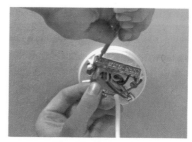

6. Connect to the terminals of the rose and hook wires over cord grips.

There are two main methods of wiring a lighting circuit. In the loop-in method the cable runs from ceiling rose to ceiling rose, stopping at the last one on the circuit, and the switches are wired into the roses. With the junction box system the cable runs to a number of junction boxes each serving a switch and a light. You may well find that both methods have been used in the same circuit to simplify and reduce the cable runs.

It's possible to connect into a nearby rose provided it's a loop-in type. To check this, simply turn off the power and unscrew the rose cover. A loop-in rose will have more than one red insulated wire going into the central terminal bank of the three in-line terminal banks. However, it can be quite fiddly to fit another cable, given that the terminal banks are very small, so you might find it easier to insert a junction box in the main circuit. And if there isn't a loop-in rose you'll have to use this method anyway.

Changing the position of a ceiling light is even easier than adding a new one. If you have a junction box system, all you have to do is to disconnect the wires from the rose and then reconnect them to the respective terminals of a new three-terminal junction box that you put in directly above the old fitting.

You can then lead off another cable from this junction box to the re-positioned ceiling rose. The switch remains unaffected.

If the rose is a loop-in type, you have to carry out a similar modification, but this time the switch wires have to be incorporated in the new junction box, which must be a four-terminal type.

EARTHING A LIGHTING CIRCUIT

Modern lighting circuits are protected by an earth. But if you've got a fairly old system (it's likely to be based on junction boxes), you might find that it doesn't have one. So when you're extending such a circuit, you're now required to protect the new wiring, light fitting and switch by installing an

CONNECTING INTO THE CIRCUIT

1. Connecting into a loop-in rose: keep all the existing wires in place.

2. Draw down about 200mm (8in) of the cable leading to the new rose.

3. Prepare to connect the new cable; sleeve the earth wire.

4. Connect the red conductor to the central in-line terminals.

5. When connecting in at a junction box, use the four-terminal type.

6. Wiring a three-terminal junction box after taking out a loop-in rose.

earth. Consequently, you have to use two-core and earth cable for the extension, which will most probably connect into the existing circuit at a junction box. You then have to run a 1.5mm² earth cable from this point to the main earthing point.

CIRCUIT ADDITIONS

Usually there's a lighting circuit for each floor of a house and in a single storey dwelling there are likely to be two or more. But it's easy to identify the individual circuits simply by switching on all the lights, turning off the power and taking out a 5A fuse from the consumer unit or switching off an MCB. When you restore the power you'll know that the lights that remain off all belong to the same circuit.

Generally speaking, a lighting circuit serves six to eight fixed lighting points. In fact, it can serve up to 12 lampholders provided the total wattage of the bulbs on the circuit doesn't exceed 1,200 watts. This means that unless other lights have previously been added – wall lights for example – there should be no problem in connecting in another light.

Remember, when adding up the bulb wattages, a bulb of less than 100 watts counts as 100 watts and not its face value.

Extensions to lighting circuits are usually wired in 1.00mm² two-core and earth PVC-sheathed and insulated cable.

THE PLACE FOR LIGHTS

Make sure that new switches are conveniently located – by a door is often the most satisfactory position. Usually they are set on the wall 1.4 metres (4ft 6in) above floor level.

For safety you mustn't install pendant lights, especially plain pendants with exposed flexible cords, in a bathroom. All light fittings here must be of the close-mounted type, preferably totally enclosed to keep off condensation. If instead you use an open batten lampholder it must be fitted with a protective shield or skirt which makes it impossible for anyone changing the bulb to touch the metal clamp.

In a bathroom, only fit a ceiling switch operated by an insulating cord.

SWITCHES

With a new light, you can either connect it into an existing switch position (fitting a two-gang switch in place of a one-gang one, for example) or a new switch. Depending on how you connect into the existing circuit, you'll have to run the switch cable above the ceiling from a rose or a junction box down the wall to where you are going to locate it.

If you want to conceal the cable on the down drop you'll have to cut a shallow channel – which will damage the existing decoration. Alternatively, you can surface-mount it in trunking.

REWIRING A HOUSE

Completely rewiring your home is a job that sounds more difficult than it really is. If you've mastered such techniques as running cable, fitting new lights and installing new socket outlets then it certainly won't present you with any major problems.

RING CIRCUITS

The advantage of this system is that it allows the cable to cope with more sockets than if it made a one-way trip; in fact, you can have as many sockets as you like on the ring so long as the floor area served by the circuit doesn't exceed 100 sq m (1,080 sq ft). What's more, you can increase the number of sockets by adding branch lines off

KNOWING WHEN TO REWIRE

1. If your fuseboard looks like this it is almost certain that rewiring is necessary throughout. This must be done with great care, but need not be difficult.

2. Any exposed cores present a risk of both electric shock and fire.

3. Wrap any damaged cores in PVC insulating tape without delay.

the ring. These are called 'spurs' and break into the ring via a junction box, a spur connection unit, or an existing socket.

Spurs are able to supply only one single or one double socket or one fused connection unit.

A ring circuit is protected by a 30A fuse. Of course, with all those sockets, there is a risk of overloading the circuit, but if the circuit does overload, the fuse will blow, or the MCB will switch off.

RADIAL CIRCUITS

Radial circuits are sometimes used in modern wiring systems where a ring circuit would be inappropriate for some reason. There are two types, the difference being their current-carrying capacity.

A 20A radial circuit comprises 2.5mm^2 cable and is protected by a 20A fuse (rewirable or cartridge) or an MCB in the consumer unit (or fuse box). It can supply an unlimited number of 13A socket outlets and fixed appliances using 3kW of power or less, providing they are within a floor area not exceeding 20 sq m (about 215 sq ft).

The other type of circuit is the 30A radial which is basically the same as the 20A circuit, but it uses at least 4mm^2 cable and can carry more power to a larger floor area (50 sq metres/540 sq ft). The circuit is protected by a 30A fuse.

These restrictions on floor area mean that several radial circuits would have to be installed to cover the same area as a ring circuit. The 'ring' is now the common method of wiring in the UK, but radial circuits can usefully supplement an overworked ring circuit.

SPECIAL PURPOSE SOCKETS

In addition to rings and radials, your home may have special circuits which supply only one outlet or appliance. Cookers, immersion heaters, instantaneous showers and the like are wired in this way and each has its own individual fuse. In effect, these circuits are just radials that have had both the cable and fuse sizes 'beefed up' so that they can cope with the often heavy demands of the appliances

they supply – for example, a large cooker might need a 45A fuse, and 6mm^2 or even 10mm^2 cable.

Because electric night storage heaters all come on together they could overload a ring circuit; consequently each one is supplied by a separate radial circuit protected by a 15A fuse. The fuses are all housed in a separate consumer unit which is linked to a sealed time clock and uses off-peak electricity.

LIGHTING CIRCUITS

Two systems of wiring lighting circuits are in common use, and it is not unusual for an installation to contain a little bit of each. One

is called the loop-in system; the other the junction (or joint) box system.

With the loop-in system, a cable (normally 1.0mm^2 but sometimes 1.5mm^2) leaves a 5A fuse in the consumer unit (or fuse box) and is connected to the first in a series of special loop-in ceiling roses. From this rose, one cable goes on to the next in the series, while another takes power down to the switch controlling the light and back up through the light itself.

The junction box system uses the same idea but, instead of going from rose to rose, the cable from the consumer unit (or fuse box) passes through a series of junction

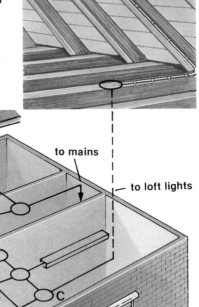

PLANNING
Making the decision to rewire is perhaps the biggest step you'll have to take and, as with any electrical installation, you should never undertake the job without knowing exactly what you want and where you want it. Detailed planning is crucial to the final results and overlooking one important socket outlet or light can cause considerable inconvenience and, in the long run, extra work. Before making any decision about rewiring your home it's a good idea to examine the existing circuitry thoroughly to make sure that it really does need replacing.

to mains

to loft lights

Start the job by rewiring the circuits in the loft. Aim to fit new switches (A), but re-use conduit for switch drops, loop-in ceiling roses (B), junction boxes for wall lights and fluorescent lamps (C) and BESA boxes (D) where there is little room for connections. Inset: when you have finished wiring lights on the floor below, you can wire up a light in the loft itself.

INSTALLING A DIMMER SWITCH

1. Unscrew existing faceplate and disconnect old switch.

2. Make connections according to the manufacturer's instructions.

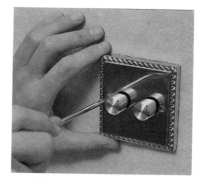

3. If installing a metal switch make sure the faceplate is earthed.

boxes. From each box, one cable goes to the ceiling rose or light, and another to the switch that controls it. This system is particularly useful, for example, when fitting wall lights, as there is usually little space at the back of a wall light fitting for looping-in.

Lighting circuits are rated at 5 amps, which means they can take a load of up to 1,200 watts. In effect, this means that they could supply 12 lamp-holders containing bulbs of 100w each or smaller.

However, as you may want to fit bulbs with higher wattages at some points, it is usual for a lighting circuit to supply up to eight outlet points, so separate circuits are required for each floor.

Strictly speaking it's better to arrange the circuits so that there is more than one on each floor – this means that you won't be in total darkness if a fuse in the consumer unit blows.

WHEN TO REWIRE

There are a number of telltale signs that will help you determine if your home needs rewiring. When you inspect your circuitry, look out for:
● old cable with brittle or cracked insulation
● cable with poor sheathing
● unsheathed cores that are touching combustible material
● loose, rusty or disconnected light gauge steel conduit
● poor earthing continuity
● damaged accessories
● obsolete accessories
● accessories that can't be earthed
● overloaded circuits
● frequent use of adaptors
● insufficient lighting points
● insufficient power points.

PLANNING THE JOB

Planning is an extremely important part of the job, as careful and

thorough preparation will mean minimum disruption to your daily routine: you'll have to move furniture around, lift floorcoverings such as fitted carpets and lino, and raise floorboards.

An obvious way of cutting down on the time spent rewiring is to have a helper, and it'll also make running cable that much easier. With some assistance you'll be able to rewire the upper floor lighting and install a light in the loft in a couple of days; so you could set aside a weekend for this section of the job. For the rest of the house you should really allow about seven days.

ESTIMATING

Cast an eye around your home and assess what your power and lighting needs really are before you buy any materials. The chances are that your current needs are going to be considerably greater than

INSTALLING A JUNCTION BOX

1. Installing a junction box: note the red sleeve on the black switch core.

2. Lay a length of cable from the lighting point and prepare the ends.

3. Connect as shown (the switch terminal is top left).

when the existing system was installed, and ideally you should aim to have one socket per electrical appliance.

When buying the equipment for your rewiring, always choose good quality cable and fittings made by well-known and established firms. Make sure that the cable you buy has been produced to the relevant British Standard. This is likely to be stamped on the outside of the sheathing.

Before visiting your supplier, make a list of your requirements. This should include both accessories and cable.

ACCESSORIES

For a typical three-bedroom house with a loft and garage, your shopping list is likely to resemble the following:
25 double socket outlets plus flush or surface mounting boxes
3 single socket outlets plus boxes
14 one-gang plate-switches and boxes

3 cord-operated ceiling switches
2 two-way switches plus boxes
8 ceiling roses
8 lampholders
2 batten holders
1 close-ceiling light fitting
4 fluorescent fittings
1 shaver supply unit plus box
1 cooker switch plus box
junction boxes (optional)
1 eight-way consumer unit
8 MCBs

CABLE

Cable requirements could include:
50-100m 1.5mm² two-core and earth cable
50-100m 2.5mm² two-core and earth cable
10m 1.0mm² three-core and earth cable
5-10m 1.0mm² flexible cord
Length of 6.0mm² two-core and earth cable
Length of 10mm² two-core and earth cable
Length of PVC-covered armoured cable

Approximately 5m 6.0mm² single core green/yellow PVC cable for bonding gas/water services
Approximately 5m 4mm² single green/yellow cable for bonding extraneous metal to earth
1m 16mm² single green/yellow cable for main earthing
10m green/yellow PVC earth sleeving

Other items you need include screws, wallplugs, nails, PVC insulating tape and cable clips.

CABLE CHECKLIST

The uses of cable vary according to its size
1.0mm² and 1.5mm² – lighting
2.5mm² – power circuit, immersion heater and small water heater (up to 5kW)
4mm² – small cooker, 30A radial circuit, water heater (up to 7kW)
6mm² – cookers up to 12kW
10mm² – large cookers

STARTING WORK

As you'll be starting work in the loft, check which existing lights are on which circuits and label them accordingly. Inspect each circuit separately, with only its fuse in position in the fuseboard at the time. Then list which lights are on it. Before starting work you must turn off the mainswitch of the fuseboard that contains the fuses controlling those lighting circuits that run in the loft. Make a note of their positions so you know which is which, but in fact, it's probably better to keep all fuses out and mainswitches off when working on the old wiring itself. You should then remove all light fittings on the floor below, that are supplied by the wiring in the loft. That includes all switches as well, but not the two-way switch in the hall that controls the landing lighting as this is likely to get its power from a different circuit. Then get up in the loft, taking with you a couple of battery-powered lights. This is extremely important. It's not worth working merely in torch light as you risk making errors in the wiring that could prove costly. It is possible to arrange electric lighting from an extension lead,

---

FITTING A BESA BOX

1. To fit a BESA box, mark the position of the terminal block.

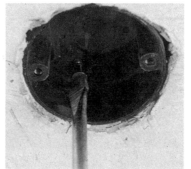

2. Cut a hole, push the box into the recess and screw it to the joist.

3. With loop-in wiring, draw the feed and switch cables into the BESA box. Wrap red PVC tape around the black core of the switch cable.

4. Connect the lives, neutral and earths to separate connectors.

but only if there is a socket outlet below which is supplied from a circuit controlled by a mainswitch independent of the lighting mainswitch.

Once up in the loft you can pull out all the old wiring and any old conduit it's run in. Only if conduits are sunk into plaster and run down to switch positions should they be left in place.

Once you've removed the cables from fittings and switches, you should find that there is only one cable left. This will be the circuit feed cable running from the mains.

LIGHTING POINTS

Before making the connections, decide whether to use a loop-in system, a junction box system or a mixture of the two. In the loop-in system, the lighting circuit cable leaves the consumer unit and is connected to the first in a series of special loop-in ceiling roses. From this first rose, one cable will go on to the next rose in the series, while another takes the power down to the switch controlling the light and back up to the light itself. The junction box system is based on much the same idea but, rather

DOWNSTAIRS WIRING

When you have completed wiring the upstairs rooms from the loft and installed a light in the loft itself, the remaining stages of the job involve tackling the light and power circuits in the ground floor ceiling void, and then the power circuits under the ground floor itself.

Install a new consumer unit in an easily accessible place and make sure that you have sufficient fuseways for your needs. All cables running up to the first floor and loft should be taken along the same route, and must be labelled clearly.

ESTIMATING

The amount of cable you'll need obviously depends on the size of your home, the number of circuits, the number of lights and the number of socket outlets you intend to install. For the average three- or four-bedroomed house that has one light and switch per room and two in the main living room and kitchen you'll probably need about ten metres of cable per light. So, as the chances are that you'll be running power to at least ten lighting points you might just as well buy a couple of 50-metre reels of cable for this part of the job. For socket outlets wired on, say, two ring circuits you'll probably need between 50 and 100 metres of 2.5mm² cable. It's a good idea to buy just one reel at first, and then, if necessary, another – or else a specific length of the cable if you don't need another whole reel. But it's certainly worth taking accurate measurements of the circuit for cookers, showers and outside power, because more expensive cable is used for these.

It's worth shopping around, but beware of special bargains or similar offers of equipment from unknown sources.

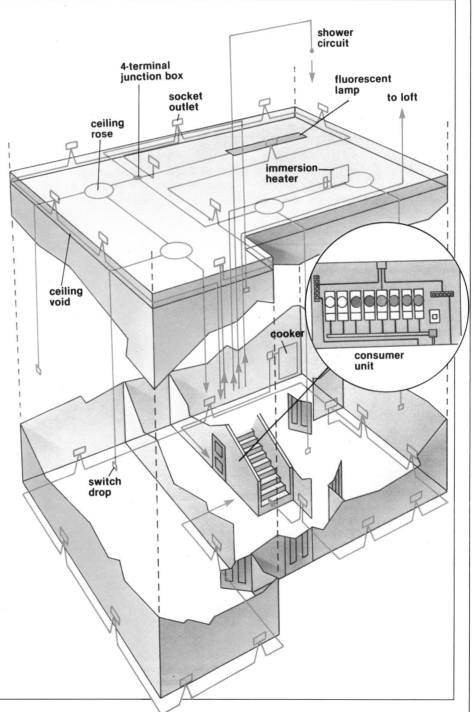

than running from rose to rose, the lighting circuit feed cable passes through a series of four-terminal junction boxes that are fixed to battens between the joists. From each box, one cable runs to the ceiling rose or light, while another serves as a switch drop and goes to the switch that controls the new light. A junction box system can prove very convenient when fitting wall lights, for example.

A mixture of the two systems is the likeliest compromise, using whichever method saves the most cable at any point.

RUNNING IN THE CABLE

The circuit feed cable should be 1.5mm² two-core and earth PVC cable and should originate at a 5A fuseway. If you're going to run it in an existing conduit you must make sure that each end of the conduit is fitted with a PVC bush to prevent the cable from getting damaged on any sharp edges. Then start running the feed cable to the lighting points in the ceiling. Push the cable through the holes and make the connections to the roses but don't, at this stage, fix the fittings to the ceiling. It's a good idea to mark the feed cables 'feed' at each point where they emerge through the ceiling so there is no possibility of subsequent confusion. You then have to run the switch cables either from the rose itself (for loop-in wiring) or from the junction box where the feed to the light is taken (junction-box wiring) to the switch position. If there is no existing conduit just pierce a hole in the ceiling above the switch position and push the cable through. You can later chase it into the plaster.

Once you have completed the wiring for the lights on the floor below, you can start wiring up a light in the loft itself, extending the feed cable to a loop-in batten-holder that is screwed to one of the rafters. Run a switch cable to a position on the landing below; the switch should be labelled 'loft'.

FIXING THE CABLE

It's generally frowned upon to drill holes in the joists in the loft as you risk weakening them, so clip the cables parallel to the joists as far as the binder – the large timber cross member linking the joists. You can then clip the cable to the binder to go across the joists.

INSTALLING THE SWITCHES

When using an existing conduit for your switch drop you must make sure that it is fitted with a protective PVC bush at each end. If you want to fix surface-mounted switches, then this can be done neatly over the end of the conduit, but flush boxes have to be fixed below the conduit. If you don't have an existing conduit you'll have to cut a chase (channel) into the wall.

FISHING CABLE ABOVE CEILINGS

1. Use a piece of stiff wire longer than the distance between holes.

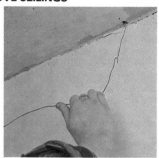

2. Feed wire into one hole, and use more wire to fish it out of the other.

INSTALLING CABLE ACROSS FLOOR JOISTS

1. Drill holes in the joists 50mm (2in) below their tops.

2. Carefully thread the cable through the holes without stretching it.

FITTING SOCKET OUTLETS

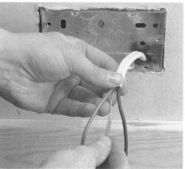

1. Sleeve the exposed earth core in green/yellow PVC.

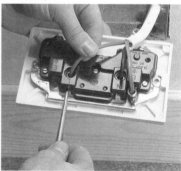

2. Connect the three cores to the relevant terminals of the sockets.

FIXING THE LIGHT FITTINGS

Once you've connected up all the ceiling roses and switches, fit two-core PVC sheathed flex and plastic lampholders to them. Special pendant fittings that have backless ceiling plates have boxes called BESA boxes. These are fixed flush with the ceiling and secured to a timber batten fixed at the relevant height between two joists or actually to one of the joists.

Finally, having installed all the lights and switches, you can make the connections at the fuseboard/consumer unit end, insert the relevant fuse and test the new circuit.

Once you've completed the loft rewiring, you can turn your attention to the rest of your home.

DOWNSTAIRS LIGHTING

It's a good idea to rewire the lighting circuit first, as that way you'll be able to have light when you do the rest of the wiring. First switch off the mainswitch controlling the circuit, and then remove the fuse and disconnect the circuit cable. Remove all fittings and switches and mark the position of the old fittings you're replacing and the new lights you plan to install. Aim to lift a board above each lighting point and also one that runs the length of each room. It's quite likely that many of the circuits will run along the landing so it's wise to raise a floorboard that runs the length of the landing so you can pull out the cables. If your floorboards run across the landing, then raise one at each end and fish the cable through. If switch drops aren't run in conduit then just cut the old cables at ceiling level and leave them chased in the wall. Work back towards the landing and then pull out the circuit feed cable running down to the fuseboard. If you find a cable that runs under numerous floorboards, it's a good idea to attach a length of stout wire to it before pulling it out: then you'll have a draw wire in place for the new cable and so avoid having to lift further floorboards.

You can then proceed as described for rewiring the loft.

INSTALLING A COOKER UNIT

1. Connect the circuit cable to the mains side.

2. Next make the connections on the cooker side of the unit.

3. Fix centre part of the face plate; redecorate before fixing the rest.

WIRING THE CIRCUIT

Before running in the circuit cable, you must drill holes in the joists where the cable crosses them. The holes should be 19mm (¾in) in diameter and at least 50mm (2in) below the tops of the joists. Where you run only one cable through the holes they can be slightly smaller in diameter. If you're using the loop-in system for the circuit then run a cable from the lighting point

nearest the mains position down to the consumer unit and mark the end of this sheathing 'lighting circuit, ground floor'. Then, as with the first floor lighting circuit, you link up the lighting points with 1.0mm^2 or 1.5mm^2 two-core and earth PVC-sheathed cable, and run in the switchdrops as well. At this stage, however, you needn't worry about taking cable to any wall lights. Remember to label all cables so that there is no chance of any confusion at a later date.

From each wall light run a cable back up into the ceiling void to a four-terminal junction box fixed centrally above the lights. To obtain power you could break into the circuit with a three-terminal junction box and extend a branch cable to the four-terminal one, or simply break into the mains with the four-terminal box. At this stage you should also run a cable to a porch light, a back door light or to any other light you want to fix outside the house. It's also a good idea to take a length of three-core and earth cable from the landing two-way switch and link it to another in the hall to give yourself two-way control of the landing and hall lights. Once you've made all the connections, you can fix the fittings to the ceiling and walls and temporarily connect the cable to the fuseway in your existing fuseboard so you can check that the circuit is working correctly.

FIRST-FLOOR SOCKET OUTLETS

After switching off at the mains and taking out the fuse carriers, remove all socket outlets and lift a floorboard running to, or alongside, the skirting board or wall where each socket was fixed. Once you've done this, you can pull out all the cables and disconnect them at the fuseboard.

Start off by running two lengths of 2.5mm^2 two-core and earth cable down to the consumer unit position. One cable should run from the first socket outlet and the other from the last, but these two are likely to be in close proximity to each other. Link all sockets with the same sized cable, with the ex-

COOKER CONNECTION UNIT

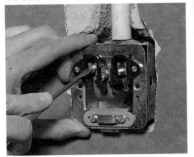

1. Chase in the cable to the cooker and run it to the connection unit.

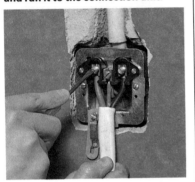

2. Undo clamp and hold the cooker cable in place while you connect it.

ception of remote sockets or fused connection units which can be supplied via spur cables wired into the nearest sockets to them. Mount socket outlets in the wall above the skirting boards and at least 150mm (6in) above the floor. Where possible it's best to install double sockets as this will cut down on the use of adaptors.

Having placed all the cables in position, and fixed all socket outlets and fused connection units, connect the two cables to one of the existing 30A fuseways in your fuseboard. You should then replace the relevant fuse carrier and turn on the mains switch. To test the circuit, fit a 13A fused plug to a portable lamp and plug it into each socket outlet in turn.

OTHER CIRCUITS

Working in the ground floor ceiling void will enable you to replace several other circuits at the same time. A new immersion heater circuit, for example, can be run along the same route as the old, but where the cable crosses joists, you

can thread it through pre-drilled holes – the old one was probably notched into the top.

If your kitchen floor is of solid concrete, you may well find that the cooker circuit is also run under the floorboards on the first floor.

With all the cables laid on the first floor, the remaining floorboards can be relaid permanently and cable chases made good. As there are likely to be many cables on the landing, it's a good idea to refix one floorboard with woodscrews so that it can be readily lifted at any time.

GROUND FLOOR WIRING

The chances are that the only wiring on the ground floor will be a ring circuit for the socket outlets and, possibly, the cooker circuit. The first thing to do is to check whether the floor is suspended or solid. If it is suspended, the cable can be run underneath the joists, so doing away with the necessity of drilling them.

Start pulling out the cables, but leave them in place if there is any chance of using them as drawstrings for the new cable. This will save you a lot of trouble, especially when it comes to getting cable up behind the skirting boards. Where there is more than one socket on any one wall it might be just as well to raise an extra floorboard about 500mm (20in) from the skirting board. This will save you both work and cable.

DEALING WITH SOLID FLOORS

If your home has a solid ground floor the old wiring, most likely in conduit, will have to be left in place; then the cables at socket outlets and at the consumer unit are chopped off flush and, together with the conduit, abandoned. New cables can be run in mini-trunking fixed to the top of the skirting board and around the architraves of doorways.

An alternative method is to run the power circuit in the ceiling void above the ground floor. Using this method, however, would involve extensive chasing and the use of a lot of extra cable.

BONDING TO EARTH
Electricity boards may require all metal pipework, radiators, baths and other metal work that could come in contact with electric cables to be connected to the earthing terminal, and it is your responsibility to cross bond the gas and water mains to the earthing terminal.

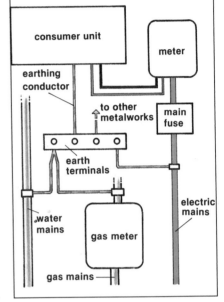

THE NEW CONSUMER UNIT

The new consumer unit must be in reach of the electricity board's service fuse which will serve as the installation's main fuse. If you want to fix the unit away from the board's fuse, fit a new mainswitch and main fuse unit next to the meter and then run a submains cable to the consumer unit. This is likely to be 16mm² two-core and earth cable, while the switchfuse should have a rating of 80 to 100A.

Before the new consumer unit can be connected you'll have to ask your local electricity board to disconnect the leads of the existing mainswitch units so you can remove them. You must give them a minimum of 48 hours' notice for this and it's best to apply for your wiring to be reconnected to the mains at the same time.

Fix the new unit to the wall, run in the new cable, make the connections and fit the MCBs or fuses in the correct order. Finally refit the cover and await the electricity board official.

Chapter 5
BUILDING PROJECTS

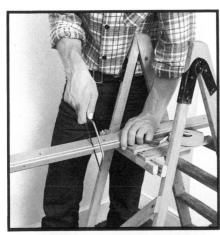

CONSTRUCTING INDOOR ARCHES

An arch can be purely decorative and need not support the wall above it. There are three ways to make an arch indoors: build a frame of timber and clad it with a sheet material such as hardboard; fix up a prefabricated arch former in the opening and plaster the surface; or buy a ready-made fibrous plaster or glass fibre arch.

MAKING AN ARCH FRAME

The arch profiles, or face panels, can be cut from 13mm (½in) thick chipboard or plywood, which you can simply glue and screw to timber mounting blocks fixed to the inside of the opening, recessed by the thickness of the panels so they

DRAWING AN ARCH SHAPE
Most arch shapes can be drawn using only a nail, string and pencil. To mark a semi-circular arch, fix the nail as a pivot with string the radius of the circle, stretched taut, and scribe the curve with a pencil (A).

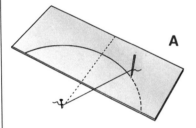

A

For an elliptical arch (B), draw base line XY the span of the arch and vertical line ZO the height; measure line ZX and drive a nail into the base line where this distance from point O bisects the line; repeat to fix the second nail. Tie a loop of string to the nails so that when it's taut the pencil rests at point O. Run the pencil within the loop between X and Y to draw out the ellipse.

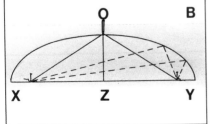

MAKING ARCH FRAMES
The simplest arch consists of a timber frame fixed under the lintel of a doorway (below) with plasterboard arch profiles nailed to it. The curved underside is made from metal mesh nailed to the profiles; the joints are sealed with hessian scrim (right) and the entire arch plastered.

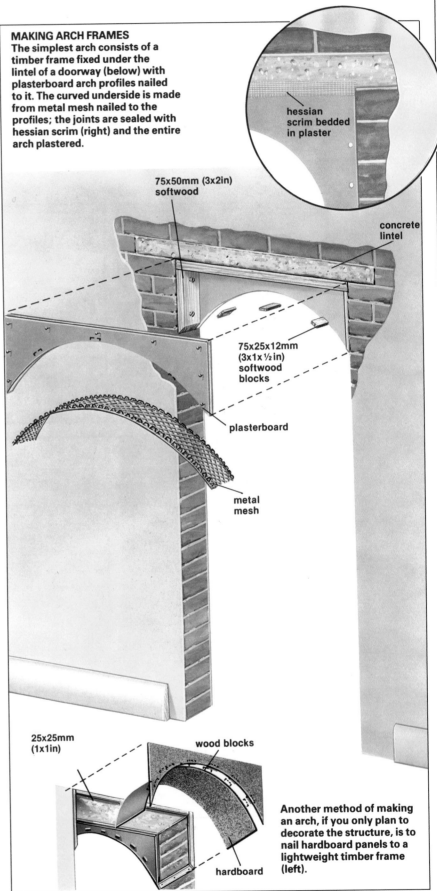

hessian scrim bedded in plaster

75x50mm (3x2in) softwood

concrete lintel

75x25x12mm (3x1x½in) softwood blocks

plasterboard

metal mesh

25x25mm (1x1in)

wood blocks

hardboard

Another method of making an arch, if you only plan to decorate the structure, is to nail hardboard panels to a lightweight timber frame (left).

will be set flush with the walls. Small, lightweight arches up to about 1m (3ft) span can be made from 3mm (⅛in) thick hardboard, but you'll need a sturdy frame of 25×25mm (1×1in) softwood.

When you've marked one panel, clamp and pin it on top of the other panel, then cut out both together.

The underside of a wood-faced arch frame can be made using a strip of hardboard – this is flexible enough to cope with most arch curves, but to make it more pliable, soak it in a bath of warm water for about 30 minutes.

To bend the board, loop string around the strip until you obtain the correct curve and leave to dry like this before fixing. Fix the strip, ridged side out, using PVA adhesive and hardboard pins, to wood blocks fixed inside the face panels.

For a plastered arch with an invisible join, nail plasterboard face panels to a 50×50mm (2×2in) softwood frame, recessed by the thickness of the board plus about 3mm (⅛in) for a skim-coat of plaster. Chip away the plaster at the perimeter of the opening to bare masonry so you can blend in the new plaster at the joint.

You can't form the arch underside from hardboard in this case, so nail a strip of expanded metal mesh under the arch to timber battens nailed between the panels. Fold 'tabs' cut along the edges of the mesh on to the face panels, and finish with a skim-coat of plaster.

INDOOR ARCHES

If you are constructing arches in a load-bearing wall, as in the photograph above, you will need to form the openings in the same way as you would for a conventional doorway: the wall and its loading is supported on metal props and needles so that a pre-stressed concrete lintel can be installed directly above each proposed opening (below).

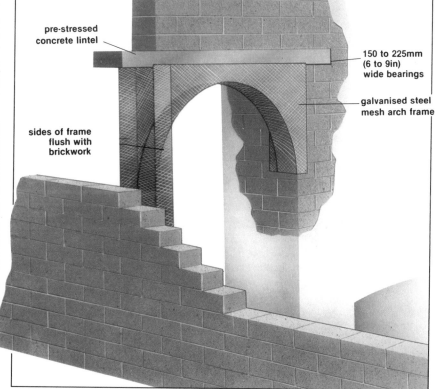

pre-stressed concrete lintel

150 to 225mm (6 to 9in) wide bearings

galvanised steel mesh arch frame

sides of frame flush with brickwork

ARCHED ALCOVES
You can fit arches in the alcoves at each side of a chimney breast with only one facing panel: the diagram shows the structural elements.

A   E

B

D   C

IMPROVISING CRAMPS

1. Use a bench vice to cramp frame against a batten fixed to the bench.

2. Tap wedges between the frame and bolts in holes in the surface.

3. Drive pairs of wedges together to cramp the freme between battens.

WOODWORK SKILLS

When you are doing woodwork it's the joints that count towards making a good job.

If you want a timber joint that's permanent, rigid and invisible, glue it together. It is true that furniture can often incorporate screws and assembly fittings in all their different varieties, but these may obstruct clean lines or free access, and lack strength. In such circumstances you need adhesives, either alone, or in conjunction with secondary fixings (nails and screws).

TYPES OF ADHESIVES

There are several different types of adhesive you can use for glued and cramped assemblies, and all have different characteristics.

G-cramps are the commonest type of cramp and will take assemblies of up to 305mm (12in).

SIMPLE BUTT JOINTS

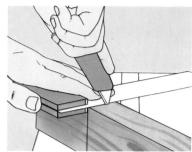

1. Use a try-square and sharp knife for accurate marking out.

2. Dovetail nailing produces a strong joint.

3. An overlap joint is best reinforced with screws.

4. For extra strength, glue and screw on a reinforcing block.

5. Plastic jointing blocks are very neat and strong reinforcements.

6. Drill chipboard to take plugs, then glue and screw the joint together.

HALVING JOINTS
Halving joints are usually used for making frameworks. Here you can see which joint to use where, and how each one is assembled.

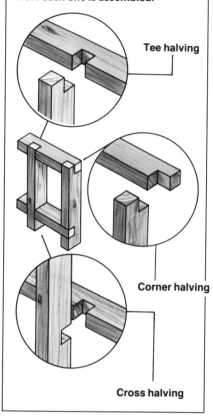

Tee halving

Corner halving

Cross halving

PVA is a general-purpose adhesive universally used for indoor jobs because it does not need to be specially mixed. It comes as a thick white liquid. It takes at least an hour or two to set properly but you can't slide the joint around after more than 15 or 20 minutes.

UF (urea-formaldehyde) is a lot more waterproof than PVA (better for outdoor work or in a kitchen, for example), rather stronger, and better at filling gaps. It comes as a powder which must be mixed with water. Once mixed, it 'goes off' – even before use – in an hour or less, unlike PVA; but again the joint should be left cramped overnight to 'cure' (set) completely.

Epoxy resins usually consist of a separate syrup and paste which harden quickly when mixed. They are extremely strong and will bond widely different materials (eg., steel/glass/wood/ceramics). Some need very brief cramping. Because

of their cost and the rather fiddly method of application, they are best kept for small jobs in which wood is joined to another material.

Scotch glue is animal glue made from hide etc., and was the only one in use until the invention of synthetics. It comes as granules or sheets which have to be soaked, then boiled up in a pot. It cracks and gives way with age, and is not water-resistant. It dries very quickly as it cools, and melts under heat. Today, its main uses are in hand-veneering and antique restoration, not in general woodworking.

Contact or *impact adhesives* are mostly used in laying plastic laminates and similar materials. They are spread on both surfaces and allowed to dry before the surfaces are pressed together to form an immediate bond, which means that no cramps are needed – unless perhaps air is trapped and needs to be pushed out.

Whenever you glue up an assembly, take great care to confine the adhesive only to mating surfaces. You can wipe away excess PVA, UF or scotch glue with a damp cloth, but removing epoxy or contact adhesives usually requires a special solvent; try methylated spirits on epoxies, and petrol on contact adhesives.

CRAMPING

Cramping (in other words, clamping) goes hand-in-hand with glueing. Unless the joint is nailed, pinned or screwed as well, you'll need something to hold the structure together until the adhesive hardens. Nails or pins driven in halfway and later removed provide a simple form of cramp. So do heavy weights; but you often need greater pressure than these can provide, and to be able to exert it in two or three different directions at once (for example, along the length and across the width of a box). Here, G-cramps will be adequate for most small jobs and sash cramps for most large jobs, but in unusual situations, you may have to improvise and use whatever arrangement seems to grip most firmly.

BUTT JOINTS

It's often thought that only elaborate joints give good results in woodwork. It isn't true. There are simple ways to join timber, and one of the simplest is the butt joint. You can use them on any kind of timber or man-made board, pro-

CROSS HALVING JOINTS

1. Cut down the width lines with a tenon saw.

2. Remove the waste by chiselling at a slight upward angle.

3. Do the same on the other side, then flatten the 'pyramid' of waste.

4. Finally clean up by trimming the fibres in the corners.

vided it isn't too thin – not under 6mm (¼in). The only problem you will run into is where you are joining chipboard: a special technique is needed here to get the screws to grip, as is explained later.

Although it is possible simply to glue two pieces of wood together, unless you add some kind of reinforcement the result won't be very strong. So in most cases, the joint should be strengthened with either screws or nails. The question is, which? As a rule of thumb, screws will give a stronger joint than nails. The exception is where you are screwing into the endgrain of natural timber. Here, the screw thread chews up the timber to such an extent that it has almost no fixing value at all. Nails in this case are a much better bet.

MARKING AND CUTTING TOOLS

The tools you will need for butt joints are measuring tape, a sharp handyman's knife, a try-square and a tenon saw

MARKING TIMBER

Butt joints are the simplest of all joints – there's no complicated chiselling or marking out to worry about – but if the joint is to be both strong and neat you do need to be able to saw wood to length, leaving the end perfectly square.

Use a try-square and sharp knife to mark cutting lines on all four faces, pressing the stock of the try-square firmly against the wood, or the last line will not meet the first.

CHOOSING AN ADHESIVE

Even if you are screwing or nailing the joint together, it ought to be glued as well. A PVA woodworking adhesive will do the trick in most jobs, or use a UF glue where the joint will have to stand up to extreme heat or moisture, such as in a kitchen.

TYPES OF BUTT JOINTS

The overlap joint is the simplest of all and is one you can use on relatively thin timber. The example shown is for a T-joint, but the method is the same if you want to make an X-joint.

MARKING DOWEL JOINTS

Make a central line on the edge where the dowel will go (above left), then divide this line into three (above right) and draw two lines at right angles.

Tap panel pins into the wood at the centre points. Snip off their heads, then hold the joint in position and press the pins in to mark the drill positions (inset).

Dovetail nailing is a simple way of strengthening any butt joint. All you do is glue the pieces together, and then drive in the nails dovetail fashion. If you were to drive the nails in square, there would be more risk that the joint would pull apart. Putting them in at an angle really does add strength.

With chipboard use screws to make a butt joint, but to help them grip, you drive them into chip-

DOWEL JOINTS

1. The through dowel joint shown here ready for assembly.

2. When assembled, the through joint shows up the dowels.

3. The dowels in a stopped joint won't be seen on the outside.

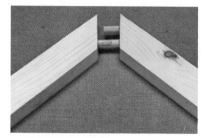

3. A mitred dowel joint – these can be very tricky to make.

BUYING DOWEL

Buying grooved dowel saves you having to groove it yourself. Pre-packed dowels are bought in packs containing short lengths of diameters such as 4, 8 and 10mm. They are fluted (finely grooved) and the ends are chamfered. Dowel pellets finish woodwork where screws have been countersunk. They should fit the hole exactly but be fractionally deeper so they can be planed back when the adhesive has set. Either buy them pre-packed, or cut your own from offcuts using a special plug attachment for an electric drill.

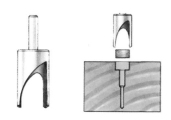

HOUSING JOINTS

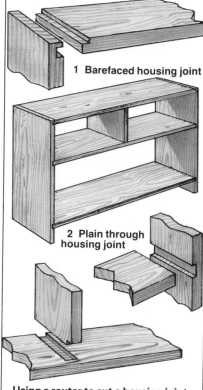

1 Barefaced housing joint

2 Plain through housing joint

Using a router to cut a housing joint.

board plugs. Chipboard plugs are a bit like ordinary wall plugs. In fact, you can use ordinary plugs, but you have to be careful to position the plug so that any expanding jaws open across the board's width and not across its thickness, where they could cause it to break up.

The joints described so far are fairly robust, but if a lot of strength is needed it's worth reinforcing the joint with some sort of block. The simplest is a square piece of timber; neater is a plastic joint block.

HALVING JOINTS

There are frequent situations in woodwork when you need a joint that's fast and simple, but also neat and strong. This is where halving joints come into their own. Despite their simplicity, they're very effective joints because the two pieces of wood are cut so they interlock together, either face to face or edge to edge, making the joint as strong as – or even stronger than – the timber itself. Halving joints are used almost exclusively for building frameworks, joining the rails (side pieces) either at a corner or in a cross absolutely flush. You end up with a frame that's neat enough to be on show and sturdy enough to need no reinforcement.

TOOLS FOR HALVING JOINTS

For measuring and marking: use a handyman's knife rather than a pencil for marking; use a marking gauge on each face of the joint – it'll be more accurate than using a tape measure; a try-square ensures accurate squaring off.

For cutting: use a tenon saw and a broad-blade chisel (25mm/1in) for cutting out cross halvings.

DOWEL JOINTS

There are two basic ways in which you can use dowels in woodworking joints. You can drive a dowel through such joints as a halving instead of using a nail or screw, or you can use them to make joints in their own right by drilling holes in one piece of wood, glueing in dowels, and then slotting these into corresponding holes in the second piece.

The dowel joint proper is used mostly in furniture-making where it provides a neat joint of great strength without intricate cutting and without the need for unsightly reinforcement. Dowels can also be used to repair furniture.

TOOLS FOR DOWEL JOINTS

You will need the following: a try-square and marking gauge – essential for accurate marking up; an electric drill, held in a drill stand for perfectly plumb holes; a mallet for tapping in the dowels; a block or ordinary plane for finishing a through joint; a cramp to hold the joint until the adhesive has set; and a dowelling jig to ensure holes

TIPS FOR BETTER HOUSINGS

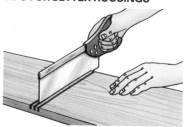

1. Make three cuts for wide housing.

2. Chisel narrow wood vertically.

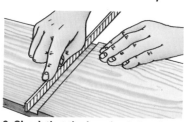

3. Check that the housing is level.

4. Marking pairs of uprights.

for dowels are accurately drilled and are square.

HOUSING JOINTS

Housing joints are very useful in constructing drawers, door frames and partition walls, among other things; but they're indispensible for fixing shelves neatly into uprights. The joint is so named because the end of the shelf fits into a square-bottomed channel or 'housing' across the upright. A

PLANNING SHELVES
When designing storage, plan ahead and think about *how* it will be used.

Keep everyday items within reach – between 750 and 1500mm (30-60in) off the ground. The deepest shelves should be the lowest; and leave an inch or two over the actual height of objects when spacing the shelves. Space brackets according to shelf thickness. Heavy loads (left) need closer brackets than light loads.

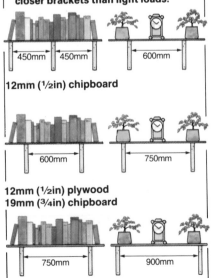

12mm (½in) chipboard
450mm | 450mm | 600mm

12mm (½in) plywood
19mm (¾in) chipboard
600mm | 750mm

750mm | 900mm

basic housing joint is as simple as that, and very easy to cut and assemble. What's more, it's ideal for supporting the weight of a shelf and its contents – it resists twisting, and it looks much more professional than the metal brackets or other fittings which can do the same job.

TOOLS FOR HOUSING JOINTS

You will need the following: a tenon saw for cutting the sides of housings, rebates and shoulders; a bevel-edged chisel the same width as the housing, plus a wooden mallet; a hand router – useful for smoothing the bottom of the housing; and a marking gauge, knife, pencil and try-square for accurate setting-out.

Power tool options include a power router – ideal for cutting all types of housing quickly and easily – and a circular saw, which will cut an ordinary housing very well, although you'll need to make several passes with it across the timber to cut the housing.

SHELVING UNITS

There are lots of ways of putting up shelves. Some systems are fixed, others adjustable – the choice is up to you. This is how both types work, and how to get the best from each.

WHICH SHELF MATERIAL?

Chipboard is usually the most economical material, and if properly supported is strong enough for most shelving. It can also be fairly attractive – you can choose a type with a decorative wood veneer or plastic finish. These come in a variety of widths – most of them designed with shelving in mind.

Natural timber, though more costly and sometimes prone to warping, is an obvious alternative. You may have difficulty obtaining some timber in board widths over 225mm (9in) but narrower widths are readily available. Proprietary solid timber for making shelves with moulded edges is also avail-

able. For wider shelves, another way is to make up the shelf width from narrower pieces. An easy method is to leave gaps between the lengths and brace them with others which run from front to back on the underside, forming a slatted shelf.

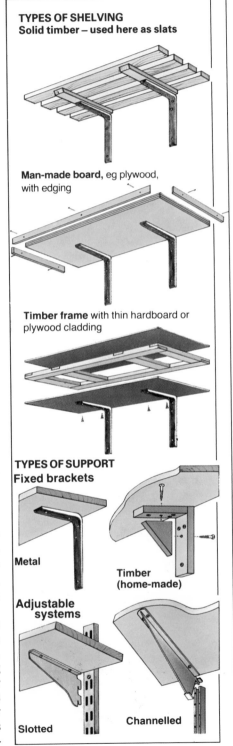

TYPES OF SHELVING
Solid timber – used here as slats

Man-made board, eg plywood, with edging

Timber frame with thin hardboard or plywood cladding

TYPES OF SUPPORT
Fixed brackets

Metal

Timber (home-made)

Adjustable systems

Slotted

Channelled

Blockboard and plywood are also worth considering. They are both a lot stronger than chipboard and have a more attractive surface which can be painted or varnished without trouble. However, in the thicknesses you need for shelves – at least 12mm (½in) – plywood is relatively expensive; blockboard is cheaper, and chipboard cheaper still. All these man-made boards need to have their edges disguised to give a clean finish. An easy yet effective way to do this is just to glue and pin on strips of timber moulding or 'beading'. Also, remember that the cheapest way to buy any of these boards is in large sheets – approximately 2.4×1.2m (8×4ft), so it's most economical to plan your shelves in lengths and widths that can be cut from a standard size sheet. Shelves needn't be solid, though. If you want them extra thick, for appearance or strength, you can make them up from a timber frame covered with a thin sheet material. Hardboard is cheap, but thin plywood gives a more attractive edge; alternatively use a timber edging strip.

FIXING SHELVES

The simplest way to fix shelves is directly to the wall, using brackets. L-shaped metal brackets of various sizes and designs are available everywhere; some are plain and functional, others have attractive

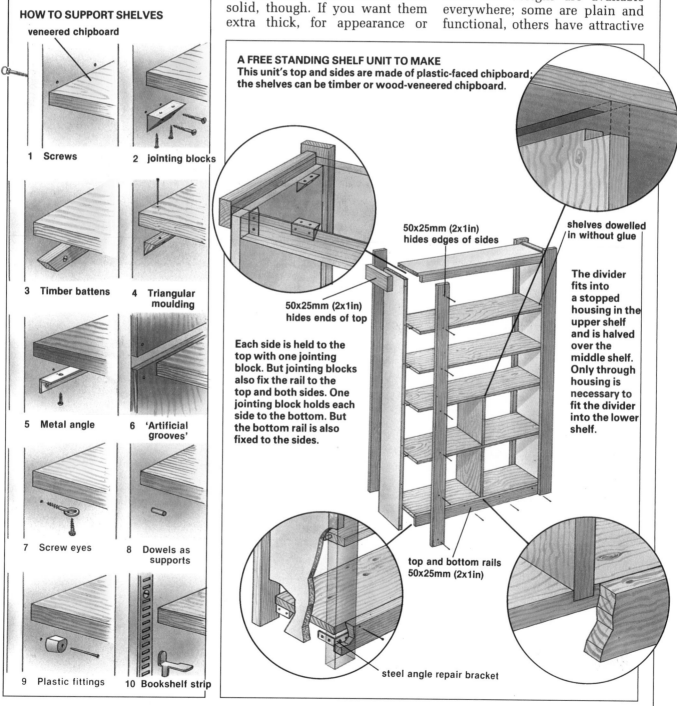

HOW TO SUPPORT SHELVES

veneered chipboard

1   Screws

2   jointing blocks

3   Timber battens

4   Triangular moulding

5   Metal angle

6   'Artificial grooves'

7   Screw eyes

8   Dowels as supports

9   Plastic fittings

10   Bookshelf strip

A FREE STANDING SHELF UNIT TO MAKE
This unit's top and sides are made of plastic-faced chipboard; the shelves can be timber or wood-veneered chipboard.

50x25mm (2x1in) hides ends of top

Each side is held to the top with one jointing block. But jointing blocks also fix the rail to the top and both sides. One jointing block holds each side to the bottom. But the bottom rail is also fixed to the sides.

50x25mm (2x1in) hides edges of sides

shelves dowelled in without glue

The divider fits into a stopped housing in the upper shelf and is halved over the middle shelf. Only through housing is necessary to fit the divider into the lower shelf.

top and bottom rails 50x25mm (2x1in)

steel angle repair bracket

lacquered or enamelled finishes. It's just a question of choosing ones about 25mm (1in) less than the shelf depth, spacing them the right distance apart and screwing them to both shelf and wall.

If you're filling up your shelves with books, the support brackets won't be seen. But if you're using the shelves for ornaments, the brackets will be visible, so choose a style that blends. Alternatively, you can make up your own brackets from two pieces of timber butt-jointed into an L-shape and braced with a diagonal strut or triangular block.

To fix the brackets, first draw a line on the wall where the shelf is to go, using a spirit level. Next, fix the brackets to the shelf and put the whole assembly up against the line. Mark on to the wall through the pre-drilled screw holes in the brackets; then take the shelf away and drill holes in the wall, filling each with a plastic plug. Lastly, drive in one screw through each bracket; then insert the rest and tighten them all up.

Because the accuracy of this method relies largely on your ability to hold the shelf level against your line, you may find it easier to work the other way round. By fixing the brackets to the wall along the guide line, you can then drop the shelf into place and screw up into it through the brackets. This works, but you must position the brackets with great care and avoid squeezing them out of position as you screw them into the wall. That isn't always easy. For one thing, some brackets don't have arms which meet at a neat right angle. They curve slightly, which makes it hard to align the top of the shelf-

FIXING BRACKET SHELVING

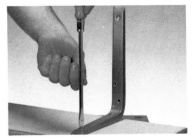

1. Screw the short arm to the shelf.

2. Mark with a pencil line the position of the top of the shelf.

3. Mark wall through screw holes.

4. Screw the shelf in position.

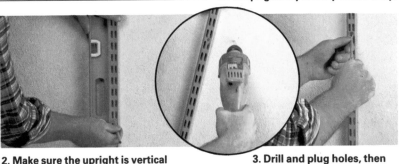

2. Make sure the upright is vertical and mark the other screw positions.

4. Screw the bracket to the shelf.

6. Notch the shelf round the upright.

FIXING ADJUSTABLE SHELVING

1. Fix uprights by the top screw only.

3. Drill and plug holes, then insert screws and tighten them.

5. Fitting brackets with lugs.

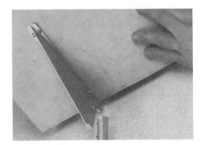

7. Using the channel system.

bearing arm with the line on the wall.

MAKING A FIRM FIXING

Remember that the strength of all brackets depends partly on the length of their arms (particularly the one fixed to the wall) and partly on the strength of your fixing into the wall. The longer the wall arm in proportion to the shelf arm, the better; but it's also important

WARDROBE ARRANGEMENTS
The standard arrangements you can choose with most kits are illustrated below.

1. Wall-to-wall, needing only a door frame or full-width sliding track.

2. Wall-to-panel, with one side panel fixed to the rear wall.

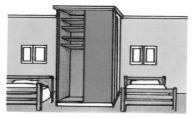

3. Panel-to-panel, with two side panels reaching from floor to ceiling.

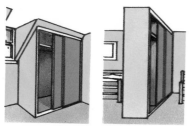

4. Units adapted for sloping ceilings (left) or to act as room dividers.

to use adequate screws – 38mm (1½in) No. 8s or 10s should do – and to plug the wall properly.

In a hollow partition wall you really must make sure that you secure the brackets to the wooden framework and not just to the cladding. Even if you use plasterboard plugs or similar devices, a lot of weight on the shelf will cause the brackets to come away from the cladding and possibly damage the wall.

Of course, there is a limit to how much weight the brackets themselves will take. Under very wide shelves they may start to bend. With shelves which have heavy items regularly taken off and then dumped back on, and shelves used as desk tops, worktops and the like, the movement can eventually work the fixings loose. In such cases it's best to opt for what's called a cantilevered shelf bracket. Part of this is set into the masonry to give a very strong fixing indeed. Details of its installation procedure obviously vary from brand to brand, but you should get instructions when you buy.

ALCOVE SHELVING

For putting up shelves in an alcove use battens screwed to the wall. Fix a 50×25mm (2×1in) piece of softwood along the back of the alcove, using screws driven into plastic plugs at roughly 450mm (18in) centres. Then screw similar ones to the side walls, making sure that they line up with the first. In both cases, getting the battens absolutely level is vital. In fact, it's best to start by drawing guidelines, using a spirit level as a straight-edge.

A front 'rail' is advisable where the shelf spans a wide alcove and is likely to have to carry a lot of weight. But there's a limit to what you can do. With a 50×25mm (2× 1in) front rail and battens, all on edge, 1.5m (5ft) is the safe maximum width.

A front rail has another advantage – as well as giving man-made boards a respectably thick and natural look, it also hides the ends of the side battens. So does stop-

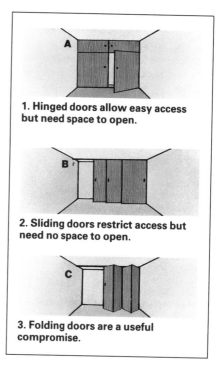

1. Hinged doors allow easy access but need space to open.

2. Sliding doors restrict access but need no space to open.

3. Folding doors are a useful compromise.

ping them short of the shelf's front edge and cutting the ends at an angle.

The shelf can be screwed or even just nailed to the battens to complete the job.

MOVABLE SHELVES

An adjustable shelving system is needed if you may want to move the shelves up and down without unscrewing them. Such systems consist of uprights, screwed to the wall, and brackets which slot into them at almost any point down the length.

There are two main types. In one, brackets locate in vertical slots in the uprights. The other has a continuous channel down each upright. You can slide brackets along it and lock them at any point along the way, where they stay put largely because of the weight of the shelf. With both types, brackets come in standard sizes suitable for shelf widths, and there's a choice of upright lengths to fulfil most needs.

Many proprietary shelving systems of this sort include a number of accessories to make them more versatile. These include book ends, shelf clips, and even light fittings.

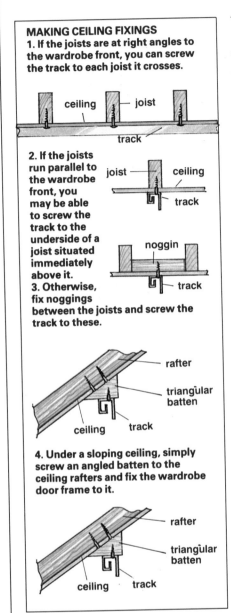

MAKING CEILING FIXINGS
1. If the joists are at right angles to the wardrobe front, you can screw the track to each joist it crosses.

ceiling — joist

track

2. If the joists run parallel to the wardrobe front, you may be able to screw the track to the underside of a joist situated immediately above it.

joist — ceiling

track

noggin

track

3. Otherwise, fix noggings between the joists and screw the track to these.

rafter

triangular batten

ceiling — track

4. Under a sloping ceiling, simply screw an angled batten to the ceiling rafters and fix the wardrobe door frame to it.

rafter

triangular batten

ceiling — track

FREESTANDING SHELF UNITS

Apart from their most obvious advantages over built-in units, freestanding units don't have to be tailored to fit any irregularities of walls and alcoves. But, because they aren't fixed in position, you have to devote a bit more time and thought to making them rigid.

This is often a matter of making a straightforward box with a back, although frame construction using wide side rails, as shown in the drawing on page 135, is possible. Either way, it is important to remember that the shelves themselves won't add much stability.

FITTED WARDROBES

If you need somewhere to store clothes there are a variety of ways to approach the problem. You can buy a free-standing wardrobe or you could build your own from scratch.

If you're an accomplished carpenter, and you are very particular about the materials you use, or you have a very unusual site in mind, then building your own wardrobe from scratch may be worth considering.

There is also a half-way option that offers some of the advantages of a made-to-measure wardrobe combined with the relative ease of installation of a ready-made product, and that is to go for one of the many self-assembly kits available.

PROPRIETARY WARDROBES

The walls of a room are seldom perfectly flat, floors and ceilings are rarely level and corners absolutely true, so it takes painstaking measuring, marking, cutting and packing out if you are to end up with a showroom finish.

The formula for success starts right at the initial planning stage. You have to measure up the space available, working accurately in the same measurements that the wardrobes are sold in – metric or imperial. (Nowadays it's nearly always metric.) Don't try to work with both systems at once; converting from one to the other is where mistakes start to creep in.

Proprietary wardrobe systems come in all sorts of arrangements to suit a classic 'chimney breast' situation, to turn a corner, to span a bed, and so on. Then you'll have the choice of sliding or hinged doors and countless internal storage arrangements.

In many instances, a given wardrobe range might be available in just a couple of sizes which might (or, far more likely, might not) fit exactly into the space you have in mind. A typical example would be in the floor-to-ceiling measurements; most will fall short and it

will then be up to you either to accept that there will be a gap below the ceiling or, if the space is just a small one, to fill it by adding a wide fascia piece. Some manufacturers supply a variety of infill pieces to bridge the gap. As far as depth and width are concerned,

FITTING SLIDING DOORS

The commonest type of sliding door gear features wheel units which you fix to the tops of the doors, plus a track which you fix to the ceiling.

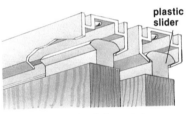

plastic slider

Also available, for lighter duty, are plastic sliders instead of wheels.

The usual way of keeping the doors on course is plastic guides screwed to the floor or frame.

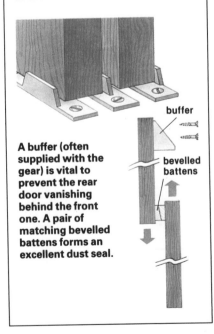

buffer

bevelled battens

A buffer (often supplied with the gear) is vital to prevent the rear door vanishing behind the front one. A pair of matching bevelled battens forms an excellent dust seal.

don't try to reduce the carcase of a wardrobe by sawing some timber off the members – once you get to this stage you would be far better off building your own wardrobe from scratch. This usually defeats the object of paying out for a shop-bought unit.

Another point to remember is that some ceilings sag downwards in places, especially old lath and plaster types. This can mean that after you have fitted full height floor-to-ceiling doors (allowing for a small amount of fascia above) a door will jam against a bulge in the ceiling when opened.

WARDROBE CONSTRUCTION

There are three standard wardrobe arrangements. Wall-to-wall units extend right across a room or a recess; sometimes the side walls serve as the side panels, in other cases the end panels are provided. A wall-to-end panel arrangement uses one wall as the side panel but the other end finishes in the middle of a wall run. And finally there is an end-panel-to-end-panel arrangement where the unit looks like a self-contained, freestanding unit independent of side walls. This system generally poses fewer installation problems.

FITTING THE WARDROBE

Right at the start of the installation it's worth marking in pencil, either on the walls or skirting boards, the

position of the panels or framework. Do this accurately so that throughout the assembly you will have a ready check as to whether or not the job is going according to plan. The exact assembly of different ranges varies in detail so it's difficult to lay down hard-and-fast rules about the order of assembly. The instructions are normally adequate, but you shouldn't try to take any short-cuts.

There are, however, some general points which apply to most situations and to many different wardrobes. In the first place it's a good idea to pin to the wall an assembly plan of the wardrobe so that it can be referred to quickly.

FITTING THE TRACK

1. You need a helper for measuring.

2. Cut the track with a hacksaw.

3. Screw the track into place.

4. Find a vertical from the top track.

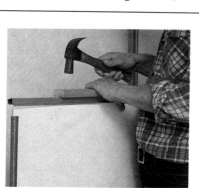
2. Tap the stiffening rails into place.

4. Offer up the doors.

HANGING DOORS

1. Cut all the panels together.

3. Hook the fascia into place.

5. Press down the nylon guide pins.

Working from memory is unnecessarily risky.

FIXING TO THE CEILING

In some cases it will be necessary to make fixings direct to a ceiling. This can apply to the sliding door track in many cases. If you are lucky then the ceiling joists above may run at right angles to the track. If this is the case you can make the fixings directly into the joists. To find the joists, go into the room above and drill down on either side of each joist. The holes made in the plaster will identify, from below, the positions of the joists. If access from above is a problem then make some trial drillings into the ceiling from the room below. As long as you make these tests inside the area to be occupied by the wardrobe they won't be visible after the installation is complete.

If the track runs parallel with the joists, you might be lucky enough to find that the required position coincides exactly with the joist. If so, the screws can go straight into the wood. It's more likely, however, that the required position will fall in between two joists. Here, provided access is available from above the ceiling, a number of 50×50mm (2×2in) noggings can be nailed or screwed between the joists to provide solid fixing points for the sliding track screws. If you can't reach the ceiling from above then the wood supports will have to be added working from below.

Manufacturers sometimes recommend making a fixing direct to a sound plasterboard ceiling (if access is not possible from above) using special cavity toggles, or similar devices. However, plasterboard is fairly thin and sliding doors are quite heavy so it's best to avoid this if possible and instead add some wood noggings.

Attic rooms and loft conversions often have sloping ceilings that cause problems when fixing door tracks. You can create a horizontal beam, either by fixing a timber fillet across the rafters, or by fixing timber angle pieces to individual rafters.

FINISHING OFF

1. Scribing the end panel.

2. Use brackets to fix the end panel.

3. Assemble side panels and shelves.

4. Lift the assembled unit into place.

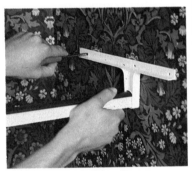
5. Finally, fix hanging rails.

FIXING TO WALLS

When fixing vertical timbers to walls, use thin slivers of wood or hardboard as packing pieces to compensate for irregularities in the wall and make sure that the timbers are vertical. Fixings can be made with normal screws and wall plugs (suitable sizes will probably be recommended in the manufacturer's instructions). The alternative is to use cavity fixings if you're fixing into a partition wall.

It is usual to fix end panels or intermediate panels to the walls at the rear edge by using screw fixings through joint blocks or metal angle brackets.

FITTING THE DOORS

Whether you are using sliding or hinged doors there will be little problem in hanging them to work efficiently provided the wardrobe aperture is square. Sliding door gear usually has a simple adjustment device to align the doors after hanging them on the track. Hinges of opening doors usually also have an inbuilt adjustment facility and the hinge screw holes are usually pre-drilled in the door end panels so you'll know where to fit them.

INTERIOR FITTINGS

Interior shelf arrangements are simple to assemble, following the same principles as for the main carcase. Some of these are free-standing, while others give greater rigidity after being screwed to the wardrobe sides. You may find that extra support bearers will have to be fixed below veneered chipboard shelves if they are to be used for books or other heavy objects. Remember that veneered chipboard tends to bow under heavy weights, so don't overload your shelves.

Hanging rails, hooks, tie racks and other fittings are quite simply screw-fixed into pre-drilled holes. Drawers, where used, are normally of the slot-together type normally supplied with fitted kitchen units.

REMOVING INTERIOR WALLS

Making a small hole in a wall – to fit an air brick, or an extractor fan, for example – is a fairly straight-forward job. All you need to do is to chop out the necessary bricks or blocks with a club hammer and cold chisel. But if you're cutting an opening to install a door, window or serving hatch, or knocking two rooms into one, you'll need to provide support for the wall, and perhaps the floors, above.

The usual way of spanning an opening is to bridge it with a horizontal beam which will take the load of the wall above, plus any other part of the building that bears upon this section.

WHAT TYPE OF WALL?

Before you can decide which beam to use you have to determine what type of wall you're dealing with. There are two basic types: load-bearing and non-load-bearing.

The first is an integral part of the structure of the house, and helps to keep it up; the second offers no support to the building whatsoever and is merely a partition.

Non-load-bearing walls usually run parallel with the joists in the floor or ceiling above; load-bearing walls run at right angles to the joists.

You can gain a preliminary idea of what type of wall you have from the direction of the floorboards – they always run at right angles to the joists supporting them.

First-floor joists, rafters and other roof beams will be either recessed into load-bearing walls, or attached to them with special 'hangers', or seated on a narrow brick ledge.

TYPES OF BEAM

Your choice of beam is dictated mainly by the structure of the wall and whether it has to bear a load. When you're spanning a very wide opening – before removing a load-bearing wall, for example – you'll need a large heavyweight beam known as a 'rolled steel joist' (RSJ) or a 'British Standard beam' (BSB). This type of beam has either an H- or an L-section and must rest on stout piers because of the heavy load it carries.

Smaller beams for door and win-dow openings are called 'lintels'. They're made from stone, wood, steel or concrete. Stone and timber have now been superseded by other materials, mainly for econ-omic reasons, but you may well come across them in older houses. Timber is still commonly used for lintels in lightweight internal par-tition walls.

Lintels of concrete reinforced

TYPES OF BEAM
Beams are made of stone, wood, concrete or steel. Your choice depends upon the structure of the wall and whether it has to bear a load.

Concrete is cast in various shapes to span large and small openings; it must be fitted the correct way up.

Steel beams combine light weight with strength; there are special shapes for different wall structures.

TYPES OF WALLS
Before choosing your beam you will need to know whether the wall in question is load-bearing or non-load-bearing. In general, if the joists in the floor above run parallel to the wall (A) it is non-load-bearing, while if they are at right angles to the wall then it is load-bearing (B). The floorboards always run at right angles to the joists supporting them, and this may enable you to work out what type of wall you have simply by inspecting the floor.

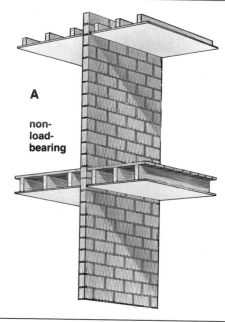

A non-load-bearing

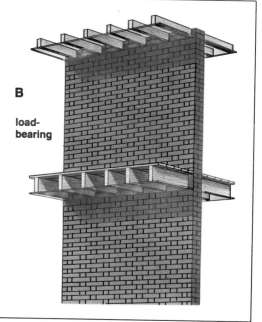

B load-bearing

SUPPORTING THE WALLS

If you're making a door or window-sized opening in a wall you must (A) temporarily support the walling above the proposed opening, and any load bearing upon it, with adjustable metal props and timber 'needles'; and (B) install a lintel resting on suitable bearings (C) above the opening to support the walling permanently.

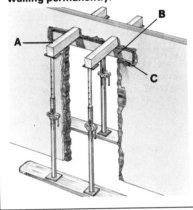

PIERS AND SUPPORTS

The ends of a load-bearing beam must themselves be adequately supported – on stubs of brickwork at each side, by allowing the beam to protrude into the cavity of walls, or by adding supporting piers – often needed at corners (see detail).

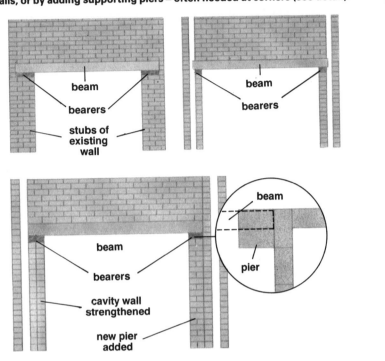

with steel rods can be conveniently precast into a range of shapes and sizes, usually in multiples of 75mm (3in) deep, so that they'll line up with courses of bricks or blocks. They're also suitable for spanning wide openings up to about 3m (10ft). The larger ones are heavy and cumbersome to fit, although you can cast them *in situ* by fixing a timber framework to the wall above the opening. Concrete lintels are usually rough-finished for rendering or plastering but 'fair-faced' types, which have a smooth finish that can be left bare, are also made. Some concrete lintels have pre-stressed (stretched) reinforcing rods; these are stronger than ordinary reinforced ones, so a thinner pre-stressed beam can perform the same job as a much thicker but unstressed lintel.

Concrete lintels for internal partition walls are usually rectangular in section, although special shapes for other functions are also cast. The 'boot' lintel, so-called because of its unusual cross-section, is for use in cavity walls where it also acts as a damp-proof course.

Galvanized steel lintels are the most extensively used type for external solid or cavity walls and internal partitions. Their main

TEMPORARY PROPS

During the work, use adjustable steel props to support joists bearing on the beam. Use timber needles too if there is masonry above it.

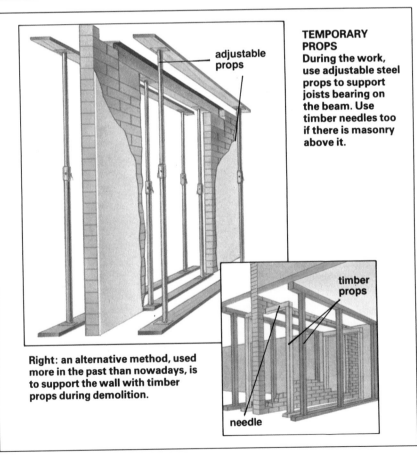

Right: an alternative method, used more in the past than nowadays, is to support the wall with timber props during demolition.

MAKING BEARINGS

To enable a lintel to support a wall and distribute its loading both ends must rest on bearings. A bearing should be a slot 150 to 225mm (6 to 9in) wider than the opening plus 25mm (1in) at each end and on top to make fitting easier and to allow for slight settlement. Trowel a mortar mix of three parts soft sand to one of Portland cement on to the bearing. Lift the lintel into place. If the lintel sits unevenly, pack out underneath with squares of slate; when level, fill the gap on top and at each end with mortar.

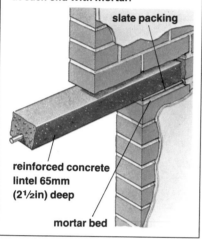

slate packing

reinforced concrete lintel 65mm (2½in) deep

mortar bed

advantage over the other types of lintel is that they're lightweight and are therefore easier to install. Some steel lintels are used in conjunction with a concrete beam.

They're rust-proofed and must be handled carefully so as to avoid damaging the galvanized layer. They come in a range of standard lengths for spanning openings of different widths and wall thicknesses. Like concrete lintels, some steel types also serve as a dpc.

PLANNING THE OPENING

Before you can make an opening in a wall – whether it's load-bearing or not – you must check with your local Building Department that what you plan to do is permissible under Building Regulations.

It's not always feasible to change the position of a window or a door in an external wall: your new location might infringe local bye-laws or, especially in the case of a window, it might simply have a poor outlook. But you can usually make a new opening in an internal wall wherever you want.

SUPPORTING THE WALL

It's possible to cut a door-sized or window-sized hole in a non-load-bearing wall without supporting the wall above while you work. If it's properly bonded and the mortar joints are in good condition, the only area that's at risk from collapse is roughly in the shape of a 45° triangle directly above the opening. In the absence of a lintel the bricks or blocks within this area would tend to fall out, forming a stepped 'arch', the walling that's left would, however, be self-supporting – although weaker than it was – up to a span of about 1.2m (4ft).

So when you've marked out the position of your proposed opening it's quite safe to chop out the triangle of bricks or blocks above and insert your lintel. When that's in position, and you've filled in the triangle, you can remove the walling below to form your opening.

However, if you're going to cut an opening in a load-bearing wall you'll have to provide temporary

MAKING A DOOR OPENING

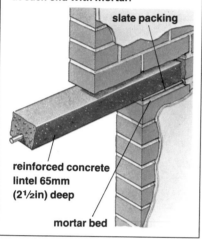
1. Measure the lintel and add on 25mm (1in) so it's easier to fit.

2. Mark the slots for the needles directly above the lintel position.

3. Cut the first hole through the wall and then slot in your needle.

4. With a helper, tighten up the metal props on both sides at once.

5. Chop around the lintel guidelines then start to remove the plaster.

6. Chop out the bricks to form the slot for the lintel.

supports not only for the walling above the opening but also for any load from floors or walls above, which bears upon the wall. To support the walling when making a door or window opening you'll need four adjustable metal props and two stout timber beams called 'needles'. For wider openings the needles should be no more than 900mm (3ft) apart.

The props work rather like a car jack, and to fit them you'll have to cut holes through the wall directly above the lintel's position at each end, and slot in the needles. You can then use the props to support each end of the needles.

If floor joists from the rooms above are resting on your wall, you'd be wise to provide extra support for the ceilings at each side of the wall. Again you can use adjustable metal props with stout boards at top and bottom.

With the wall supported in this way you can safely chop out a slot in the brickwork or blockwork directly below the needles and insert your lintel.

MARKING OUT THE OPENING

When you have selected the best location for your opening you'll have to mark out its shape on the wall. Take the overall measurements of your frame and add on about 25mm (1in) to give fitting tolerance; then transfer these dimensions to the wall. You might have to move your proposed opening along the wall fractionally so that both its edges line up with a vertical mortar joint; this keeps the number of bricks or blocks you have to cut to a minimum.

If the wall is plastered you could chip away a section about 500mm (1ft 8in) square from the centre of your proposed opening to reveal the bricks or blocks beneath. With this small area uncovered you'll be able to measure from a mortar joint to your line marking the perimeter of the opening. If the lines at each side don't correspond with a mortar joint you'll have to move them over until they do.

When you're satisfied with the position of your opening you can

7. Trowel mortar on to the bearing then lift the lintel into position.

8. The lintel must sit firmly and perfectly level on its bearings.

9. Replace the bricks on top of the lintel, copying the original bond.

10. Point the mortar joints flush with the face of the brickwork.

draw its shape on both sides of the wall more accurately using a pencil held against a spirit level.

You will also have to mark the position of the lintel on the wall directly above the line that marks the top of the opening. Make it wider than the opening by about 150 to 225mm (6 to 9in) to give a sufficiently sturdy bearing, plus an extra 25mm (1in) at each end and on top to make fitting the lintel easier.

CUTTING THE LINTEL SLOT

Before you can chop out any bricks or blocks you'll have to rig up your temporary supports for the wall.

If you're using a heavy or long lintel, you'd be wise to place it across two trestles in front of your proposed opening before you rig up the props and needles, to save having to haul it in later.

Set up the adjustable props and needles first. If you're making a doorway or narrow window you'll need 100×75mm (4×3in) thick needles about 1800mm (6ft) long made of sawn timber. For larger openings, the needles should be 150×50mm (6×2in) and can be up

FINISHING TOUCHES
When forming two rooms into one, it is most important to encase the beam to protect it from the effects of fire, and this is a requirement of the Building Regulations. The most common way of encasing a beam is to drive in wooden wedges and to pin battens to these to carry a plasterboard skin. You can make the cladding wider than the beam by fixing hangers to the joists away from the beam and adding wider-than-usual horizontals.

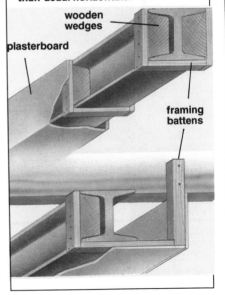
wooden wedges / plasterboard / framing battens

to 2.7m (9ft) long. You'll have to chop out equivalent sized holes in the wall and then feed the needles through. Support each end of the needles with an adjustable prop resting on a timber board on the floor. The props mustn't be more than 600mm (2ft) from either side of the wall.

You may need to provide temporary supports for the ceiling. Do this, if it's necessary, by erecting adjustable props between stout planks measuring approximately 100×50mm (4×2in) top and bottom and 1m (3ft) apart.

If you're working on a brick wall you can simply remove a single course of bricks in order to fit the lintel, but if the wall is made of blocks you'll have to remove a whole block and fill the gap above with a row of bricks. Start to cut out the bricks or blocks directly below the needles by chopping into the mortar joints with a bolster chisel and club hammer to loosen them.

When you've cut the slot for the lintel, trowel a bedding mortar mix of three parts soft sand to one of Portland cement on to the bearings at each side and lift the lintel into place. If the walling and its load is to bear evenly on the lintel you'll have to make sure that it's bedded perfectly level. You can hold a spirit level below it and pack out where it rests on the bearings with squares of slate until it's level. Fill the 25mm (1in) fitting tolerance gap above and at each end of the lintel with mortar.

Wait for about 24 hours for the mortar to set before you move any of the bricks and blocks below the lintel.

If you're making a doorway you will have to prise away the skirting board first, using an old chisel and a mallet if necessary. Alternatively, you might be able to chisel away just the section of skirting within your proposed doorway, although you'll probably find it easier to cut it with a saw when it has been removed, and then to re-fix the cut sections to the wall.

Next, using a bolster chisel and club hammer chop along the guide lines to give a fairly clean, straight edge through the plaster surface and minimize the amount of making good that will be necessary later. Hack off the plaster within this area to reveal the brickwork or blockwork beneath.

Don't forget to wear old clothes, stout gloves and goggles to protect your eyes from flying fragments.

Start to remove the masonry just below the lintel, cutting into the mortar joints of the first brick or block, then lever it out with your chisel.

Once you've removed the first couple of bricks or blocks the rest shouldn't be too difficult to remove. The best way to work is to chop into the vertical joints first, followed by the horizontals; you should then be able to lever the individual brick or block out.

Cut off the half or three-quarter size bricks that project into the opening on alternate courses as you come to them. Don't leave them until last to cut off, or you could weaken their joints in the sides of the opening by hammering. It's always best to cut on to a solid surface.

Where there's a difference in floor levels between the two rooms you've connected, you'll have to make a step with floorboards or by laying concrete inside simple formwork.

11. Hack off the plaster.

12. Chop out bricks below the lintel.

13. Do the second leaf of brickwork.

14. Lift the frame into place.

15. Cement in brick fillets.

16. Trowel out mortar smoothly.

When you've formed your opening you can tidy up the perimeter by filling any large cracks and voids at the edges with mortar.

If you're making a doorway you will have to fit a frame within the opening, to which you can attach a stop-bead, door and decorative architrave.

You can fix the lining frame to the sides of the opening with galvanized metal frame ties set into 'pockets' cut into the walling, or, alternatively, simply by screwing the frame to the masonry if it's fairly level.

You can fix a window frame with frame ties or by inserting timber wedges between the masonry and the frame and then screwing through both.

REMOVING A CHIMNEY BREAST

Great care must be exercised when considering removing chimney breast walls.

Chimney breasts are key structural features of a house. Building Regulations approval will definitely be required before one can be removed.

In some cases you may need to provide some form of support for the upstairs section of the chimney breast, perhaps by corbelling out the wall, but it's always best to seek professional advice from a structural engineer.

REPLACING A WINDOW

There are numerous reasons why you may decide to remove or replace a window or, indeed, to install a new one. The most common one, however, is likely to be age. Whether your windows are made of wood or metal, they're likely to deteriorate unless you maintain them regularly. It's possible to make minor repairs to the frames, but if the damage is widespread, the only solution to the problem is to fit a new window.

Equally, your reason for replacing a window may be aesthetic rather than practical. Previous renovations might have included the fitting of new windows that you think are incompatible with the original style and age of the property.

Another possibility is that you feel there aren't sufficient openings to give adequate ventilation, or that the existing ones are in the wrong places. You may also want to make adjustments to the position of your windows within an area of wall to fit in with a new decorative scheme.

If you're replacing your existing window with one of the same size you won't have to worry about providing any support for the opening while you remove the old frame and fit your new one. If you're increasing the width of the frame or making an entirely new window opening, you'll have to install a rigid beam or lintel to support the walling you've removed.

PLANNING PERMISSION

Before going ahead with plans to replace your windows you must contact your local Building Inspector with details of what you intend to do. Local planning bye-laws may dictate the type of window you can fit. At all events, you will have to adhere to the Building Regulations, which ensure that you carry out the work safely and that the structure, when complete, is sound. This is particularly important if you are enlarging the window opening.

CHOOSING A REPLACEMENT

It's important to choose a window that's compatible with the style and age of your house; there are many styles of traditional and modern windows, made in a variety of materials, commonly wood or steel, and nowadays aluminium and sometimes even plastic. Some of these materials, especially if they are badly maintained, will only have a limited life.

Steel windows, although tough and long-lasting, are prone to rust

HOW EXISTING WINDOWS ARE FIXED

outside face of wall

frame

225mm (9in) solid wall

1. Wooden window frames may be fixed within the opening with galvanized metal frame ties screwed to the frame and embedded in the mortar joints of the wall.

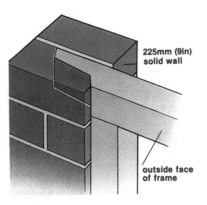

225mm (9in) solid wall

outside face of frame

2. Alternatively they may be fixed with the horns built into the brickwork (above), or by screws driven into wooden plugs or into plugged holes in the masonry.

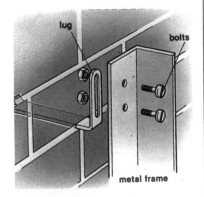

lug

bolts

metal frame

3. Metal frames may be fixed with metal lugs inserted into the mortar joints and bolted to the frame as shown, or with screws to a timber frame fixed to the masonry.

REPLACING A WINDOW

and, like plastic and aluminium, don't always lend themselves to older-style homes, although you can conceal their starkness by painting them. Wood, although it can rot, comes in the widest range of styles and can be painted to match other woodwork in your choice of colour.

Plastic window frames are much

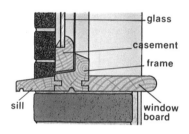

POSITIONING THE NEW FRAME
The position of your new window frame within the opening depends on whether there's a sub-sill.

1. If there isn't a sub-sill, place the frame near the outside face of the wall with its integral sill overhanging the brickwork by about 25mm (1in), leaving reveals for plastering on the inside of the opening.

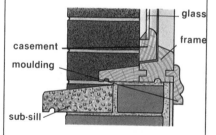

2. If there is a sub-sill, place the frame flush with the inside face of the wall, reducing the amount of plastering necessary.

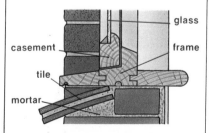

3. Alternatively place it centrally within the opening, leaving reveals on both sides of the window.

more durable than the steel types. They require little maintenance, but have the disadvantage that they don't take paint well, so you are limited to the factory-made colour – usually white. Unless you're making new timber frames to your own specification, you'll be limited in your choice of window size and style by the standard dimensions available. these range from 600 to 2400mm (2 to 8ft) wide and from 450 to 2100mm (18in to 7ft) in height. If you can't find a standard frame size or style that fits your opening – and it's not possible to enlarge or decrease the size of the opening – you can either adapt a standard frame of similar size by dismantling it and cutting it down to the required size, or make a frame specially designed to fit the opening.

CLOSING A CAVITY WALL

If you have cavity walls, you will have to close off the gap between the two leaves and insert a damp proof course to prevent the cavity being breached by moisture.

You must also fit a vertical dpc at the sides of the opening. Chop out the half bricks on alternate courses of the inner leaf and tack a strip of bituminous felt to the outer leaf. Mortar nearly whole bricks into the recesses left by the removal of the half bricks; position them header-on, at right-angles to the inner leaf so they butt up to the felt strip and close the cavities. Fill in the gaps on alternate courses at the reveals with fillers of brick. Allow the felt strip to project into the reveal so it can butt up to the window frame or locate in a narrow groove in the jamb. You'll also have to fit a strip of dpc along the bottom of the opening separating the two leaves.

REMOVING THE FRAME

Window frames are fixed to the masonry within the opening in a variety of ways. It is helpful to know how your frame is fixed before you attempt to remove it.

First unscrew any hinged sashes within the frame, to make the unit lighter to carry. Also consider re-

moving any fixed panes of glass in case you accidentally drop the frame on removal. If you're careful you may even be able to save the glass for use elsewhere. Chop around the putty with a hacking knife, remove the glazing sprigs or nails holding in the glass, then lift out the pane and set it aside.

The screws holding a timber frame in place will probably be covered by layers of paint and their heads may even be countersunk and concealed with filler or dowels: scrape away the paint to locate them. You may be able to chisel out the dowels or filler to reach the screw heads but if they are awkward to withdraw – or if nails have been used – simply insert a hacksaw blade between the frame and wall and saw through them.

Use a couple of bolster chisels – or even a crowbar – to lever the old frame from the opening – you can work from the outside or the inside, but you'd be wise to enlist the help of someone to support the frame while you lever it out and, if it's large, to lift it away.

If you're not intending to save the frame for use elsewhere you can saw through the sill, transom and head near each corner and remove it in pieces.

Clear away any loose mortar, projecting nails and plugs from the opening. If there's a separate concrete or tiled sub-sill you can remove this by breaking the mortar bond with the masonry and levering it free.

Where possible you should try to have the new frame ready to fit as soon as you've removed the old one, but if you're going to alter the size of the opening you won't be able to complete the job in one day. Cover the opening with a large sheet of heavy gauge polythene held in place with timber battens lightly pinned to the wall with masonry nails to keep out draughts and rain.

ALTERING THE OPENING SIZE

You can fit a deeper window frame in your opening without rigging up any temporary structural support for the walling, but if you're intending to increase its width or height you'll have to prop up the masonry with adjustable metal props and stout timber 'needles' while you reposition the lintel or fit a new, wider one to support the wall and its loading.

When you have positioned the props you can mark out where the lintel is to be fitted, cut a slot for it and then fit the lintel in place.

REMOVING THE OLD FRAME

1. If enlarging the opening, support the wall above.

2. With the masonry suitably propped, chop out the lintel.

3. Lever out the old frame with bolster chisels or a crowbar.

Once it's installed, you can safely chop back the reveals to the new window width.

It's much easier to increase the depth of the opening: you can simply cut out the brickwork at the bottom to the new depth.

Your new depth of opening may not conveniently fall at an exact number of bricks, so you'll have to lay a course of split bricks to bring the opening to the correct level.

Making the opening narrower is also possible, but you'll need a supply of bricks that match the existing masonry for filling in, or the finished job will look patchy, unless, of course, the exterior walls are going to be rendered. Continue the brick bond in your narrower opening by carefully knocking out all the half bricks down the sides and saving them. Mortar into both sides of your 'toothed' wall the required number of whole or cut bricks you'll need to decrease the width of the opening then use the half bricks to fill in between. Any cut bricks at the reveals should be mortared in cut end fiirst, so you have a neat, square edge within the opening.

If you're increasing the width of your opening you should also 'tooth out' the reveals to fill in with cut bricks.

HOW FRAMES ARE FIXED

Once you've adapted the size – or even the shape – of your opening to accept the frame you should leave the structure for about 24 hours so that any new mortar sets. You can then remove any props or arch formers and fit the frame into place.

There are various ways in which you can secure your frame within the opening. A steel or aluminium frame, for instance, can be either bolted to metal lugs inserted in the mortar joints, or first screwed to a timber subframe which in turn is screwed or nailed to the surrounding masonry.

A timber frame can be secured with galvanized metal 'frame ties', which are screwed to the jambs (sides) of the frame and embedded in the mortar joints. An alternative

method of fixing a timber frame is to drive screws or nails through the jambs into wood wedges set in the mortar courses of the brickwork. But the simplest method of all is to screw the frame into plugged holes drilled in the masonry, although this type of fixing isn't as tough and long-lasting as the other methods.

Some new frames have projecting 'horns' at each side of the sill and head piece. Although they're intended to protect the corners while in storage or transit, you can build them into the masonry at top and bottom for a really tough fixing. It's quite common for the head horns to be cut off flush with the jambs and for the sill horns alone to be built into the masonry.

POSITIONING THE FRAME

The position of your frame in the opening depends on whether you want to fit a sub-sill or whether the sill built into the frame is going to rest on the masonry at the base of the opening. If you want to make a concrete sub-sill you can cast one in formwork when you've fitted the frame, which you'll have to wedge up to the require height. You can, on the other hand, fit a timber sub-sill. Thirdly, you can simply bed the frame's integral timber sill on a mortar bed.

If you're installing the frame in a cavity wall, you'll have to fit a vertical damp-proof course (dpc) between the two leaves of the closed-off cavity and set them in a groove

INSERTING THE LINTEL

4. Cut a slot for the lintel at each side of the opening.

in the jambs to prevent moisture seeping through; you'll also need to fit a dpc beneath the sill.

You may also want to locate the frame within the opening so that it sits flush with either the inside or the outside face of the wall, or recessed from each face to leave 'reveals' on each side.

FITTING A TIMBER FRAME

Before fitting a timber frame you should treat all its surfaces – especially those that will be inaccessible when the frame's fitted – with a coat of wood primer. A new, off-the-shelf frame will probably come ready-primed – it's usually pink in colour – but you'd be wise to give it another treatment in case the factory-applied coat has been damaged in transit.

If you intend to secure the frame by its horns, you should chop out slots for them in the masonry at the sides of the opening using a club hammer and bolster chisel. Be very careful, when cutting the holes for the horns, that you don't weaken the bearings, which support the lintel and its load. If you did, and the masonry 'dropped', you wouldn't be able to return it to normal without substantial rebuilding.

To screw the frame into wallplugs you must drill the holes in the sides of the opening – three at each side – and insert the plugs. As your frame must be perfectly level and the fixing holes accurately positioned, you'd be wise to drill the jambs of the frame first, wedge it temporarily in the opening level and square and then mark the wall through the holes.

Remove the frame, then drill and plug the holes in the masonry. Return the frame to the opening, set it level and square again, and drive in the fixing screws. Check that the frame is level and square and adjust it if necessary by re-drilling the fixing holes.

If you are going to fix the frame to timber wedges you can chop out the mortar joints at two points on each side of the opening and hammer in triangular-shaped timber wedges, cut with a chisel from a length of 50×25mm (2×1in) softwood. Don't cut them too thin or they'll simply split and the fixing nails won't hold securely.

Lift the frame – unglazed – into the opening. Temporarily wedge it in place with blocks of wood while you ensure that it is level and square. The jambs should be tight against the triangular wedges; if not you'll have to adjust them.

Hold your spirit level against the jambs to make sure that the frame is sitting truly vertical and adjust it if necessary, by tapping gently with the handle of your club hammer. When you're satisfied that it's straight, transfer the spirit level to the top of the sill to check that the frame is truly horizontal. Insert more packing underneath, or remove the existing packing, to set the level. Don't forget to leave a small gap beneath the lintel at this stage. Re-check the vertical once more in case your horizontal ad-

REPLACING A WINDOW

1. Starting at the top, chop out the bricks below the lintel.

2. Make up a timber arch former if you want to copy a soldier arch.

3. Remove the timber arch former if one has been used.

4. Insert wedges at the sides of the opening.

5. Lift the new frame into the opening.

6. Use a spirit level to check that the frame is truly horizontal.

justments have knocked the frame out of square again, then nail or screw it to the wedges. Check again with your spirit level that the frame hasn't moved; if it has you may have to release some or all of the fixings and adjust the position of the frame. Once the frame is securely and accurately fixed in the opening you can remove the temporary timber packing.

If you've set the frame above the base of the opening, intending to install a concrete or timber sub-sill in the gap, you'll have to brick up under the frame on the inside face

7. Use a spirit level to check that the frame is vertical.

8. Nail into each wedge, punching in their heads.

9. While the sub-sill is setting, glaze the window.

of the wall. You may have to insert bricks split along their length if the gap is less than a course deep.

Mortar in bricks to cover the horns of the frame at the top and bottom, and point in the gap between the jambs and the masonry on the inside of the window frame with mortar, covering up the triangular timber wedges. Leave a gap of about 3mm (⅛in) so that you can spread on a layer of finishing plaster flush with the rest of the wall.

MAKING GOOD THE WALLS

Leave the window for 24 hours or so for the mortar to set before making good the wall round the perimeter of the opening with plaster.

SEALING AND GLAZING

Fill the gap between the frame and brickwork with mortar to within about 10mm (⅜in) of the outside edge of the frame then, when the mortar has set, apply a flexible non-setting mastic over it and between the lintel and the frame.

REPLACING A CEILING

If only a small section of a ceiling is damaged you can make a patch of plasterboard. To do this, tidy up the edges of the hole and remove any loose laths, or, if the ceiling is plasterboard, either cut out the damaged section or remove the whole board. Cut a new piece of board to fit just inside the hole.

Fix the panel to the joists, grey-side-down, with plasterboard nails. Wet the edges of the board and spread on undercoat plaster to fill the gap between the board and the ceiling. Leave the plaster 3mm (⅛in) below the surface of the ceiling to allow for a skim-coat of finish plaster. Apply a skim-coat of Thistle Board Finish to the entire surface of the patch to bring it flush with the rest of the ceiling.

When the plaster has stiffened, trowel it smooth using water to lubricate your trowel. You could then paper the ceiling or apply a textured paint.

If the problem's more serious or if you think that the ceiling looks particularly shabby, it's usually better to take it down completely and start again from scratch.

HOW CEILINGS ARE MADE

Older houses usually have ceilings consisting of thin wooden battens called 'laths' nailed to the under-

WEATHERPROOFING WINDOWS
Fill the gap between the window frame and the masonry with mortar to within 10mm (⅜in) of the outside edge of the frame.

When the mortar has set fill the gap with a non-setting mastic applied with a special gun.

FITTING THE WINDOW BOARD

screws

A

window board

To make a shelf or 'window board' on the inner face of the sill, fit a ready-made window board to an off-the-shelf frame notched to take it.

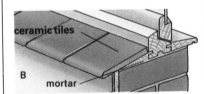

ceramic tiles

B

mortar

Alternatively, set ceramic or quarry tiles on a mortar bed, sloping the shelf downwards for a decorative effect.

side of the joists above, and clad with a thin coat of lime plaster reinforced with hair fibres to give a smooth, flat surface. This is the type that most frequently needs replacement.

Modern ceilings, however, are made in a much simpler way: sheets of plasterboard are nailed to the joists and can be decorated directly or plastered first.

MAKING A NEW CEILING

Before you can put up your new ceiling you'll have to hack off the original lath and plaster surface

REPAIRING A SMALL SECTION

1. Fix up a plasterboard patch.

2. Plaster over the repair.

Make T-shaped supports from softwood to wedge between floor and ceiling boards.

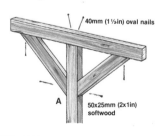

40mm (1½in) oval nails

A   50x25mm (2x1in) softwood

to reveal the joists. This is a very messy job, so clear the room and wear old clothes and a dust mask. You can then nail up sheets of plasterboard and finish off the surface with a skim of plaster or simply decorate with paper, paint or a textured finish.

There are a number of types and thicknesses of plasterboard and it's important to choose the right one for the job. The standard type is British Gypsum Gyproc wallboard. One side has a smooth, ivory-coloured surface suitable for direct decoration, and the other face a grey surface, which you fix outermost when you're going to finish the ceiling with plaster.

If you're replacing the ceiling of an upstairs room, use a special board called Gyproc vapour-check wallboard, which has a water-vapour-resistant, blue-tinted plastic film bonded to the grey side, leaving the ivory surface exposed for direct decoration. The plastic film stops water vapour from inside the building passing into the roof space above. There is also insulating wallboard, which has a veneer of aluminium foil on the

2. Remove all the lath-fixing nails.

4. Fix noggins between the joists.

grey face. It's also useful for upstairs ceilings.

FIXING THE PLASTERBOARD

With the joists exposed and clear of nails, you should mark their centre points on the adjacent walls as a helpful guide when positioning the fixing nails.

The board should be fixed with the long, paper-covered edges lightly butted together at right angles to the run of the joists, with the grey, foil or polystyrene surface against the joists. The ends of the boards should be located centrally over a joist, which means that you'll probably have to cut them to the correct length.

PREPARATION

1. Remove a section of plaster.

3. Mark joist centres on the walls.

5. Fix noggins by skew-nailing.

If the joists are spaced more than 450mm (18in) apart, you'll also have to support the edges of the boards by nailing 100×50mm (4×2in) timber battens called noggins between the joists at these positions. Fix up the noggins by skew nailing before you start to nail up the boards. The noggins will ensure that your new ceiling is set perfectly flat and rigid.

Secure the boards to the joists with galvanized plasterboard nails. Use nails 30mm (1¼in) long for 9.5mm (⅜in) thick boards; 40mm (1½in) long for· 12.7mm (½in) boards.

To reach the ceiling you'll need to rig up a platform such as a hop-up or planks between stepladders. Alternatively, you can make T-shaped timber supports which will either wedge between floor and ceiling to support the boards, or which will enable your helpers to hold up the boards at each end from floor level.

Drive home the nails firmly but without the head fracturing the paper surface; the final hammer blow should leave a slight depression, which you can fill later. Nail each board to every joist and noggin at 150mm (6in) centres, starting at the centre of each board and working outwards. Nails should not be closer than 13mm (½in) from the ends of the boards and 10mm (⅜in) from the edges.

Try to arrange the boards so that the cut edges fit into the internal angles at the sides of the room. When you're forced to have cut edges within the ceiling area, you should stagger the end joints and arrange the boards so that they fall midway over a joist, with a 3mm (⅛in) gap between each.

SEALING THE JOINTS

If you're going to plaster your new ceiling, you have to seal the joints with hessian scrim and spread on a skim-coat of special Board Finish plaster.

But if you just intend to decorate the surface with paint or paper you should seal the joints with paper tape – see pictures on the opposite page.

FIXING PLASTERBOARD

1. Set angles on a profile gauge.

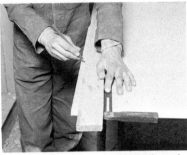

2. Cut waste from the plasterboard.

3. Position first plasterboard sheet.

4. Nail up the board.

5. Mark the centre of each joist.

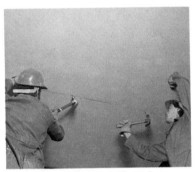

6. Butt up subsequent boards.

PLASTERING

If you want to plaster the surface of your new plasterboard ceiling, fix up the sheets grey-side-down, using plasterboard nails. Spread a thin layer of Thistle Board Finish plaster along the joints, about one arm's length at a time, then embed 75mm (3in) wide hessian scrim in the band of wet plaster using your trowel and leave to set. Spread a 3mm (⅛in) layer of plaster over the entire surface of the ceiling, and when the plaster has stiffened, trowel over the ceiling without any plaster, to polish the surface. Lubricate your trowel blade with flicks of water.

PLASTERING TECHNIQUES

Patching small areas of plasterwork is a fairly straightforward job, but sometimes you'll need to replaster a whole wall. This is skilled work, therefore before you can start, you have to learn the basic techniques.

TOOLS FOR REPLASTERING

There are a number of specialist tools for plastering but the following are the basic requirements: hawk – a 300mm (1ft) wood, aluminium or plastic square with a handle, used to carry plaster to

FINISHING OFF

1. Press jointing tape into the filler.

2. Spread joint finish over the joint.

your working area; plasterer's trowel – the basic tool for applying plaster to the wall, it has a thin rectangular steel blade measuring about 250×115mm (10×4½in) and shaped wooden handle; wood float – generally used to give a flatter finish coat to plaster, it is rectangular in shape and can be converted to a devilling float for keying surfaces by driving in two or three nails at one end so that their points just protrude; rule – a planed softwood batten measuring about 75×25mm (3×1in) and 1.5m (5ft) long, used to level off the floating coat when applied between screeds, grounds or beads; water brush – used to dampen the wall and to sprinkle water on the trowel when finishing; and a spirit level – for accurate positioning of the timber grounds and angle beads.

In addition, for plastering angles and reveals you will need a metal angle bead of the appropriate type, plus tinsnips and hacksaw for cutting it to length; an angle trowel; a reveal gauge for gauging the plaster thickness within the reveal, plus a try-square.

For mixing plaster you'll need the following equipment: a trough about the size of a galvanized bath for large amounts, or a tea chest lined with polythene; a 22-litre (5-gallon) bucket for small amounts; a clean bucket containing clean water for adding to the plaster mix; a bucket to transfer mixed plaster to the spot board; a clean shovel for stirring large mixes.

MAKING A SPOT BOARD

The spot board is used to hold the mixed plaster near the work area. Make one from a 1m (3ft) square panel of exterior grade plywood and mount it on an old table or tea chest so it's at a convenient height. Make sure it projects over the edge of the stand so you can place the hawk underneath when loading with plaster.

TYPES OF PLASTER

Gypsum-based plasters have now largely superseded cement-based plasters. They are quicker-setting, and usually available in pre-mixed form, which requires only the addition of clean water to make them workable. Another point in their favour is that they contain lightweight aggregates such as perlite and vermiculite instead of sand, so they're easier to use.

Ready-mixed plaster is usually spread on to the wall in two parts. The first is a backing, base or 'floating' coat; it is applied fairly thickly – up to 10mm (⅜in) – to take up any unevenness in the wall. The second is a finishing coat, and it is spread on thinly – up to 3mm (⅛in) – and finished to give a smooth, matt surface.

Carlite is the most widely-used lightweight pre-mixed gypsum plaster and it's available in various grades for use on different wall surfaces, depending on how absorbent they are: the plaster will crack if the wall to which it's applied draws moisture from it too quickly. Common brickwork and most types of lightweight building blocks, for instance, are described as having 'high suction', which means that their absorption rate is rapid. Concrete engineering

APPLYING A SKIM COAT

1. Apply a thin layer of board finish.

2. Next apply a second coat.

3. Finally polish the plastered surface.

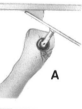
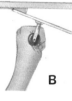
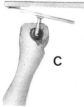

How to use the plasterer's trowel to spread the plaster on to the ceiling evenly and to the correct thickness: keep the trowel at 30° to the ceiling with its back edge 1-2mm (¹⁄₁₆in) away from the board (A). Push the trowel away from you (B). Close the leading edge of the trowel to the board near the end of the stroke (C). Pinch in the plaster at the end of the run. You can reverse this action if you like, pulling the trowel towards you.

TOOLS FOR PLASTERING

(A) Hawk, for carrying plaster to your working area.

(B) Plasterer's trowel.

(C) Wood float.

(D) Angle trowel.

bricks, dense building blocks and plasterboard, on the other hand, have 'low suction'.

You can recognize which walls are high or low suction by splashing on a little clean water. If it's absorbed immediately, the wall is high suction, but if it runs off the surface the wall is low suction. If after this test you're still unsure, you can treat the wall with a coat of PVA bonding agent or adhesive, which turns all backgrounds into low suction, and both seals and stabilizes the surface.

For a high-suction background you will need Carlite Browning plaster for the base coat; for low suction choose Carlite Bonding plaster. Use Bonding where the wall is of a composite nature (containing both high- and low-suction materials). Carlite Finish plaster is used as the final coat on Bonding and Browning plaster.

BUYING PLASTER

Large quantities of plaster are sold in 50kg (110lb) bags, and smaller amounts for patching are sold in 2.5 to 10kg (5½ to 22lb) bags.

10kg (22lb) of Carlite Browning laid 10mm (⅜in) thick will cover about 1.5 sq m (1.8 sq yd).

10kg (22lb) of Carlite Bonding laid 10mm (⅜in) thick will cover about 1.6 sq m (1.9 sq yd).

10kg (22lb) of Carlite Finish will cover about 5 sq m (6 sq yd).

PREPARING THE SURFACE

If replastering an old wall of bricks or blocks, hack off all the old plaster and examine the mortar joints.

MIXING PLASTER

1. Sprinkle dry plaster on to water.

2. Stir thoroughly with a stout stick.

4. Scoop plaster on to the hawk.

3. Tip plaster on to a spot board.

5. Push the trowel upwards.

If they're soft and crumbly, rake them out and repoint. Lightly dampen the wall.

Smooth surfaces such as concrete and timber (used as lintels over openings, for example), must be keyed to accept the plaster. You can do this either by nailing expanded metal laths or plasterboard to them, applying PVA bonding agent, or by hacking shallow crisscross lines on the surface.

APPLYING THE PLASTER

Plaster is applied to the wall in a series of sections called 'bays'. These need to be marked out, usually with timber battens called 'grounds' lightly nailed vertically to the wall.

The distance between the markers can vary according to your skill in applying the plaster, but 1m (3ft) is an easily manageable width for the beginner. Grounds are essentially guides that enable you to apply the backing coat to the correct thickness, and when the plaster's been applied to one bay it's smoothed off level with them using a timber straightedge called a 'rule'.

When you've plastered one bay using timber grounds as guides, leave the plaster until it is partially set; then remove one of the battens and move it along the wall about another 1m (3ft), then refix it.

Plaster this second bay using the edge of the first one as a thickness guide, and carefully rule off the surface. Carry on in this way until you've covered the whole wall.

To ensure that the finishing plaster will adhere to the backing coat the latter must be 'keyed' using a tool called a devilling float. This is a wooden or plastic block with nails driven in from the top so that their points just protrude through the base. It's used to scratch lightly the surface of the backing coat.

Two thin coats of finishing plaster will give a smooth and flat surface. The first coat is applied from bottom to top, working left to right if you are right-handed, right to left otherwise, and is then ruled off. The second coat is applied straight away and then flattened off to produce a matt finish. When this has been done you return to the starting point and, with the addition of a little water splashed on to the wall, you trowel over the entire surface. When the plaster has hardened, trowel the surface again several times, applying water to the surface as a lubricant to create a smooth, flat finish.

COPING WITH CORNERS

If you're plastering large areas, you'll have to cope with corners sooner or later.

To tackle an internal corner, where you have a hard surface to work to, apply your floating coat to the wall in the normal manner. Then rule the plaster outwards from the corner, using the wooden rules vertically. Key the plaster well with a devilling float and then cut out the internal angle. Do this by laying the trowel flat against the finished surface so that it is at an angle of 30° to 40° to the vertical and then moving it into the corner until the tip of the toe cuts into the fresh plaster. Move the trowel up and down the angle and then repeat the procedure with the trowel

APPLYING THE FLOATING COAT

1. Start at the bottom of the bay.

2. Spread on the plaster in rows.

3. Use a timber batten to rule off.

4. Fill any hollows with more plaster.

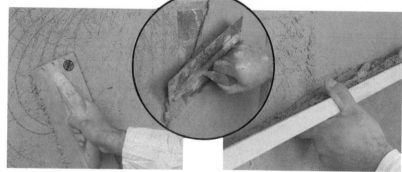

5. Key the floating coat before it sets.

6. Move ground, then fill the gap.

flat against the floated surface and its tip against the hard plaster. This will cut out the corner neatly. Leave it to harden.

Next apply the finishing plaster, ruling vertically away from the angle with a feather-edge rule, and cut into the corner as before. The second coat of finishing plaster should be trowelled in to form a flat surface. Just before the plaster hardens fully, pass a wooden float up and down the angle.

When you are satisfied that the angle is straight, you can finish it off. To do this, hold your trowel so that its toe is flat against the finished wall with one corner just touching the new plaster at the

angle. By moving the trowel down the entire length of the corner you should be able to produce a clean and sharp internal angle.

When plastering two adjacent walls at the same time, the procedure for dealing with the internal angle is basically the same, but extra care is needed because there is no hard surface to work from. You can use a special internal angle trowel for finishing off the angle smoothly.

Metal angle beads make it easy to get a perfect external corner every time. They allow simultaneous plastering of both walls and give an extremely durable corner. The other method is to use a timber

APPLYING THE FINISHING COAT

1. Mixing the finishing plaster.

2. Scoop plaster on to your hawk.

3. Work from bottom to top.

4. Polish the surface.

FITTING ANGLE BEAD

1. Preparing to fit angle bead.

2. Positioning the angle bead.

3. Spread plaster over the mesh wings.

The two basic types of metal angle bead are illustrated below.

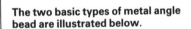

plasterboard
galvanised nails

Below: dealing with reveals.

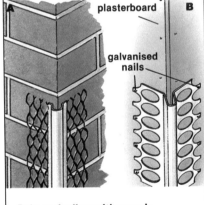

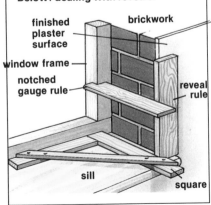

finished plaster surface
window frame
notched gauge rule
brickwork
reveal rule
sill
square

rule to form first one side of the angle and then the other.

Two versions of metal angle bead are available: one that will take the full thickness of a floating and finishing coat of plaster, and another that is shallower for use with plasterboard. The latter is called a 'thin coat' bead.

The first type of beading is fixed by means of 30mm (1¼in) thick dabs of backing plaster which are applied at 600mm (2ft) intervals to both sides of the angles. After pressing the bead into place on the dabs, it is trued up and straightened with the aid of a straightedge and spirit level. Then the plaster dabs are allowed to harden before the floating coat is applied.

Thin coat bead is usually fitted by nailing (with galvanized nails) through the side wings into the wooden batten behind the plasterboard.

Whatever type is being used, the bead can easily be cut to length, using tinsnips to cut through the wings and a hacksaw to cut the nosing.

If you have to join two lengths of angle bead, fix the first length to the angle and insert a dowel – a short length of stout wire or a headless galvanized nail – into the nose of the bead. Then position the second length over the dowel and bed it into place.

Once the bead is secure, it may be used as a screed for the floating coat. When this has become sufficiently hard, it should be cut back with a steel trowel to just below the level of the bead nose to allow room for the finishing coat. This coat is applied in the normal way, using the bead as a guide. When the finishing coat has been trowelled off to the angle bead, a sharp, clean and hard corner will be left exposed.

If a wooden rule is used as a guide for plastering an external corner, nail it first to one of the walls so that it projects beyond the corner ready to act as a ground for floating the other wall. Once the floating coat has hardened on the first wall, the rule is removed and nailed to the wall just floated to enable the second wall to be treated in the same way.

DOOR AND WINDOW REVEALS

The narrow strips of wall at door and window openings, which are normally at right angles to the main wall surfaces, are known as reveals.

To ensure that reveals are plastered squarely and with a uniform thickness of plaster, use a piece of softwood about 75mm (3in) larger than the reveal depth. Lay it in the reveal, against the angle rule or bead, and parallel to the blade of the square, and mark one end to match the margin on the frame. Cut out a notch and use the gauge as a short rule to level the plaster within the reveal.

BUILDING AND CLADDING A PARTITION WALL

Building a partition wall gives you two rooms where you only had one before. Surprisingly, you don't have to be a skilled craftsman.

A timber stud partition consists of: a timber sole plate, which runs the length of the partition at floor level; a timber top plate, which runs the length of the partition at ceiling level; vertical timber studs at intervals along the partition, their centres coinciding with joins in the plasterboard; horizontal timber noggins nailed between the studs to strengthen the structure and provide support for the plasterboard cladding.

PLANNING

At the planning stage, think about lighting, ventilation, and positioning of doors. You do not need planning permission, but you cannot be too careful where the Building Regulations are concerned; they deal with things like fire hazards and proper ventilation. Consult the council, who will be able to tell you whether your plans conform.

Also consider how the ceiling joists run. This is important, as you'll have to fix your partition to them, and not just into the ceiling plaster. They're probably spaced regularly, but you'll have to find their exact positions by tapping and making small holes, or by removing the floorboards above. If they lie at right angles (or nearly) to the intended line of your partition, there's no problem. If you want the partition to run in the same direction as the joists, think carefully. You'll either have to position it directly underneath a joist, or fit a new joist and fix it to that, or fit 50×50mm (2×2in)

FINISH AN EXTERNAL CORNER

1. Apply a floating coat.

2. Level the backing plaster.

3. Draw the trowel down the wall.

4. Apply coat of finishing plaster.

FINISH AN INTERNAL CORNER

1. Apply a floating coat.

2. Apply two finishing coats.

Trim off the ridge of excess plaster.

TOOLS

You will need the following tools for building a timber stud partition: pencil, plumb line, spirit level, hammer, pincers, electric drill, assorted drill bits, screwdriver, try square, steel measuring tape, tenon saw, panel saw, mallet, assorted chisels.

For plastering you need a steel trowel for the plaster; a hawk of wood or aluminium to hold small amounts of plaster; a spot board to hold large amounts, and two 14-litre (3-gallon) plastic buckets for mixing plaster and for clean water.

FRAME JOINTS

1. Wide housing joint (for studs).

2. Rebate joint (for corners).

FIXING TOP AND SOLE PLATES

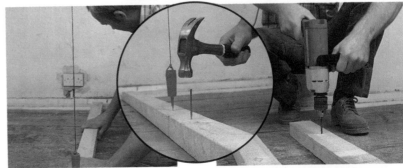

1. Cut and position the sole plate.

2. Cut the top plate to length.

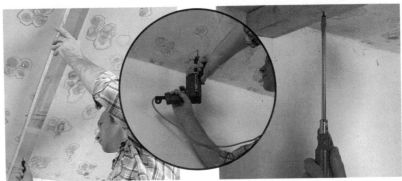

3. Mark the top plate screw positions.

4. Screw the top plate into place.

bridging pieces between existing joists at regular intervals and fix the top plate to them. Moreover, an especially long and/or tall partition may be too heavy for the floorboards alone to support – so you might have to make similar decisions about the floor joists.

CONSTRUCTIONAL DETAILS

Studs set at 600mm (2ft) centres (ie., with their centres that distance apart) give what is really the maximum spacing, and 400mm (16in) will provide an even more rigid structure.

Also take into account the sizes

of whatever cladding material you will be fixing to the wooden framework. Plasterboard, for example, is standardized at 2440×1220mm (8×4ft) and 3000×1220mm (10× 3ft). You might therefore want to arrange the studs so that there's one every 1220mm (4ft). Putting them at either 600mm (2ft) centres or 400mm (16in) centres would ensure this.

The door opening, of course, will need to be wider. Take its size from the size of the door you plan to use, adding 3mm (⅛in) clearance either side and the thickness of extra lining pieces of, say, 100× 25mm (4×1in) wood, fixed round its inside at top and sides. These should be wide enough to cover the edges of the cladding on both sides of the partition. A window opening should be lined in the same way.

It's unlikely, of course, that you will be able to fit an exact number of whole sheets of cladding from wall to wall or floor to ceiling, so you'll need to cut some sheets to fit. Besides, the walls or ceiling

may not be dead straight or true, so you'll need to mark and cut the edges of the sheets which adjoin them, to make them fit snugly. Luckily, plasterboard is extremely easy to cut.

Noggins need only be placed 1220mm (4ft) above the floor, and again at 2400mm (8ft) if the ceiling is any higher – assuming that you are using 2400×1200mm (8×4ft) sheets.

USING JOINTS

Although skew-nailing will make quite a strong framework, it is better to use a wide housing joint instead. Mark out the housings across both plates at the same time with a try-square. The four corners of the frame will have rebate joints; so will the bottom corners of the door opening.

All timber (except for door and window linings, which are added later anyway) is the same cross-sectional size. 75×50mm (3×2in) is quite big enough for most purposes, and 75×38mm (3×1½in) will sometimes do for the top and

FIXING STUDS

1. Screw and plug studs to side wall.

2. Check that each stud is vertical.

3. Nailing a stud to the sole plate.

sole plates. Buy ordinary sawn softwood.

STARTING WORK

Cut away the existing skirting board and cut or chip away the ceiling moulding, if any, so that the corners of the framework will fit closely into the angles between wall and floor and between wall and ceiling. This will help to make the structure rigid and secure.

Then cut the sole and top plates to length. (Keep each as a single piece of timber if at all possible.) Screw the top plate to the ceiling joist or joists, and use a plumbline to position the sole plate directly underneath it. Then nail or screw

the sole plate through the floorboards and into the floor joist(s), or screw into a solid floor with the aid of fibre or plastic plugs.

ADDING THE STUDS

Now you can start on the studs. You'll have to measure separately for the length of each one, in case floor and ceiling aren't quite parallel. For an exceptionally sturdy job, cut housings across the plates with a tenon saw and chisel, and simply fit the ends of the studs into them.

The last stage in building the framework is to cut and fix the noggins. Be careful not to make them too long. If you do, you'll probably still be able to squeeze them into position, but they'll bend the studs out of true.

The lintel (the noggin above the door opening) should be housed in the studs at each side for stability. If you are intending to mount cupboards on the wall, you may find it helpful to fix bearers for them in the same way.

Next, screw the door lining to its frame; the top piece is fitted to the side pieces with either rebate or barefaced housing joints.

PIPES AND CABLES

The final job before putting on the cladding (though you can do it after cladding one side) is to bore holes in studs and perhaps noggins, and run any essential pipes and cables through them.

CLADDING THE PARTITION

To give your partition a suitable surface for plastering you'll have to nail sheets of plasterboard to the studs.

Boards have a grey side intended for plastering and an ivory-coloured side specially prepared for decorating directly with paint or wallpaper. If the boards are fixed with the ivory-coloured side outwards, the partition is finished by painting the surface with a drywall top coat.

Plasterboard cladding is simply nailed to the wooden framework of the partition wall.

To fit the first sheet of plaster-

COMPLETING THE FRAME

1. Mark across one edge of studs, where tops of the noggins are to go.

2. Skew-nail through the end of the noggin above the steadying block.

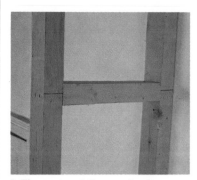

3. The centre of the noggin aligns with the top edge of the cladding.

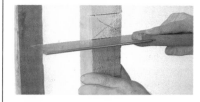

4. The noggin above a door opening needs a firmer fixing: cut housings across the studs.

5. Above the opening, nail noggin horizontally through the studs.

6. Cut away part of the sole plate to complete the door opening.

7. Finish the frame by screwing on lining pieces of planed timber.

COVERING THE FRAME

1. You'll probably have to cut a sheet to width at the end of the partition.

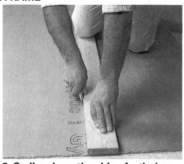

2. Scribe along the side of a timber straightedge and cut off the waste.

3. To fit the board tightly into the ceiling angle you'll need a 'footlifter' made from two offcuts of wood, which you use to lever up the sheet.

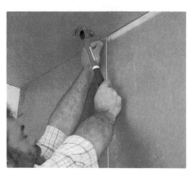

4. You'll now have both hands free to nail the plasterboard to the studs.

board measure the height of the partition and if it's less than the length of the board, transfer this dimension to one face and subtract about 12mm (½in). Scribe a line against a straightedge across the board, using a sharp trimming knife, and 'snap' back the waste piece. Then run the knife up the opposite side to cut through the paper and free the waste piece.

It's important that the sheet is fixed tightly at the ceiling, so offer it up to the wall, pushing it up with a footlifter so that there is a 12mm (½in) gap at the floor.

This simple footlifter device for levering the plasterboard in position is a tool you can easily make yourself from a small block of softwood and a thinner strip which fits on top. It works like a seesaw, levering up the board from the floor so you can make the first fixings at both sides.

When you've hammered in a few nails at each side, you can remove the footlifter and hammer in the remaining nails.

Use only galvanized plasterboard nails 30mm (1¼in) long, evenly spaced about 150mm (6in) apart and no closer to the edge of the board than 12mm (½in) or there's a danger that the edge will tear away. Hammer in the nail so that the head just grips the surface of the paper without tearing or punching its way through. Continue along the partition, nailing up whole sheets of plasterboard.

Your last sheet of plasterboard will probably be narrower than a full sheet so you'll have to cut it to size. If the adjoining wall is fairly straight and vertical (test this with

a spirit level) just measure the width of the gap, transfer this to the board and cut off the waste. Fit the board in the same way as the others. If the wall is untrue you'll have to cut the cladding to fit.

Hold the sheet against the partition, using your footlifter, and butt its edge up to the wall. Make sure the opposite edge is parallel with the edge of the last fixed sheet or stud. To scribe the shape of the wall on to the face of the plasterboard, hold a small block of wood and a pencil against the wall and draw it along to mark the profile of the wall on the face of the board. Lay the board flat on the floor and carefully cut along the guideline with a sharp knife. Return the board to the wall and butt the cut edge up to the wall. Mark the opposite side where it falls halfway between the last stud. Cut off the waste and nail the sheet in place.

When you've covered one side of the partition you can move to the opposite side and clad that in the same way. Now is the time to add some form of thermal or sound insulation to the cavity between the two skins.

PLASTERING THE PLASTERBOARD

You can apply a finishing coat of plaster to the partition as soon as you've nailed all the plasterboard sheets in place. First seal the joints between the sheets so they won't show through on the finished surface. This is done by embedding a strip of hessian called 'scrim' in a thin layer of plaster covering each joint.

To stick the scrim to the wall, spread a thin 100mm (4in) wide strip of Thistle Board Finish along the first joint with a steel trowel. Drape one end of the scrim over the top of your trowel and position it on the screed at the top of the wall. Keep the trowel blade at about 30° to the surface of the wall and draw it down the joint, feeding the scrim on to the plaster strip with your free hand. Don't press too hard. Scrim the second joint in the same way, forming a 'bay' between the two joints. When the plaster has begun to set it'll turn from dark pink to light pink in colour, and when this happens, spread a thin layer of plaster over the bay, working from the bottom left hand side of the wall. This will bring the whole plastered surface to the level of the scrimmed joints. Scrim the remaining joints and plaster the bays between them.

By the time you've applied the first coat of plaster to the entire wall the surface will be set hard enough to accept the second, finishing coat. Apply an even layer of plaster 4mm (just over ⅛in) thick to the entire surface of the wall, again working from the bottom left, but this time make the strokes long, light, and sweeping to avoid ridges in the plaster.

When the finishing coat has almost set, go back over the area with your trowel – without any plaster – to give a smooth finish. Finally, when it's completely set, trowel again but splash a little clean water on to the wall from a brush to lubricate the trowel and create a polished and perfectly smooth surface.

PLASTERING THE PARTITION

1. Cut scrim to cover joints.

2. Spread plaster along the joint.

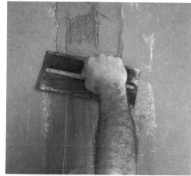
3. Press scrim into wet plaster.

4. Spread on the plaster in the bays.

5. Spread on the finishing coat.

6. Polish and flatten the surface.

HANGING A DOOR AND FITTING LOCKS

Replacing old doors that squeak, stick or let in draughts is one of the quickest ways of improving your home in terms of both appearance and comfort. And whether it's a bedroom door, cupboard door or front door, large or small, the techniques you will use are basically the same. They involve nothing more complex than planing, chiselling and sawing.

DOOR TYPES

Panel doors have two vertical stiles and horizontal rails that enclose panels of plywood, solid timber or glass. *Moulded panel doors* have the classic look but each face is shaped from a sheet of wood, fibreboard or plastic which is bonded to a timber frame. *Flush doors* have a narrow timber frame around a solid, semi-solid or cellular core. They are faced with plywood or hardboard; many have thin lipping; some are reinforced where hinges and locks are to be

Saw and chisel a housing in scrap wood and press in a wedge.

fitted. *Fire-resistant doors* are usually flush, but are thicker and more robust. They should be used with hardwood one-piece rebated frames.

THE HANGING PROCESS

Even though you'll choose a door for the exact size of opening, it may still not quite fit. This could mean offering it up to the door-frame, marking it and planing or sawing it down to make adjustments. Often, you can wedge the door in place on scraps of wood while you mark it, and you can hold the door on edge while you plane it, either by clamping it into the jaws of a portable folding workbench, or using chocks and wedges.

Probably, you'll have to make your door smaller. To take off large amounts you'll need a ripsaw or a powered circular saw; guide it along a batten firmly cramped to the door. After sawing, plane the edge smooth.

Alterations like this are relatively easy on panel doors – but remember to saw similar amounts off both opposite edges to avoid lopsidedness, and be careful not to destroy the joints.

A flush door, unless the core is solid, is a very different proposition. A cellular core (which may be made of wood strips laminated together, or a honeycomb of kraft paper), a narrow timber frame, and the hardboard or plywood faces are all there to make the door lightweight. And you risk mutilating any or all of them if you try to alter the width by more than about 10mm (the height's all right, for you can make a new piece to glue

and nail in at the top or bottom if you need to).

So, if you need to take off more than a little, buy a panel door. If you must have a flush door and you can't get one that fits or is about 10mm (³⁄₈in) larger, buy one slightly undersize and add lippings all round.

FINISHING

Once the door fits the frame with a gap of about 2mm all round, you can add the hinges. If you're re-using the existing hinge recesses in the frame, support the door in the opening parallel to the upright and mark on it where their tops and bottoms are. If you're cutting new ones, mark their positions on both door and frame. For internal doors the positions should be 125-150mm (5-6in) from the top and 175-230mm (7-9in) from the bottom. Use 75mm (3in) or 90mm (3½in) steel or brass butt hinges. Heavy or external doors need a third hinge halfway between the other two. Use 100mm (4in) steel or brass butt hinges.

Remove the door and, using a try-square and marking-gauge, mark out all new recesses – a hinge should fit flush with both the door edge and the edge of the frame. Carefully chisel out the recess and screw one side of the hinges to the door, checking that they lie neatly in place.

HANGING A DOOR

1. Check the height of the door.

2. Plane edges, top and bottom to fit.

3. Mark the hinge positions.

4. Hold door firm and mark recesses.

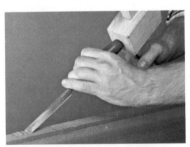

5. Make recesses and fix hinges.

6. Mark and drill central holes.

7. Put screws in central holes first.

Support the door in position once more, and fix the hinges to the frame with one screw each. Check whether the door swings and closes properly; if not, you can take it off again and make various adjustments to the way the hinges sit in the frame. Finally, you can fit a lock.

FITTING A MORTISE LOCK

Chisel out a rectangular recess for the mechanism in the thickness of the door. Then drill a hole for the keyhole, and again for the handle spindle, if any.

FITTING A RIM LOCK

The casing is simply screwed to the door face. You also bore a hole for the cylinder. In order to fix the staple (the box which receives the tongue) you may have to chisel into the frame as well.

FITTING THE STRIKING PLATE

After fitting the main lock mechanism to the door, push the door almost closed and mark out the matching position of the striking plate or staple on the jamb. Chisel out a recess for the main body of the striking plate, or for the lip of the staple. If necessary, chisel recesses for tongues to enter, or for the box of the striking plate.

FITTING A STRIKING PLATE

LAYING A TIMBER FLOOR

Timber floors are both durable and long-suffering. But eventually they may become loose, worn, damaged by woodworm and sometimes cracked, and then it's time to think about laying a new floor.

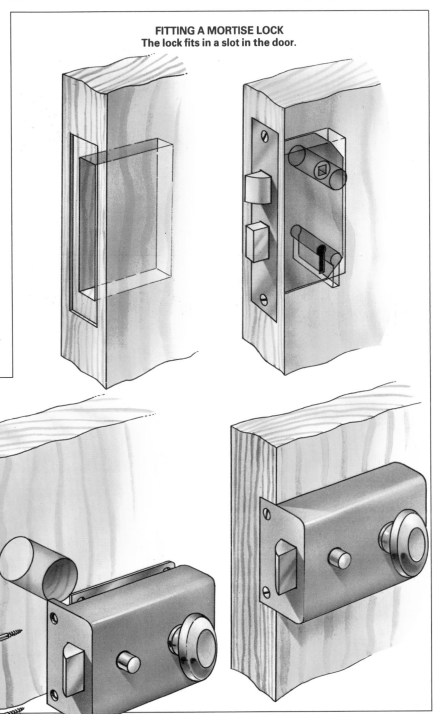

FITTING A MORTISE LOCK
The lock fits in a slot in the door.

FITTING A RIM LOCK
The casing is simply screwed to the door face. You also bore a hole for the cylinder, or – with the lever type – one for the keyhole and one for the spindle. Fixing the staple (the box which receives the tongue) may mean chiselling into the frame as well.

LAYING A TIMBER FLOOR

1. Lever up the end of a board.

2. Use a piece of timber as a lever.

3. Use packing pieces, if required.

4. Scribe to fit round obstacles.

5. Nail down the first board.

6. Ends must be supported by joists.

7. Loose-lay the boards, then nail.

8. Use pairs of wedges as cramps.

9. Punch nail heads below surface.

Consider chipboard as an alternative to a timber floor. Special flooring grade chipboard can be obtained; it is usually 19mm (¾in) thick, and it may have tongued-and-grooved edges, providing greater rigidity.

Chipboard is cheaper than solid timber floorboards, and it doesn't shrink; but it is more work to fit, and removing it is harder.

BUYING FLOORBOARDS

Floorboards are made of planed softwood, and come in two varieties: square-edged, and tongued-and-grooved (T & G). In the latter type each board has a tongue down one edge and a matching groove down the other. T & G boards take a little more effort to lay (the tongues fit the grooves very tightly), but they repay that in being draught-proof, and in their greater strength; once laid, they form what is in effect a solid sheet.

The tongues and grooves aren't centred in their respective edges. Boards should be laid with the tongues towards the bottom. Standard widths for floorboards (i.e., across the face, excluding the width of the tongue) are 100mm (4in) and 150mm (6in), although these vary slightly with suppliers. The standard nominal thickness is 25mm (1in), planed down from sawn timber to 19mm (¾in) or so.

Boards planed down to a finished thickness of about 25mm (1in) from 32mm (1¼in) are also available, and they make a fine substantial floor; but they cost more. Remember, too, that if they are thicker than the old boards they probably won't fit under the existing skirting. You'll either have to butt them up against it (which may create problems when it comes to supporting their ends, since the last joist may be flush with the wall surface) or replace the skirting too.

Floorboards must, of course, be laid across the joists, not parallel to them. To work out how much timber you'll need, make careful calculations, dividing the length of the room by the width of board to find how many lengths to buy. A good tip is to visit your timber merchant even before this, to find out the exact width of the boards he stocks.

If possible, buy boards which will just span the width of the room with a little to spare. In any case, make sure you get enough to cover the total length you need.

Buy the boards a week or two before doing the job, and stack them flat inside the house. This will give them time to dry out and therefore shrink a bit before you lay them.

REMOVING OLD FLOORBOARDS

Lever up the first board with a bolster and, if necessary, a claw-hammer. If the old floorboards are tongued-and-grooved, you'll need to cut through the tongue first with a pad saw, a floorboard saw, a tenon saw, or a circular saw whose depth of cut is set to the floorboard thickness. Be very careful not to cut into the joists.

After you have lifted one end, by far the quickest way to continue (and to lift all the other boards) is to use a long piece of substantial timber – say 75×50mm (3×2in) – as a lever, and a shorter piece as a fulcrum.

LAYING NEW BOARDS

Before starting to lay the floor, place a straight-edged piece of timber (a floorboard will do) across the joists to check whether their top edges are in line. If not, cut packing pieces (planing them to the right thickness, or using hardboard) and pin them in position.

Lay the first board in position with the groove facing out into the room, and scribe it to fit against the wall. Then cut it to shape, removing the waste from the tongue side, and nail it down to each joist in turn through its face.

After that, the basic procedure is to lay the boards on the floor in sequences of four or five (inserting the tongues, if using T & G boards, into the grooves), cramp them tight and nail them down.

There are two ways to cramp floorboards. You can use pairs of wedges, cut from 75×50mm (3×2in) planed softwood, tapped together between the last board and another piece of timber nailed across the joists. Or you can hire flooring cramps, which clamp themselves on to the joists while

FITTING THE LAST TWO BOARDS
After planing the tongues off two lengths (A and B), place A against the last nailed board, and scribe it to fit the wall – using a piece the same width as B.

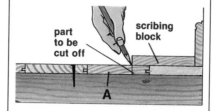

Remove A, replace it with B, then cut A as scribed and put A next to the wall. Then press them both in place and nail down.

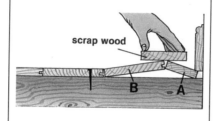

being tightened against the floorboards.

The right nails to use for fixing are cut floorbrads about two and a half times as long as the floorboards are thick. These are blunt and thus won't split the timber. Drive two through each board wherever it crosses a joist. Make quite sure at all times that you know where pipework and electrical wiring runs. A nail through a gas pipe or mains cable is no joke.

MAKING BOARDS FIT

No room is without various irregularities in, and protrusions from, the walls at floor level, and you'll have to cut the boards to fit round them. The first and last boards must be scribed to fit along the walls, and you'll also need to cope with the chimney breast (if any) in a similar way. A combination square is ideal for scribing round small obstacles.

A fitted cupboard can create problems if the floorboards run into rather than parallel with it, but these aren't insurmountable. You can remove the bottom cross piece in its frame, and replace it

after laying the floorboards. Or you can leave the cross-piece there, saw through the old floorboards immediately in front of it, and then butt the ends of the new ones up against them. In the latter case, the remaining old boards (those under the cupboard) may no longer be supported; if not, you'll have to screw down through the cross-piece to hold them in position.

In places where you need access to pipes and wiring, you can include a trap-door in the form of a short board such as an offcut (or a full-length board cut into two), held down by countersunk screws instead of nails. In the case of T&G flooring, you'll have to plane or chisel the tongue off the adjacent board first.

FINISHING THE JOB

You can't, of course, use wedges or cramps to get the last couple of boards tight, because there's no room for them. An alternative procedure is as follows.

After cutting the last two boards to length and planing the tongues off both, place one of them next to the last board already nailed. Next wedge it tightly against the board by using a chisel as a lever. Then scribe the profile of the wall on it, using a block of wood the same width as the boards. Even if the wall were dead straight and parallel to the board edges, you'd still need to do this in order to find out the width to which you need to cut the last board down: it would be quite a coincidence if a full-width board fitted exactly into the gap.

Cut the board along the scribed line, lay the whole board next to the last board nailed, and place the cut board next to the wall. Now you can spring them both into place at once – using a piece of timber to press them flat – and nail them down.

When you've laid all the boards, punch all the nail heads below the surface. Then look at how neatly the boards fit under or butt against the skirting. If the effect is ragged, you can improve it enormously by nailing quadrant moulding to the skirting in the angle.

LEVELLING SOLID FLOORS

1. Hack off the old floor covering.

2. Concrete surfaces may need priming.

3. Mix up the levelling compound.

4. Pour a small quantity on to the floor.

5. Spread the compound smooth.

SOLID FLOORS

There are two common faults with solid floors. They may be quite sound, but have an uneven surface which can be corrected by applying a smoothing compound.

Alternatively, the floor may be badly cracked and damp, and in this case the only remedy is to dig up the floor and re-lay it.

LEVELLING COMPOUNDS

There are two main types of levelling compounds: they are either water-based or latex-based. Both types come as a powder which is then mixed to a slurry and spread over the floor in a very thin layer. They must be trowelled out to an even thickness but there is no need to finish off the surface as they are self-smoothing and any trowel marks will disappear.

The water-based type is the most common and widely available. It is also easier to use. It is most suitable for levelling concrete floors and Terrazzo or quarry tiles.

The latex-based compounds are harder-wearing and slightly flexible. Some types can also be used to level joints and nail-holes in a timber floor. It is also best to use a latex compound on an impervious surface such as vinyl tiles, as it will bond more successfully. Even harder wearing acrylic-based compounds are also available.

USING THE COMPOUND

The levelling compound should be applied to a floor that is absolutely free from grease and polish.

The compound must be no more than 3 or 4mm (about ³⁄₁₆in) thick; any irregularities deeper than this should be filled first.

The compound should be mixed up in accordance with the manufacturer's instructions. Only mix up a small amount first, as much as you can use in 15 minutes, as after this time it will become too stiff to spread. It is then poured on the floor and smoothed out to an even layer with a steel trowel. Since the compounds are self-smoothing any trowel marks will disappear as the compound dries. But it is *not* self-levelling, so you must trowel it until the surface is as flat as you can manage. If you don't get a good finish, sprinkle water over the surface and trowel again. It is usually possible to walk on it after one or two hours and will be thoroughly dry in 8 to 10 hours.

REMOVING A SOLID FLOOR

If you are replacing a solid floor, first break up the surface using a pick-axe, or hire an electric power breaker, which will make the job much easier. Nevertheless, it's a very messy job, so you'd be wise to wear old clothes or, better still, overalls, stout shoes, gloves, and goggles to protect your eyes from flying fragments. You'll probably need to hire a skip in which to dispose of debris, although you can keep any large pieces of concrete to use in your new foundations as hardcore.

Prise off the skirting boards and door frames and look for the dpc in the walls. You should be able to pinpoint its position from outside: it should be visible as a narrow line of slates, or a black bitumen layer, or one or two courses of hard blue bricks. It might be necessary for you to hack off a margin of plaster inside to expose the dpc.

PREPARING THE BASE

When you've removed all of the original floor surface, excavate the earth to at least 300mm (12in) below the finished floor level. To help make a level base, hammer sturdy timber 'datum' pegs at intervals of about 1.2m (4ft) over the entire floor area. Their tops should be level, and 50mm (2in) below the finished floor level if you're making a conventional solid floor, to allow for a finishing screed 50mm (2in) thick; 175mm (7in) below the finished level if you're laying an insulated floor, to allow for 50mm (2in) thick expanded polystyrene slabs, 75mm (3in) of concrete, and a 50mm (2in) screed; and 69mm (2¾in) below finished floor level if you are 'floating' a chipboard floor over polystyrene slabs, to allow for 50mm (2in) of polystyrene and 19mm (¾in) of chipboard.

Use a long, straight-edged board with a spirit level on top to get the tops of the pegs the same height. Next, shovel in your hardcore and spread it over the entire floor area, ramming it down with a tool called a 'punner', which you can hire, or a stout fence post, so it's about 150mm (6in) below the top of the datum pegs. While you're laying the hardcore, you should incorporate any ventilation ducts that are needed. When you've laid the hardcore and have compacted it thoroughly, spread on a layer of damp sand to fill any voids in the surface. Use a long straight-edged board to smooth and level the surface.

Lay a concrete mix consisting of 1 part cement, 2½ parts concreting sand and 4 parts coarse aggregate over the entire area, bringing the surface to the top of your datum pegs. Tamp the concrete firmly to remove any air pockets and to leave the surface flat.

LAYING A NEW SOLID FLOOR

Your new floor needs adequate foundations consisting of a layer of hardcore about 150mm (6in) deep, topped with a blinding layer of damp sand to fill in any voids in the surface and provide a flat, smooth bed for the concrete subfloor. This should be a 100mm (4in) thick slab of concrete, on which you can lay a damp-proof membrane (dpm) which should then be followed by a 50mm (2in) thick mortar screed.

PROVISIONS AGAINST DAMP

The dpm can be a thick polythene sheet called '1000-gauge' or 'sheet 1000' PVC, butyl rubber, or bitumen emulsion.

You must 'link' the dpm with the damp-proof course (dpc) in the walls of your house. If your new floor level is to be below the existing damp-proof course (dpc) in the wall take the liquid or sheet damp-

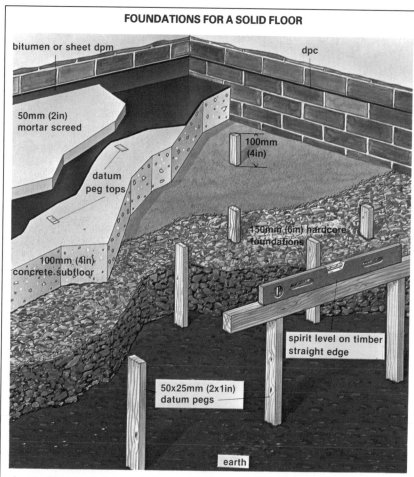

FOUNDATIONS FOR A SOLID FLOOR

bitumen or sheet dpm

dpc

50mm (2in) mortar screed

100mm (4in)

datum peg tops

150mm (6in) hardcore foundations

100mm (4in) concrete subfloor

spirit level on timber straight edge

50x25mm (2x1in) datum pegs

earth

A solid floor needs foundations of well-compacted hardcore topped with a 100mm (4in) concrete subfloor. On this you can lay a damp-proof membrane and mortar screed. Use datum pegs to ensure that levels are set properly.

proof membrane (dpm) up the wall to touch the dpc.

If your new floor level is to be above the dpc in the wall, paint bitumen down the wall to the dpc

and up the wall to the finished floor level.

INSULATING THE FLOOR

You can insulate a solid floor in

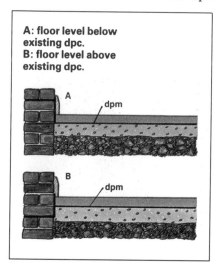

A: floor level below existing dpc.
B: floor level above existing dpc.

A

dpm

B

dpm

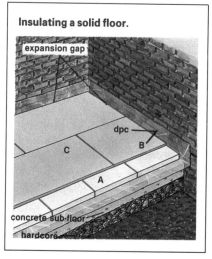

Insulating a solid floor.

expansion gap

dpc

C

B

A

concrete sub-floor

hardcore

HOW FIREPLACES ARE BUILT

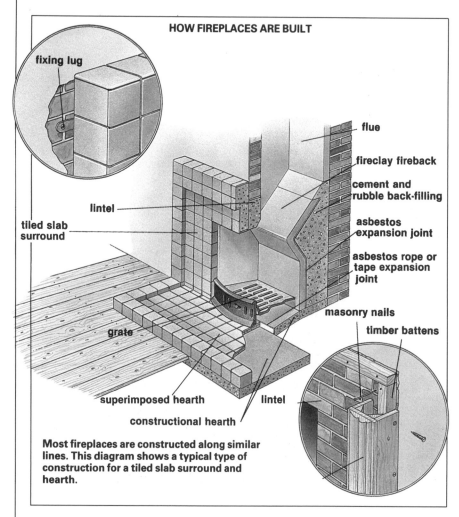

fixing lug

flue

fireclay fireback

cement and
rubble back-filling

asbestos
expansion joint

asbestos rope or
tape expansion
joint

masonry nails

timber battens

lintel

tiled slab
surround

grate

lintel

superimposed hearth

constructional hearth

Most fireplaces are constructed along similar lines. This diagram shows a typical type of construction for a tiled slab surround and hearth.

FIREPLACES AND FIREPLACE SURROUNDS

If you've a drab, old fire surround that detracts from your decor, or a fireplace made redundant by central heating, you can remove it and either block off the opening, or build a new fire surround.

SURROUNDS AND HEARTHS

There are many types of modern and older-style fireplaces, but they're usually fixed to the wall in

REMOVING A SURROUND
To remove tiled surround you will have to expose the metal lugs which hold it to the wall, then release the lugs, and, finally, insert a crowbar behind the surround to lever it free from the plaster.

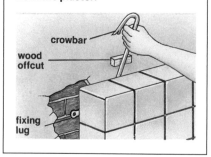

crowbar

wood
offcut

fixing
lug

one of two ways. Loose-lay 25 or 50mm (1 or 2in) thick slabs of expanded polystyrene over the floor surface, on top of the damp-proof membrane, staggering the joins, or loose-lay 2400×1200mm (8×4ft) sheets of 19mm (¾in) tongued-and-grooved flooring-grade chipboard over the slabs, staggering the

joins. Leave an expansion gap of about 6mm (¼in) at the perimeter of the floor.

Alternatively, you can loose-lay the polystyrene slabs directly on the dpm, spread a 75mm (3in) layer of concrete over the entire surface, and lay a 50mm (2in) thick mortar screed on the concrete.

a similar way. If the fire surround is a decorative cast-iron type, it will have four or six integral 'lugs' at the sides, through which are inserted the screws that fix it to the wall.

This type of surround is very heavy, so you would be wise to dismantle the separate sections

REMOVING A FIREPLACE

1. Lift off the mantelshelf, if any.

2. Next pull the columns free.

3. Pull away the cast iron centrepiece.

BRICKING UP THE OPENING
The most durable way to block off your fireplace opening is to brick up the recess and then to plaster the surface to match the rest of the chimney breast.

The first steps in bricking up your opening are to remove the hearth and surround, make good the floor and chop away the plaster from around the opening to reveal the old brickwork.

Chop out the half bricks at the sides of the opening so that you can 'tooth in' the new brickwork to make a firm, bonded joint. Lay an airbrick just above skirting level to allow for ventilation in the flue.

Continue bricking up the opening, toothing-in the bricks at alternate courses; then plaster the surface when complete to match the rest of the chimney breast. Don't plaster over the airbrick. Fit a plaster grille on the finished surface.

before you try to remove it from the room. This type should also have a good re-sale value.

Surrounds may also be made of brickwork or stonework; they're built like a wall flat against the chimney breast, and sometimes they're bonded to the wall. You can remove either type by dismantling them piece by piece.

Timber fire surrounds, whether elaborately moulded, carved, or simple hardwood frames, are usually screwed to timber battens fixed to the wall, sometimes as a separate mantelshelf and side pieces. They often have a central tiled area, which may be fixed directly to the wall or stuck on a slab and secured to the wall with metal lugs and screws. Cast-iron and wooden surrounds can be valuable and some types are much sought-after, so you may think yours is worth selling. You'll have to take great care when removing it so you don't damage it.

Concrete slab surrounds are usually clad with ceramic tiles and

have wire mesh or steel rod reinforcement, and fixing lugs set in the concrete at the sides.

Most decorative or 'superimposed' hearths are made of reinforced concrete, often clad with tiles, or stonework. The decorative hearth is set in mortar on a concrete slab called the 'constructional' hearth, which is set flush with the floor surface. It forms the base of the fireplace opening and also extends into the room.

Inset tiled hearths are found mostly in upstairs rooms. You probably won't need to remove the tiles if your floorcovering conceals them, but you may have to lay a concrete screed over them or glue hardboard on top to bring the surface level with the floor.

FIREBACKS AND LINTELS

There will be a fireclay fireback cemented inside the cavity, which protects the brickwork of the chimney breast from the heat of the fire. You can remove this by chopping out the mortar which

BOARDING UP THE OPENING

1. Fix a timber frame in the opening.

2. Nail supporting battens at corners.

3. Fix plasterboard and install a grille.

4. Spread on Thistle Board finish.

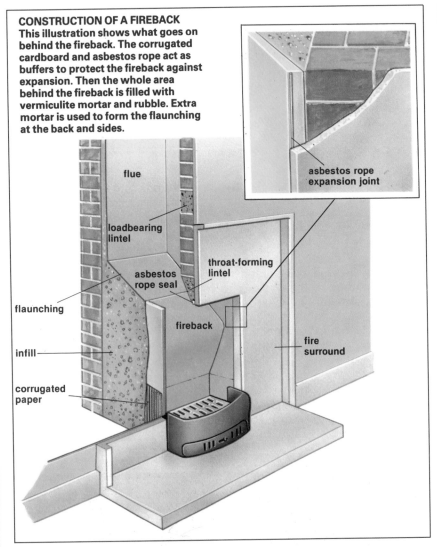

CONSTRUCTION OF A FIREBACK
This illustration shows what goes on behind the fireback. The corrugated cardboard and asbestos rope act as buffers to protect the fireback against expansion. Then the whole area behind the fireback is filled with vermiculite mortar and rubble. Extra mortar is used to form the flaunching at the back and sides.

flue

loadbearing lintel

asbestos rope seal

throat-forming lintel

flaunching

fireback

infill

fire surround

corrugated paper

asbestos rope expansion joint

secures it, but if on the other hand you think you may want to restore the fire to working order later, leave it in place.

The builder's recess itself is formed in the chimney breast and has a concrete lintel or iron bar and brick arch above to support the walling above the opening.

Removing your fireplace can be a messy job. Before you start, have the chimney swept to remove any loose soot.

REMOVING THE HEARTH

The decorative hearth is the first thing to remove. However, if the surround has been laid on top of the hearth, you'll have to remove this first.

Use a club hammer and bolster chisel to loosen the mortar bond

between the two hearths and ram a crowbar or garden spade underneath to prise them apart.

REMOVING THE SURROUND

When you've located all the lugs, chip away about 50mm (2in) of plaster at each point to expose them, using a club hammer and cold chisel.

Undo the fixing screws or drill out their heads using a drill bit the size of the screw shank, or saw them off with a hacksaw.

Wedge a crowbar behind the edge of the surround near the top lugs and insert an offcut of timber behind it to protect the wall and give better leverage. Lever the surround away from the wall slowly and lower it gently to the floor; you may need someone to help you.

BUILDING A FIRE SURROUND

A chimney breast and fireplace are among the first things you notice when you enter a room. You can make them into the room's centrepiece by installing an attractive fire surround. Building a new surround in stone or brick is relatively straightforward.

REPAIRING A FIREBACK

The fireback within the fireplace opening is constructed from fireproof clay and usually comprises two separate pieces which are assembled in situ. If the fireback is cracked then it should be repaired or, if badly damaged, replaced.

You can fill cracks with plastic fireclay cement, available from a builder's merchant. Don't use the fireplace for at least 24 hours beforehand because it has to be cold for the filler to adhere properly. You should undercut the cracks, clean away any dust, soak them with water and trowel in the cement. Wait 48 hours before you light the fire.

If a replacement is needed then you can use a club hammer and bolster to remove the old fireback, plus any hardcore behind it. This is an extremely messy job, so wear gloves and a dust mask.

The new fireback must comply with BS1251: part 1: 1969. Place the lower half squarely and centrally in the opening. Check that it is horizontal; if necessary, pack up below. Place a double layer of corrugated paper or a thin piece of strawboard at the back (this allows for expansion to prevent cracking). Then infill using a mix of 1 part lime: 2 parts sand: 4 parts broken brick (very small pieces). Don't use cement as this will be too strong. If, however, the chimney is against an outside wall then a better mix for infilling is 1 part cement: 5 parts vermiculite (a granular material, a different grade of which is more commonly used for loft insulation). This mix has insulating qualities which will ensure that heat is prevented from escaping through the outside wall.

Place a layer of flat asbestos tape

FITTING A FIRE BACK

1. Remove old fire back and clean up.

2. Splitting along the break line.

3. Make up mortar to infill.

4. Insert a layer of cardboard.

5. Put fire cement along break line.

6. Finish with a wet brush.

on the top edge of the lower half of the fireback and then lift the top half into place either flush on the lower half or set back by up to 3mm (⅛in) to prevent its lower edge from burning; it must not protrude forwards.

Fill in behind the top half as before, and then carefully chamfer off the area from the knee of the fireback to the throat of the flue. Use either a cement: vermiculite mix or a mortar mix consisting of 1 part cement: 3 parts sharp sand. The chamfer must be smooth and should follow the same angle as the knee.

BUILDING THE SURROUND

After you have designed a good working plan (or looked at the one supplied by the kit manufacturer) it's worth laying the stones out on the ground so that the complete fireplace is created exactly as it will appear in situ on the wall. This gives you the opportunity to make any modifications which may be necessary to make it fit.

Get as much cutting or dressing of the stones as is needed com-

pleted first to avoid hold-ups once building is under way.

For bonding you can buy ready-mix mortar or mix one yourself. A suitable mortar mix for bedding stone blocks to form a surround is a readily workable (but not sloppy) mix of 1 part masonry cement to 6 parts sand; for a hearth use 1 part cement to 4 parts sand. Mortar joints play an important part in the final effect of the stonework, so consider carefully which mortar will best complement the stone you are using. Some sands, particularly dark orange types, tend to give a strongly coloured mortar and you might feel that lighter coloured sand and white (rather than grey) cement, which will produce a paler mortar, would be more suitable for the surround.

Especially where you intend to have an open fire it's worth lining the lower edge of the lintel above the fireplace opening and also the front edges of the fireback from top to bottom with a piece of soft asbestos rope, fixed in place with fire cement. This allows for expansion and contraction of the fireback and

lintel without pushing the surround away from the wall.

Similarly, when you come to lay a lintel stone across the opening during construction of the surround, you can bed it on a mild steel flat bar about 75mm (3in) wide and also put in a metal plate deflector to protect the lintel from the heat.

You build up the stones using 10mm (⅜in) joints throughout, course by course, making sure the courses are level. An improved bond between the stone and the wall will be gained by nailing lengths of expanded metal to act as a key for the mortar and, as work proceeds, you can drive masonry nails or staples into the wall to project into the mortar joints between the courses of stones.

To prevent staining of the hearth stones from spilled liquids later it is advisable to treat them with a sealing liquid; the most effective types can be obtained from a specialist supplier of stone cleaning materials.

To build a brick or briquette surround, follow the same techniques as for basic brickwork. Safety details such as tying-in the surround to the backing wall and the use of asbestos rope are the same as for stone surrounds and you should again leave the pointing until the surround has been built. It's best to choose mortar of a colour which harmonizes with the brick colour.

One point concerning a hearth for either a brick or stone surround is that the Building Regulations require the new hearth to be at least as deep and wide as the concrete constructional hearth built into the floor. For solid fuel use the hearth should be 125mm (5in) thick; for use with a gas appliance a 12mm (½in) thick hearth will suffice.

HOME INSULATION

If your home is uninsulated then heating it efficiently is likely to prove an expensive business. The chances are that up to 75% of the heat generated will be completely wasted: it just escapes through the roof, walls, floors, windows and doors. Insulating your home will cut down on heat loss quite considerably and therefore make it that much warmer. And if it's a particularly hot summer then you'll find that insulation can work in quite a different way: it will keep out the heat and so keep your home pleasantly cool.

Most parts of the home are suitable for some kind of insulation. Windows should be dealt with by double glazing. Doors and other windows can be draught-proofed. Other parts of the home should be insulated, and choosing the right material for the job will be your first step.

LOFT INSULATION MATERIALS

There are three types of insulation that the householder can fit in a loft. Glass fibre or mineral fibre blankets are probably the most common: they are laid between the joists, and are available in 75mm (3in) and 100mm (4in) thicknesses. The thicker it is, the better,

BUILDING A NEW FIREPLACE SURROUND

1. Trim-up the existing surround.

2. Check that the edges are vertical

3. Spread mortar along the hearth.

4. Check that the mortar is level.

5. Build up the courses evenly.

6. Bed first course on the other side.

7. Build second side symmetrically.

8. Carefully bed the lintel.

9. Continue above the lintel.

10. Bed the hearth blocks in mortar.

but a blanket thicker than 100mm (4in) won't really be practical as it will sit above the tops of most joists and so will obstruct movement and storage. Blankets are available in a number of widths from 300mm (1ft) to 1200mm (4ft), the most common being 400mm (16in). This leaves you a little to turn up against the joists at each side.

Lengths range from 5m (16ft) to 9.4m (30ft), and to calculate how many rolls you'll need to insulate your loft fully, simply multiply its length by its width. One roll usually covers about 2sq m (23sq ft). Remember that blanket insulation can be irritating to the skin, and so when handling it do make sure you wear gloves, old clothes and a mask.

Loose-fill insulation comes in bags and is simply tipped into the joist space and smoothed out to an even depth. Vermiculite, expanded polystyrene granules, loose mineral wool and cellulose fibre are all available. You'll have to make sure that you lay it to an even depth, and if your loft is draughty you'll probably find that the granules will blow about.

You will also have to block the eaves to make sure the granules don't spill into the wall cavities.

LAGGING THE PIPES
You can lag pipes in the loft space with:
proprietary foam tubes slit down their length so they can be slipped on the pipe

or with **mineral fibre rolls wrapped on diagonally like bandages and secured with wire, adhesive tape or string.**

You needn't lag the pipes if they're contained within loose-fill insulation or they'll be covered with blanket insulation.

LAGGING THE TANK
Your cold water storage tank in the loft must be insulated. You can use: **sheets of expanded polystyrene**

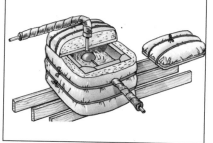

or lengths of **blanket insulation**. Other materials include proprietary lagging kits and loose-fill insulation.

Loose-fill insulation material usually comes in 110 litre bags, one of which will be sufficient to insulate an area of about 0.9sq m (9½sq ft) to a depth of 125mm (5in).

Sheet insulation can be used in lofts, although getting it up there might prove tricky as most loft openings are quite narrow. It is most commonly used to insulate between the rafters and on flat roofs and on floors.

INSULATING TANKS AND PIPES

If you've insulated the floor of your loft, the air within it will be considerably colder than before. In that case you have to insulate all

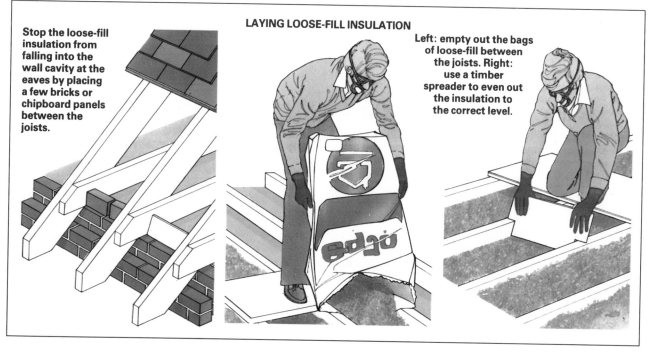

Stop the loose-fill insulation from falling into the wall cavity at the eaves by placing a few bricks or chipboard panels between the joists.

LAYING LOOSE-FILL INSULATION

Left: empty out the bags of loose-fill between the joists. Right: use a timber spreader to even out the insulation to the correct level.

LAYING BLANKET INSULATION

1. Unroll blanket between the joists.

2. Blanket lies between the joists.

3. Butt up adjoining rolls.

4. Don't cover electric cables.

5. Attach cables to the side of a joist.

tanks and pipework to stop them from freezing during the winter.

Cold water tank jackets normally consist of one piece of polythene filled with glass fibre insulation. They are available in many different sizes, and finding one to suit your tank should be very easy. Their advantage lies in that they are so easy to fit – you simply pull

them into position over the tank and then tie them in place with the fixing bands usually supplied.

Expanded polystyrene kits can be used to insulate square or rectangular cold water tanks. Alternatively, you can simply buy sheets of the material and make up a box for the tank. The pieces will have to be joined with tape, string or polystyrene adhesive and you'll have to make sure that you fill all gaps left from cut-outs for pipework.

Glass or mineral fibre blankets can also be successfully used on tanks. A 50mm (2in) thickness will be the most manageable. You have to tie it round the tank, making sure that each layer overlaps the previous one. Cover the tank top with hardboard to which more insulation is tied.

Cylinder jackets are used on hot water tanks. These consist of four or eight separate sections filled with glass fibre insulation and covered with flame-retardant PVC. They are normally supplied with a minimum of two fixing bands, and a cord for securing the top of the jacket to the hot water supply pipe.

Split sleeve insulation is usually made from flexible foamed plastic

and is simply pushed on to water pipes to insulate them. It comes in a variety of lengths ranging from 1m (3ft 3in) to 2m (6ft 6in). When buying this type of pipe insulation you'll have to specify your pipe's outside diameter so you can get the correct-sized sleeving.

INSULATING WALLS

The problem with insulating cavity walls is that, unless you do so at the building stage, you'll have to employ a contractor to inject the insulation into the cavities. The alternative is to regard them as solid walls and to insulate them by applying an extra layer of material to the inside surface. There are two methods. With the first, thermal insulating board is fixed directly to the wall surface. Alternatively, the material is attached to battens on the wall so a layer of still, trapped air is formed. This latter method is similar to dry lining a wall (see page 41).

DRAUGHT-PROOFING

Besides making your home more comfortable to live in, draughtproofing could also save you a considerable amount of money, and this will more than pay for the cost of the work.

USING FOAM STRIP

Foam strip is probably the most common draught-proofing material and is easily available in a variety of forms and thicknesses. It's also cheap, but not very longlasting. However, all you have to do when it wears out is to peel it off and stick on a new strip. Invariably some of the adhesive backing will

SILICONE SEALANTS
As an alternative to strip excluders use silicone sealant to make a tailormade gasket. It's ideal for badly warped doors and windows. Coat the closing face with petroleum jelly. Apply a thin bead of silicone to the face of the frame's rebates and to the side of the rebate on the hinge side. Leave silicone overnight to cure.

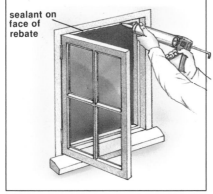

sealant on face of rebate

be left behind when you do this, but you can remove it from the frame by rubbing it with a cloth soaked in white spirit (turps).

The strip has to be stuck on the rebate of the frame so that the door or window compresses it when closed and does not slide across its surface. For this reason, on the hinge side of the frame you have to position the strip on the *side* of the rebate.

WEATHERSTRIP

Being made of metal or plastic, these excluders are more substantial than foam strip. They work on a hinge principle – some are in the form of a flap; others have a V profile which bridges the gap between the frame and the window or door. The strip can either be fitted to the frame (in the same places as you fit foam strip) or to the window or door itself. If you are installing it round a door then you can't run it down the lock/handle edge: you'll have to use the frame for this part. Generally speaking, fixing to a door is more tricky and you may find it easier to take the door off the hinges first. Weatherstrip can be fitted to the bottom edge, but check that it doesn't drag across the carpet as the door is opened and closed.

RIGID AND FLEXIBLE STRIP

In contrast to the excluders just described, these strips are fitted to the inner face of the door or window frame on the outside, rather than in the rebate. They consist of a plastic or aluminium holder with a flexible insert (either a PVC flap or tube) against which the door presses when it's closed. For this reason it's best to position the strip with the door shut so you can see that the flexible strip touches the door along its entire length. You can then open the door to make nailing easier.

DOUBLE GLAZING

Installing double glazing in your home not only cuts costly heat loss but also reduces unpleasant noise from the outside.

There are two ways of obtaining double glazing. The first is to buy it from a specialist company and the second is to buy it in kit form and install it yourself. A double glazing kit is a much cheaper way of installing secondary double glazing. Conventional kits, while varying in detail, are all similar in principle: a framework of UPVC (a rigid, weather-resistant plastic) or aluminium is made up to accept the glass and the whole thing is then fixed directly either to the existing frame or to the walls of the reveal. These panels can be fixed permanently, but hinged or sliding panels are an advantage as they give ready access to any openable windows and make cleaning that much easier.

WHERE TO FIT DRAUGHT STRIP

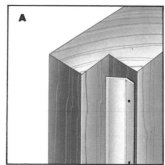

(A) to the side of the rebate.

(B) to the outside edge of the frame.

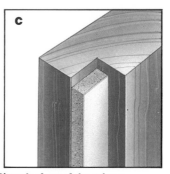

(C) to the face of the rebate.

WHERE TO FIT FLAPS

Simple flaps (A) fit inside the door; automatic hinged flaps (B) tend to fit outside.

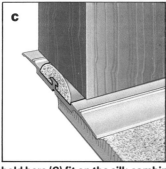

Threshold bars (C) fit on the sill; combination types (D) fit to sill and door.

HOME SECURITY

It isn't easy to keep out a really determined burglar, but most of the ones who break into houses are petty thieves who are out looking for easy spoils; they prefer to rob and vandalize homes which are not well protected, rather than organize a proper crime.

Hinged panes are usually fitted to frequently opened windows. They should incorporate special felt fins to prevent any possible heat loss or draughts when they are closed. Most DIY manufacturers produce kits that are hinged at the sides or top of the secondary pane. If you have metal window frames you might have to fit a wooden subframe.

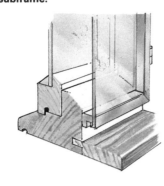

Vertical sliders: these systems are designed to act as secondary glazing on sliding sash windows. They allow access to either the top or the bottom of the original window and so make opening it easy. The finger-operated catches that feature in some kits allow you to set the secondary panes at whatever position you like for ventilation.

Fixed panes: these are a simple form of secondary glazing designed for use on small windows that are seldom opened. Frames that are made of UPVC, anodized aluminium or wood can be fixed to the window reveal or the existing frame itself, and they can usually accommodate glass, perspex or thick polystyrene. As with all secondary glazing, the fixed pane should be fitted on a dry and cool day to lessen the risk of condensation occurring later.

Horizontal sliders are usually fitted within the reveal, but some DIY kits can be fixed to an existing wooden window frame provided they are not impeded by the window stays and catches. The kits are simple to fix and the corners are neat as the cut edges are usually concealed within the vertical tracks. Kits usually cater for two frames, but multi-pane kits are also available. The glass itself is housed in special gaskets and then fitted into the channels.

WHERE TO FIT DOUBLE GLAZING

There is a wide range of DIY kits and they can be fitted to different parts of the window and its reveal.

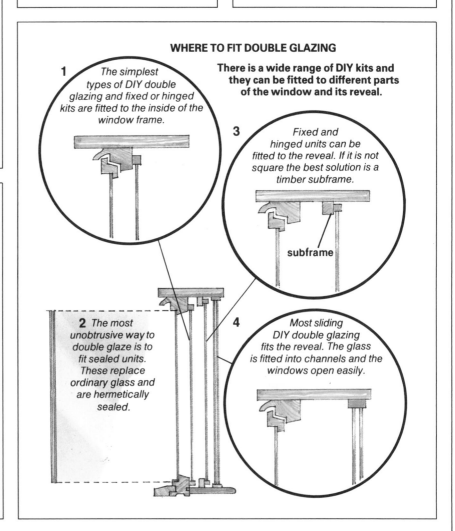

1 The simplest types of DIY double glazing and fixed or hinged kits are fitted to the inside of the window frame.

2 The most unobtrusive way to double glaze is to fit sealed units. These replace ordinary glass and are hermetically sealed.

3 Fixed and hinged units can be fitted to the reveal. If it is not square the best solution is a timber subframe.

subframe

4 Most sliding DIY double glazing fits the reveal. The glass is fitted into channels and the windows open easily.

SECURING WINDOWS

Windows come in many shapes and sizes. Some have side or top-hung casements, others pivot at the centre. Horizontal and sliding sashes and vertical sliding sashes are also common. To complicate matters further these windows are made in wood, aluminium and steel. So you may think you'll need a tremendous range of devices to make them secure against burglars. Fortunately, this isn't the case. Many bolts are made to fit a variety of windows, but there are also fittings specially made to fit specific window types.

RACK BOLTS

These bolts are suitable for wooden doors and windows. Apart from securing exterior doors they can also be fitted to interior ones to isolate each room in the house. In this situation the bolt has to be operated from the hallway side so the intruder can't see it from the room side of the door.

Rack bolts are dead-locking. The lock section is mortised into the door or window and the striking plate is fitted into the frame. For added security, the key is removable. You'll only need to fit one bolt to the middle of a small window, but on longer windows fit two, top and bottom. Likewise French doors should be fitted with two – one in the top of the frame, the other in the sill.

STAY BOLT

This type of lock is screwed either to the stay retainer or the frame to lock a casement window. Models are available for both metal and wooden frames and for stays with

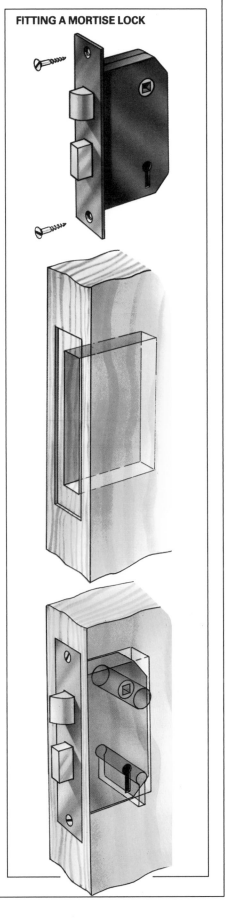

FITTING A MORTISE LOCK

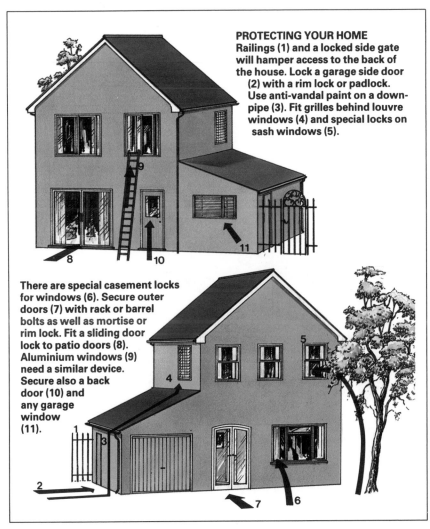

PROTECTING YOUR HOME
Railings (1) and a locked side gate will hamper access to the back of the house. Lock a garage side door (2) with a rim lock or padlock. Use anti-vandal paint on a down-pipe (3). Fit grilles behind louvre windows (4) and special locks on sash windows (5).

There are special casement locks for windows (6). Secure outer doors (7) with rack or barrel bolts as well as mortise or rim lock. Fit a sliding door lock to patio doors (8). Aluminium windows (9) need a similar device. Secure also a back door (10) and any garage window (11).

and without holes, so make sure you buy the right type.

One seeming advantage of these bolts is that the window can be locked slightly open to give some ventilation. But no self-respecting burglar would take longer than a few seconds with a hacksaw to cut through the stay.

CASEMENT LOCK

Although designed primarily for hinged casements, this type of lock is also suitable for some pivoted wood-framed windows. The lock is fitted to the opening window and the bolt engages into the striking plate which is on the fixed frame. A catch is used to secure the lock and it is released with a key.

Another type of lock has been specially designed so that it can be fitted to windows which have narrow wooden opening frames. With this device the body part, incorporating a screw thread, is fixed to the frame itself. When the window opening is closed the screw is driven with a special key into a stud fitted to the opening.

COCKSPUR LOCK

For hinged metal casement windows you can fit a key-operated lock. This is positioned below the cockspur handle and when the bolt is locked the handle is immobilised. Different types are made; some screw to the frame, others slot into its metal channel.

TRANSOM LOCK

This secures a metal transom window by clamping the metal stay to a fixed location bracket using a key. It isn't a permanent fixture.

SLIDING LOCK

This device is intended solely for horizontal sliding metal windows. It clamps in position on the window channel and is locked in place with a special key or by depressing a button. The lock can only be released using the key.

Sliding patio doors need to be fitted with a special lock that prevents the doors sliding past each other and stops them from being lifted out of their tracks.

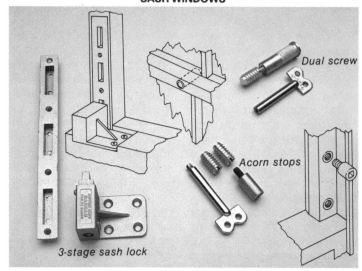

SASH WINDOWS

Dual screw

Acorn stops

3-stage sash lock

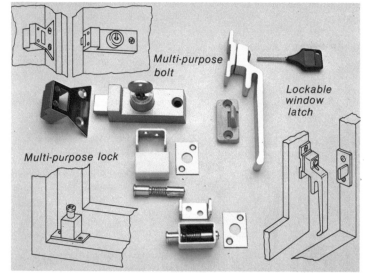

OTHER LOCKS AND LATCHES

Multi-purpose bolt

Lockable window latch

Multi-purpose lock

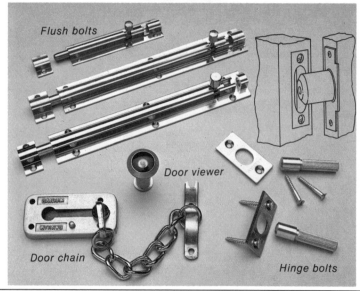

HINGED DOORS

Flush bolts

Door viewer

Door chain

Hinge bolts

DUAL SCREW

Any type of wooden window can be secured with a dual screw, but most commonly it is fitted to vertical sliding sashes. This is a concealed fixing made by drilling through the inner sash into the outer one. A barrel containing a threaded screw is then inserted into the inner sash and a special key is used to drive the screw into a stud fixed into the hole on the outer sash. Thus the two sashes can be fixed together. (With this type of fitting it's not possible to secure the window slightly open for ventilation.) Normally two of them are fitted to each window.

SASH LOCK

This is a more sophisticated version of the dual screw and is used on sliding wooden sash windows. It's best to fit one on each side on top of the inner sash. In fact the lock is screwed to the inner sash and a bolt goes into a hole drilled in the outer sash. You can place the locks so that slight ventilation is possible. Likewise, a 3-stage lock enables you to secure a sash in three open positions, all of which are too small to allow a burglar access.

SECURING DOORS

The first line of defence for securing a door, particularly an exterior one, is a good lock.

LOCKS AND LATCHES

The main advantage of a *mortise lock* is that, once fitted, its mechanism is inaccessible. On the other hand, you need a lot of care to cut a mortise into which the lock will fit snugly; and cutting the mortise itself may weaken the door.

The door must be at least 45mm (1¾in) thick, and you should also check that the stile (the upright part of the frame) is wide enough – though some locks are available in narrow-stile patterns.

Rim locks and latches are generally easier to fit because they don't need a hole cut into the thickness of the door. With a thin door a rim lock may be your only option;

most makes will fit doors as thin as 38mm (1½in). But in the case of rim cylinder locks, there is sometimes a maximum door thickness of about 60mm (2⅜in). Again, some models come in narrow-stile patterns. Rim locks have a 'staple' (a matching box that is fixed to the door jamb) instead of a simple striking plate.

BOLTS

After locks, the most popular form of additional security is a flush or barrel bolt. This is screwed to the door and then the integral bar is shunted across into a housing fixed to the frame. Obviously, the bolt can only be operated from the inside so it's not suitable for a front door, but it does give good security to a back door provided long fixing screws are used.

An automatic locking bolt is a useful bolt which can be fitted to wooden doors and to certain aluminium and other metal doors. It is easily mounted on the surface of

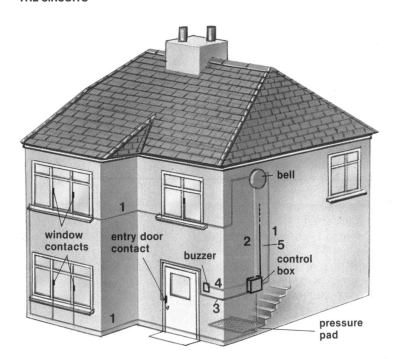

THE CIRCUITS

A typical burglar alarm system consists of circuits that link door and window sensors of various types to a central control unit. In the system illustrated here there are five circuits in all. **1** main loop to doors/switches. **2** circuit to alarm bell. **3** circuit to front door. **4** circuit to warning buzzer. **5** circuit to panic switch.

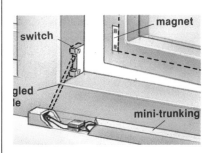

Make contacts less obtrusive by recessing them into the woodwork.

Positioning pressure pads.

the door and for added security the screws are concealed when the door is shut. The bolt is ideal for doors that are too thin to accept a mortise-type lock. A simple push action locks the bolt automatically and a special key is necessary to release it.

Hinge bolts are especially useful on outward-opening doors to prevent them being forced inwards on the hinge side. They come into operation as soon as the door is closed.

You have to drill a hole in the edge of the door to take the bolt, which is tapped home tightly. You then have to drill another hole in the door frame to accept the bolt as the door is closed.

Another type has a tongue that fits a slot chiselled into the door frame.

BURGLAR ALARMS

DIY burglar alarm kits usually consist of a master control box (powered by mains electricity or batteries), door and window sensors, pressure mats, an internal audible warning device and an exterior alarm bell.

However, components do vary from system to system, as does their method of operation.

In essence, the sensors are fixed to windows and doors and will detect a door or window being opened or glass being broken. The pressure pads are placed below floorcoverings and will react to the foot pressure of someone walking over them.

Ultrasonic alarms consist of a simple battery-operated unit resembling a hi-fi speaker which is placed so that its field of 'vision' covers the most vulnerable part of the house – perhaps the living room where you may have expensive TV, stereo and video equipment. When switched on, the piercing alarm will be triggered by anyone (and that includes a pet!) moving within its field of vision. These systems are extremely easy to install, primarily because they only include one sensor unit. They usually also include a time delay switch.

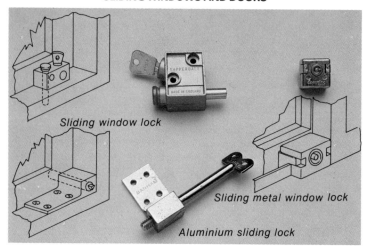

SLIDING WINDOWS AND DOORS

Sliding window lock

Sliding metal window lock

Aluminium sliding lock

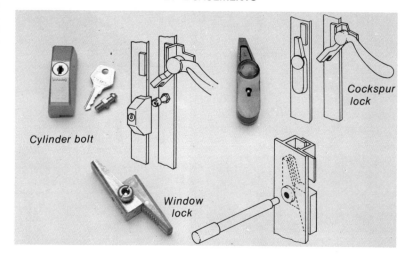

METAL CASEMENTS

Cylinder bolt

Cockspur lock

Window lock

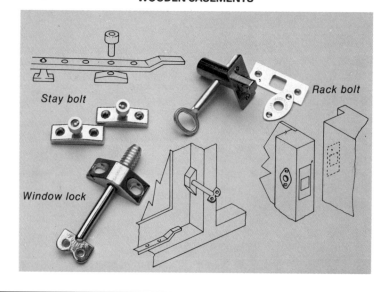

WOODEN CASEMENTS

Stay bolt

Rack bolt

Window lock

Chapter 6
EXTERIOR REPAIRS

DRAINS AND GULLIES

If a house was built before about 1955, its underground drainage system will almost certainly be constructed of socketed, glazed stoneware pipes, 100mm (4in) internal diameter and 600mm (2ft) long.

Drains of this kind were at risk from subsoil settlement, which could crack joints between sections and cause a leak. For stability, the trenches in which they were laid were first filled with concrete 150mm deep and 450mm wide (6in deep and 18in wide). The drains were laid and joined on this concrete raft and then given further stability by 'haunching' up the concrete so that it half-encased the stoneware drain.

If drains are to be self-cleaning and free from recurring blockages, they must be laid to a steady fall so that water flows through them at a reasonable rate. In pre-war days, 100mm (4in) drains were laid at a gradient of 1 in 40 (75mm in 3m), and 150mm (6in) drains, which might be used where several properties were drained in common, at a gradient of 1 in 60. If the drain was perfectly laid to an even fall this gave an adequate flow velocity, but such perfection was rarely obtained and so these rule-of-thumb falls made allowance for the retarding effect of the drain's many joints.

MANHOLES

Drains had to be laid in straight lines and provision had to be made for every part to be accessible for rodding in the event of a blockage. This was achieved by providing inspection chambers or 'manholes' at junctions and changes of direction. These chambers were built in 112mm (4½in) or 225mm (9in) brickwork, depending upon their depth. They had a concrete base in which was set a stoneware 'half channel' (in effect a stoneware drainpipe split down the middle). Branches joined this half-channel in special bends that di-

TYPES OF DRAINAGE SYSTEM
In some areas separate drains are provided for carrying household waste water and rainwater. All the soil and waste outflow is taken via inspection chambers to the house's main underground drain, which runs into the local authority's main sewer.

high-level vent pipe

inspection chamber (manhole)

yard gully

storm drain to deal with rainwater

public sewer

Rainwater runs in a separate drain to the authority's surface water drain, which usually runs alongside the main sewer. Any new downpipes must be connected to this surface-water drain.

rected incoming water into the main drain in the direction of flow.

The concrete was built up on either side of the half channel and the branch channel-bends to form a slope (called benching) that was trowelled to a smooth easily-cleaned surface. It was usual to render the walls of the inspection chamber with a sand-and-cement mixture to make them watertight. The inspection chamber was covered with a removable cast iron manhole cover, with two handholds, set in a frame of the same material.

At least two drain inspection chambers are likely to be found in the driveway – or side path – of small detached or semi-detached houses built in the immediate pre-war years. The manhole nearest

the house will bring together the lower end of the house's main soil and vent pipe and the outlet of the yard gully over which the branch waste pipes of the sink, bath and wash basin discharge.

The other inspection chamber will be found near the boundary of the property, and may well have no branch drains connected to it. At its outlet, however, will be seen the inlet of an 'intercepting trap' with, immediately above it, the stopper of a rodding arm that gives access to the length of drain between the final inspection chamber and the sewer. A fresh air inlet – a metal box with a grille at its front, behind which is a hinged mica flap – may also be found near this inspection chamber and connected to it by a length of pipe.

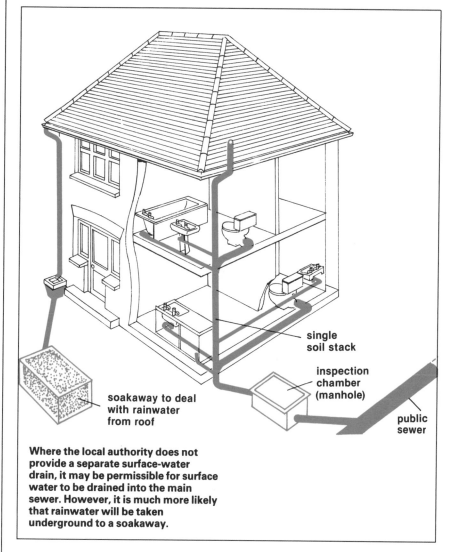

single
soil stack

inspection
chamber
(manhole)

public
sewer

**soakaway to deal
with rainwater
from roof**

**Where the local authority does not
provide a separate surface-water
drain, it may be permissible for surface
water to be drained into the main
sewer. However, it is much more likely
that rainwater will be taken
underground to a soakaway.**

remain undetected for weeks, even months. Unable to flow through the trap, the waste water in the inspection chamber soon rises to the level of the rodding arm and flows down it to the sewer. The problem only becomes obvious when the sewage in the base of the chamber has become so foul that its smell attracts attention. Whenever unpleasant smells are noticed near the front boundary of a property, look for a nearby drain inspection chamber and raise its cover. The chances are that this will be the cause of the trouble.

DRAINS TODAY

Nowadays, drains must still be laid in straight lines to an even fall and there must still be access to every part for rodding purposes. However, cement-jointed stoneware drains are no longer used. Household drains today may be of glazed stoneware with patent flexible push-fit joints, or long lengths of UPVC plastic pipe joined with ring-seal joints, or they may be of pitch-fibre with ring-seal or fusion joints. Trenches must still be carefully prepared and filled in, and suitable sand, gravel and other bedding and covering materials will have to be used. However, the flexible joints of modern drains are able to accommodate minor subsoil settlement, and it is no longer considered necessary or desirable to provide artificial stability with a 150mm (6in) thick concrete base.

Falls as steep as 1 in 40 are nowadays not considered necessary, as it has been found that falls as shallow as 1 in 60 or 1 in 70 will perform quite satisfactorily. Too steep a fall can, in fact, be as undesirable as one that is too shallow, as liquid wastes may run ahead of solids, leaving the latter behind to create a blockage.

Access must still be provided to every part of the drain, but there is a wide choice of the form that this access should take.

Conventionally-built brick inspection chambers are still in common use and these can be used quite satisfactorily in conjunction with drains of more modern mat-

The intercepting trap was there to prevent foul air (and possibly rats) entering the house drains from the sewer. The fresh air inlet was to ensure the adequate ventilation of the drain. The idea was that air would enter this inlet and flow constantly through the drain to escape through the main soil and vent pipe at high level. Drain air was supposed to be prevented from flowing out through the fresh air inlet by the hinged mica flap.

It rarely, if ever, worked quite like that. Moreover, fresh air inlets are particularly susceptible to accidental damage and vandalism. If your drainage system has one there is at least an even chance that the box will be damaged, the grille broken or the flap jammed open or shut. Many householders remove

the box and seal off the inlet. It serves little useful purpose and can itself be a source of unpleasant smells.

Intercepting traps are now considered to be more of a nuisance than they are worth: they are easily the most common site of drain blockages and they can produce a particularly unpleasant form of partial blockage that is a source of annoyance and embarrassment to the householder.

This is likely to happen when a sudden heavy storm temporarily fills the public sewer to capacity. Back pressure of the extra water pushes the stopper out of the rodding arm and inevitably it falls into the intercepting trap immediately below – creating a stoppage. It is, however, a stoppage that may erials. Nowadays, though, their walls are not rendered internally with sand and cement. This was liable to flake off and fall into the half-channel to form a blockage. If waterproof rendering is considered to be necessary it should be applied to the exterior of the chamber walls before the earth is backfilled around them.

Alternative forms of inspection chamber are those built up from pre-cast concrete sections with a conventional base and pre-formed GRP (glass-fibre-reinforced plastic) chambers with a choice of base configurations. These pre-formed chambers are circular in plan and can be sawn off to shorten them to the exact depth required.

Another relatively recent development has been the production of sealed-access drains and inspection chambers. The inspection chambers of sealed-access UPVC drainage systems have no need to be watertight. Nor is there any possibility of drain smells seeping out from under their manhole covers. Access is provided within the inspection chambers by access caps fitted tightly over the points at which branch drains join the main drain. A look into such a chamber will reveal just one or two round plastic access caps set into the flat concrete base of the chamber.

No matter how an inspection chamber is built and drain access provided, intercepting traps and fresh air inlets are never

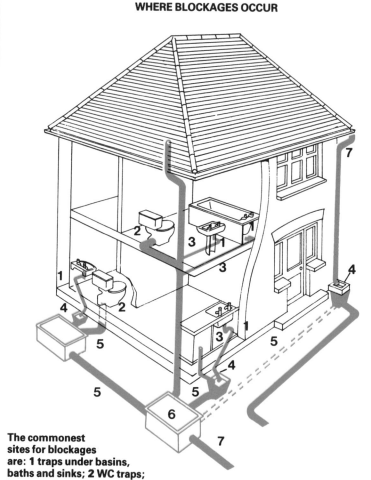

WHERE BLOCKAGES OCCUR

The commonest sites for blockages are: **1** traps under basins, baths and sinks; **2** WC traps; **3** waste pipes running to soil stacks, hoppers or gullies; **4** rainwater or yard gullies; **5** underground drain runs between house and manhole; **6** intercepting chambers; **7** underground drain runs between manhole and sewer.

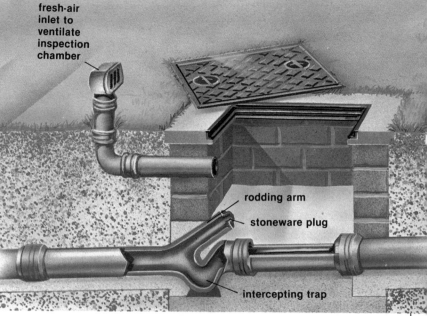

to public sewer

stoneware pipe (modern drainage systems have PVC or pitch fibre pipes)

fresh-air inlet to ventilate inspection chamber

rodding arm

stoneware plug

intercepting trap

used with present-day drainage systems. There should be no rats in well-maintained sewers and, with the sewer adequately ventilated by the main waste and vent stack of every property connected to it, there are no unpleasant sewer gases. The absence of the intercepting trap and the long lengths of smooth-bore pipe that are used in modern drainage systems have made drain blockages in such systems a very rare occurrence indeed.

RAINWATER DRAINAGE

In very old urban properties, gullies taking rainwater from roofs and yard surfaces may discharge into the same drain and by the same sewer as the household's waste drainage. Many years ago, though, sewage authorities realised that this was a thoroughly wasteful and inefficient practice. It meant that the flow of sewage to their treatment works was totally unpredictable, that they were having to provide larger sewers than would otherwise be necessary and that, during wet weather, their expensive-to-run sewage treatment plants were treating vast volumes of virtually clean rainwater.

Today in many areas separate drainage systems are provided – one for household sewerage and one for surface water. The latter drain, with its contents untreated, will discharge straight into a convenient river or stream. Where a dual system of drainage is provided, it is vital that any new connection – eg. from a new ground-floor WC suite, or from a new gully taking drainage from a utility room sink – should be connected to the drainage sewer. The connection of household sewerage to a surface water drain could result in serious pollution of a watercourse.

Where a separate surface water drain is not provided by the local authority, that authority may require householders to dispose of roof drainage water to a soakaway or soakaways. In such a case there is no need for the rainwater downpipes from the roof to discharge over a yard gully. The pipes can be taken underground to empty direct into the soakaway. Typically, this might be a pit 1.5m (5ft) deep and 1.2m (4ft) square, filled to within 200mm (8in) or 225mm (9in) of the surface with broken bricks and builders' rubble and covered with topsoil.

COMBINED DRAINS

It has, for many years, been the practice when developing new housing estates to drain anything up to fifteen or even more houses in combination. There are, for the building contractor, very con-

siderable economies to be made by this. The road needs to be opened only once instead of ten times and there is only one connection to be made to the public sewer. However, the blockage of a combined drain like this can be a fruitful source of neighbourly discord, and it is important that householders who use such a drain should be fully aware of the legal position before trouble arises.

This position depends on when the drain was built. Combined drains built before 1 October 1937 (when the Public Health Act 1936 came into force) are defined as public sewers, but those using them retain a certain direct responsibility for them. The sewerage authority (nowadays the Area Water Authority) is responsible for their repair, maintenance and cleansing. It can recover the cost of any repair and maintenance from the owners of the properties using them, but must pay for any cleansing itself.

Cleansing is usually taken to include clearing blockages, so, if

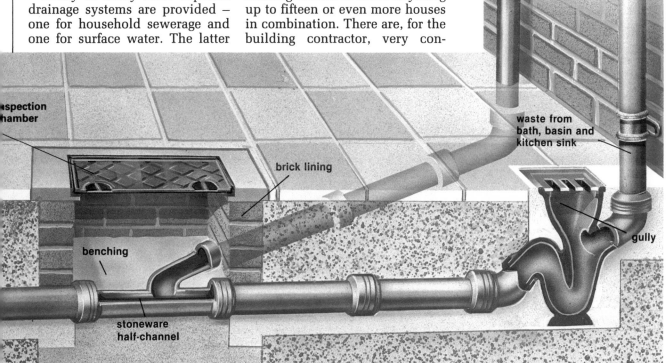

inspection chamber

brick lining

benching

stoneware half-channel

WC soil pipe

waste from bath, basin and kitchen sink

gully

your home is served by a pre-1937 combined drain, you can reasonably hope to have any blockages cleared free of charge.

If, on the other hand, the combined drain was constructed after 1 October 1937, it is a 'private sewer' for which the owners of the properties draining into it are responsible in every respect. If you think your house may be drained by a private sewer, consult your deeds and the plans of the property. If still in doubt, seek the on-

DRAIN-CLEANING TOOLS
You can hire a set of flexible rods for drain cleaning. These have various attachments and screw together to form the length you need.

drain cleaning rods and heads

Intercepting traps can cause blockages when a heavy storm fills the public sewer, causing back pressure to push the stopper out of the rodding arm. This can then fall into the trap to form a blockage. To stop this happening, remove the stopper from the rodding arm inlet and replace it with a disc of glass lightly cemented into place.

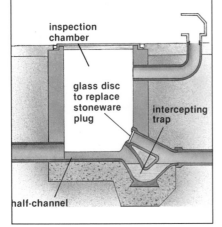

inspection chamber

glass disc to replace stoneware plug

intercepting trap

half-channel

CLEARING BLOCKED DRAINS AND GULLIES

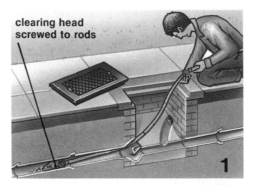

clearing head screwed to rods

1

How you go about clearing a blockage in your main drain depends on where the blockage is. If all the manholes are full of water, the blockage must be between the last one and the sewer. Clear this by rodding towards the sewer, via a rodding eye if one is fitted.

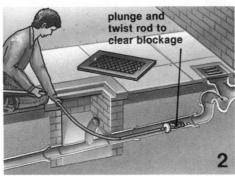

plunge and twist rod to clear blockage

2

If only the first manhole is full, rod from it towards the house; if you need to twist the rod, do so in a clockwise direction, *never* anti-clockwise, or you risk unscrewing sections of the rod and leaving them stuck in the drain.

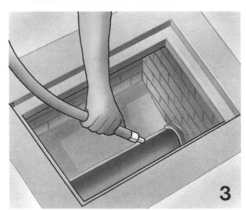

3

When the blockage has been cleared, flush with water from a garden hose. Leave the water running for a few minutes in order to remove silt that may have accumulated behind the blockage.

the-spot advice of the Council's environmental health officer. If you find that you are connected to a private sewer, make sure that everyone else whose property is connected to it is aware of the position and of his joint responsibility for dealing with blockages and other defects.

CLEARING A BLOCKED DRAIN

You'll know you have a blocked underground drain if you find a flooding yard gully, water seeping from under the cover of an inspection chamber or by a WC which, when flushed, fills with water almost to its rim and only very slowly subsides.

To clear a blocked drain you'll need a set of drain rods, which can be hired from a local tool hire firm. But first, find the blockage.

Raise the manhole covers. You will find that one or more drain inspection chambers are flooded. If your drain has an intercepting trap, it is probable that the blockage is at this trap and that it can be cleared by plunging. Screw two lengths of drain rod together and screw a drain plunger (a 100mm rubber disc) on to the end. Lower the plunger into the intercepting trap chamber and feel for the half channel at its base. Move the plunger along the half channel until it reaches the drop into the intercepting trap. Plunge down sharply three or four times. There will be a gurgling sound and the flooded inspection chamber will empty.

In an emergency you can improvise, using an old-fashioned mop or even a broom stick with a bundle of rags tied firmly to its end as a drain plunger.

If the blockage is in a length of drain, screw two or three lengths of drain-rod together, and lower the end into the flooded inspection chamber nearest the sewer. Feel for the half channel at its base and push the rod along this and into the drain towards the sewer. Add more rods as necessary and

keep pushing until you encounter and clear the obstruction. Twisting the rods clockwise may help them to push along the drain – but whatever you do, NEVER be tempted to twist anti-clockwise. If you do the rods will unscrew and some will be left irretrievably in the drain, leaving you with a problem far worse than you started with.

After clearing the drain, flush the sides of the inspection chambers down with a garden hose, and leave the water running down the drain for a few minutes to wash away silt that has accumulated behind the blockage.

Where a gully is overflowing but the manholes are clear, scoop out debris by hand from the gully trap and, again, flush through with water from the garden hose.

CLEARING BLOCKED GULLIES

If a gully overflows, the likeliest site for a blockage is in the gully trap itself. To clean it, lift off the grating or cover, then scoop out solid debris with a gloved hand or an old tin. Mop out all the water, then scrub the gully and trap with hot water and soda. Flush it out with clean water from a garden hose. If the blockage is between the gully and the next inspection chamber, rod the branch drain from the chamber to clear it as described earlier for drains.

The remedy for blocked grids is to discharge the kitchen and bathroom wastes into the gully *above* the water level but *below* the grid. To this end, back-inlet and side-inlet gullies are manufactured.

PLASTIC GULLIES

The revolution which produced the present generation of yard gullies came with the widespread development of plastics in underground drainage, and (at about the same time) with the Building Regulations of the early 1960s which insisted upon under-grid discharge in all new drainage work.

REPAIRING AN OLD MANHOLE

1. Use cardboard to catch debris.

2. Clean up the edge of the manhole.

3. Remove any damaged bricks.

4. Lay a mortar bed for the frame.

5. Replace the frame and level it.

6. Smooth over the whole area.

REPLACING A GULLY CHANNEL
The earthenware half-channel in an old gully may cause damp if it is cracked or the rendering in which it is set has become porous. To replace it, break out the old channel, rendering and gully surround. Buy a straight half-section of glazed earthenware pipe, lay it on a bed of sand and cut it to the length required with a cold chisel and club hammer. Bed the channel in mortar at a slight slope towards the gully. Build up the gully surround with new bricks, mortared into place. Slope mortar upwards and smooth off.

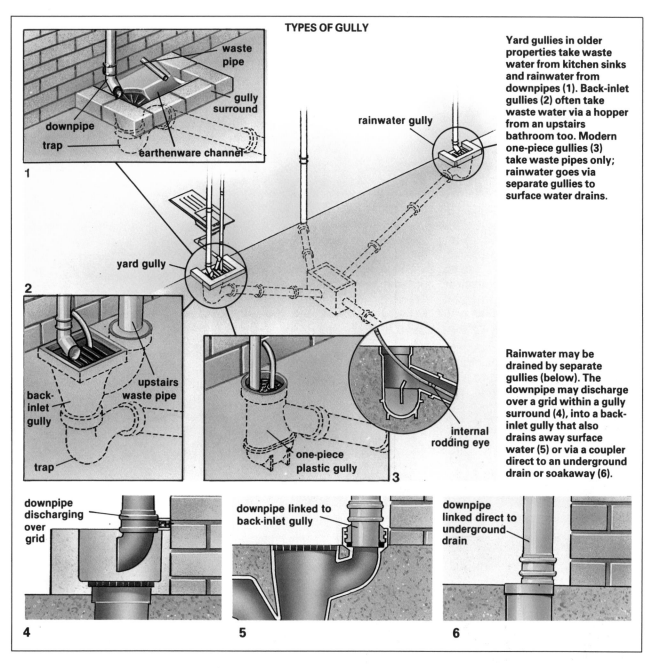

TYPES OF GULLY

waste pipe

gully surround

downpipe

trap

earthenware channel

1

rainwater gully

Yard gullies in older properties take waste water from kitchen sinks and rainwater from downpipes (1). Back-inlet gullies (2) often take waste water via a hopper from an upstairs bathroom too. Modern one-piece gullies (3) take waste pipes only; rainwater goes via separate gullies to surface water drains.

yard gully

2

back-inlet gully

upstairs waste pipe

trap

one-piece plastic gully

3

internal rodding eye

Rainwater may be drained by separate gullies (below). The downpipe may discharge over a grid within a gully surround (4), into a back-inlet gully that also drains away surface water (5) or via a coupler direct to an underground drain or soakaway (6).

downpipe discharging over grid

4

downpipe linked to back-inlet gully

5

downpipe linked direct to underground drain

6

A typical modern plastic gully assembly comprises three components – the gully inlet with two or more socket inlets for waste and rainwater pipes, the trap itself, and the outlet pipe. One-piece gullies are also available. Some manufacturers provide an access cap on the outlet pipe, eliminating the need for an inspection chamber at the point where the branch from the gully joins the main drain. Blockages occurring here can be cleared by removing the cap and inserting rods through the opening.

These components are usually solvent-welded into one unit on the site, care being taken to ensure that the gully inlet is positioned so as best to accept the waste pipes to be connected to it, and that the gully trap is positioned with its outlet pointing towards the main drain. To make solvent-welded joints, the surface of the spigot and the inside of the socket are roughened with medium-grade abrasive paper. Then an even coat of solvent cement is applied both to the spigot and to the interior of the

socket, using a wooden spatula to stroke the cement along (rather than round) the surfaces to be joined together.

To assemble the joint the spigot is pushed into the socket with a slight twist, and is held in position for a few seconds. The joint can be handled within minutes, but the gully should not be used for at least 24 hours.

Ring-seal push-fit joints may be used instead of solvent-welded ones to link the gully components. To make a joint of this kind, first clean the recess inside the socket and insert the sealing ring. You should then smear a small amount of petroleum jelly round the ring to lubricate it, and push the spigot firmly past the joint ring into the socket (or thrust the socket over the spigot if this is more convenient). Finally, you have to withdraw the spigot by 10mm (⅜in) to allow for expansion.

GULLY REPAIRS

An existing one-piece stoneware yard gully can be converted to under-grid discharge by discarding the existing metal grid and replacing it with a modern plastic one, provided with a slot through which the waste pipes can pass. All that is then necessary to convert the gully into a modern self-cleansing one is to lengthen the waste pipes so they pass through this slot to terminate below the grid but above the water level.

Stoneware gullies, once installed, are virtually impervious to damage but the same cannot be said about the cement-rendered gully surround. The cement rendering is very liable to crack, chip or flake off, leaving cracks into which potentially smelly waste water can seep. Defects of this kind can be repaired using a pre-packed sand and cement rendering mix. Add a PVA bonding agent to the mix to ensure good adhesion of the new mortar to existing surfaces.

REPLACING A GULLY

Occasionally it may be necessary (or at least desirable) to replace an existing glazed stoneware gully with a modern plastic one. As with so many plumbing and drainage operations, the most difficult part is likely to be the removal of the old fitting.

You will, of course, first have to excavate the surrounding surface to expose the old gully and its connection to the stoneware branch drain. Using a cold chisel and a club hammer, deliberately break the old gully so as to leave only the jagged end of its spigot outlet protruding from the drain socket. Remove the main part of the gully. Now attempt to remove the spigot and its jointing material from the drain socket *without* damaging the socket. Proceed carefully and with patience, using the cold chisel and a hammer. Keep the blade of the

INSTALLING A NEW GULLY

1. Install a PVC-to-clay adaptor.

2. Bed the gully trap in dry concrete.

3. Push trap outlet into the adaptor.

4. Lubricate the sealing rings.

5. Push the extra pipe into place.

6. Next position the gully hopper.

7. Check the depth of the hopper.

8. Back-fill round the gully.

9. Finish off with fine concrete.

SIMPLE GUTTER REPAIRS

1. Inspect your guttering regularly.

2. Get rid of debris with a trowel.

3. Strip rusty areas to bare metal.

4. Treat bare metal with a primer.

5. Coat inside with bitumastic paint.

efficient removal of rainwater is important to keep your outside walls sound. Any missing, damaged, or blocked guttering will result in water cascading down the face of your wall, leading to dampness, and eventually mortar and brick decay. You may be able to repair it; or you may be faced with having to replace whole sections or the complete system.

LEAKING JOINTS

Joints in cast iron gutters are made by overlapping the two lengths of gutter, and bolting them together with a layer of sealant in between to form a watertight seal. As this sealant begins to deteriorate with age, the joint starts to leak.

To make the repair, first remove the bolt holding the joint together. Often this is too rusty to undo, so hacksaw off the bolt between the nut and the guttering, or drill out the rest of the bolt. Lever the joint apart with an old chisel, and scrape away all the old sealant. Clean up the joint with a wire brush, then apply a finger-thick sausage of new sealant and bolt

chisel pointing inwards towards the centre of the socket and try to break the spigot right down to the shoulder of the socket at one point. Having done this, the rest of the socket will probably come away fairly easily. Alternatively, cut through the drain pipe just beyond the socket using a cutting disc and an angle grinder.

The manufacturers of UPVC drainage systems provide various means of connecting plastic gully outlets (or other UPVC drainage components) to existing stoneware drains. Typically, a 'caulking bush' component is provided; this is either solvent-welded or push-fit-jointed to the gully outlet. The

other end of the caulking bush is then connected to the socket of the stoneware drain with a gasket (to centre the bush and to prevent mortar entering the drain) and the joint completed with mortar.

GUTTERS, HOPPERS AND DOWNPIPES

The gutters on your home are supposed to capture all the rain falling on the roof and channel it to one or more downpipes. In turn these downpipes take the water into the main drain, a storm drain, or to a soakaway in your garden. This

FIXING JOINTS

1. Loosen fascia screws by tapping.

2. Make a new seal with mastic.

3. Fit a new nut and bolt through joint.

HALF-ROUND GUTTER FITTINGS

This is the most common style of fitting available for gutter work. The means of joining varies according to manufacturer.

gutter with seal end

union

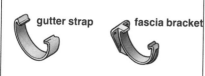

gutter strap

fascia bracket

ogee to half-round adaptor

An ogee/half-round adaptor will help to join gutters of different profiles. Other adaptors will connect new PVC guttering to half-round and square cast iron profiles.

90° gutter angle

Different gutter angles are available to get round corners which are not square.

120° gutter angle

running outlet

stop end

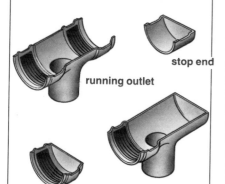

stop end with seal

stop end outlet

The gutter outlet should fit *inside* the top of the downpipe. Measure the downpipe diameter before you buy a new outlet.

the sections back together using a new nut and bolt and a couple of washers. Scrape off any sealant that has oozed out before giving the repair a coat of bitumen-based paint on the inside of the gutter.

DEALING WITH RUST

If one bit of guttering has rusted right through, it won't be long before the rest follows suit, so you may as well save yourself a lot of trouble and replace it all. If in the mean time you need a temporary repair, there are several suitable repair kits on the market. They consist of a form of wide metal sticky tape which you apply inside the guttering and over the holes with bitumen adhesive.

CHOOSING A REPLACEMENT

Assuming you won't be using cast iron again (you'll have a job getting hold of it and even more of a job putting it up, apart from the fact that it's expensive) your choice is between aluminium and plastic. Plastic guttering is made of UPVC (unplasticized polyvinyl chloride). It's probably the better choice for a do-it-yourself installation: it is far more widely available than aluminium, and has the edge in terms of cost and durability.

It is important to buy the right size of gutter. Too small, and it will be forever overflowing; too large, and you will have paid more for the installation than is necessary. It's all to do with relating the amount of water the guttering can carry to the amount of water likely to come off the roof during a heavy rainstorm. These calculations are complicated, but you can assume that they were done when the guttering was originally installed. Just measure the existing guttering at its widest point to find its size, and buy the same again. The most commonly available sizes are 75mm (3in), 100mm (4in), 112mm (4½in), 125mm (5in), and 150mm (6in). If in doubt, consult the manufacturer's literature.

The actual cross-section of the gutter may vary from brand to brand; this can make it difficult to join with existing guttering: for

SQUARE GUTTER FITTINGS

These fittings may be preferred to the half-round profile, although they are slightly less efficient at discharging water.

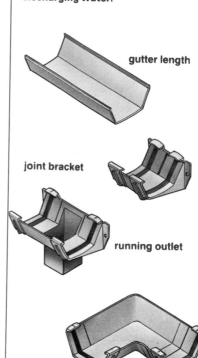

gutter length

joint bracket

running outlet

90° gutter angle

stop end outlet

long stop end

ogee adaptor

short stop end

Remember that if you have old square or ogee profile cast iron guttering matched with round downpipes, you will have to replace the downpipes as well when you fit new square-profile guttering.

example, the guttering belonging to a neighbour on a semi-detached or terraced house. Most firms offer adaptors to link their product with cast iron guttering, or with a different size from within their range. However, they tend not to offer adaptors to tie in with the equivalent size from another brand, so if possible stick to one brand throughout the installation. If you have to link up with a neighbour's gutter, find out which brand was used, and try to use the same.

There are many different fittings as well as lengths of guttering available on the market. Before you start buying your new guttering get hold of a manufacturer's brochure from the stockist you use and carefully check to ensure you have all the fittings you will need. Make sure you understand how the particular system works before you buy anything.

TAKING DOWN OLD GUTTERING

Cast iron guttering is heavy, and may also be rusted into place, so removing it can be tricky. But there is no need to be gentle with it: it doesn't matter if it breaks. The important thing is to work in safe conditions. If you are wrenching things apart, do it in a controlled way so you don't fall off the ladder, and so that great chunks of gutter don't fall down. Try not to drop cast iron guttering to the ground: it shatters easily, and, if it lands on a hard surface, dangerous fragments can fly off. If you toss the guttering clear of the house you might overbalance and fall off the ladder, so aim to lower larger sections gently to the ground with a rope.

Begin with the section linking gutter and downpipe. Cut through the old bolts holding the sections together. Then, if you lift the gutter slightly, you should be able to pull it free from the downpipe. Once it's out of the way, unmake the joints between the sections of gutter (as if you were repairing them), and lift the guttering off its supporting brackets. It may, of course, be screwed directly to the fascia board.

You can now turn your attention to the brackets themselves. These are usually screwed to the fascia board just beneath the eaves of the roof, and can either be unscrewed or levered off with a claw hammer. In older houses the brackets may be screwed to the tops or sides of the roof rafters, to support the weight of the iron guttering. If there is a fascia board to which

PUTTING UP PLASTIC GUTTERING

1. Joining to a neighbour's gutter.

2. Fix a string at one end of the run.

3. Fix the other end level.

4. Fix brackets at 1m (39in) intervals.

5. Fit the first section of guttering.

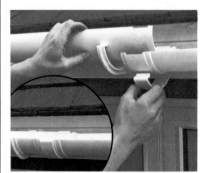

6. Joining the sections with a clip.

7. Cut the last section squarely.

8. Fix last section to the downpipe.

you can fit the new gutter, the ends of the brackets can be hacksawed off. Otherwise, you will have to lift off some of the roofing to remove them.

When all the old guttering has been removed, inspect the fascia board to make sure it is sound and securely fixed. If it is, fill the old screw holes and paint it before fixing the new guttering. If it isn't, it will have to be replaced.

FIXING NEW GUTTERING

At the end of the run furthest from the downpipe, fix a gutter support bracket as high up the fascia as possible, about 150mm (6in) from the end. The fixings here, and elsewhere, are made with 25mm (1in) screws. Choose galvanized ones to stop them rusting. Insert a nail into the fascia board level with the bottom bracket.

At the other end, 150mm from the downpipe, fix another nail; tie a length of string tightly between the two, and use a spirit level to check that the string is level. When it is, lower the second nail by the amount needed to ensure that the guttering runs downhill towards the outlet. This 'fall' varies according to the type of guttering, so check the manufacturer's recommendations. Usually, it is in the region of 5mm for every metre of gutter run. Once you've found the right line for the gutter, fix another bracket level with the lowest nail.

The next job is to fix the next bracket 1m (39in) from the one at the downpipe end of the run, using the string as a guide to set it at the correct level. Use these two brackets to support a length of gutter with the downpipe outlet attached.

Work your way along, building up the gutter run as you go and adding additional support brackets as required, again using the string as a guide.

In most cases, you will need a bracket every metre, plus one on each side of every join – although some ranges contain combined unions and support brackets. So check the manufacturer's recommendations.

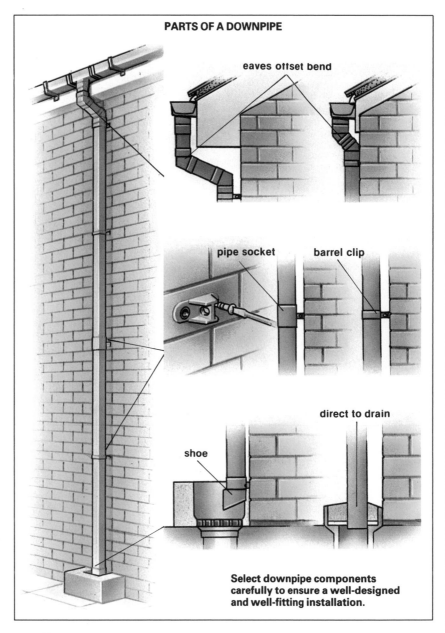

PARTS OF A DOWNPIPE

eaves offset bend

pipe socket   barrel clip

direct to drain

shoe

Select downpipe components carefully to ensure a well-designed and well-fitting installation.

The only problem you may run into is when you have to cut the guttering to length, either to go round a corner, or to finish the run with a stop end. Do the cutting on the ground using a hacksaw, making sure that you cut the end square. Any roughness left by the saw should be cleaned up with a file. If you want to turn a corner, fix the corner piece before cutting the straight piece of gutter to length. You can then use it to work out exactly how long the straight gutter length needs to be. When cutting to finish at a stop end, it is usual to leave about 50mm (2in) of gutter projecting beyond the ends of the fascia.

When you've finished the job and checked to see that all the joints are properly connected, take a bucket of water to the highest point of the gutter and pour it down. If the gutter doesn't drain all the water then go back and check your work.

MAINTENANCE OF DOWNPIPES

The faults that occur with downpipes are very much the sort of thing you get with gutters. For instance, you may occasionally get a blockage, caused by dirt, leaves

PARTS OF A DOWNPIPE

Downpipe fittings are available from various manufacturers, but they are all basically similar and your choice can be decided by convenience as much as anything else – just get whatever is sold by your local supplier. All the different sorts of downpipe fittings which you are likely to require are illustrated below. They are available in the square profile as shown or in the traditional round profile. Colours tend to be grey, white and black.

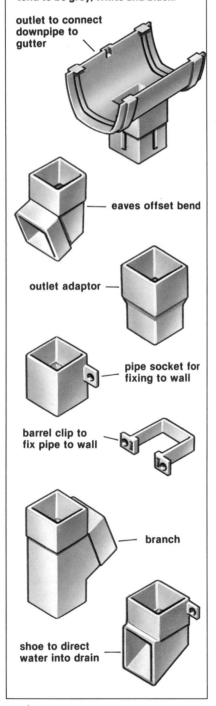

outlet to connect downpipe to gutter

eaves offset bend

outlet adaptor

pipe socket for fixing to wall

barrel clip to fix pipe to wall

branch

shoe to direct water into drain

or other debris being washed off the roof. You should clear this out as soon as possible, otherwise the surrounding wall of your house will get soaked with escaping water, and damp could find its way inside the house, You will see at a glance in which section of a downpipe the trouble has occurred because the joins between various lengths are not sealed. Thus when, during a downpour, water bubbles out of a join, you will know that the trouble lies in the section below.

The fact that the sections are just loosely joined also means that a blocked one can be taken down for clearance. You merely lift it up and pull it away, rather like a sliding door that operates in a groove.

On a straight run, you can probably push out the blockage with a long stick, although in stubborn cases you might have to tie a wad of rags to the end of the stick to make a sort of plunger. Bends have to be poked clear with a length of wire or cane. Then clean them by pulling through a piece of rope with a rag tied to the end of it.

Should the system have a hopper head, scoop debris out with a trowel. You should wear protective gloves as you do this. Take care not to push anything *down* the pipe; in fact, it's a wise precaution to push a rag bung into the top of the pipe as you work. When everything has been cleared up, fit netting to the top of the pipe so that the trouble will not occur again.

When one length of downpipe becomes defective, you can replace it with a new one, and there is no problem about inserting a length of plastic pipe in a cast iron system. It merely sits loosely in place, so you do not have to worry about sealing joints, as you do with gutters.

However, if one section of pipe corrodes, it is a good bet that all are coming to the end of their useful

FIXING A DOWNPIPE

1. Attach the outlet to the gutter.

2. Measure the length you need.

3. Attach the shoe to the last section of pipe with solvent-weld cement.

4. Connect downpipe to the outlet.

5. Screw the brackets to the wall.

FITTING A PVC GUTTERING SYSTEM

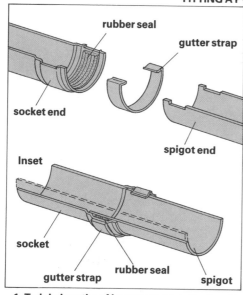

rubber seal

gutter strap

socket end

spigot end

Inset

socket

gutter strap

rubber seal

spigot

1. To join lengths of heavy-gauge guttering, fit spigot into the socket and clip on the strap.

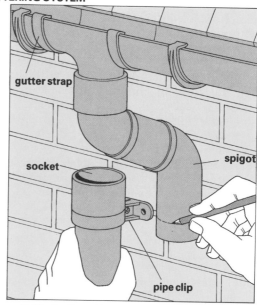

gutter strap

socket

spigot

pipe clip

2. Mark off an offset connector before cutting.

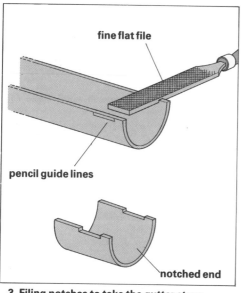

fine flat file

pencil guide lines

notched end

3. Filing notches to take the gutter strap.

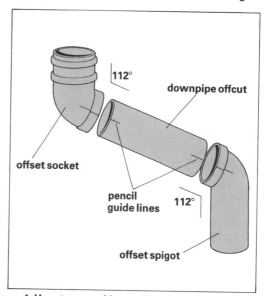

112°

downpipe offcut

offset socket

pencil guide lines

112°

offset spigot

4. How to assemble an offset connector.

FITTING A NEW HOPPER

1. Mark position of new fixing holes.

2. Use rustproof round-headed screws.

3. Seal joins with bitumen mastic.

life. And, of course, if the whole system becomes ramshackle, it is time to replace the lot – especially if you are fitting new gutters.

PUTTING IN NEW PIPES

There are a number of brands to select from, but little to choose between them, so settle for one which is available from a convenient store. If you are fitting new gutters, the pipes should be of the same brand, to ensure that you can link the two at the eaves. With a short length of guttering, consider replacing the whole gutter and downpipe system.

Inspect the existing system, and note down the exact replacements you will need. The pipes come in three common diameters – 75mm (3in) for extensions and the like, 100mm (4in) for most normal houses, and 150mm (6in) for very large roofs. Your pipes must, of course, match the gutters in size.

You have to begin the work with what is really the only troublesome part of the job, and that's taking down and discarding the old metal or asbestos pipes. Once you have freed each section you can lower it gently to the ground. Don't drop it as it may shatter. The clips holding the pipe to the wall can now be removed. If held by screws, there's a fair chance they will have rusted into place, and will be virtually impossible to turn. However, there is a trick you can use to start the screw moving: insert the screwdriver blade in the slot of the screw, then give the

handle a short sharp blow with a wooden mallet. This should free the screw so you can turn it. Alternatively, the brackets may be held in place by large galvanized nails cemented into the mortar – these will have to be prised out; if all else fails, cut everything loose with a hacksaw.

The pipe itself comes in a series of standard lengths and you'll probably have to join two or more sections together with a special socket, or cut one down to size, to make up the required run. You should leave an expansion gap of 10mm at the end of the pipe.

Plastic pipes are held to the wall with a series of small clips. These may come, according to the make, as one unit, or in two parts – a separate back-plate and clip. A clip should be placed at each joint socket, and at the manufacturer's recommended spacings in between – possibly every 2m (6ft 6in). Incidentally, there is no need to go to the trouble of drilling holes in brickwork to take the plugs for the screws that hold the clips in place. The pipes are so light that you will get a fixing by drilling holes into the mortar.

On a simple structure, such as a garden shed, the gutter may well be fitted directly into the top of the pipe without being sealed, and this makes it easier to locate and to deal with blockages. However, houses have eaves, which means the gutters won't be flush with the wall on which the downpipe is situated. So some form of fitting is

1. Prepare brickwork for repointing by chopping out the old pointing.

2. First chop out the horizontals, then go on to the verticals.

3. Use an old paintbrush to clean out debris from the joints.

needed to make the connection: this is known as an offset or 'swan neck'. You can make one of these yourself from an offset socket, an offset spigot, and a short length of pipe – perhaps an offcut from one of the main lengths. The joins between the gutter outlet and the offset socket and spigot should be solvent-welded, for these do need to be watertight.

With the top clip in place, you can plumb the drop of the pipe and mark the positions of the clips on the wall with chalk, so that they will all be directly underneath each other. Then fix these clips in place, and fit the pipe sections.

If your downpipes discharge into an open gully at the bottom, a curved or angled end, known as a shoe, is fitted.

REPOINTING TOOLS YOU CAN MAKE

To make a hawk, nail a 150mm (6in) length of broom handle or 25mm (1in) diameter dowel to a 200mm (8in) square piece of exterior grade plywood 19mm (¾in) thick. For weatherstruck pointing you need a frenchman: clamp an old table knife in a vice and heat the blade with a blowtorch, then bend the blade into a right angle. Make a pointing rule from planed timber with two square blocks screwed on as shown.

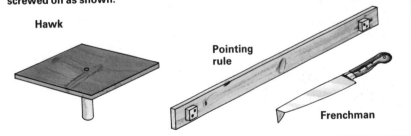

Hawk

Pointing rule

Frenchman

MORTAR FINISHES

1

2

3

4

5

A number of finishes are commonly used for mortar joints, depending partly on the conditions and partly on your personal preference. **1** Flush joints are best for bricks with crumbly or damaged edges. **2** Rounded or concave joints are an inconspicuous treatment for exposed walls. **3** Recessed joints are vivid, especially in angled sunlight, but are not suitable for use on exposed walls. **4** Struck joints have a bevelled profile which drains quickly. **5** Weatherstruck joints have a tiny overhang to throw water clear.

STARTING TO WORK

1. Begin by wetting joints (but not the brick faces) with a paintbrush.

2. Scoop up a small sausage shape of mortar on the back of the trowel.

3. Press the mortar into the vertical joints first, then the horizontals.

REPOINTING BRICKWORK

When pointing starts to crumble or crack, it needs repointing – a job that involves chipping out the old mortar and replacing it with new.

Complete repointing of a wall is only necessary if the damage is extensive. If the damage is restricted to small patches you should be able to make a neat repair. If you intend to paint your outside walls full repointing in flush pointing is desirable, but if the pointing is fairly new and fault-free you can get away with a little patching up.

STRUCTURAL DAMAGE

Pointing and brickwork that is badly cracked in clearly-defined runs across the face of the wall could be caused either by structural movement due to 'heave' or subsidence in the wall foundations, or by vibration from heavy traffic on a nearby road. Any such damage should be inspected by a builder or surveyor. Chimneys that need repointing may also be suffering from serious structural defects, and if not in use should be demolished by a builder.

Joints are the weakest point of the wall structure. If you are in any doubt about the condition of your brickwork, consult an architect or builder but don't try to patch up the damage.

EXPERIMENTING WITH COLOUR

If you are completely repointing a wall you may want to colour the mortar; if you are patching small areas you will need to try and match the colour of the existing pointing so that the patches don't show up. Different coloured sands give a range of mortar colours and your builder's merchant can tell you what is available. Cement colouring can also be bought and added to the mix – it is usually combined with a plasticizer and is available in black, brown, green, yellow, red and orange.

Experiment with any colouring before you tackle the whole job. If you are trying to match mortars you won't know if you've got it right until the pointing is dry. It's best to leave a sample for a couple of weeks before going on. Special colours will also be a different shade when dry.

STRUCK AND WEATHERSTRUCK JOINTS

1. For struck joints, recess one edge of the vertical, then the other.

2. Bevel the horizontals by drawing the edge of the trowel along.

1. With weatherstruck joints, run the trowel along to leave an overhang.

2. Run a frenchman along the pointing rule to trim off the overhang neatly.

TOOLS FOR POINTING

You will need the following tools: a club hammer and 12mm (½in) cold chisel to chip out old pointing (a pointing chisel with angled tip is better still); a pointing trowel – like a brick trowel but only 125mm (5in) to 175mm (7in) long; a hawk for carrying the mortar (a bucket is easier to carry on a ladder).

MORTAR MIXES

Use dry-mixed mortar for small jobs; it is obtainable in bags ready to mix with water. Buy a mix labelled 'sand/cement' or 'rendering' mix. It is usually grey in colour when dry.

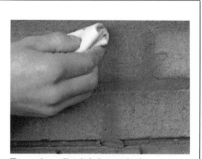

To make a flush joint, rub the surface of the pointing when nearly dry with a piece of sacking.

For larger jobs, mix cement and soft (bricklaying) sand in the ratio of 1:6 and add a plasticizer to make the mix more workable and frost-resistant.

Take care when using coloured mortar for pointing; you may get patchy results unless you are meticulous in measuring out quantities of pigment.

METHOD OF WORKING

Frost will damage your new pointing and very hot weather will cause the surrounding bricks to dry out, however much you soak them, sucking moisture from the mortar and weakening it. Work on a mild, dry day.

Start raking out at the top left-hand side, and work across and downwards (reverse the procedure if you're left-handed). Work on no more than 2 sq metres (21 sq ft) at a time. Be careful not to damage the edges of the brickwork and keep the groove square. Brush out the joints thoroughly to remove all old mortar fragments and dust.

The amount of mortar you mix up depends on how quickly you can work – in average conditions a mortar mix will be workable for a couple of hours. Roughly speaking

you will need 2½ bucketfuls for 1 sq metre of wall – allowing for wastage and provided that you are filling to a depth of about 15mm (⅝in).

Try to get a workable but stiff consistency. Drag the edge of a trowel across it; this should leave 'wrinkles' if the consistency is dry enough.

Dampen the joints with clean water, using an old brush – this should prevent the bricks from absorbing water too quickly from the mortar and thus weakening it. Transfer some mortar to the hawk, pick up a small sausage of it on the back of a trowel and transfer it to the first joint, pressing it in firmly to fill the gap completely. Start off by filling in all of the vertical joints (perpends) in your working area and then go on to the horizontals (bed joints).

It is very easy to splash the wall below your working area with mortar, which may be difficult to get off, especially if your mix is too wet. Hang a polythene sheet or an old linen sheet over the wall below, with long battens to prop it in place. If the bricks do get spattered don't attempt to wipe off the mortar with water as this makes a worse mess – leave it to dry and then brush it down with a stiff-bristled brush.

There are a number of different pointing finishes to be done when you've filled the joints in the area on which you're working. You'll obviously want to match the existing finish on a small repair job, but you have a free choice if you are completely repointing a wall.

For recessed joints, form the joints (left), and then trim the edges with a home-made scraper.

To make rounded joints, draw a piece of metal piping along the joints to form a rounded indent.

For an exterior wall in an exposed position weatherstruck joints are best as they are angled to throw rainwater off very effectively. Rounded (or concave) joints are quite common and can be made with a length of plastic piping, while struck and recessed joints show very little mortar and they give the brickwork an interesting shadowy appearance – but this is not the most protective of pointing finishes and is not recommended on exposed walls. Flush joints are used where the edges of the bricks are damaged and crumbly or when the surface of the wall is either to be decorated later on with paint, or rendered.

REPLACING A DAMAGED AIRBRICK

A damaged or broken airbrick can allow vermin to get under the floors of the house where they can multiply.

To remove a damaged airbrick, use a hammer and cold chisel to break out the pieces and clear mortar from around the opening in the brickwork. Buy a new airbrick

To replace a damaged brick, chip it out carefully and replace with one of the same colour if possible.

of the same style and size as the old one. Modern airbricks are produced in metric sizes and rather than have an airbrick that is considerably smaller than the existing opening, it is better to choose the next size up and enlarge the opening instead.

In a solid wall it is unlikely that the opening in the wall will be lined, but in a more modern house with cavity walls the cavity between the inner and outer skins of the brickwork should be sealed to prevent dissipation of the airflow into the cavity instead of beneath the floor. This is done with pre-formed clay ducts or by lining the opening with slates. If the cavity is found not to be sealed when the old airbrick is removed, a duct should ideally be formed in the opening before the new airbrick is fixed in place.

Replacement airbricks will be of clay, cast iron or cast aluminium, and in all cases they fit flush with the surface of the wall, being bedded on cement mortar. The mix to use is 1 part cement to 6 parts sharp sand, with a little plasticiser to improve workability.

Assuming that your replacement airbrick is the same size as the old one, just dampen the opening, spread some of the mortar in the bottom of the hole, ease the airbrick into place, and press more mortar in around the brick. Strike off excess mortar level with the wall surface.

RENDERING

Rendering is a mortar mix made of Portland cement, sand, some lime and possibly a few additives and pigments.

It is very important to use the correct type of sand, so make it clear to your supplier that you want a sand for rendering. It will be a type of sharp sand; soft sand and builder's sand for bricklaying mortar are not suitable.

The correct proportions for different mixes are shown on page 200. But to save time in buying and

The commonest type of airbrick is the square hole pattern (A and B); airbricks with rectangular holes (C) or louvres (D) admit more air.

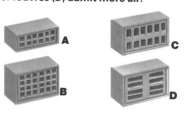

FITTING AN AIRBRICK

1. Push the new airbrick into place.

2. Force mortar deep into the gap.

3. Trowel the mortar to a neat finish.

mixing the materials, some part-mixed and completely pre-mixed products are available.

Ready-mixed dry materials for rendering are available in paper sacks, and all you need do is add water. The manufacturers have accurately batched the ingredients and they may have included additives to improve workability and setting. Don't make your own additions to the mix.

Masonry cement is a ready-mixed blend of ordinary Portland cement with additions to improve the mortar. It should be added to sand alone to produce a complete mortar. Don't add anything else.

Lime and sand mixtures can be supplied but make sure you order one specially for rendering. The supplier can also offer to include certain additives to improve the mix. These materials need to be measured out carefully so it is best left to the specialist supplier. The mixture is bought slightly damp and it should be kept in this state. You can store it for a week or more on a clean drained surface, but protect it with a tarpaulin or polythene sheet to prevent it getting wet or drying out too quickly.

When you come to use it, it must be mixed with the correct amount of Portland cement – check with your supplier to find out what proportions are needed. Use ordinary or sulphate-resisting Portland cement, but not masonry cement.

RENDERING EDGES AND CORNERS
Use expanded metal beading at edges and corners for a neat, strong finish. Use stop bead around windows, doors and other openings (A) and angle bead at internal corners (B).

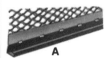

A   B

Don't render over the dpc. It's best to stop the render above the dpc, in which case you can use a bell cast or flared render stop. This shape directs water away from the wall.

If the render is carried below the dpc, cut a slot in the render sloping down towards the ground to throw off the rainwater.

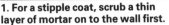

1. For a stipple coat, scrub a thin layer of mortar on to the wall first.

2. Load the brush and go over the same area with a stippling action.

Fibre-reinforced rendering mortar is another ready-mixed product available in bags. Strands of glass fibre are mixed in with the mortar and allow the mortar to be applied in a layer only 6mm (¼in) thick. The fibres reinforce the rendering to prevent shrinkage and cracking and the finished surface has a good resistance to impact and wear. Again, follow the maker's instructions and do not use additives.

PREPARING THE SURFACE

You will have to fix beading at external corners and around window and door openings and at the bottom edge so you have a hard edge to work to.

Fix temporary battens to the wall to divide the area into manageable bays. Their thicknesses should be equal to the thickness of the render coat. There's no need to fix battens at the bottom edges since the beading will provide a firm edge. Finally, before the first coat is applied, dampen the area to even out the suction.

TOOLS AND EQUIPMENT

You will need some or all of the following tools: a hawk to hold the mortar up to the wall; a plasterer's trowel – this is a rectangular steel trowel with a central handle; a steel float for smooth textures; a wood float for texturing the final coat or tamping pebbledash into place; a scoop for applying spatterdash or pebbledash; a comb – this consists of a wooden handle with protruding nails for scratching a key into the undercoat; a screeding board for levelling the surface – this is usually 125mm (5in) wide, 15mm (½in) thick and about 1200 to 1500mm (4 to 5ft) long; a spot board to hold the mixed mortar before use, approximately 700mm (30in) sq; a Tyrolean machine for applying a Tyrolean finish.

A cement mixer is desirable for all but the smallest jobs; it can be hired by the day or week from plant hire shops.

You may also need a wheelbarrow, shovels, watering can,

CHOOSING THE RIGHT MORTAR MIX

Type	cement:lime:sand	masonry cement:sand
1	1:0-¼:3	—
2	1:½:4½	1:3½
3	1:1:6	1:5
4	1:2:9	1:6½

| Background to be rendered | Smooth/scraped/ textured finish | | Rough cast/ pebbledash |
	Sheltered conditions	Exposed conditions	For all conditions
Strong, dense	2/3	2/3	2/2
Fairly strong, porous	3/4	3/3	2/2
Fairly weak, porous	4/4	3/3	—

polythene sheeting, buckets, hammer and nails and possibly ladders or scaffolding or a platform tower.

APPLYING THE FIRST COAT

Many surfaces benefit from a thin stipple or spatterdash coat before the main coats of render are applied. These coats will improve the key of a wall and they will even out the suction too. Before application, the wall must be brushed clean of any loose material and damped down if it is absorbent.

Spatterdash is a mix of 1 part Portland cement and 2 parts coarse sand, with just enough water to produce a thick slurry. It must be kept well stirred. All you have to do is pick up a small amount in a hand scoop and fling it on the surface, working from top to bottom. Build up a 3 to 5mm (⅛ to ³⁄₁₆in) layer and do not smooth or level it off in any way.

A stipple coat is a mix of 1 part Portland cement and 1½ parts sharp sand. Again it is mixed to a thick slurry but instead of using water, a mix of equal parts water and PVA building adhesive is used. This slurry is brushed vigorously on to the wall with a banister brush (dustpan brush) and then immediately stippled with it to provide the key.

MIXING THE MORTAR

The materials for an undercoat or top coat should be mixed together dry until a uniform colour is obtained. Then add water a little at a time until just sufficient has been added to give a workable consistency. The mix must not be too wet or it will slump down the wall. Continue mixing for about two minutes after the water has been added, then turn it out on to a spot board and take to the work.

It is a good idea to cover the bulk of the mix with polythene to prevent it drying out. If the mix does stiffen up, retemper it by turning with a shovel. Add more water only if absolutely necessary, and then only with a watering can fitted with a rose. All mortar from a batch should be used within two hours of mixing.

APPLYING THE UNDERCOAT

The undercoat may be up to 15mm (⅝in) thick, but on dense backgrounds the *total* thickness of render should not exceed 15mm, and in this case the undercoat will be much thinner.

Work with the hawk in one hand and the trowel in the other. Place about half a shovelful of mortar on the hawk and hold it to the wall. Then, starting at the top, press the mortar on to the surface a little at a time.

When the hawk is empty smooth over the area before picking up some more mortar.

When one bay is covered, use a screeding board or long straight-edge to rule off excess mortar. Then, when the coat has stiffened, comb the surface with scratches about 5mm (³⁄₁₆in) deep. This will form a key for the following coats. However, take care not to scratch right through the coat, and do not scratch at all if you are going to apply a Tyrolean finish.

Cover the surface with polythene to retain moisture while the mortar is setting – for about four days – then remove it to allow the mortar to dry out for another three days. You can then apply the next coat. Any fine cracks that may develop in this coat will not affect the final render.

APPLYING SMOOTH RENDERING

1. For smooth rendering, clean off the bricks and roughen them up.

2. Nail up battens, then lay on a thin coat of render and scratch it.

3. Let the scratch coat set for a day, then lay on the second coat.

4. Use a straightedge held across the battens to rule off the render.

5. Remove the battens, then fill the gaps with mortar, pressing in well.

6. Leave to set for half an hour, then apply a smooth finishing coat.

ROUGHCAST RENDER

1. Roughcast is mortar mixed with crushed stones or pebbles.

2. Use a scoop or trowel to pick up a small amount of the mix.

3. Fling the mix at the wall from a distance of about 500mm (20in).

APPLYING THE TOP COAT

How you apply the top coat will depend on the type of finish you want. Smooth and scraped finishes are laid on with a trowel; with pebbledash the final coat is trowelled and pebbles or stones are thrown on to it. Rough-cast and Tyrolean are wet mixes thrown on to the wall either by hand or machine.

Whatever finish you choose it is essential to protect the surface while the mortar dries out. Any covering must be held clear of the surface, as uneven setting may cause a patchy appearance. Try not to let wind blow under the covering as that could increase evaporation and make the mortar dry out too quickly. If the surface does start to dry out early, careful spraying will help – mostly during the first three days.

ROUGH-CAST

Rough-cast gives a very rugged-looking and rough-textured finish. Pebbles or crushed stones are mixed with the mortar, which is then thrown at the wall as a wet dash. As the pebbles or stones are mixed in the mortar this is a very long-lasting and hard-wearing finish.

The mix consists of 1 part Portland cement, ½ part lime, 3 parts sharp sand and 1½ parts shingle or crushed stone. The maximum size of the coarse materials may vary from 5 to 15mm (³⁄₁₆ to ⅝in). Add water until the mix has a fairly wet, plastic consistency.

The mix is taken to the work in a bucket and a hand scoop is used to fling the mix on to the wall. Great care must be taken to get an even texture and consistent thickness. If you make a mistake don't attempt to trowel the surface; instead, scrape off the mix while it is still wet and try again.

PEBBLEDASHING

This is one of the most popular finishes and is produced by throwing small stones or pebbles on to a freshly-laid mortar coat. It is sometimes called dry dash. The undercoats for this finish should include a waterproofing additive.

The finishing mortar coat which receives the pebbles is called the butter coat. It is a mix of 1 part cement, 1 part lime and 5 parts sand, with enough water to make a slightly wetter mix than you use for smooth finished render. It should not dry out too quickly and to help this the background may be dampened to reduce its suction. The butter coat is laid 6 to 10mm (¼ to ⅜in) thick and a straightedge can be used to level off the surface.

The pebbles or stone chips must be washed and drained first. Place the stones in a bucket and fling

TYROLEAN FINISH

1. Load the machine with 5-6 trowels full of the special mix.

2. Turn the handle of the machine to flick the mixture at the wall.

3. Go over the wall again until it is evenly covered.

them into the wet finish coat with a hand scoop. Try and obtain a close and even texture. When a large area has been covered, *lightly* tamp the surface with a clean dry wooden float for a good bond.

A lot of the dry dash will fall off during the application, so spread a clean polythene sheet at the base of the wall to catch it. Use a sieve and watering can or hose to clean the stones, and re-use them.

SCRAPED FINISH

This is a fairly smooth-textured finish. The final coat of mortar is laid on with a trowel, levelled off with a straightedge, then trow-

FORMING ASHLAR JOINTING

1. An effective finish for smooth render is lines imitating stone blocks.

2. Using a straightedge, draw in the lines on marks made previously.

3. The vertical lines are marked in exactly the same way.

elled smooth with a steel float and allowed to harden for several hours. Then the surface is 'torn' or scraped with a suitable tool – an old tenon saw blade is ideal. This breaks up the cement-rich surface and drags out some of the coarser particles of sand. Take care to scrape the surface evenly, and when complete brush the surface with a soft brush to remove any dust and leave a crisp texture.

TYROLEAN FINISH

This is a spattered finish applied with a hand-operated machine which flicks wet mortar on to a base coat. The result is an even, coarse, open honeycomb texture which is very attractive. The finish coat is made up from a prepacked mix which is available in a range of pale colours. These mixes vary so you should follow the makers' instructions regarding the amount of water to add. The hand spray machine can normally be hired from the supplier of the Tyrolean mix or from plant hire firms.

ROOF REPAIRS

Roof tiles are made either of clay or concrete. They're available in a wide range of shapes, sizes and colours, with a shiny or matt glaze, and in a wide variety of profiles.

The basic tile used on the main part of the roof measures 265× 165mm (10½×6½in), and it has a slight bevel or sometimes a double camber so that each tile is bedded down evenly on its neighbours.

There's also a wider 'tile-and-a-half' tile, which you use at the edge, or 'verge', of the roof to maintain the bonding pattern without having to cut tiles. Shorter 'ridge under' and 'eaves under' tiles are made for use at the top and bottom of the roof slope respectively, in addition to numerous half-round and angled tiles to seal the ridge and 'hip' of the roof.

Plain tiles are usually simply hooked on to the fixing battens by the two integral 'nibs' under their top edge; they also have two holes below the nibs so that they can be nailed to the battens at every third or fourth course to make the structure more secure. The tiles are set out on the roof in a 'double lap' pattern in which each tile overlaps two tiles below it and is itself overlapped by the two tiles above it. This means that the whole roof is covered by at least two thicknesses of tiles and three at the lap.

REACHING THE ROOF

It's vital that you work safely and securely while on the roof. You'll need either a ladder or scaffold tower to reach gutter level and a roof or 'cat' ladder to enable you to move about and work on the roof slope and at its apex.

You must secure your ladder to the house at the top by tying it to a ring bolt at the soffit to prevent the ladder sliding sideways as you climb on to it from the roof ladder. If your house has overhanging eaves you'll have to use a ladder stay to position the ladder out from the wall; but you'll need to secure it as well.

Otherwise like a conventional ladder, a roof ladder has a large hook at the top, which secures it to the ridge of the roof, two wheels for running it up the slope, and pressure plates, which spread the load over the fragile surface of the roof. Crawlboards are an alternative to a roof ladder. They usually

PEBBLEDASHING

Work from the top, covering the wall with an even layer of stones.

comprise slot-together sections of slats having footholds at right-angles, a ridge hook, wheels and pressure plates.

REPLACING A PLAIN TILE

Because replacement of a single plain tile is easy and cheap it isn't worth attempting to repair a single damaged tile, except as a stop-gap. In which case you can trowel thick mastic into the crack, or cover the tile with a strip of self-adhesive flashing strip, tucking the top under the tile in the course, or row, above. If a piece of tile has broken off you can temporarily stick it back with epoxy putty or glass fibre resin repair paste.

Replacement of damaged tiles is, however, the best solution. To make this task easier you need two small wedges made from offcuts of softwood about 25mm (1in) thick, 150mm (6in) long and tapering almost to a point. Push the wedges under the sides of the two tiles in the row above the one you're going to replace. The wedges will hold these tiles clear of the damaged one, allowing you to slide the point of a bricklaying trowel underneath, lift its nibs clear of the batten and remove it.

Tiles are usually held at every third or fourth course with nails. If the damaged tile is one of these you may be able to loosen the nails by working the tile from side to side, but if this fails you may have to pull them free with a pair of pincers, or saw off their heads by inserting a hacksaw blade underneath them.

Try to buy a replacement tile of exactly the same size, style and colour as the one that you have removed. Rest the new tile on your trowel and, with the wedges still in place, simply guide the tile upwards until its nibs hook over the batten. When it's correctly positioned, remove the wedges and the job is complete.

REPLACING AN AREA OF TILES

If a small area of roof is to be renewed, first remove the damaged tiles from the top course within this area and then work down the roof until all the tiles are removed from the defective area, leaving the felt (if present) and battens exposed. You'll probably find a lot of dust and debris on the felt surface, which you can brush away carefully with a hand brush.

Replace the broken tiles with new ones by hooking them over the battens, working upwards course by course from the lowest point. Fit the tiles in the top course using the method previously described for replacing single tiles.

REPLACING INTERLOCKING TILES

Single lap interlocking tiles are usually made of concrete and they are widely used on modern houses

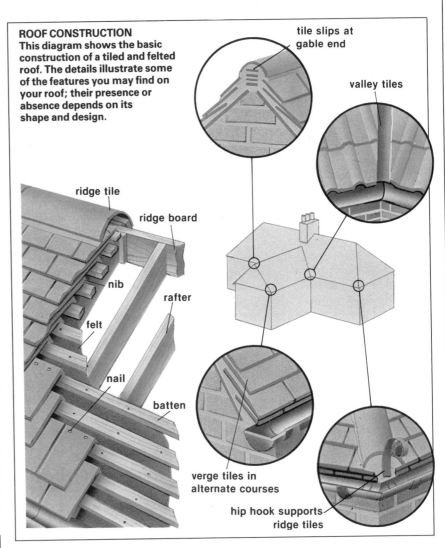

ROOF CONSTRUCTION
This diagram shows the basic construction of a tiled and felted roof. The details illustrate some of the features you may find on your roof; their presence or absence depends on its shape and design.

tile slips at gable end

valley tiles

ridge tile

ridge board

nib

rafter

felt

nail

batten

verge tiles in alternate courses

hip hook supports ridge tiles

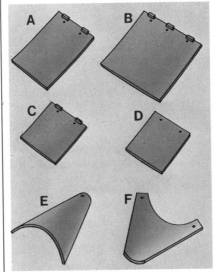

ROOF TILE TYPES
Roof tiles, basically described as 'plain' or 'single lap' are made of clay or concrete in a range of shapes, sizes, colours and profiles. *Plain tiles* include: (A) standard tiles for use within the roof area – they're flat, or curved to ensure they're bedded evenly; (B) wider than tile-and-a-half tiles for use at the ridge; (C) shorter ridge-under tiles for use at the ridge; (D) nib-less, half-length eaves-under tiles, nailed under the last tile to give a double thickness at the eaves; (E) hip tiles to seal the external angle between two slopes; (F) valley tiles to seal internal angles. *Single lap* tiles include: (G) concrete interlocking tiles for use within the roof area; (H) pantiles, nailed in place or interlocked.

A

B

C

D

E

F

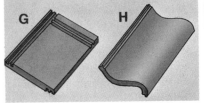

G

H

and on houses that have been re-roofed. Adjacent tiles interlock with one another and it's usual for each course to overlap the one below.

Replacement of defective tiles follows basically the same guidelines as for plain tiled roofs; tiles in the course above are lifted with wedges, which makes it easier for you to lift and remove the damaged tile below.

This type of tile is often nailed at every course and therefore you'll have to remove or cut through the nails. Additionally, interlocking tiles may be fastened with clips hooked over the interlocking ridge and nailed to the battens; in a case like this you'll have to lever out the clips first. A single replacement tile of this type can be replaced without a clip.

Some clay pantiles are simply hung on to the battens and if these tiles become displaced or need replacement it's best to refix them by drilling each with a masonry bit to make a hole near the top edge so that they can be nailed to the

ERECTING A ROOF LADDER

1. Make sure your access ladder is secure, then haul up the roof ladder.

2. Turn the ladder over so that the hook latches over the ridge.

batten. The last tile in the repair, which you can't nail because the surrounding tiles overlap it, can be held with epoxy putty or a gap-filling building adhesive.

FITTING NEW VALLEY TILES

Valley tiles are frequently found as an alternative to a metal-lined valley at the junction of two roofs. They can be used on plain and interlocking tile roofs but they can be tricky to replace. Usually they

are fixed with nails and the adjacent tiles interlock into them. Consequently you may have to remove a larger number of tiles in order to gain access to the fixing. If possible, you can attempt a simple repair using self-adhesive flashing strip tucked under the tile above.

REPAIRING RIDGE TILES

Ridge tiles, which seal the apex of the roof, are held in place with mortar. It's common for the mortar

REPLACING A SINGLE TILE

1. Open up a gap using wedges.

2. Remove the broken tile.

3. Guide the new tile into place.

REPLACING AN AREA OF TILES

1. Again use wedges to free the tiles.

2. Work from the bottom upwards.

3. Reposition the wedges as you work.

REPLACING A RIDGE TILE

1. Soak the edges of the ridge tile and press it firmly into a mortar bed.

2. Check that the tile is level, then smooth off the mortar joints.

between the individual ridge tiles to crack and fall out of place, but if the tiles are firmly fixed you can fill narrow cracks easily by injecting a bead of flexible non-setting mastic using a special gun for application. This mastic is available in various colours, including fawn and brown to tone with most roof tiles, so the repair shouldn't be too obtrusive.

Larger gaps can be refilled with mortar, using a one part cement to five parts sharp sand mixture to which you've added some PVA bonding agent to improve its workability. First rake old, loose mortar out of the gaps between the ridge tiles, with a cold chisel, and brush out any dust. Then dampen the cracks with water, splashed on from a paint brush; this prevents the new mortar from drying out too quickly and cracking. Brush on PVA bonding agent to aid adhesion, allow it to become tacky before trowelling in the new mortar, and smooth it off.

Loose ridge tiles should be removed, and the apex cleared of old mortar, before they are rebedded on fresh mortar. Soak the ridge tiles in water, and dampen the topmost course of roof tiles too, then trowel on mortar in strips at each side of the apex to coincide with the edges of the ridge tiles. Butter the end of the adjacent ridge tile with mortar to seal the two together. It's important to keep most of the underside of the ridge tile free of mortar to leave an air space, which keeps the timber ridge board (to which the rafters are fixed) dry; this also minimizes the chance of the ridge tiles cracking. Smooth off the mortar around the edge of the ridge tiles, forming a bevel to ensure good drainage of rainwater.

Seal the open end of the ridge tile at the edge of the roof with pieces of broken tile called 'tile slips', bedding them into place in a cement mortar filling.

FITTING HIP TILES

Hip tiles are half-round ridge-type tiles that are fixed along a sloping roof to the eaves. They can be repaired or replaced as described for ridge tiles, except that it's usual to fix a metal bracket called a 'hip iron' at eaves level as a safety precaution to help prevent dislodged hip tiles from sliding off the roof. The hip iron is simply screwed to the hip rafter using zinc-plated screws. Then the hip tile covering it is re-bedded on mortar with tile slips to help fill the cavity at the end.

SLATE ROOFS

Although slate is hardwearing, it does deteriorate with age. From the ground it may look in a good state of repair, but close up there are a number of tell-tale signs to indicate that all is not well. So although you can check for broken, slipped or missing slates from the street, it's far better to get up a ladder and have a closer inspection. If a slate has a flaky or powdery surface, then it isn't doing its job effectively, likewise with hairline cracks and split edges. And if some

ROOF TILE LAYOUT
Roof tiles are laid out in either single-lap or double-lap fashion. Single-lap tiles overlap their neighbours on one side and are overlapped by their neighbours on the other side; similarly the overlap is a single tile above and below (A). Double-lap tiles overlap two tiles below and are overlapped by the two tiles above; the overlap is double at the side also (B).

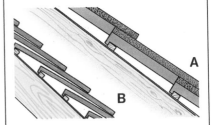

INTERLOCKING TILES
There are several designs of interlocking tiles. Some are nailed to the battens on alternate rows as well as hanging on nibs; others are fixed with tile clips to the battens.

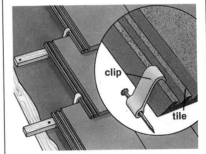

MAKING A BONNET HIP
To make a bonnet hip at the external angle between two roof slopes, nail the bonnet hip tiles to the hip rafter from the eaves up to the ridge; fill the cavity between each tile with mortar to bed them in place, and mortar in tile slips at the last tile cavity.

tile slips at gable end

REPLACING A SINGLE SLATE

1. Insert the slate ripper.

2. Break the nail fixing.

3. Slide the damaged slate out.

4. Next fit the lead strip in place.

5. Work the new slate into position.

6. Ensure slate is correctly aligned.

slates have slipped or fallen from the roof, check that the others have not deteriorated around the nail holes. Slipped tiles could also result from corroded fixing nails – a fault known as 'nail sickness'.

HOW SLATES ARE FIXED

Slates are usually nailed at either side to the battens which run at right angles to the rafters. The position of the fixing holes can vary up or down the slate and ideally they should be centre-nailed as opposed to head-nailed because there is then less chance of the slate being lifted by the wind. Head-nailing tends to be used for small slates. But whatever method you find, you'll have to copy it when replacing an area of slates.

REPLACING A SINGLE SLATE

If you're lucky you may only have to replace a single slate, and this shouldn't be too difficult or expensive to get hold of. While it's important to get a replacement of the same thickness (otherwise the new slate will not bed in correctly with the surrounding ones) you can always cut a larger one down to size. Also try to get one of a similar colour to the rest of the roof so the repair isn't conspicuous. Slates vary in size from 225×150mm (9× 6in) to 610×355mm (24×14in).

There are two ways of putting in the new slate. The traditional method uses a bent metal strip called a 'tingle'; and there is also a new proprietary method which uses a specially manufactured fixing bracket called a Jenny Twin.

But regardless of the method you intend using you first have to remove the damaged slate. To do this you'll need to hire a specialist tool called a slate ripper.

The slate ripper is a flat tool with cutting barbs at the end. To use it you slide it under the centre of the damaged slate and then move it to one side and pull it down so that the barb engages one of the fixing nails. You then have to give the handle a sharp tug or hammer blow to cut through the nail or pull it out. Repeat the process for the other nail and the slate should then be free to slide out.

What will now be obvious is that the course of slates above the one you've removed masks the fixing batten, so you can't just nail the new slate in place. The traditional fixing method gets round this problem using a tingle – a strip of lead, zinc or aluminium about 200mm (8in) long by 25mm (1in) wide. You have to fix one end of this strip to the batten just visible between the slates of the row below the displaced slate. You can use an aluminium alloy or galvanized clout nail to do this. Then push the replacement slate into position so that it is level with the

THE 'JENNY TWIN'
Use a proprietary fitting called a 'Jenny Twin' to fix single slates.

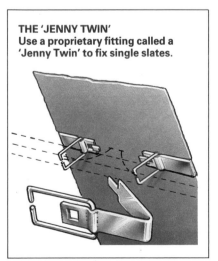

other slates in the row. You can even use the ripper to guide it into place. Finally, bend the tingle over the lower edge to secure the slate. In fact what you're doing is hooking it in place. A tip worth noting is to double over the end of the clip so that it is less likely to be bent flat by melting snow. Some people prefer to use stronger copper wire for the tingle because it is less conspicuous than the strip material.

This is where the hidden clip method can come in useful, because it too makes a repair that can't be seen, and it also has other advantages over the tingle. However, it can only be used on slate roofs attached to battens and not where slates are fixed direct to a boarded roof – one where planks

have been nailed over the rafters, and where battens are not used. You have to drill holes in the sides of the slate and fit special clips that will coincide with the top of the batten. You then slide the slate permanently in position.

CUTTING SLATES

Cutting slates isn't as difficult as it may appear but you should always do cutting work on the ground. When you have marked out the slate, score deeply over the lines with a tile cutter tool. Then support the slate on a flat timber board and tap a wide bolster chisel along the lines until the slate is cut.

Alternatively, you can hold the slate over the edge of the timber and chop along the line with a

builder's trowel. Another alternative is a slate cutter: once you've marked out the cut you just snip along the line – it results in a good clean edge.

FELT ROOFS

Although a felt roof may be perfectly adequate, it's susceptible to blistering and cracking of the covering. This can allow rain to penetrate and form damp patches on the ceiling and, if undetected, can even lead to the onset of rot in the roof timbers.

Look inside first for any signs that the roof might be defective. The most obvious signs are damp

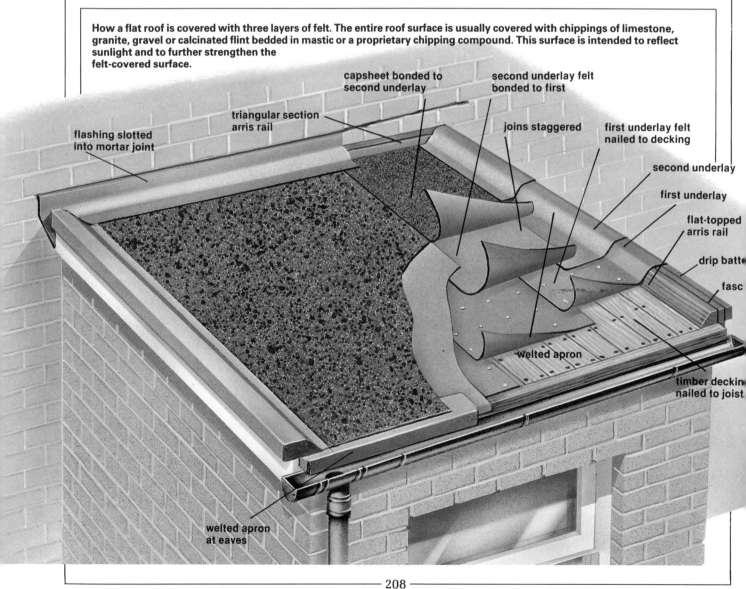

How a flat roof is covered with three layers of felt. The entire roof surface is usually covered with chippings of limestone, granite, gravel or calcinated flint bedded in mastic or a proprietary chipping compound. This surface is intended to reflect sunlight and to further strengthen the felt-covered surface.

flashing slotted into mortar joint

triangular section arris rail

capsheet bonded to second underlay

second underlay felt bonded to first

joins staggered

first underlay felt nailed to decking

second underlay

first underlay

flat-topped arris rail

drip batte

fasc

welted apron

timber deckin nailed to joist

welted apron at eaves

patches or even drips of water seeping through. But the source of the leak might not be immediately above this point; water can travel quite some distance on top of the ceiling before it eventually finds its way through and down.

ACCESS TO THE ROOF

You'll probably be able to reach your roof with just a ladder and it's usually perfectly safe to walk on the surface, as long as you wear soft-soled shoes. But, if you suspect that the decking or structural joists are rotten, you'd be wise to spread the load by laying scaffold boards across the roof so that you can walk safely.

It's best to check your roof after particularly hot weather because intense sunlight can cause cracks and bubbles in the felt. Look for pools of water on the surface after long periods of rain, as this could indicate a sagging in the structure of the roof. This sagging is another cause of cracks appearing.

REPAIRING MINOR FAULTS

You can usually seal small cracks simply by spreading on a bitumen mastic, but bubbles, caused by moisture seeping underneath the felt and then swelling in the heat of the sun, require different treatment.

First burst the bubble by making a cross-shaped cut in it with a sharp trimming knife, peel back the four triangular leaves you have formed and allow the moisture to dry out. Then bed the felt back in a cold bitumastic compound. Apply more compound on top of the repair, and then sprinkle a few chippings on top of it, pressing them into the mastic.

If the roof covering appears to be sound, yet there's still evidence of dampness, it's likely that the flashing strip has come away from the wall, allowing water to trickle behind. If this has happened, prise it away completely and rake out the mortar joint into which it was slotted, using a pointing chisel. Brush away any dust and debris, dampen the joint with water so the new mortar won't dry out too rap-

idly and crack, then mortar the flashing strip back in place and repoint the joint.

REPAIRING LARGE AREAS

If there aren't any obvious signs of localized damage, you will have to suspect extensive failure of the felt covering. You can either apply a waterproofing treatment to the existing roof, or strip off all the felt and re-cover it.

A waterproofing treatment can be given in two ways, depending upon how bad the damage is. The simpler method is to brush off as many of the loose chippings from the roof as you can, along with any other dirt and debris and then to

seal any cracks with mastic. Then brush on a bitumastic waterproofing liquid, applying a further coat of liquid followed by chippings.

But if the condition of the roof is poor it's advisable to remove the

LAYING FELT

1. Position a strip of underlay felt.

2. Nail the felt to the decking.

3. Paint on a thin margin of adhesive.

4. Nail on the second strip of felt.

5. Coat first underlay with adhesive.

6. Smooth out any air bubbles.

7. Finish with handfuls of chippings.

FITTING A CORRUGATED ROOF

1. Drill using a bit of a suitable size.

2. Clip caps over the screw heads.

3. Place the next sheet in position.

4. Drill through sheets and timbers.

felt and replace it. Estimate how much you'll need, buy it well in advance and cut it to the required lengths with a sharp trimming knife. Leave it flat for a few days, weighted down, to uncurl, or you could find that it won't stick properly and bubbles in the surface might result.

REMOVING THE OLD FELT

Start to strip off the old, bonded layers of felt using a tough wallpaper scraper or even a garden spade with a sharp blade. When you reach the last layer you'll need a claw hammer to remove the roofing nails that secure it.

When you have stripped the roof of felt completely, give the decking a thorough sweeping and then in-spect the boards for defects. You should replace any boards that are rotten and treat the new wood with preservative; don't use creosote, which is incompatible with bitumen materials used for re-felting.

LAYING NEW FELT

If you've a conventional planked or sheet timber roof, nail the first underlayer of felt to the decking, parallel with the drainage fall, using 20mm (¾in) extra-large-head galvanized clout nails. Start nailing in the centre of the sheet and work outwards, nailing at 150mm (6in) centres. Overlap the second and subsequent sheets by about 50mm (2in), seal with bitumen mastic and nail along the overlap at 50mm (2in) centres.

The second underlay must be bonded to the first with a bitumen mastic or special proprietary adhesive. You will find it easier to tackle half a length of felt at a time; lay the strip flat on the roof, roll half of it back and then paint the mastic on to the surface of the first, nailed underlay. Unroll the second underlay on to the mastic and press it into place, making sure that there aren't any air pockets trapped underneath; you can tread the strip down if you're careful. Roll back the other half, apply the mastic, then smooth this half into place.

You can fix the top layer of felt, the capsheet, in the same way. Cover the edges of the roof with felt strips called 'welted aprons'.

Finish off the roof by applying a coat of mastic or chipping compound to the entire roof, working in easily manageable sections towards your ladder. Then scatter on handfuls of 12mm (½in) chippings. You'll need about 100kg (220lb) of chippings for every 5 sq m (6 sq yd) of roof.

CORRUGATED PLASTIC SHEETING

Corrugated sheeting comes in various sizes and shapes. Plastic types are commonly available with a round or box profile. The most popular type is 75mm (3in) round profile, with the distance between each peak being about 75mm (3in). Other common profiles are 38mm (1½in) and 150mm

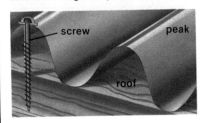

Where to nail corrugated plastic sheeting: for roofing, fix nails or screws through the peaks (crests) of the corrugations. For vertical situations (wall fixing) nail or screw through the valleys.

screw
peak
roof

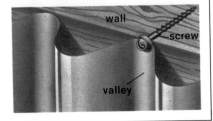

wall
screw
valley

Fitting a snowguard: if you live in an area of heavy snow, fit a snowguard to the eaves above a conservatory.

(6in). Sheet widths vary, though 760mm (2½ft) wide is a common width and lengths may be as long as 3050mm (10ft).

With some brands of plastic sheeting the material may start out clear but will become opaque or will 'yellow' when it is exposed to the weather. If you require a sheeting which remains clear in use you should therefore go for a brand which guarantees clarity; this will usually be more expensive but it will give you the result you want.

When you buy, check for quality. The sheets should be in good condition without cracks, splits or discoloration. When you get them home, store them so they are laid flat to prevent warping; cover them up if you're leaving them outside so they will be protected from the weather.

At the same time as you're buying the sheeting you will also need to think if you require any flashing material to seal the joint between the cladding or roofing and the existing wall. You might decide to buy pre-formed foam eaves filler strips so you can make a draught-proof seal at the ends of the corrugations, or special tape to seal the joints between the sheets. Follow the sheeting manufacturer's instructions as to the type of fixings you will need (these often come with special protection to prevent water from penetrating the fixings and cladding).

One of the advantages that plastic sheeting has over other corrugated materials is that it is easier to cut, but you should still work carefully to avoid splitting or tearing the plastic. Use a fine-toothed tenon or panel saw, holding it at a shallow angle as you cut, and support the material on both sides of the cutting line. Awkward or small parts can be cut with strong scissors or a pair of tinsnips.

Plastic sheeting is easier to cut when warm, so store it for a day indoors before you start working with it.

DRILLING AND FIXING

You will have to drill holes to take the fixings. You can use a hand

WEATHERPROOFING A CORRUGATED ROOF

You can seal the joint between the roofing and the wall with flexible, self-adhesive flashing tape (1). Prime the wall first with bitumen primer. Lay the first length of tape carefully along over the primed surface so it's in the exact position you want it to be (2). To prevent water penetration at any point, flatten any folds and the edges of the tape (3), and smooth out any wrinkles.

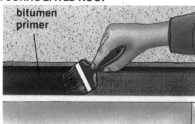

1. Use an old paintbrush to apply bitumen primer to the wall.

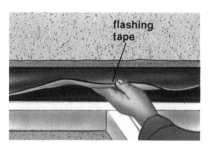

2. Leave the lower half of the tape free for the time being.

3. You can use a hammer and a wood offcut to get a neat finish.

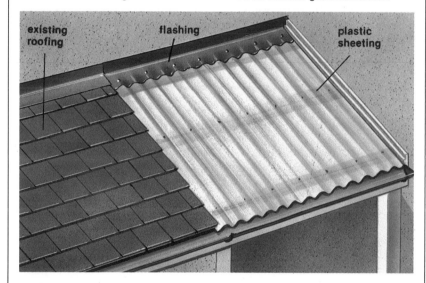

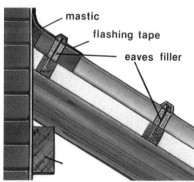

4. Where corrugations run at right angles to the wall, a combination of flashing tape and mastic can be used.

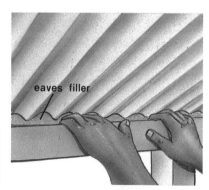

5. Press a strip of pre-formed plastic foam eaves filler into the gap along the top of the wall.

drill with an ordinary twist bit but a power drill will, of course, make the job go faster (to make drilling even easier you can make pilot holes with a bradawl first). You may find with plastic sheeting that a slightly blunt bit makes a neater hole than a new one.

The fixings should normally be spaced about 450mm (18in) apart. If there is not enough support beneath a crest in the corrugations to allow you to drill without distorting the sheet, you can get around this by marking the positions of the fixing holes, then turning the

---

USING A ROOF LADDER
To reach a chimney that's within the roof slope or at its apex, you'll need a roof or 'cat' ladder. This has a large hook (1) for securing it to the ridge of the roof, two wheels (2) for running it up the roof slope, and pressure plates (3) to spread the load over the fragile roof surface.

To fit the ladder, first turn it on its back and run it up the roof slope on its wheels. At the apex, turn it over so the hook anchors over the ridge. When climbing, use your hands on the rungs. Take one step at a time.

---

sheet over so that the crests become valleys and are easier to drill through. When you have drilled, turn the sheet back over again and fix it in place with the fixings passing through the crests.

The holes should be slightly larger – by about 3mm (⅛in) – in diameter than the shanks of the screws or nails, to allow for expansion and contraction of the sheet-

ing material. To avoid rust, use galvanized nails or non-ferrous screws; any fixing washers should also be galvanized. Make sure you don't over-tighten screws; a spiral ratchet screwdriver will make driving them in a simpler task.

CHIMNEY STACKS

A chimney isn't in the most accessible of locations: to reach it you will need special ladders and even scaffolding. You would be wise, therefore, to keep a regular check on its condition in case any damage becomes widespread.

Start your examination indoors: look for signs of dampness on chimney breast walls, and in the ceilings around chimney breasts in upper floor rooms: dampness here indicates that water is penetrating the flashings and running down the walls.

Stand away from the house to examine the stack: you'll find it much easier to spot defects if you use a pair of binoculars. Faults to look for include cracked or leaning pots, missing mortar pointing between the bricks, and cracked or damaged rendering or pebble-dashing. More seriously there may be cracks or large bulges in the masonry, or even a leaning stack: tell-tale signs that the structure is in a dangerous condition, and could even collapse during high winds.

In addition to making good any defects in the stack you may also feel it's worthwhile sealing off a disused chimney against rain, or even cutting down a tall, disused stack to a lower level for safety.

For work on tall chimneys that can't be reached from a roof ladder, and for more major jobs such as replacing or removing the chimney pot, you'll need a secure, flat working platform. There are specially designed chimney scaffolding sets available for hire, or you may be able to build a platform around the chimney using conventional scaffolding, which you can also hire.

DEALING WITH DAMPNESS

Dampness high up on a chimney breast wall and on a ceiling close to a chimney stack usually indicates problems with the flashings around the chimney stack, which seal the join between the roof and the base of the stack.

If the dampness is lower down the chimney breast wall, then the problem could be due to the flue and the fireplace having been completely sealed. In cases like this you should introduce a supply of air into the flue; the usual way is to fit an airbrick or ventilator grille in the blocked-off fireplace, and a chimney pot cap.

RENEWING THE FLASHINGS

Flashings may be triangular fillets of cement mortar, although sheet metal flashings made from lead or zinc are much more reliable.

At the sides of a chimney it's usual to have stepped metal flashings, which are tucked into the horizontal mortar joints at the base of the stack, and fold on to the roof, where they cover 'soakers' (separate pieces of lead or zinc interleaved between tiles or slates adjacent to the stack).

With modern single lap interlocking tiles, and occasionally with slate and plain tiled roofs, the stepped flashings may simply be beaten down or 'dressed'.

The flashings at the sides of a stack may be either the soaker or apron types, but invariably the flashing at the lower face of the stack is of the apron type. If the chimney isn't built on the apex of the roof, the upper side of the stack is weatherproofed with a metal channel and flashing, called a 'back gutter'. A chimney built into the ridge should be fitted with a 'saddle' flashing.

Each of these flashings can give trouble, often parting from the masonry or roof material to admit rain. With cement fillet or tiled flashings it's common for gaps to appear where the fillet moves away from the brickwork. In this case, if the fillet is sound, you can simply inject a bead of non-setting mastic into the crack. Such mastic comes in a cartridge and is applied by a special gun.

But if the fillet is badly cracked or crumbling, chip it away with a club hammer and cold chisel and replace it with a new flashing. You can use either fresh mortar or a metal-faced self-adhesive flashing strip, which is available in rolls. These strips are sold in various widths, 150mm (6in) wide being the most useful, and with an aluminium foil face or a grey finish that resembles lead.

Rolls of flashing are usually supplied with a small tin of primer, which you paint on to ensure good adhesion of the strip to the bricks and tiles; but it's not necessary to use this on slates. The primer is a black bituminous liquid, which

you apply in a band to the angle between the brickwork and the roof where the flashing is to go. After the primer has dried you can cut the flashing strip to length, peel off its backing paper and then press the strip carefully down into position. Roll it down firmly using a wallpaper seam roller. It's best to seal the lower face of the chimney first, followed by the sides and finally the back, or upper part, folding the flashing on to the previously laid strips in each case.

Original metal flashing may be torn, corroded or displaced, and this may allow rainwater to trickle behind and down the wall.

Displaced flashings usually pull away at the top where they're tucked into the horizontal mortar joints in the stack. If this has hap-

pened you should rake out the mortar joints and tap the flashing back into place with a hammer. Cut small strips of lead, roll them up and use them as wedges to hold the flashing in place. Spray water into the mortar joints from a house plant sprayer to prepare them to take new mortar and then repoint the joints using a mix of one part cement to five parts of sharp sand plus a little PVA bonding agent.

The best way to repair slightly corroded or torn metal flashings is to patch them with pieces of self-adhesive flashing strip. In the case of a leaking back gutter it's best to line it completely with a self-adhesive flashing strip. To ensure good adhesion, key the area to be repaired by rubbing it over with medium-grade abrasive paper.

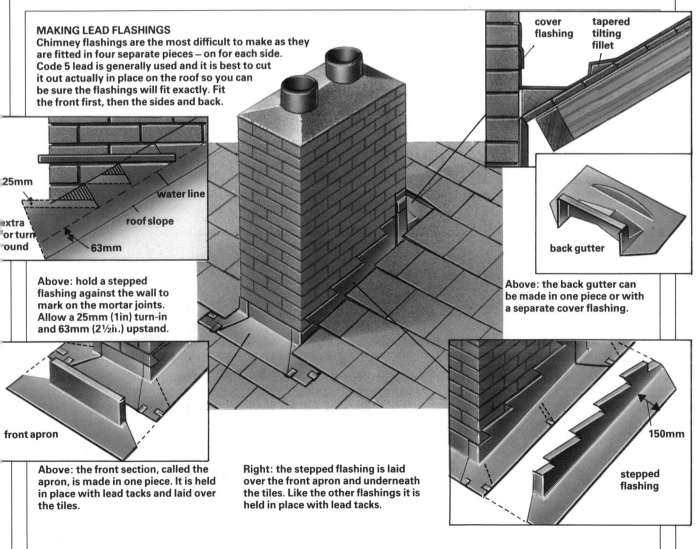

MAKING LEAD FLASHINGS
Chimney flashings are the most difficult to make as they are fitted in four separate pieces – on for each side. Code 5 lead is generally used and it is best to cut it out actually in place on the roof so you can be sure the flashings will fit exactly. Fit the front first, then the sides and back.

cover flashing

tapered tilting fillet

25mm

water line

extra for turn round

roof slope

63mm

back gutter

Above: hold a stepped flashing against the wall to mark on the mortar joints. Allow a 25mm (1in) turn-in and 63mm (2½in.) upstand.

Above: the back gutter can be made in one piece or with a separate cover flashing.

front apron

150mm

stepped flashing

Above: the front section, called the apron, is made in one piece. It is held in place with lead tacks and laid over the tiles.

Right: the stepped flashing is laid over the front apron and underneath the tiles. Like the other flashings it is held in place with lead tacks.

If a flashing is badly corroded the simplest solution is to remove it completely and replace it with self-adhesive flashing strip, which you can apply around the base of the stack without the need for stepping or inserting it into the mortar joints.

Leave any soakers in place as this will make it unnecessary to disturb the tiles or slates and will give a useful second line of defence.

Fitting a new lead stepped flashing around a chimney is best for the sake of traditional appearance – especially in an old house – and for long-lasting weather-proofing.

REPAIRING THE MORTAR JOINTS

If the mortar between the bricks in your chimney is missing or crumbling away it's likely that moisture will penetrate, soak into the bricks and, in winter, cause the masonry to crack. You should repoint the joints. The technique is the same as for conventional brickwork repointing (see page 197).

DAMAGED FLAUNCHING

Minor cracks in mortar flaunching can be repaired with stiff mastic pressed into the cracks. However, when the flaunching is badly damaged it's best to replace it completely. When you've removed the flaunching, check that the brickwork at the top of the stack is secure, and if necessary re-lay loose bricks using a 1:5 cement:sand mortar mix. Dampen the top of the stack and then spread on the new flaunching mortar using a mix of one part cement to four parts sharp sand to which you've added some PVA bonding agent to improve its workability.

The mortar should be thickest around the base of the pots and slope down to about 20mm (¾in) thick at the edges. The actual maximum thickness of flaunching mortar depends on the size of the stack: 65mm (2½in) close to the pot is about right on a small single-pot chimney. On very large chimneys with several pots you'll have to pack out the flaunching at the centre with broken bricks to give a

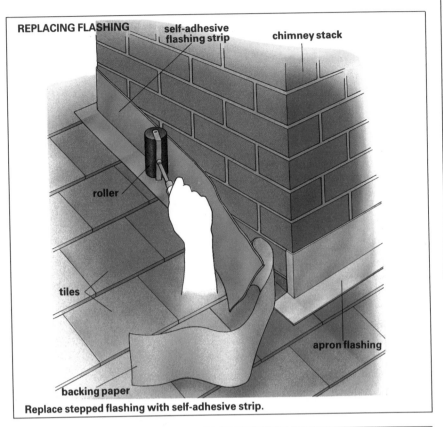

Replace stepped flashing with self-adhesive strip.

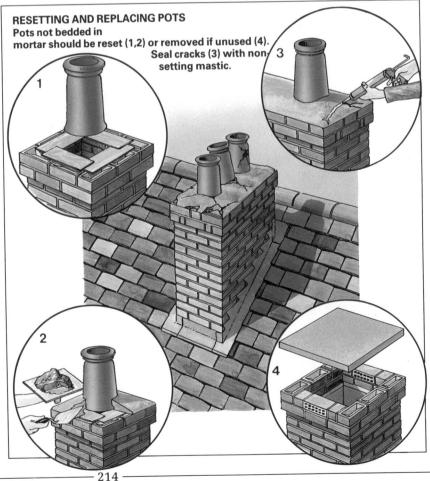

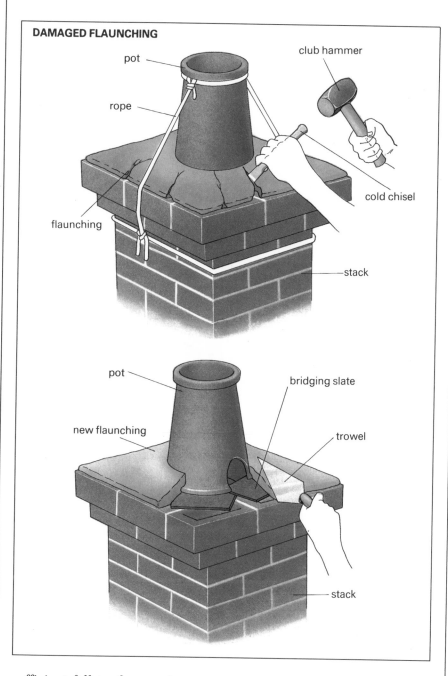

DAMAGED FLAUNCHING

pot

rope

club hammer

flaunching

cold chisel

stack

pot

bridging slate

new flaunching

trowel

stack

flue with airbricks. Then seal the top of the flue with a paving slab bedded on 1:5 cement to sand mortar mix, or cover it with slates and then spread new flaunching all over the top of the stack. When the mortar has dried, paint the entire stack with a clear silicone water repellent: this will prevent water from soaking into the stack.

RENDER AND PEBBLEDASH REPAIRS

To repair hairline cracks in smooth render, first widen the crack with a chisel. Undercut the edges to improve the bond, and brush out debris from the crack. Apply PVA bonding agent, then press a mortar mix of 5 parts sand to 1 part cement into the crack and smooth flush with the surrounding surface.

To repair 'blown' render, cut back the damaged section to sound edges. Undercut the edges, rake out the mortar joints and brush out dust and debris. Apply PVA bonding agent, then trowel on a new mortar mix of 1 part cement to 5 of sand and smooth off with a straight-edged timber batten.

To repair a pebbledashed area, first prepare the hole as for smooth render, then throw handfuls of matching pebbles on to the wet mortar and press them into the surface with a wooden float.

sufficient fall to throw rainwater clear of the stack.

CHIMNEY POTS

Leaning pots can be reset in new flaunching mortar, but cracked pots can't be repaired and should be replaced. Before you start work, secure the pots with rope to the stack; then hack off the flaunching.

Pots with a square base are available to fit the flue exactly, but pots smaller than the size of the flue opening will have to be supported on strips of slate.

SEALING THE FLUE

If the flue is no longer used, it's a good idea to seal it to prevent rain getting in. However, it's vital that you maintain an air supply inside to keep it dry and free from condensation. A simple solution is to clip a metal ventilator cap into the chimney pot. Alternatively, a clay type ventilator cap can be set into the pot, bedded in mortar.

A better solution is to remove the pots and replace at least two bricks from opposite sides of the

EXTERIOR PAINTING

The main parts of the house that have to be painted are the woodwork, metalwork, and possibly the walls. Plastic gutters and pipes do not need to be painted. It's up to you whether you paint the walls or not. Brick, pebbledash, stone and rendering can all be left in their natural state, but if the walls are in need of repair or are porous, stained and dirty, a good coat of paint will both protect the surface and brighten up the house.

The first thing to do is to take a long, critical look at your house to assess what needs to be done. Search for any defects that may affect the final paintwork. It is very important that you remedy every fault you find before you begin to paint, or the paint won't be able to do its job and your house will only deteriorate further. Preparation will usually be the most time consuming part of the decoration and will often be quite hard work. But it has to be done if you want your new paintwork to last.

WHAT TO PAINT FIRST

There is a good, logical painting sequence which holds for nearly all houses. In general it's best to start at the top and do larger areas before smaller ones. So if you're going to paint the whole of your house try to follow this order: do the fascia boards and barge boards first, followed by the gutters. The rendering (if any) comes next, then the windows and doors and finally the downpipes.

The reason for sticking to this sequence is that splashes of paint that drop on to the wall beneath a fascia or gutter, even if wiped off immediately, will leave a mark; but subsequent painting of the wall will cover it up.

WORKING IN SAFETY

To paint the outside of your house in comfort and safety you need the right tools and equipment. Always work from a step-ladder or an extension ladder and make sure

ACCESS TO WORK
A safe working platform is essential: you can use ladders or scaffolding.

WORKING WITH LADDERS

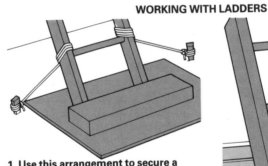

1. Use this arrangement to secure a ladder on soft ground.

2. Securing a ladder at the eaves.

3. Ladder accessories make working at height more comfortable.

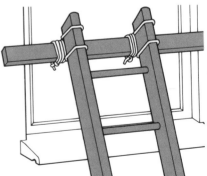

4. Arrangement for supporting a ladder at a window.

it stands on a firm and level surface. If the ground is uneven, push wedges under a board until the board is level then stand the ladder on this. You'll have to put down a board on soft ground too. If you're working on grass there's a danger of the board slipping, so drive in two stakes on either side of the ladder and tie the ladder to these with rope. On a slippery surface put down some canvas or sacking. Don't use plastic sheeting as a dust sheet, because the ladder could slip on it.

If you're working high up it's best to tie the ladder to something solid at the top. Don't tie it to the gutter or downpipe as these are not designed to take the extra weight and wouldn't support a ladder if it started to slip. The best way is to fix big screw eyes into sound woodwork such as a window sill, fascia or barge boards and tie the ladder to these. Or, if convenient, you can tie the ladder to the centre mullion of an open window. If there's no sound woodwork, it's advisable to drill and plug the wall to take the screw eyes. Fix them at intervals of about 2m (6ft) and leave them in place when you've finished so they're ready the next time you have to decorate.

Be sure to position the ladder square against the wall so it won't wobble, and lean it at the correct safe angle of 4 to 1: that is, for every 4m of height the bottom should be 1m out from the wall.

When working on a ladder don't lean out too far as it's all too easy to lose your balance. Never work from the very top of a step ladder as you'll have nothing to hold on to. A paint kettle is an essential piece of equipment as you can hook it on to a rung of the ladder, leaving both hands free.

A safer alternative to a ladder or step ladder is a tower platform which you can hire from most hire shops. The tower comes as a set of interlocking sections which you build up to the required height; you then lay boards across to provide the platform. A handrail fits around the top and there is plenty of room for tools and paint. The

THE TOOLS YOU'LL NEED

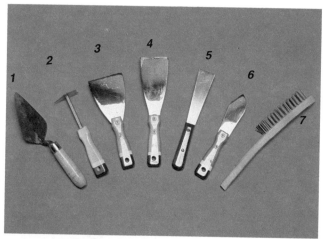

1 Small trowel for repointing; 2 combination shavehook; 3 scraper; 4 filling knife; 5 narrow filling knife; 6 putty knife for reputtying windows; 7 wire brush.

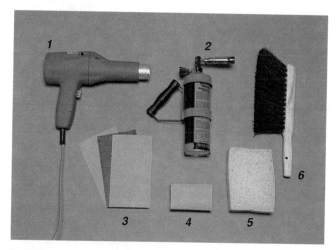

1 Hot air electric stripper or 2 gas blow lamp; 3 various grades of sandpaper and emery paper; 4 sanding block; 5 sponge; 6 stiff brush for removing dust.

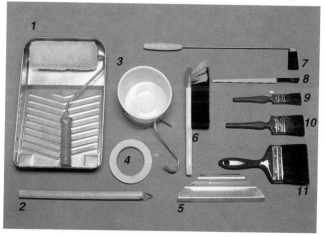

1,2 Long pile roller with extension handle, and tray; 3 paint kettle and hook; 4,5 masking tape and shield; 6 banister brush; 7,8,9,10 a selection of brushes for wood and metalwork; 11 wide brush for smooth surfaces.

towers can be extended over bay windows or round chimneys, so you can reach all parts of the house in safety.

WALLS

Wall surfaces can become cracked and dirty and a coat of paint will cover up repairs that don't match the original surface, and protect the wall from further damage. Examine the pointing and, if it has deteriorated, repoint with fresh mortar (see *Brickwork*, page 197). Don't worry about hairline cracks as these will easily be covered by the paint. The white crystalline deposit which sometimes appears on brickwork is known as efflorescence. It is caused by water-soluble salts in the brick being brought to the surface, and should be brushed off with a dry brush. Don't try to wash it off as this will only make it worse.

Pebbledash deteriorates faster than the other types of render, causing the pebbles to loosen and fall out. Paint will bind in the pebbles and protect small cracks.

Stop up cracks with mortar, using a mix of 1 part cement to 5 parts sand. Chip away very wide cracks until you reach a firm edge, then undercut this to provide a key for the new mortar. Dampen the surface, then stop up with a trowel. Use a float if the surface is plain, or texture the surface to match the surrounding area. See *Chimney stacks* (page 212) for other repairs.

MOULD AND STAINS

If there are any signs of mould or algae on the wall, treat this next. Mix up a solution of 1 part household bleach to 4 parts water and paint this on the affected area. Be generous with the solution and cover the area well. Leave for 48 hours for the bleach to kill off all the growth, then wash off thoroughly and brush down with a stiff brush. Proprietary fungicide treatments are readily available.

Rusty gutters, pipes and metal fittings can all cause stains if rusty water drips down the wall. So cure any leaks first and clean and prime

all metal to ensure there's no trace of rust. Mould and algae thrive on damp walls; even if you can't actually see any growth on a damp patch, there may be some spores lurking there, so you should make absolutely sure that you sterilize all stains with the bleach solution just to make sure.

DUSTY OR CHALKY WALLS

All walls, whether dusty or not, must be brushed down thoroughly to remove any loose material. But if, after brushing, the wall is still dusty or chalky, if a cement-based paint was used previously to decorate it, or if the wall is porous, you

COPING WITH FAULTY SURFACES

1. Brittle, crazed paint on roughcast rendering: stabilize and repair gaps by stippling on rendering.

2. Iron staining: prise off pebbles that cause the staining. Cover stains with aluminium leafing primer.

3. Common brick blistering: scrape off flaking paint, then apply a waterproofing solution.

4. Paint film failure: rake out old filler, remove all flakiness and repair with exterior grade filler.

5. Movement cracks: stabilize, fill, then apply bitumen waterproofer, glass fibre strip and a sealer.

6. Chalkiness: remove with a stiff bristle brush, apply a stabilizer and paint over.

will have to brush on a stabilizing solution. This will bind together loose particles to allow the paint to stick and it will seal a porous surface and stop paint from being sucked in too much.

WOODWORK

If paintwork on windows frames is in good condition all you need do is give them a wash and a light sanding. If the paint is cracked and flaking, a little more preparation is needed. Occasional chipped or blistered portions can be scraped off and cut back to a firm edge. As long as the edge is feathered smooth with glasspaper, it should not show too much. If previous coatings are too thick for this treatment, build up the surface with outdoor grade hard stopping until it is just proud of the surrounding paint, then sand level when it's dry. Don't allow the stopping to extend too far over the edge of the damage or it'll be difficult to sand it smooth.

There comes a time, however, when the condition of the old coating has become so bad that complete stripping is advisable. A blow-torch or electric hot air stripper are the quickest tools to use to remove old paint.

A chemical paint stripper is the best method to use near glass in case the glass cracks under the heat.

KNOTS, PUTTY AND HOLES

Check the woodwork for any live knots which are oozing out resin.

PAINTING WALLS

1. Load the roller, pressing against a short plank of wood in the bucket.

2. Using the roller, cover a strip on your right hand side.

3. Paint a second strip.

4. Protect pipes with newspaper.

If you find any, strip off the paint over them and then play a blow-torch or electric hot air stripper over them to burn out the resin. Sand lightly and treat with knotting, then prime when dry.

You should also check the putty fillet round each pane of glass, and if any has disintegrated, rake it out with an old knife. Then sand and prime the wood and bed in new putty using a putty knife. Use linseed oil putty on wood and metal glazing putty on metal frame win-

dows. All-purpose putty can be used on either. Smooth the putty and leave it for about a week before painting.

Rake out any cracks in the wood and cut back wood which is starting to rot. If a large amount of wood is rotten – usually along the bottom edge of a sash window – a larger repair is needed. Prime the bare wood, working the primer well into cracks and end grain as this is where the weather gets in. Small cracks can be filled with

TEXTURED WALLS

1. Use a 'banister' or 'dust-pan' brush for painting rough-textured finishes.

2. Paint brickwork with a well-loaded old brush. First fill any large cracks.

3. Alternatively use a roller on brick to give a thicker coat of paint.

REPLACING OLD PUTTY

1. Rake out old, damaged putty. Clean glass with methylated spirit.

2. Work new putty in your hands, then press it firmly into the gap.

3. Smooth the new putty level with the old using a putty knife.

putty, but larger ones should be filled with exterior grade hard stopping or filler. A complete wood repair system is available under a proprietary name. Sand level when dry, and spot-prime. Gaps between the window frame and wall should be filled with a flexible, waterproof, mastic compound applied with a special gun.

Finally, sand down the whole of the woodwork to make it ready for repainting.

TYPES OF PAINT

There is a wide range of paints available for exterior walls. As for tools, a 100mm (4in) brush is the easiest size to handle; anything larger would put too much strain on the wrist. An alternative is a long-pile roller which has the advantage of being much quicker to use – about three times quicker than a brush. An extra long-pile roller is needed for roughcast or pebbledash; choose one with a pile 32mm (1¼in) deep, or use a banister brush instead. Use cheap disposable brushes or rollers for cement paints as they are almost impossible to clean afterwards.

A large plastic bucket or paint kettle is essential when working up a ladder. Stir the paint thoroughly first, then pour some into the bucket until it's about one-third full. If you're using a roller, use a special roller tray with a large paint reservoir, or else stand a short plank in the bucket to allow you to load the roller evenly.

Hook the bucket or tray onto a rung of the ladder with an S-hook to leave both hands free. Lay a dust sheet below to catch any drips, and you're ready to start.

CEMENT PAINT

This is the cheapest of all outdoor paints and, in spite of its name (which refers to what it's made of) it's suitable for most types of previously unpainted brick, concrete and cement rendering, pebbledash and asbestos sheeting. Porous surfaces should first be damped down (this stops the paint drying out too quickly) and the paint applied while the surface is damp.

Cement paint is not especially

PREPARING WOODWORK

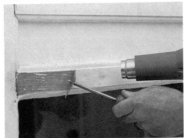

1. Start preparing woodwork by scraping or stripping flaking paint.

2. Sand and prime all bare wood, then leave the surface to dry.

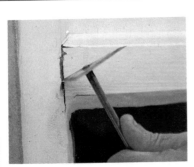

3. Clean out any loose debris from joints that have opened up.

4. Fill large cracks with exterior grade filler or wood filling system.

5. Fill gaps between frame and wall with a mastic compound.

durable, and turns powdery in time. The choice of colours is limited and it is mainly sold by builders' merchants rather than decorating stores. If you intend to paint over a cement paint, an alkali-resisting primer/sealer must first be applied.

EXTERIOR GLOSS

Based on various resins modified with drying oils, full gloss paints have very good weather resistance. Though mostly thought of as *the* major decorative finish for timber, it can also be used on primed and undercoated concrete, brickwork and building boards.

Exterior gloss flows well and can easily be applied by brush, roller or spray gun. It will be tack-free in 4-6 hours, though it should be left overnight to dry before a second coat is applied. The clean-ing solvent is turps. It's quite expensive when you add in the cost of all-surface primer and under-coat that are needed. A new paint type, microporous, is used to save wood. It resists flaking and blister-ing as it allows wood to breathe.

EXTERIOR GRADE EMULSION

Also known as plastic paint, this is the weather-resistant version of emulsion used indoors. Based on

PAINTING SEQUENCES
Windows and panelled doors are tricky areas to paint properly but you shouldn't have any trouble if you follow the correct sequence of painting as shown in these diagrams.

Painting a window (right): start with the rebate on the frame (1), then paint the outside edge of the window (2). Do the putty (3) next, followed by the glazing bars (4) and the rails and stiles (5 to 8). Paint the frame and sill (9 to 13) last.

Painting a door (far right): wedge the door ajar and paint the frame and the hinged edge of the frame and door (1 to 3). Do mouldings and panels next (4 to 13) followed by the muntins (14, 15), the rails (16 to 19) and finally the stiles (20, 21).

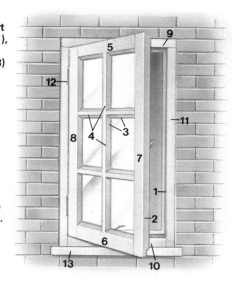

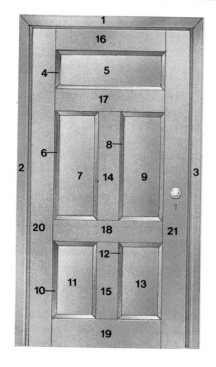

Painting sliding sash windows: these need to be painted in two stages. Pull down the top sash and paint the top rail of the inside sash (1) and the sides as far as you can go (2). Do the runners at the top of the frame (3) and a short way down the outer runner (4).
Almost close the windows, then paint the bottom runners (5, 6), and the remainder of the bottom sash to meet the other paint (7 to 10). Paint the whole of the top sash including the bottom edge (11 to 15) and finally the window frame (16 to 20).

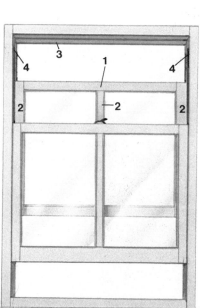

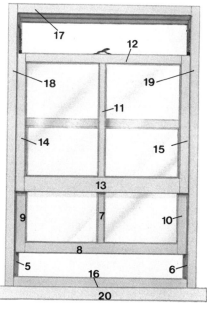

acrylic polymers, which give excellent adhesion, it's easily applied with a brush, roller or spray gun. Equipment can be cleaned in water – but do it immediately after use. It's suitable for most surfaces (although not those painted with masonry paint) and it gives a good seal to brickwork, cement rendering, stucco and asbestos.

Emulsion dries very quickly – within 4 to 6 hours – but perhaps most important, it's fairly inexpensive.

STONE PAINT

The name doesn't mean you can use it only on stone, for in fact the paint is similar to exterior grade emulsion but gives a textured finish. The resins on which it's based are more robust and to help it cope with cracks, holes and natural movement in the building, it's 'beefed up' with various fibres and mineral powders (such as granite, stone or rock). It adheres well and is weather-resistant. Its major drawback is its low coverage rate. You can improve on this by applying an undercoat of cement paint.

Only masonry paint outdoes it for durability, but stone paint has the added advantage of one of the best colour ranges. You brush on a thickish coat, then 'work' the surface with a fine rubber stippler (or the brush) to create the effect you want. This paint can be difficult to brush on if you don't have an artistic flair, but you can use a roller or spray gun (this must be fitted with a modified nozzle to cope with the added fillers).

MASONRY PAINT

A durable, oil-based paint producing a smooth semi-gloss finish, this is the most expensive of the outdoor finishes but can be used on brick, stucco, concrete, cement rendering and asbestos sheeting. It's also the type with the most drawbacks. Although it can be applied quickly with a brush, roller or spray gun, you first have to prime the wall, then wait at least 12 hours for the first coat to dry and finally clean your equipment in turps/white spirit.

The colours offered are mostly pastel shades. It is extremely durable, and is resistant to airborne dirt and pollution.

Water-based masonry paint is tough and flexible and has additives such as mica or nylon fibres to give reinforcement and texture. It both protects and decorates new and old cement rendering, brickwork, concrete, pebbledash, stucco and asbestos sheeting. Apply by brush, roller or spray gun. Water is the solvent, but even so it is often difficult to remove all fibrous material from brushes or rollers and these cannot be used again for a finishing coat.

Primers are only ever needed on masonry if the surface is defective and would prevent the paint adhering. Very powdery surfaces will need a stabilizing solution to seal the surface.

PAINTING WINDOW FRAMES

1. Apply undercoat to the frame rebates first.

2. Paint the rebates on open casements next.

3. Close the window slightly and paint the area along the hinged edge.

4. A paint shield may help you to achieve a neat paint line on the glass.

5. Do the cross bars first, then the uprights, and the sill last.

6. Sand down the undercoat, then apply the top coat in the same order.

INDEX